CHINESE
AESTHETICS
AND
LITERATURE

SUNY SERIES IN

ASIAN STUDIES DEVELOPMENT

ROGER T. AMES AND PETER D. HERSHOCK, EDITORS

CHINESE
AESTHETICS
AND
LITERATURE

a reader

EDITED BY

CORINNE H. DALE

STATE UNIVERSITY OF NEW YORK PRESS

Grateful acknowledgement is given to the following for permission to reproduce previously published material: Pauline Yu and Theodore Huters, "The Imaginative Universe of Chinese Literature," copyright © 1994 by Trustees of Columbia University in the City of New York, from Barbara Stoler Miller, ed., *Masterworks of Asian Literature in Comparative Perspective: A Guide for Teaching* (Armonk, N.Y.: M. E. Sharpe, 1994), pp. 21–36. Reprinted with permission; Roger T. Ames, "Language and Interpretive Contexts," adapted from "Introduction," *Interpreting Culture Through Translation: A Festschrift for D. C. Lau*, Eds. Roger T. Ames, Chan Sin-wai, and Mau-sang Ng (Hong Kong: The Chinese University Press, 1991), xiii–xxvii; Tu Wei-ming, "The Continuity of Being: Chinese Visions of Nature," from *On Nature*, ed. Leroy S. Rouner, copyright 1984 by University of Notre Dame Press, Notre Dame, IN 46556. All rights reserved. Used by permission; Wilt Idema and Lloyd Haft, "The Central Tradition in Traditional Society," from *A Guide to Chinese Literature*, © 1997 by Center for Chinese Studies, The University of Michigan. Reprinted with permission; Larson, Wendy, Excerpts from "Woman, Moral Virtue, and Literary Text," in *Woman and Writing in Modern China*, copyright © permission 1998 by the Board of Trustees of the Leland Stanford, Jr., University. With the permission of Stanford University Press, *www.sup.org*; Stephen Owen, "Omen of the World: Meaning in the Chinese Lyric," from *Traditional Chinese Poetry and Poetics*, © 1985. Reprinted by permission of The University of Wisconsin Press; "Paul S. Ropp, The Distinctive Art of Chinese Fiction," from *Heritage of China: Contemporary Perspectives on Chinese Civilization*, copyright © 1990 The Regents of the University of California, published by the University of California Press; Elizabeth Wichmann, "Beijing Opera Plays and Performance," from *Listening to Theatre: The Aural Dimension of Beijing Opera*, copyright © 1991. Reprinted by permission of The University of Hawaii Press; Leo Ou-fan Lee, "Reflections on Change and Continuity in Modern Chinese Fiction" from *May Fourth to June Fourth: Fiction and Film in Twentieth-Century China*, edited by Ellen Widmer and David Der-wei Wang, pp. 361–83, Cambridge: Harvard University Press. Copyright © 1993 by the President and Fellows of Harvard College. Reprinted by permission of the publisher; Yan Haiping, "Theater and Society: An Introduction to Contemporary Chinese Drama," adapted from Yan Haiping, ed., *Theater & Society: An Anthology of Contemporary Chinese Drama*, copyright © 1998 by M. E. Sharpe, Inc. (Armonk, N.Y.: M. E. Sharpe, 1998), pp. ix–xlvi. Reprinted with permission; Howard Goldblatt, "Border Crossings: Chinese Writing, in Their World and Ours" from *China beyond the Headlines*, ed. Timothy B. Weston and Lionel M. Jensen, © 2000 by permission of Rowman & Littlefield Publishers, Inc.

Published by
STATE UNIVERSITY OF NEW YORK PRESS, ALBANY

© 2004 State University of New York

For information, address State University of New York Press,
90 State Street, Suite 700, Albany, NY 12207

Production, Laurie Searl
Marketing, Anne M. Valentine

Library of Congress Cataloging-in-Publication Data

Chinese aesthetics and literature: a reader / Edited by Corinne H. Dale.
  p. cm.—(SUNY series in Asian studies development)
  Includes bibliographical references and index.
  ISBN 0-7914-6021-5 (alk. paper)—ISBN 0-7914-6022-3 (pbk. : alk. paper)
  1. Chinese literature–History and criticism–Theory, etc. 2. Chinese
literature–Philosophy.   3. Chinese literature–Aesthetics.   4. Popular culture–China.
  I. Dale, Corinne H.   II. Series.

PL2261.C48 2004
895.1'09–dc21
                                                                              2003052620

10 9 8 7 6 5 4 3 2 1

CONTENTS

PREFACE

TO BE EDUCATED requires us to transcend our own cultural world-view. Increasingly, American high school and college teachers are challenged to internationalize the curriculum not only to complement global efforts in business, politics, and the arts, but also to satisfy the intellectual needs of students who are now introduced in lower, middle, and high schools to Asian, African, and other non-Western cultures.

I was fortunate to begin my study of Chinese culture at the East West Center in Honolulu, where in the summer of 1999 I joined a small group of professors from a variety of disciplines for a three-week intensive study of Chinese, Japanese, and Korean cultures. Asian Studies Development Project seminars, cosponsored by the East West Center and the University of Hawaii, promote the infusion of Asian studies into the undergraduate curriculum. During the seminar, as I studied the histories, philosophies, and social practices of these cultures, I began to develop more informed responses to non-Western literary and other artistic expressions rather than to read them as distorted reflections of my own familiar Western worldview.

As I struggled to destabilize my Western-bred expectations in order to understand more fully the accomplishments of these sophisticated and ancient cultures, I was also encouraged to think of how to support my colleagues in opening up the curriculum. How could we teachers educate ourselves well enough to teach texts from these very different cultures? Listening to my colleagues at the ASDP seminar as they thanked Nancy Hume for her book *Japanese Aesthetics and Culture: A Reader* (Nancy G. Hume, ed., New York: State University of New York Press, 1995), I recognized the need for a companion reader, *Chinese Aesthetics and Literature*. With Nancy Hume's encouragement, I undertook to imitate her work with this book; I offer it as the sincerest form of flattery.

As a Visiting Fellow at the East West Center during my ensuing sabbatical year, I began to explore the extensive resources available at the library of the University of Hawaii. Many scholarly works on Chinese culture can be found in major academic libraries. The difficulty for a nonspecialist is to select from these vast resources, especially since many scholarly essays are aimed at sinologists. The majority of general anthologies and comprehensive critiques of Chinese literature do provide excellent historical views yet do not focus on the aesthetic contexts crucial to reading these texts.

The essays collected in this volume introduce nonspecialists to the philosophy and aesthetics of Chinese art, especially literature, including the major modern genres of poetry, fiction, drama, and film. Translation issues are also addressed, including the selection of English diction and also the selection of Chinese texts, both of which determine the accessibility of Chinese texts for most Western readers. I have chosen standard essays written for a general reader by recognized scholars in the fields, believing that many who read this book will seek out other works by these experts. The annotated bibliography, which follows the essays, will help guide the reader to the many excellent resources for further study.

Though this volume is not a literary history, the essays are arranged to reflect the development of Chinese aesthetics: they begin with the philosophical concepts revealed in nature and human society, including literature, and expressed in Daoism, Buddhism, and Confucian thought; proceed to the traditional expressions of lyric, narrative, and theater; then focus on the crisis of aesthetics in twentieth-century China. The traditional philosophies of Chinese culture still inform modern literature, even film—in spite of the crisis precipitated by the sudden impact of Western cultures on modern China when these traditions were rejected, criticized, and revised in the series of revolutionary appropriations of Marxism and Capitalism.

Clearly, this book depends on the scholarly achievements of the essayists represented here; I gratefully acknowledge their contributions to this project. In addition, although I take full responsibility for my judgments and comments, I depended on consultations with Cyndy Ning on cinema, David McCraw on poetry, Giovanelli Vitiello on fiction, Elizabeth Wichmann-Walczak on drama—all at the University of Hawaii. I also learned much from conversations with Daniel Cole, Henry Rosemont, and Steve Goldberg. Roger Ames and Peter Hershock provided wise guidance and encouragement as well as friendship. My teachers and my partners in learning at the ASDP seminar were inspirations. Betty Buck and the staff at the East West Center offered gracious hospitality and support. I thank them all.

At Belmont University, I relied on the support of the Provost George Sims, the Dean of Arts and Sciences Richard Fallis, and the Chair of Literature and Languages Maggie Monteverde. I continued my studies with my China Reading Group at Belmont—Marcia McDonald, John Paine, Dan Shafer, Jon Thornton, Rebecca Coke, and Ronnie Littlejohn. My trip to China with Belmont University faculty and students dramatically reinforced my intellectual learning. Especially, I thank Ronnie Littlejohn, for his unflagging inspiration, enthusiastic leadership, logistical support, and hard work on behalf of this project. I hope that this book does justice to the wise counsel and friendly encouragement provided by all of them.

INTRODUCTION

CHINESE CIVILIZATION is, for many Westerners, a site of the exotic—a set of traditions so radically different from those dominant in the West that it challenges the very presuppositions underlying Western ways of thinking, believing, speaking, and acting. Yet, China's five-thousand-year-old civilization—the oldest sustained civilization in the world—has not been hermetic. It continues to be a dynamic tradition that expresses a strong sense of cultural identity interwoven with and strengthened by cultural borrowings.

The Chinese historically called themselves the Middle Kingdom—that is, the central kingdom and also the centered kingdom. An eclectic and expanding culture, China has traditionally disdained outside cultures, which were often viewed as barbarian. But it also fused elements of these foreign cultures into Chinese civilization. Thus, Buddhism has profoundly transformed and been transformed by Chinese culture for some two thousand years since it reached China from India. Since the early nineteenth century, China has been most impacted by Western culture, including the ideologies of Capitalism and Marxism. Twentieth-century China has suffered a wrenching series of cultural revisions as traditional Chinese culture has clashed with Western values. Despite the diversity of experience in China and despite the crisis of the modern, it can be argued that a distinctive Chinese aesthetic tradition persists, a set of values that informs art and literature and expresses China's dynamic civilization.

Because of China's radically different worldview, Westerners must come to terms with aesthetic values and artistic practices that may initially seem incomprehensible or even alienating. "Aesthetics" is a hotly debated philosophical concept, Western in origin, denoting meanings that range from a sense of what is beautiful in art and literature to a highly articulated system of meta-theories. Modern aesthetic theory emerged in China at the turn of the twentieth century as a self-conscious and defensive response to the encounter with Western culture. Chinese aesthetics, in the fundamental sense of artistic values or preferences, are based on philosophically informed understandings of human experience as part of the dynamic world's natural and harmonious balance. Daoist, Buddhist, and Confucian teachings promote this persistently open worldview; revolutionary thought in modern China has interpreted and critiqued these teachings.

Traditionally in Chinese culture, art is an expression of essence—the meaning, often the emotion, of a moment within the flow of the dynamic and harmonious natural world. Further, art in China has traditionally been a practice that is transformational and continuous, both an act of self-cultivation and an interpretation of a rich, dynamic tradition. Thus, traditional Chinese aesthetics value modification rather than the radical reformations commonly valued by Western aesthetics, and creativity is expressed in variations rather than in deviations. The traditional Chinese apprehension of art does not valorize difference, conflict, and alienation, although contemporary Chinese culture does reflect these modern Western values. The inherent moral optimism of the traditional Chinese worldview precludes tragedy in the Western sense; it minimizes the importance of individual development, inner experience, and free will, all of which are highly valued in Western art. Instead, Chinese art traditionally presents the long view of human experience as revealing a continuously unfolding and harmonious order.

The essays collected here identify this aesthetic tradition as it is embedded in Chinese culture, language, art, and literature, demonstrating the continuity of that tradition even in these turbulent times. This collection of essays is intended for nonspecialist Westerners who seek to learn about Chinese culture, especially about the ways in which art and particularly literature express that culture. Although we cannot ultimately go native, leaving our Western culture entirely behind, we can and must educate ourselves, seeking to understand Chinese culture as a valid response to human experience. By coming to terms with Chinese aesthetic values, Westerners can better appreciate Chinese literature and other artistic practices and also develop a better understanding of the core values of Chinese culture. Only then can we truly begin to understand ways in which these values resonate within Western culture and enrich our own experience.

The essays were chosen because of their accessibility to nonspecialist Western readers, their scholarly merit, and their discussion of Chinese artistic practices in the context of the aesthetic traditions of Chinese civilization. These essays have all been previously published and thus do not pose new theories; together, they provide the reader with an authoritative introduction to the vocabulary and traditions of Chinese aesthetics and literature. The essayists present extended definitions of key concepts that resist translation into English; for this reason, a glossary has not been included. The essayists are eminent scholars of Chinese culture, steeped in the language, philosophy, history, and aesthetic traditions. As experts in their fields, they present Chinese aesthetics from a deep base of knowledge, and readers will do well to seek other works by them.

The first essay in this collection defines Chinese literary aesthetics in the context of Daoism, Buddhism, and Confucianism, and discusses characteristics of traditional Chinese literature. In "The Imaginative Universe of Chinese Literature," Pauline Yu and Theodore Huters describe the integration of literature within the Chinese culture, explaining that the word for writing, *wen*, also means "culture, civilization, learning, pattern, refinement, and embellishment." Examining the ancient creation story of Pangu, Yu and Huters identify aesthetic values that express the organic, correlational, and holistic worldview of traditional Chinese civilization.

The next two essays further develop these aesthetic values as they are grounded in the philosophical traditions of Daoism and Buddhism in China and as they contrast with a Western philosophical worldview. These essays offer the reader further understanding of the traditional Chinese worldview, without which Western readers may find Chinese art and literature incomprehensible or simply lacking in interest. In "Language and Interpretive Contexts," Roger T. Ames contrasts Chinese correlative thinking to Western dualism, explaining *yin* and *yang*, correlative thinking, and complementary relationships. But Ames also identifies correspondences between the traditional Chinese worldview and the native pre-Christian Anglo-Saxon tradition whose values are embedded in the Anglo-Saxon vocabulary of the English language. Thus, Ames suggests that traditional Chinese literature, so different aesthetically from most Western literature, does resonate with those many English-speakers who must rely on the imperfect art of Chinese-to-English translation.

In "The Continuity of Being: Chinese Visions of Nature," Tu Wei-ming continues the discussion of the Chinese correlative worldview, explaining why Chinese art valorizes conformity and communal harmony rather than the Western tropes of individuality and tragedy. Tu explains Chinese cosmogony, focusing on the concept of *qi* as the "vital force" that infuses the dynamic and wholly immanent world. In the traditional Chinese worldview, each moment is significant in revealing the Dao (the Way or dynamic process of the world), and individual experience is always significant in relationship to other moments, other people, institutions, nature, the arts, and literature.

The tradition of Chinese literature has flourished for over three thousand years, embracing philosophy, history, civil documents, lyric, music, calligraphy, and drama, as well as official documents—all of which were admired for stylistic excellence and social and political importance. Classical Chinese culture developed interpenetrating art forms, and poetry infuses narratives, dramas, painting, and theater. The essays that follow reflect modern concepts of literary genres, both in China and the West, focusing on poetry, fiction, drama, theater, and film. The first group considers the role of writers in the community, the next group considers major traditions of classical Chinese literature, and the final group considers the development of literature and the arts in modern China.

In "The Central Tradition in Traditional Society," Wilt Idema and Lloyd Haft consider literature and art as a practice of the central tradition of Confucianism. The Dao (the pattern or ordering principle of the dynamic world) is revealed in human social practices as well as in art and nature. Just as nature expresses eternal essence as revealed by Daoism and Buddhism rather than transitory material reality, so human society also reveals the essence of the cosmic order as ritualized hierarchical relationships of Confucian tradition.

Confucian thought, with its tradition of interpretations, explores human correlationships and social behaviors as revelations of Dao. Thus a self is not simply an individual in Western terms, but a child, a parent, a leader, a worker, etc. The literati, gentlemen-scholars, practiced literature in reading, writing, and calligraphy as an act of expressing the Dao and as a practice of self-cultivation that became the official demonstration in the civil examination system of eligibility for public office.

Literati were traditionally men; virtuous women were nonliterary by definition in the Central Tradition. In the next essay, adapted from "Woman, Moral Virtue, and Literary Text," Wendy Larson argues that *de* (moral virtue) and *cai* (literary talent) are gendered concepts that historically served to limit women's development of literary talent. Although there were many challenges and exceptions to traditional gender roles even in classical China, virtuous women were defined in opposition to literati until the twentieth century when these concepts were criticized and redefined by revolutionaries seeking to overturn Chinese social traditions. Thus, women writers in classical China were rare and an affront to the traditional worldview.

For two thousand years poetry was the most esteemed form of literature in China, manifesting the mastery of classical written language, literary tradition, and calligraphy and demonstrating the self-cultivation of the literati, who were interpreters of the tradition and models of Chinese civilization. Stephen Owen's "Omen of the World: Meaning in the Chinese Lyric" treats the dominant tradition of lyric poetry (*shi*) as a manifestation of the cosmic order. Developing in the second century and reaching full flowering in the tenth-century Tang dynasty, the *shi*, with its many variations, is a lyrical evocation of essence through concrete imagery describing a particular moment. Owen discusses the concept of occasional poetry as an act or manifestation of the order inherent in the immanent world, rather than, as in Western poetry, a symbolic revelation of transcendent truth.

Whereas poetry has traditionally been the central elite literary form, the classical tradition of parallel prose also features stylistic formalism in parallel sentence structure, formal diction, imagery, and allusions. Vernacular fiction in China developed as a minor form, a popular genre derived from folk stories and historical events and read as didactic entertainment, only later becoming more valued as serious explorations of life and values. Extended prose narratives developed in the fourteenth through the eighteenth centuries, yielding a number of great episodic narratives, which continue to be popular today, adapting well to television serials, sometimes with eighty or more episodes.

In "The Distinctive Art of Chinese Fiction," Paul S. Ropp describes the popular genre of traditional Chinese vernacular fiction, comparing the aesthetics that shape it to those of Western fiction, especially the optimistic moralism of the Chinese tradition, which precludes the tragic view of life so important in Western fiction. The optimistic view of a moral and balanced universe promotes narratives with multiple plots and many characters, and deemphasizes the inner development of an individual hero. Ropp illustrates the aesthetic principles of Chinese narrative in short discussions of the great traditional Chinese novels.

Just as in poetry and fiction, drama in China traditionally demonstrates an aesthetic that values emotion, rather than plot or action, as revealing the essence of a situation. The Chinese theatrical tradition is musical and has many varieties, some regional, some popular, some elite. In her essay "Beijing Opera Plays and Performance," Elizabeth Wichmann-Walczak presents Chinese theater as a synthesis of literature, music, dance, acrobatics, acting, singing, costume, and makeup. Wichmann-Walczak explains the aesthetics of the beautiful and its expression in all the performative aspects of the Beijing Opera, the most highly developed opera and still a popular theater form.

The most persistent challenge of the last one and one-half centuries has been the impact of Western culture on classical Chinese traditions. Chinese literature has been challenged by Western art theories such as social realism, by Western genres such as the spoken drama, and by Western technologies such as cinematography. The final three essays address the modern impact of the West on Chinese aesthetics and literature.

Since the Literary Revolution of 1917, there has been renewed Chinese interest in the narrative tradition along with the demand for social realism to promote communist reforms. Chinese art has always been an ethical practice, and governments in China censored and controlled art, valuing it as promoting cultural ethics rather than as individual expression. The Cultural Revolution of 1966, led by Jiang Qing, Mao Zedong's wife, exerted particularly harsh suppression of literature, especially theater, which was the actress Jiang Qing's greatest interest. "Modern revolutionary dramas" were demanded to glorify peasant heroes and socialist revolutionaries; traditional theater was banned. After Mao's death, Deng Xiaoping relaxed political control of the arts, allowing for more individual views. Still, as the Tian'anmen Massacre in 1989 made clear, the Chinese government continues to censor individual expression as it promotes community good, a traditional value reinterpreted by Chinese communism.

Leo Ou-fan Lee analyzes the impact of turbulent social developments on modern Chinese fictional realism in the essay "Reflections on Change and Continuity in Modern Chinese Fiction." Lee evaluates contemporary writers' efforts to develop an aesthetic of subjectivity by transcending the communal aesthetics that had been tied to Chinese tradition and then differently politicized by communism's demand for social realism.

Spoken drama is a modern Western-derived form, adapted to Chinese tradition. Although spoken drama features colloquial speech and more realistic performance style than traditional theater, it continues the Chinese traditions of ethical purpose and expresses emotion as the essence of a particular situation. The art of cinematography offers a particularly fascinating example of the Chinese adaptation of a Western art form, since film was developed entirely within the capitalistic framework of western technology and ideology. Following the social realism demanded by the communist regime, the Fourth and Fifth Generation of Chinese film directors in the late 1970s established a New Cinema Movement, making Chinese cinema an international success by its infusion of classical traditions into modern film.

Yan Haiping's "Theater and Society: An Introduction to Contemporary Chinese Drama" explains the aesthetic development and sociopolitical contexts of contemporary drama and film, focusing on five texts: *Bus Stop* (1983), *WM* (1985), *Pan Jinlian: The History of a Fallen Woman* (1986), *Sangshuping Chronicles* (1988), and *Old Well* (1986). Yan discusses the experimental modernism of post-Mao Chinese dramatists such as the 2000 Nobel Prize-winner Gao Xingjian, who appropriates Western-style existential anxieties but rejects alienation in "rediscovered humanism."

The final essay, Howard Goldblatt's "Border Crossings: Chinese Writing, in Their World and Ours," reminds us of the crucial role of the translator for the Western reader in choosing which texts will enter the English-speaking world. Contemporary dissident writers reject the social realism demanded by the earlier Communist regime, Goldblatt argues; consequently, contemporary Chinese texts, in their violence and alienation, are more accessible to English readers than traditional Chinese texts, but still express a difference in worldview that enriches our own literature and culture.

Learning about Chinese culture, we necessarily learn about ourselves because we are destabilized, jarred into an awareness of the philosophical platform on which Western civilization stands. Knocked off our Western feet, we can view our Western cultural presumptions from a new perspective as valid ways, but not the only valid ways, of considering human experience. This understanding is essential in order to proceed effectively with pragmatic international issues such as human rights, democracy, feminism, science and medicine, environmental conservation, and business relations. Moreover, Chinese culture, though radically different, still resonates within traditional Western culture, giving expression to values that we also affirm and that we sometimes labor to articulate, such as the natural ecological balance of the world and the correlative position of the individual within the family and the community.

Learning about Chinese culture also helps us come to terms with our own nation's cultural diversity: Chinese American and other Asian cultures within the U.S. are illuminated by a better understanding of the Asian heritages that help shape Western culture. Native American, African American, and women's cultures are other embedded traditions that differently express what it means to be human. Learning about Chinese culture, and thus problematizing our dominant patriarchal and Eurocentric worldview, radically educates us, leading us both within our cultural heritage and also beyond it to take our places as responsible citizens in a diverse world where borders are increasingly permeable.

NOTES ON LANGUAGE AND PRONUNCIATION

CHINESE WRITTEN characters developed probably in the early second millennium B.C.E. as pictograms, stylized illustrations of objects or actions. The earliest pictograms extant are engraved on oracle bones; later characters were written on metal, stone, silk, and paper with brushwork.

The early pictorial forms were sometimes modified or doubled or tripled to add meaning. Pictograms gradually became more abstracted into ideograms and also were combined into compound ideograms. Combining the characters for "to speak" and "pen" thus yields the compound ideogram for "book." Sometimes a rarely used word was substituted for a different word with the same sound. Such loan characters, indicating sound, are often combined with another character that suggests the general meaning, making phonetic compounds. But subsequent changes in pronunciation have made the phonetic elements of such words unreliable guides to modern readers.

The classical Chinese is still sometimes written and read today, even though vernacular writing is popular and modern romanization is increasingly used. Today, there are more than fifty thousand characters, though most are rarely used. Scholars today know usually about ten thousand characters; modern Chinese primary schools teach about three thousand characters. Beginning in 1979, the Chinese began using the pinyin system of romanization in their foreign-language publications, and today the pinyin is the standard form for romanization of written Chinese, a system that has replaced the now increasingly obsolete Wade-Giles. Thus, in pinyin, *Mao Zedong* replaces the Wade-Giles *Mao Tsetung*, and *Beijing* replaces *Peking*. The forms of romanization in the essays collected here follow the usage of the authors; for this reason, the forms are not always consistent: *shi* (lyric poetry) is sometimes rendered *shih*, for example.

The written script sustains a three-thousand-year-old literary tradition that is still accessible to modern readers. Moreover, Chinese characters often contain latent pictograms—visual images embedded in the characters. The classical Chinese language is compact, with grammatical brevity, no tenses or punctuation, and often little syntactical order. Each word is a cluster of meaning, understood correlationally to the other characters around it; thus, groups of words often yield a number of possible meanings. These properties make classical written Chinese an especially rich medium for imagistic poetry.

Furthermore, pronunciation is tonal and thus innately musical. Rather than a stressed and unstressed syllabic system as in English, Chinese words are pronounced with rises and falls of the voice, producing patterned alterations of tones. The four tones of classical Chinese are as follows: 1) level; 2) rising; 3) falling (actually the tone falls and then rises slightly); and 4) entering (short, abrupt).

Pinyin (romanized) words are pronounced as expected by English-speakers with the following exceptions:

Q: pronounced as a hard *ch* (*Qing* dynasty is pronounced *Ching*)
X: pronounced with a hiss as in *hs* (writer *Lu Xun* is pronounced *Lu Hsun*)
C: pronounced *ts* at the beginning of a syllable (writer *Shen Congwen* is pronounced *Shen Tsungwen*).

In addition, the pronunciation of the following Pinyin vowel sounds are different from what an English native speaker might expect, as indicated:

AI = *AYE*
AO = *OW (POW)*
EI = *A (NEIGH)*
EN/ON = *UN*
IE = *YE (YET)*
IU = *YO*
OU = *OW (SLOW)*
UAI = *WI (WILD)*
UE = *UE (DUET)*
UI = *WAY (SWAY)*

A BRIEF OUTLINE OF
LITERARY HISTORY

ca. 5000–2000 B.C.E.	Neolithic cultures.
ca. 2200–1750 B.C.E.	Xia dynasty.
ca. 1750–1100 B.C.E.	Shang Dynasty. Inscriptions on tortoise shells and sheep scapulae.
ca. 1100–256 B.C.E.	Zhou Dynasty. Oral literature from this period is later collected as *Classic of Documents*, sayings and speeches attributed to early kings.
ca. 600 B.C.E.	*The Book of Odes* (or *The Book of Songs*), anthology of over three hundred lyric poems from as early as the twelfth century B.C.E., said to be compiled by Confucius.
551–479 B.C.E.	Confucius lived.
403–221 B.C.E.	Warring States period.
221–206 B.C.E.	Qin Dynasty. Great Wall begun. Unification of China. Suppression and destruction of all writing without imperial approval including *Book of Songs* and other Confucian classics. Standardization of written script.
202 B.C.E.–220 C.E.	Han Dynasty. Buddhism comes to China from the west.
ca. 100 C.E.	Paper made from bamboo stems on scrolls replaces bamboo strips and silk for writing purposes. Rise of great historical writing; *Records of the Historian* completed. *Fu* (rhyme-prose) becomes popular. Reestablishment and development of Confucian tradition. Civil service examinations begin.
220–581 C.E.	Minor Dynasties/Period of Disunity. Rise of Buddhism and Daoism.
581–618	Sui Dynasty. Reunification of China
618–906	Tang Dynasty.
ca. 700–850	Great age of poetry, especially *shi*. Beginnings of Confucian revival. Height of Buddhist influence in China. Invention of block printing.

907–960	**Era of the Five Dynasties** (in competition for rule of China).
960–1279	**Song Dynasty.** Consolidation of civil service examination system and rise of literati as gentleman-scholar statesmen. Growth of vernacular literature.
1271–1368	**Yuan Dynasty.** Classical age of Chinese drama. Beginning of the novel.
1368–1644	**Ming Dynasty.** Archaists urge imitation of traditional models in classical literature; in reaction, rise of vernacular literature, especially long novels.
ca. 1400	*The Men of the Marshes (Outlaws of the Marshes* or *Water Margin)* and *Romance of the Three Kingdoms* published.
ca. 1570–1600	*Journey to the West (Monkey)* published.
1644–1912	**Qing (Manchu) Dynasty.** Further development of fiction and poetry.
ca. 1750	*The Scholars* completed.
1782	Completion of the *Complete Library in Four Categories* (thirty-six thousand volumes of edited and censored Chinese literature).
1792	*Dream of the Red Chamber (Story of the Stone)* published.
ca. 1875	Modern printing techniques developed.
1912–1949	**Republic of China.**
1917	Literary Revolution calls for new vernacular literature aimed at popular audience in rebellion against the formal speech and classical structures of earlier literature as well as in criticism of Chinese civilization itself.
1919	May Fourth Movement (beginning of New Culture Movement).
1930	Founding of the League of Left-wing Writers.
1942	Mao Zedong's "Talks at the Yan'an Forum on Literature and Art" directs literature and art to be enlisted in the socialist reformation.
1949	**People's Republic of China.** National writers' union formed. Socialist realism in literature required.

1952	*Jüben* (*Drama*) founded.
1957	"Anti-Rightist movement" suppresses the "Hundred Flowers" policy that had briefly encouraged critical speech.
1966–76	Cultural Revolution, led by Jiang Qing (Mao's wife). Massive political persecutions of writers and others; most art since 1949 denounced and banned; traditional culture attacked. *Jüben* (*Drama*) suppressed.
1976	End of Cultural Revolution, death of Mao Zedong, the Gang of Four falls.
1978	Deng Xiaoping's reforms ease restrictions on writers.
Late 1970s	"Literature of the new period": first wave, "scars literature," condemns persecutions of Cultural Revolution. Fourth Generation of directors begins New Cinema Movement. *Jintian* (*Today*) publishes experimental poetry.
1979	*Jüben* (*Drama*) resumes publication.
1980s	Second wave of "literature of the new period" includes "school of critical realism" in drama and the "New Realism" in fiction exposing social problems in PRC, *Xungen* or "Search for roots" literature, and experimental modernism. Fifth Generation of filmmakers establishes "New Wave" in film.
1989	Tian'namen protests, June 4 Massacre.
21st century	Postmodern avant-garde fiction, characterized by violence and pessimism, presents personal rather than nationalistic visions.

chapter one

THE IMAGINATIVE UNIVERSE OF CHINESE LITERATURE

Pauline Yu and Theodore Huters

Editor's note: Yu and Huters stress the integrated place of writing in Chinese civilization, explaining that the word for writing, *wen*, also means "culture, civilization, learning, pattern, refinement, and embellishment." Examining the creation story of Pangu, the authors contrast traditional Chinese aesthetic values to Western aesthetics: Chinese aesthetics reflect a holistic and correlative worldview in which art describes concrete phenomenon, the writer exists in a network of relationships, and literature interprets and resides within the historic tradition.

ANY UNDERSTANDING of the fundamental principles and assumptions underlying the writing and reading of Chinese literature should begin with a consideration of the larger cultural context in which those conceptions were embedded and which they to a large extent articulate. Indeed, it is no mere coincidence that the very word for writing in classical Chinese, *wen*, embraces a multitude of meanings beyond that of literature alone— among them culture, civilization, learning, pattern, refinement, and embellishment. The notion of literature as the primarily aesthetic phenomenon of belles lettres arose only very late in China—as indeed was the case in the West as well—and never took deep or exclusive root in the tradition. Much more compelling were the presumptions that literature was an integral element of the cosmos and of the sociopolitical world, and that in writing of the self one spoke ineluctably to and of society as well: the forms and patterns of one's writing corresponded naturally with those of the universe itself.

Needless to say, the tradition was not a monolithic one: significant voices were heard over time to question some of these presuppositions, and it could also be argued that the very need to reiterate them constantly suggests some fundamental uncertainty as to their validity. Moreover, these presumptions became increasingly tenuous and problematic over time. But it is undeniable that they represent the vision that the dominant literati culture continued to perpetrate of itself.

By examining what was at one time considered to be an important creation myth of the culture, we may find an example of the worldview that is implicit in notions of the nature and function of literature in China. According to this legend, the universe was once an enormous egg that one day split open, with its upper half becoming the heavens, its lower half the earth, and the first human, Pangu, emerging from within it. Each day the heavens grew ten feet higher, the earth ten feet thicker, and Pangu ten feet taller until, after eighteen thousand years, he died. His head then opened up to form the sun and the moon, his blood filled the rivers and seas, his hair became the fields and forests, his breath the wind, his perspiration the rain, his voice the thunder, and his fleas became our ancestors.

Even the most cursory reading of this myth allows us to infer certain basic presumptions about the world that produced or received it. We might conclude, for example, that the universe is an uncreated one, generating itself spontaneously from a cosmic egg whose own origins are unspecified; that the elements of the universe are, from their very beginnings, organically and inextricably linked with one another; and that within those relationships the human being does not occupy a particularly glorified position. These conclusions are further confirmed by evidence that the myth is not indigenous to China at all, since it appears so late in the tradition and has so many well-known parallels in Indo-European cultures. The Chinese evidently were not concerned earlier in their history with questions of creation at all, or at least not creation by the hand of some divinity or force outside the cosmos itself—the ultimate sanctions for human activity could therefore be sought solely within the mundane realms of nature, human society, and human history. To be sure, recent archaeological discoveries have suggested that creation myths of other sorts did arise and circulate, but they never occupied the prominent place within the culture that, for example, the Book of Genesis held in the West, indicating a relative lack of interest in the question itself.

Although the Pangu legend has been shown to possess roots in foreign soil, its implications are nonetheless borne out by other evidence of more assuredly Chinese origin. These implications of the legend can be suggestively extended to the realm of literature, where they yield a number of immediately apparent observations. In what follows the foreign myth simply serves as a useful focus for the isolation of what were pre-existing and prevailing ideas within the Chinese tradition—this may also, of course, explain why it eventually appealed to Chinese sensibilities.

A first observation might be that the tradition lacks the figure of some anthropomorphic deity whose creative actions and products serve as the model for human literary activity, as in this well-known formulation from Sir Philip Sidney's *Apology for Poetry*:

Only the poet, . . . lifted up with the vigour of his own invention, doth grow in effect another nature, in making things either better than Nature bringeth forth, or, quite anew, forms such as never were in Nature. . . . Neither let it be deemed too saucy a comparison to balance the highest point of man's wit with the efficacy of Nature; but rather give right honour to the heavenly Maker of that maker, who, having made man to His own likeness, set him beyond and over all the works of that second nature: which in nothing he showeth so much as in Poetry, when with the force of divine breath he bringeth things forth far surpassing her doings. . . .[1]

In contrast to the modern Western tradition, Chinese theories of the arts did not emphasize the notion of creation ex nihilo—Sidney's "invention," and its attendant values of originality and uniqueness—choosing instead to stress the importance of continuity and convention. It is important to keep in mind that these were emphases rather than exclusions: the culture was by no means a static or unimaginative one, but the privileging of tradition and pattern shaped critical discourse in powerful ways.

Second, the Chinese evidently did not view the work of art itself as the image or mirror of some suprasensory reality, whether successful, as in Romans 1:20 ("For the invisible things of Him from the creation of the world are clearly seen, being understood by the things that are made, even His eternal Power and Godhead"), or inevitably incomplete or flawed, as in the Platonic theory of mimesis. Literature did not claim to represent a realm of being fundamentally other from that of concrete phenomena; it embodied principles transcendent to any one individual object in the sensory world (dao [tao]), but the very essence of those principles lay in the fact that they were at the same time immanent in and inseparable from those objects, rather than residing on some altogether different level of being. In contrast to the dualistic view of the universe that lies at the basis of Western notions of poiesis, mimesis, and fictionality, there was in early Chinese literary theory no true dichotomy between the real and the ideal. Rather, literature spoke of the things of this world—and it was but a short step to the assumption that it spoke of the actual personal, social, and political circumstances of the historical author. From this arises the persistent impulse to contextualize the elements of a literary work—to assume that they referred directly, even if veiled, to the author's empirical world, rather than representing the products of a fictive imagination. Thus a poetic oeuvre could serve to construct a biography, and known biographical facts, conversely, could explicate the poetry; extended works of fictional narrative would similarly be construed as chronicles—no matter how disguised—of the author and his or her personal circumstances.

Another way of understanding this attitude, or a third implication of the Pangu myth, is to see it as a manifestation of the holistic, unitary notion of the universe, within which all things are organically connected. Just as our human ancestors are only one small yet integral element of a larger whole, so the writer in traditional Chinese formulations exists in a network of relations with the worlds of nature and society that provide the impetus, forms, and subject of his or her works. We can see this totalizing view clearly in the following passage from the "Great Preface" to the sixth-century B.C.E. canonical anthology of poetry, the *Book of Songs*:

> Poetry is where the intent of the heart goes. What in the heart is intent is poetry when issued forth in words. An emotion moves within and takes form in words. If words do not suffice, then one sighs; if sighing does not suffice, then one prolongs it [the emotion] in song; if prolonging through song does not suffice, then one unconsciously dances it with hands and feet.
>
> Emotions issue forth in sounds, and when sounds form a pattern, they are called tones. The tones of a well-governed world are peaceful and lead to joy, its government harmonious; the tones of a chaotic world are resentful and arouse anger, its government perverse; the tones of a defeated state are mournful to induce longing, its people in difficulty. Thus in regulating success and failure, moving heaven and earth, and causing spirits and gods to respond, nothing comes closer than poetry.[2]

This is a classical statement of the expressive-affective conception of poetry that the Chinese tradition shares with other Asian literatures as well. Certain basic ideas resemble those in the West—the importance in poetry of song, emotion, and patterning—but others seem quite distinctive. Later texts would make explicit the tacit assumption here that the "intent" or emotion that moves within represents a natural response to the stimulus of the external world, be it that of nature or the body politic. Certainly the "Preface" emphasizes the latter and thus takes for granted that what is internal (emotion) will naturally find some externally correlative form or action, and that song can spontaneously reflect, affect, and effect political and cosmic order. We should not underestimate the pervasive power of this assumption throughout much of the tradition—that a seamless connection between the individual and the world somehow enables the poem simultaneously to reveal feelings, provide an index of governmental stability, and serve as a didactic tool. Whether or not these could be demonstrated to everyone's agreement, the literary work certainly was never regarded as a heterocosm—an autonomous being that could serve as an end in itself and be read independently of its context and tradition. The very notion of "literature" itself embraced pragmatic forms such as epitaphs, mnemonics, dispatches, and memorials to the throne that the West generally does not include. And the act of writing even such a "high" form as poetry was an eminently social and political, as well as personal and interpersonal, form of communication. It was a skill any educated person was presumed to possess and be able to use on a regular basis—at social gatherings large or small, court festivities (and there often on command), leavetakings and reunions, births and deaths, and at any of the countless events that merited commemoration. The earliest historical works also recount incidents when allusions to poems provided a means of conveying information and opinions obliquely in delicate diplomatic situations. For several hundred years, furthermore, the ability to write poetry to set topics was tested on the civil service examinations that represented the officially sanctioned route to government office—the only acceptable career for the well-born and educated individual. This emphasis on the didactic function of all writing and the obsession with the political dimension of expression distinguishes the Chinese tradition notably from that of Japan, with which it otherwise shares several basic ideas.

A fourth possible set of implications for literature centers on the attitudes to history that the Pangu myth reveals, both overtly and implicitly. Even the myth itself demonstrates the typically felt need to place its account within some precise if meager temporal framework—note the specific mention of the "eighteen thousand years" that elapsed until Pangu's death. More important is the tacit assumption that the passage of time inevitably involves a movement from fullness to diminution, here literally from the wholeness of the original egg to its fragmentation into the elements of the cosmos. At the same time, however, no element of causality or true linear sequencing enters into the account; the egg simply opens up, and the myth focuses on what comes into existence through natural transformation rather than exploring or exploiting the possibilities of a more "vertical" set of relationships. This leads to the fifth implication: the absence of some divinity or demiurge who, like the God of the Judeo-Christian tradition, not only brings the world into being but also provides it with its laws. The lack of such a god places the burden for providing those norms and values on history itself.

These notions are related to each other and were enormously influential and persistent within the culture as a whole. The belief that history is the story of decline from some earlier golden age is basic to Confucianism. This tradition locates the perfection of sages in some dim era of mythical culture heroes, and more recently in the founding years of the Zhou dynasty, whose ideals Confucius (six hundred years later) claims merely to "transmit." This belief is shared as well by early Daoist texts like the *Dao de jing* (*The Classic of the Way and Its Power*), which advocates a return to values and modes of behavior that were possible—unself-consciously, at least—only at some prior stage of civilization. These attitudes are certainly not unfamiliar to Western culture, which locates itself somewhere and sometime after the Fall. However, the Chinese—and more particularly the Confucian—responses to this given differed significantly. Perfection did lie in the past, and earlier works were generally by definition superior to those that followed. The impulses in favor of archaism and imitation were powerful ones; innovations were therefore often best disguised as "returns" to some prior mode. At the same time, however, as the notion of "return" suggests, perfection was recuperable to the extent that one was able truly to study and emulate the past, because the exemplars were not only human—of the same order of being and therefore in theory totally imitable—but also carefully demonstrated to be genealogically related to the founders of the political order. History thus served much the same function that revelation did in the West, providing didactic models and principles to be studied and, perhaps even more importantly, embodying those ideals in concrete human figures to whom one could trace one's lineage directly and thereby be assured of the possibility of return. In literary terms these attitudes are particularly evident in the fondness for allusions to and reiterations of past texts and in the obsession with tracing the progenitors of one's own works; the descent lines are rarely fleshed out in any coherent chronological fashion, but the sources are identified. And finally, this lack of interest in a fully developed logical or temporal sequencing is significant especially for later narrative, as discussed below.

Despite this concern with history and historicity, that is, the impulse to place literature both within its own tradition and within a larger cultural context, we should note that linearity—at least in the Aristotelian sense of a shaped movement from beginning to middle to end—is conspicuously absent as a structuring principle in traditional Chinese literature, historical or otherwise. The reasons for this are extremely complex, and one can only speculate at best. It may have something to do with the primary place of the short lyric, with its values of brevity, immediacy, and momentariness, as the first and foremost paradigm for written expression (as opposed, say, to longer narrative forms like epic or drama), although here one runs into classic chicken-and-egg type questions. It may have something to do with the Chinese view of history itself. Although history suggests a linear mentality in positing a diminishment of the perfection of some distant past, it does not in Chinese formulations possess a determinate point of origin or a clear line of devolution, and does not move teleologically toward some future apocalypse or redemption. This lack of linearity certainly also has something to do with the absence mentioned earlier of a distinct creator figure who might suggest that literature itself, analogously, creates an autotelic world as well. Rather than representing a metaphoric substitution for some realm of an ontologically different order, the work—and its author as well—are construed as being metonymically related to the only world there is. Indeed, the characteristic mode of reading a poem in traditional China consisted of a synecdochic filling-in of what had only been suggested.

Most of these notions are associated most directly with the Confucian tradition in China, although many are also shared with Daoism and, later, Buddhism as well. Daoism certainly takes for granted the integral relationship of all beings in the universe while denigrating, of course, the primary position Confucianism assigns to the human. And while the other-worldly orientation of Indian Buddhism is undeniable, the uniquely Chinese development thereof that proved to be the most enduring, Chan (better known by its Japanese pronunciation, Zen) shared with the indigenous systems of belief the notion that insight into true, transcendental reality was best gained by an appreciation of the concrete things of daily life.

While the actual extent of the impact of these philosophical and religious traditions cannot be measured here (they have been and are still being examined in a number of scholarly works), a few general points can be made, with particular reference to poetry. The interest in Daoist texts as a mystical, intuitive apprehension of reality proved attractive to early literary theorists, who then wrote of a transcendence of sensory perception and spatiotemporal limits that precedes the act of composition. Discussion of the ineffability of writing itself, its curious blend of conscious craft and spontaneous outpouring, found prototypes in anecdotes centering on the marvelous accomplishments of various artisans in texts like the *Zhuang Zi* [*Chuang Tzu*]. Classical Chinese poetry was an extremely demanding and highly crafted form, but the ultimate goal came to consist in producing a poem that, exquisite, left no visible traces of the artistry that had labored to produce it.

Daoism and Buddhism also shared a distrust in the power of language to express meaning with any degree of adequacy, an issue that obsessed poetic theorists as well. The preference for short lyric forms throughout the tradition may reflect not only certain conditions imposed by the language itself—its heavily monosyllabic character, the proliferation of homophones, and the resulting limited number of rhymes—but also an acknowledgment of the incommensurability of words and meaning and a consequent preference for the evocative and unstated, for suggesting a "meaning beyond words." A slightly different version of this ideal was embraced by Confucius himself as well, who expressed an impatience with students for whom everything had to be spelled out in its entirety. Indeed, the overlaps among systems of thought that to Western eyes might appear to be mutually exclusive and antagonistic are numerous. Perhaps the most important point to be made in connection with the relationship of these systems to the culture and literature of China is that they are best viewed as mutually necessary complements. There is a strong disinclination historically to extremism and an equally strong preference for harmony, evident on as minute a level as the love for balanced pairs and parallelism in both poetic and narrative forms. Thematically, especially in poetry, the most persistent issue focuses on the obligation of the scholar-bureaucrat to serve the state versus the powerful attraction of life in retreat. Confucianism dictated the former, except in extraordinary circumstances; Daoism and Buddhism sang the lure of the latter. In some instances the two possibilities were able to coexist: the integration of public and private was presented as the image of culture from its very origins. Yet in other cases, the contradictions between the public and the private, the needs of society and those of self, began to call into question this integration of the two.

Indeed, such questions were posed from the inception of the written tradition, in poems like "Encountering Sorrow" (fourth to third centuries B.C.E.), whose author, Qu Yuan, was forced to confront an inexplicable unwillingness of those around him to recognize the true nature of his self and to trust the motives behind his public actions. He was left with no recourse but escape, whether into death or shamanism, depending on what tradition of reading one follows. The poem expresses the disjunction between the individual and the body politic; later commentary tried to put them back together. Similar questions are suggested in the first comprehensive work of history, the *Records of the Historian* of Sima Qian (145–90? B.C.E.). Like Qu Yuan, Sima Qian had been unjustly accused of disloyalty to the state and suffered the severe penalty of castration in order to be able to continue pursuing his craft. Understandably, his work often focuses on the nature of justice in the world, or—more to the point—on why there seems, on the whole, to be so little of it. He delves into this issue by repeatedly asking why, if people behave honorably, they are not thereby guaranteed at least recognition of their virtue, if not conspicuous success in life. Sima Qian allows himself to ponder this matter at some length in his biography of Bo Yi and Shu Qi, two earlier and paradigmatic victims of this noncoincidence of virtue and happiness (loyal to the Shang dynasty ruling house, they refused on principle to eat the grain of the usurping Zhou rulers, retired to "eat ferns" on Mt. Shouyang, and died there of starvation). Toward the end of the essay he quotes Confucius and comes to the sensible conclusion that since the rewards of riches and glory appear to be in no way correlated to virtue, one might as well choose the path of virtue: one prefers it, after all, and it will as likely lead to worldly success as any other approach. He seems at this point to be heading toward the larger conclusion—one very comfortable for the contemporary Western reader—that living out his own shame for the sake of his writing and pleasing himself by doing good is thus a good in and of itself. Sima Qian sums up this attitude by saying, "When the whole world is in foul and muddy confusion, then is the man of true purity seen. Then must one judge what he will consider important and unimportant."

The biography does not end there, however; instead it goes on immediately to lament that "the superior man hates the thought of his name not being mentioned after his death," and that merely doing good is a waste if others do not learn of it. The ultimate value of virtue is measured in a public sphere—the only place where it really gains any meaning. In considering the question of why anyone does anything—and this must be seen, finally, as a meditation on the nature of his literary art—Sima Qian ultimately concludes that public recognition is prerequisite to any real private value. Sima Qian and his attitude here, already adumbrated in the situation of Qu Yuan, loom large in the Chinese literary history and thought of later centuries. This is so, owing both to his position as one of the first writers in China to manifest self-consciousness concerning one's very creative motivation and to his paradigmatic role as someone concerned in equal measure with his own integrity and with the political health of the realm.

The historian's ultimate valorization of a public life has an important theoretical dimension behind its practical side. In granting precedence to the context in which one lives rather than to any individual existence that can subsist outside that context, Sima Qian points to the pervasive feature of Chinese literature mentioned above: the sense that the individual exists more as part of a network of other beings than as an entity unto himself. This overwhelming sense of context also helps explain why Chinese narratives are characterized more by metonymic progression from a given point to a closely related point within an extremely broad range than by stories that develop a limited number of elements to reach a definitive climax and denouement.

The very form of Chinese history writing best illustrates this point. Chronological sequences centered on a story with a beginning and an end are rare; more common instead are collections of a large series of individual essays and biographies. These are accompanied perhaps by a bare listing of significant dates and events, all of which taken together provide a picture of a period as a whole. Later, when novels developed, they tended to take the same shape; often they did not focus on a single set of characters for more than a few chapters before introducing a completely new group. And even when the same protagonists are retained throughout (as in *The Story of the Stone/Dream of the Red Chamber*), whole sequences of events and characters that bear very little apparent causal relationship to or acknowledgment of the needs of straightforward plot development occupy large portions of the narrative. This is also the case with *Journey to the West*, where the series of episodes in which the book's heroes are tested continue with little regard for how the events in each episode move the plot toward its conclusion. As with history, the metonymic universe of narrative discourse encompasses the whole sweep of earthly existence and is thus theoretically infinite; narrative closure becomes an arbitrary and almost insignificant act. That many novels also present themselves as either real or imagined elucidations of historical writings illustrates, in turn, how the whole genre of *xiaoshuo*—in fictional narrative—in itself exists in a contiguous relationship with other forms of narrative. Rather than being a distinct and clear-cut entity circumscribed with definite and definitive conventions, fiction shades imperceptibly into the more "factual" genre that it so much resembles. It is perhaps needless to say that the converse holds for early history writing in China as well.

With history at the forefront of narrative concern, and with the persistent assumption that interests of the individual inevitably implicate a larger context, it is perhaps only natural that politics often comes to dominate novelistic discourse. One reason for this, of course, is the position of Confucianism within Chinese thought, already adumbrated above. As an ideology concerned above all else with the happy survival of the state, Confucianism inevitably placed concerns of state in the foreground within all varieties of written expression, while subordinating all other discourses. Given the extremely broad definition of concerns of state, however, the politics of the novel are at once broader and more subtle than we are accustomed to thinking of them. Since everything has a political dimension, for an author to introduce political concerns into his work does not require the overt signification that political literature has taken in the West; on the other hand, everything, whatever else it has, has a political reading as well. The point at which these horizons merge, however, was concern for maintenance of the overall context that guaranteed meaning to each fragment of life that was represented.

Since Confucianism harbored at its core the faith that state and society could perfectly mirror one another, depiction of any sort of discord, no matter how personal it might seem to us, automatically had profound social overtones. The relations of contiguity implicit within the structure of Chinese thought wrought its effect on the arrangement of values within the system. While the paramount values were assuredly positioned within a decidedly hierarchical order, they existed at the top of this order side by side in such a way that it was almost impossible to adjudicate among them. For instance, loyalty to family and loyalty to state were seen as complementary, but certainly of a higher order than loyalty to self. If, however, family and state loyalties happened in practice to come into conflict, choosing between them was an almost impossible task—particularly in light of the virtually universal narrative awareness that the major Confucian values were usually debased in their actual historical existence. The necessity of choosing between two imperfect values provides the major source of tension in traditional Chinese narrative, in both its ironic and pathetic modes. Chinese irony and Chinese pathos both force people to make untenable choices between ideals that have become seriously flawed somewhere in the course of their implementation, but irony makes light of the result while pathos stresses how unfortunate the consequences can be.

This type of structure is in a sense writ small within *Journey to the West*, in which each major character represents a particular concatenation of imperfect values that clashes with that of each other character. The final submergence of these differences through realization of the transcendent doctrines of Buddhism finally confirms the comic nature of the earlier episodes, but only perfunctorily resolves the problems raised by the juxtaposition of the differing virtues. What renders *The Story of the Stone* so painful is the degree to which the faulty implementation of the dominant values of Confucian society destroys any possible honorable accommodation to them. In Cao Xueqin's novel, the belief that society and its ideology faithfully represent one another has turned into a disabling fear of the consequences that would ensue if the claim were true. The characters' corrosive inability to find alternative means

to lodge their subjective impulses accompanies this disillusion with the prevailing order. This inability is a powerful foreshadowing of the crisis of modern
literature, in which the fabric of traditional values has become so tattered that
there can be no meaningful response to the situation.

CHINESE LITERATURE IN THE TWENTIETH CENTURY

With the widespread realization among the educated that traditional culture
was increasingly unable to meet the political challenge presented by the
coming of Western power, a sense of cultural crisis marked intellectual discourse in China after 1895. For a variety of reasons, but perhaps primarily
because it was the only field of endeavor regarded as having the broad scope
required, literature became a focal point of efforts to meet the new demands
made upon the Chinese conceptual order. The years after 1895 witnessed the
publication of a spate of novels that wove their net of social relations with
an irony calculated to demonstrate the bankruptcy of the network as a whole.
This gloomy picture of the whole is punctuated by tentative efforts to establish the possibility of individual perception independent of what was seen as
the tyranny of a received wisdom that insisted upon a uniform view of social
events. More often, however, the cause of individual perception is mocked by
a relentless epistemology that puts true understanding of events at a level of
complexity far beyond the capacity of the individual knowing mind.

In this sense, the wide metonymic scope of the traditional conceptual
order presents a devastating paradox at its moment of crisis: the very com-
prehensiveness that had at one time insured a place for everything now
defeated any attempts to separate out discrete perceptions that would shape
events into some new order. If the old order could continue to move along
on its own terms by not changing its conception of the relationship of parts
to whole, the new context represented by the wider world had rendered the
old context radically contingent and finite by making Chinese civilization
merely one narrative among others. It was at the point where the relentless
exploration implicit within the old system suddenly discovered its new boundaries that the ultimate cultural crisis exploded in modern China.

Of the writers of the iconoclastic period that began around 1917, Lu Xun
comes closest to the crux of the problem in his brief accounts of individual
failures to communicate at any level with the rest of society. His characters
are continually obsessed with their inability to transmit their own notions
about a society that is constitutionally unable to live up to its own promises
to itself. This in turn casts a negative light upon the tradition of a literature
that had always vowed to itself that depicting a representative sample of experience would satisfactorily encompass the whole—and it is decidedly negation that Lu Xun seeks. For if to be understood one must become part of
an extended network of meaning, Lu Xun and his various personae would

emphatically reject the invitation. Thus another paradox of literature in modern China centers on the desire of authors to escape being integrated within the framework of traditional understanding by destroying the relationships of meaning they find around them. But the destruction of these networks in an important sense also destroys the possibility of representing any entity beyond the writer's own tormented self-consciousness. In response to the pervasive objectivity of events that no longer seem to add up to anything, writers retreat into denial and intransitive subjectivity. This inability to move the focus beyond themselves painfully blocked out any possibility of fulfilling the desire to express the full dimensions of the cultural crisis that had caused them to turn to literature in the first place.

The extraordinary frustration implicit in this reduced posture perhaps best explains why Chinese writers were so drawn to Marxism. As an ideology that offered powers of rational explanation of the same order as Confucianism, while at the same time—at least initially—utterly rejecting the particulars that the tradition had based itself upon, Marxism offered a restoration of context that took into account the extraordinary changes that had so disordered the Confucian worldview in its final years as the orthodoxy. Marxism also had the considerable virtue of building a context that included the whole world and all its history. With the metaphoric sweep of its dynamic view of historical change, Marxism turned Confucianism on its head even as it maintained the contextual range of old patterns of thought. That the ideology of revolution had a ready explanation as to why intellectuals were restricted to wallowing in their subjectivity only made it that much more appealing. The literature that Mao called for in his famous utterances of 1942 (*Talks at the Yan'an Forum on Literature and Art*) specifically denied the legitimacy of any further explorations of the personal worlds of the authors; the remarkable acquiescence this prohibition encountered testifies as powerfully to the desperate situation writers had worked themselves into as it does to the brute power of state enforcement.

With literature now enlisted in the campaign to create a new context for China, it was at the same time reinvested with tremendous powers of signification. It was the job of literature to demonstrate the existence of the new order, and writers, well aware of the alternative, threw themselves into the task. But as the new context either failed to materialize or, far worse, began to manifest alarming similarities with the tradition, writers were also assigned the duty to find out why—with the important caveat that the Communist Party could never be at fault. Ruling out the Party and its class allies left writers with a set of familiar targets: the bourgeoisie, the intellectuals, and, above all, themselves—or perhaps more accurately, other writers. The sad reality left to literature by the time of the Cultural Revolution combined the worst features of the traditional and the modern: a vulgar and utterly mechanical didacticism combined with the renewal of doubt about the legitimacy of the authorial voice. It is no wonder that literature after 1979 began with a veritable orgy of subjectivity: denied both subjectivity and objectivity for so long, writers quite naturally began the painful task of reconstruction by attempting to gain a new sense of themselves. This new subjectivity, however, had it remained fixated upon itself, threatened to take Chinese literature back to the indulgences of the May Fourth period.

In the past several years a number of new voices have come on the scene, working out new techniques to explore a broader horizon. Perhaps the happiest result of this reaching outward is represented by the work recently translated as *Chinese Lives*.[3] Superficially a collection of reportage, this work, in presenting the profound differences among a variety of people, perhaps marks the beginnings of the sense of a new context that modern Chinese literature has promised itself for so long.

NOTES

1. Walter Jackson Bate, ed., *Criticism: The Major Texts* (New York: Harcourt Brace Jovanovich, 1970), 85, 86.

2. Author's translation.

3. Zhang Xinxin and Sang Ye, *Chinese Lives*, ed. W. J. F. Jenner and Della Davin (New York: Pantheon Books, 1987).

chapter two

LANGUAGE AND INTERPRETIVE CONTEXTS

Roger T. Ames

Editor's note: Ames explains the fundamental difference between Western and Chinese worldviews as the contrast been dualistic and correlative thinking. The Western dualistic worldview distinguishes a primal, permanent, and perfect universal order that transcends the transient material world. The Chinese philosophical tradition, in contrast, embraces a dynamic, spontaneous world in which order is immanent and revealed in correlative and complementary relationships—*yin* and *yang.* Yet embedded in the English language is an Anglo-Saxon vocabulary that expresses a pre-Platonic, pre-Christian philosophical tradition. Translators are able to minimize the dualistic worldview that is inherent in the English language by invoking the Anglo-Saxon underpinnings of English culture—its oral tradition and correlative philosophy.

THERE ARE OBVIOUS REASONS for being curious about exotic cultures. It is surely the appreciation of cultural difference that attracts the scholar's interest and inspires growth. With the Western and the Chinese traditions, the worldviews that separate them make each of them arguably the most remote and exotic high culture from the other's perspective. To move back and forth between the Western and the Chinese worlds, then, is perhaps to traverse humanity's greatest cultural divide.

The civilizations that share the Indo-European group of languages are certainly many and diverse, but by virtue of trade, population movements, and the imperceptible dissemination of ideas, they have over past millennia developed a cultural family resemblance. This relationship does not extend to the centripetal Chinese, for whom the Great Wall has been as much a cultural screen as a physical barrier.

The prominent French sinologist Jacques Gernet argues with persuasion that when the two great civilizations of China and Europe, having developed almost entirely independently of each other, first made contact in about 1600, the seeming inaptitude of the Chinese for understanding Christianity and the philosophic edifice that undergirded it was not simply an uneasy difference in the encounter between disparate intellectual traditions, but a far more profound difference in mental categories and modes of thought, and particularly, a fundamental difference in their conceptions of human agency.[1] Much of what Christianity and Western philosophy generally had to say to the Chinese was, for the Chinese, quite literally nonsense.

The West fared little better in its opportunity to appreciate and to appropriate the Chinese contribution. In fact, it fared so badly that the very word "Chinese" in the English language came to denote "confusion," "incomprehensibility," "impenetrability"—a sense of order inaccessible to the Western mind.[2] The profound difference between prevailing Western senses of order and those dominant in the Chinese worldview plagued Europe's encounter with this antique culture from the start. With Eurocentric savants seeking corroboration for their own universal indices in the seventeenth century, they idealized China as a remarkable and "curious land" requiring the utmost scrutiny.[3] Their esteem for Chinese culture, however, plummeted from these romantic "Cathay" idealizations to the depths of disaffection with the inertia of what, in the context of their own industrial revolution, was cast as a moribund, backward-looking, and fundamentally stagnant culture.

There is a profound distinction between the European and Chinese worldviews that can be captured in the contrast between dualistic and correlative thinking. And there is a profound ambiguity that has emerged from the frequent eliding of these two radically different senses of order which has inhibited understanding in the fretful encounter between China and the West. It is this fundamental ambiguity of order that has, within the bounds of Western philosophical reflection, hobbled attempts to give Chinese philosophy and culture its integrity and its full measure of difference, and that has severely limited the impact of Western cultural influences on the Chinese experience.

To establish a working contrast, the gross lines of that sense of order dominant in the Western tradition might be sketched in the following terms. I say "gross lines" because the tradition is rich and varied, and counterexamples abound. Still, I would claim that one real contribution of comparative philosophy is that it does enable us to identify certain continuities and emphases in the dialectic of Western thought that are peculiar to it. And this brief characterization is made more persuasive by virtue of the fact that it is the dualistic sense of order, so prominent in Western philosophic thinking, which has been the target of its own internal critique—Vico, Nietzsche, the Pragmatists and Existentialists, and much of contemporary Continental reflection.

The Western cultural experience, going back to ancient Greece, is grounded in a two-world, reality-appearance distinction. This distinction challenges the ultimate reality of change and has largely defined the work of philosophy as the pursuit of the permanent behind the transitory. In Plato, this proclivity separated an immortal soul from the temporality of physical, sensual existence; it separated the universal and objective form of beauty and justice and all things good from their shadowy reflections in particular phenomena; it separated rational principle as some Archimedean point in the changing world of experience; it separated and elevated "scientific" knowledge available for discovery and contemplation (*theoria*) over practical and productive knowledge. With the melding of Greek philosophy and the Christian tradition, the immortality of the soul was guaranteed, the universal principles of truth, beauty, and goodness came to reside in a transcendent Godhead, and a rational theology promised that an understanding of the world constructed by the light of reason was consistent with and a complement to that higher knowledge available through revelation and faith. In this tradition, just as God's punishment imposed on human beings for their initial sin is mortality and change, so His reward for obedience is permanence.

The signal and recurring feature of Western civilization that emerged to dominate the development of its philosophical and religious orthodoxy was the presumption that there is something permanent, perfect, objective, and universal that disciplines the world of change and guarantees natural and moral order—some originative and determinative *archē*, an eternal realm of Platonic *eide* or "ideas," the One True God of the Judeo-Christian universe, a transcendental strongbox of invariable principles or laws, a geometric method for discerning clear and distinct ideas. The model of a single-ordered world where the unchanging source of order stands independent of, sustains, and ultimately provides explanation for the sensible world is a dominant if not an often unconscious assumption in this tradition.

The dominant Western sense of order, then, dating back to a pre-Socratic pursuit of some underlying *archē*, tends to be cosmogonic, assuming an initial beginning and privileging the primal, unchanging principle that causes and explains that origin and everything that issues from it. Hence the weight given to analytic thinking, linear, causal explanations and the dualistic categories in which these explanations are couched. There is implicit in this worldview a primacy given to some transcendent principle: the source of a top-down, disciplining order which can be discerned as unity and intelligibility, whether it exists external to us as Deity or purportedly internal to us as the hardwiring of our essential nature. It is a "given"—a source of order independent of our own actions and experience.

How do we escape these presuppositions of our own tradition, then, to discern and articulate the internal impetus that gives definition to both change and order in the Chinese world view? Jacques Gernet, in comparing the two traditions, observes that

> according to Aristotle, it is normal for all things to be at rest, whereas for the Chinese, in contrast universal dynamism is the primary assumption.[4]

In describing the largely failed encounter between the Jesuit missionaries and the Chinese intellectuals, Gernet ascribes the mutual misunderstanding to this contrast between externally imposed order assumed in our tradition, and the Chinese assumption that order is immanent in and inseparable from a spontaneously changing world. It is for this reason that the Chinese invested little importance in the conception of a willful Godhead:

> Believing that the universe possesses with itself its own organizational principles and its own creative energy, the Chinese maintained something that was quite scandalous from the point of view of scholastic reason, namely that "matter" itself is intelligent—not, clearly enough, with a conscious and reflective intelligence as we usually conceive it, but with a spontaneous intelligence which makes it possible for the yin and the yang to come together and guides the infinite combinations of these two opposite sources of energy.[5]

Yin 陰 and yang 陽 (or alternatively, Heaven and Earth, or ch'ien 乾 and k'un 坤) are correlative modalities, expressing the mutuality, interdependence, diversity, and creative efficacy of the dynamic relationships that are immanent in, pattern, and valorize the world. The full range of difference in the world—intellectual and physical, change and continuity, quality and quantity, nobility and baseness, fact and value, substance and accident—is explicable through these correlative and complementary relationships. Although there is an omnipresent hierarchical distinction obtaining between these complementary aspects—yang defines a dominant relationship and yin a subordinate one—these opposing modalities are resolutely continuous and inseparable. Yin and yang as correlatives are not universal principles that define some essential feature of phenomena, but are explanatory categories that report on a creative tension in specific differences which makes the immediate concrete things of the world intelligible. Important here is the primacy of the particular. Things of the same kind are not defined in terms of essences or natural kinds, but by virtue of the kinship resemblances that associate—"family resemblances." Hence, describing any particular phenomenon does not require the discovery of some underlying determinative and originative principle—a basis for making many one—but a tracing out and unravelling of the relationships and conditions of the phenomenon's context, and its multiple correlations.[6] The language of a classical Chinese epistemology has more to do with "mapping" and "unravelling" than with the grasping of some underlying formal essence presupposed in classical Western epistemology. Whereas in the classical Western model, the formal essence reduces the many to one, in the Chinese model, one evokes many. Each phenomenon in suggesting other similar phenomena has the multivalence of poetic images. Yin and yang, far from being universal essences, are invariably a perception from some particular perspective that enables us to unravel patterns of relationships and interpret our circumstances. They provide a vocabulary for sorting out the relationships that obtain among things as they come together and constitute themselves in unique compositions.

Now, disparate cultures, exotic for each other, are not available for wholesale import. They can only be appropriated respectively through the currency of their own language and experience. And it is in the vagaries of translating one culture through the medium of another that the important differences which have justified the project of translation in the first place are put at risk. Given this fundamental distance between Chinese correlativity and Western dualism, how then has D. C. Lau as an interpreter moved between them and, in translating them for each other, been so effective in using the language to minimize the problem of equivocation?

A distinctive characteristic of his translations is Lau's uncommon preference for the Anglo-Saxon vocabulary of the English language. This feature of his translations goes beyond the general stylistic distinction we can make between the sensibleness of British academic prose and its more free-wheeling North American counterpart. While the former works for the clarity and simplicity possible with the English language (think of Russell, Bradley, Stevenson, and of course, Ryle), the latter is willing to sacrifice ordinary language for the demands of more grand theoretical schemes. It is certainly Lau's preference for the Anglo-Saxon language that gives his readers the impression of simplicity and clarity. Compare Lau's *Lao Tzu* 61 with the distinguished American translator F. W. Mote:

大邦者下流也天下之牝也天下之交也牝恆以靜勝牡為亓（其）靜也故宜為下也故大邦以下小邦則取小邦小邦以下大邦則取於大邦故或下以取或下而取故大邦者不過欲兼畜人小邦者不過欲入事人夫皆得其欲則大者宜為下

D. C. Lau:

A large state is the lower reaches of a river—the female of the world. In the intercourse of the world, the female always gets the better of the male by stillness. It is because of her stillness that it is fitting for her to take the lower position.

Hence the large state, by taking the lower position, annexes the small state;
The small state, by taking the lower position, is annexed by the large state.
Thus the one, by taking the lower position, annexes;
The other, by taking the lower position, is annexed.
Thus all that the large state wants is to take the other under its wing;
All that the small state wants is to have its services accepted by the other.
Now if they both get their desire,
It is fitting that the large should take the lower position.

F. W. Mote:

A great country can be compared to the lower drainage of a river. It is where the world converges; it is the female of the world. The female, by its quiescence, always overcomes the male. By quiescence it assumes the lower place. Thus it is that a great state by condescending to small states, gains them for itself; and that small states, by abasing themselves to a great state, win it over to them. In the one case, the abasement leads to gaining adherents; in the other case, to procuring favor. Large states want merely to annex and accumulate people, while small states want merely to be brought in and given services to perform. Both, indeed, can gain their objectives, so the large state should assume the more lowly place.[7]

The contrast between these two renderings can be described in terms of Lau's concern to separate prose from verse and in the concreteness of his images, but perhaps the most subtle difference is the clarity that comes with his almost exclusive use of Anglo-Saxon vocabulary.

One of the virtues of Anglo-Saxon words is that they have by and large remained ordinary expressions in use in everyday communication. "Ordinary" in this sense means that they have escaped being drafted into the technical vocabulary of philosophy, and are therefore unencumbered by philosophical content that is bound to introduce distortion.

There are many examples of Lau's conscious avoidance of the technical language of philosophy. Where the vast majority of interpreters of Chinese classics have used Being and Non-being as equivalents for *yu* 有 and *wu* 無, Lau has consistently over the years used Something and Nothing instead. Being and Non-being are fraught with the assumptions of an essentialist ontology alien to the traditional Chinese view of the world. Being is the abstract quality shared by all things that are. Non-being is the opposite abstract quality of all things that are not. *Yu* 有, on the other hand, is not a shared abstract quality of things, but some things that exist (for example, *wan yu* 萬有), or the totality of things that exist. Something might not be adequate to express this latter meaning, but the advantages of Something over Being outweigh the disadvantages.

What is it about Anglo-Saxon English, in many ways a language within a language, which recommends it in moving between Chinese and English? I would suggest that there are at least three fundamental and complementary explanations for Lau's appeal to the Anglo-Saxon vocabulary. Firstly, this return to a pre-Latinized language is at the same time an appeal to a pre-Christianized world view. Secondly, the orality of the classical Chinese text and the conditions that distinguish an oral tradition from a literal one are most comfortably captured by the language of another oral tradition—in this case, Anglo-Saxon. And thirdly, there are identifiable characteristics in the nature and operation of the Anglo-Saxon language that recommend it for capturing linguistic concerns important to Chinese.

Nietzsche and Heidegger return to the conceptual clusters of pre-Socratic Greek as a strategy for getting behind the dualistic metaphysics bedrock in the received Platonic-Aristotelian-Christian tradition, and for exposing alternative philosophical possibilities. Both philosophers are persuaded that a particular worldview is sedimented in the language of a culture and in the systematic structure of its concepts, encouraging certain philosophical possibilities while discouraging others. As Nietzsche speculates,

> The strange family resemblance of all Indian, Greek, and German philosophizing is explained easily enough. Where there is an affinity of languages, it cannot fail, owing to the common philosophy of grammar—I mean, owing to the unconscious domination and guidance by similar grammatical functions—that everything is prepared at the outset for a similar development and sequence of philosophical systems; just as the way seems barred against certain other possibilities of world-interpretation.[8]

In fact, Nietzsche goes on to suggest even within the Indo-European family of languages, the closer a people's language is to Latin, the stronger and more entrenched is its commitment to the amalgamated Platonic-Christian world view:

> It seems that Catholicism is much more intimately related to the Latin races than all of Christianity in general is to us northerners—and unbelief therefore means something altogether different in Catholic and Protestant countries: among *them*, a kind of rebellion against the spirit of the race, while among us it is rather a return to the spirit (or anti-spirit) of the race. We northerners are undoubtedly descended from barbarian races, which also shows in our talent for religion: we have *little* talent for it.[9]

Other Western thinkers who have been self-conscious about sidestepping the underlying dualistic tendencies of Western philosophy have produced alternative linguistic strategies. Whitehead and Pierce invented neologistic categories which could be defined in such a way as to skirt traditional presuppositions. The phenomenologists proposed an explicit methodology for precluding implicit metaphysical assumptions. The hermeneuticists, in challenging "method" itself, have sought to expose "the myth of the given."

In the case of Lau's translations, the conscious appeal to Anglo-Saxon vocabulary and the exclusion of the Greek and Latin has precisely the effect of returning to the "spirit" of a pre-Christianized Old English. The "Latinization" of Britain was undertaken systematically by a wave of distinguished monks, scholars, and teachers who constructed their schools and church-sponsored institutions on a platform of classical learning in Latin and Greek. It is demonstrable that the most typical vocabulary introduced into Old English by these scholastic Christians was intimately related to the mythology of the new religious doctrines and to the details of institutional organization. The transformation that Augustine and his followers wrought on Britain was by no means superficial—it was a calculated and profoundly successful attempt by Rome to change the philosophy of a nation. Within a century and a half of their arrival in 597, England had risen to a position of intellectual leadership in Europe—a leadership that was justified by the successful transplantation and flowering of the alien high culture in a previously Anglo-Saxon land.[10] The classical Western worldview was digested and assimilated to the extent that the native Anglo-Saxon resources were conscripted into its service, and Old English itself responded creatively to the new cultural demands. God (not dĕus) becomes a hero rather than a transcendent deity; Christ is no longer some abstract force, but is cast as an Anglo-Saxon warrior whose crucifixion was an act of courage and daring; the cross is no longer an abstract symbol of human redemption, but is a tree with a particular history relating its own intensely dramatic story of humiliation, humility, and pride.[11]

There is a second significant change which occurred with the Latinization of Old English that has a bearing on the appropriateness of the original Old English for translating classical Chinese culture. With the rapid spread of Latin high culture, Britain was progressively transformed from a fundamentally oral culture into a chirographically controlled literal culture. The English language moved from the orality of a rhapsodic and "living" Old English toward the kind of literacy promoted by an analytic and "dead" Latin and classical Greek. Culture as the immediate revelation of the heroic unconscious of a living people gradually gave way to the abstractions of a learned academy.

But what are the specific features that distinguish an oral culture from a literate one? Walter J. Ong argues persuasively that the differences are fundamental and can be articulated in terms of significantly different thought processes, conceptions of personal agency, and social structures.[12] Much of what he has to say is familiar to us from the distinction between poetry, which evokes (presents) a world, and expository prose, which describes (represents) one. Paraphrasing and augmenting Ong's insights and observations, the oral mind can be distinguished from the literate in the following terms.

An oral tradition tends to be formulaic, patterned, and dependent upon mnemonic devices such as metrically tailored sequences, parallels, proverbs, aphorisms, and riddles. Recurrent quasi-historical allusions to memorable figures and events are repositories through which experience is stored and continued. It proceeds additively rather than through the patterns of subordination we find in literate culture: "And . . . And . . . And . . ." rather than ". . . who . . . which . . . that . . . ." Oral language tends to be aggregative, epithetic, and even clichéd where literate language is analytic (not oaks and soldiers, but repeatedly "sturdy oaks" and "brave soldiers"). The oral "text" tends to be redundant or "copious," and does not have the sparsely linear pattern of literate prosody. The oral presentation is characterized by minor variations on old and familiar formulas and themes, and hence tends to be conservative and traditionalist when compared to the more innovative possibilities of the literate text. Oral expression generates a complex history of variations and redactions, resisting the verbatim repetition we associate with the written word.

The order of the oral and literate presentations is different. The oral culture follows no strict chronological or linear order, but tends to introduce boxes within boxes created by thematic recurrences and allusions. There is no tight climactic plot. It tends to be rhapsodic: a medley of miscellaneous images patched together and collected sometimes rather randomly in recitation. Pieces of "text" are sown together correlatively out of concrete situations and operations ("axe, chop, tree, sap") creating images rather than following conceptually and logically ("tools") in the more categorical and abstract mode of linear, sequential exposition.

Given the immediacy and temporality of the oral culture, orality favors contact with concrete human experience and tends to express the abstract, distant, and objective by assimilating it to the immediate and familiar: a preponderance of colorful images and metaphors rather than the more stark language of concepts.

The hearing-dominance that attends oral expression encourages empathy and participation—it incorporates, unifies, and harmonizes, and fosters homeostasis in the communal organism. The scop or "historian-minstrel" would shape his familiar story to accommodate the interests and responses of his audience. The story line would be interactive and negotiated in a co-creative process that would seek middle ground between the talents of the orator and the dispositions of his audience. On the other hand, the sight-dependence of literature tends to separate, isolate, and dissect—it entails exteriority and alterity, separating the intention of the author irrevocably from the particular sentiments of the reader.

We can appropriate Ong's distinction between an oral and a literate culture for our discussion of Lau's translations on two levels. Firstly, anyone familiar with the general nature and structure of a classical Chinese text recognizes many similarities between it and the oral tradition as Ong is inclined to describe it. This similarity is undoubtedly a function of the role that orality plays in the birthing process of a written Chinese text. Since a written text can be the record of an oral tradition and can preserve many of the organizational features of its oral origins, the distinction between an oral culture and a literate one is at best tentative. Lau recounts in some detail the process whereby a text is standardized in his description of the gradual emergence of the *Lao Tzu*. He rehearses the principles of compilation that can be adduced from the *Lao Tzu* and other contemporaneous works, and attempts to lift the infrastructure of the *Lao Tzu* text to the surface by dividing its 81 chapters into 196 distinguishable sections. He sets off its rhymed passages, notes what is seemingly interpolated commentary, and does whatever is necessary to mark off further layers of arrangement without dissolving the traditional order.

According to Lau, perhaps the most familiar pattern of composition is the correlation of seemingly isolated passages on the basis of some topical similarity, where relevance of association can be as thin and elusive as the mere repetition of one or two catchwords, if it exists at all. In all of this effort to identify the seams between the shorter units, to reveal the looseness of the stitching, and to caution the reader against any linear and sequential reading of text, Lau is as worried about an order or logic that we might unwittingly impose upon the text as one that we might overlook.

The oral use the text would be put to even after it had congealed into a literate form is another factor that associates the Chinese text with the oral tradition. As Lau again suggests, the aphoristic passages of the literate text might well have served as rote centerpieces for oral commentary and discussion. The orality implicit in the development and use of the Chinese text would seem to recommend Anglo-Saxon over Latinized English as its medium for translation.

A second level on which Ong's characterization of oral culture can be related to the Chinese tradition can be seen in his claim that people resident in oral traditions think differently from members of literate cultures. This difference between the "correlative" mode of thinking associated with orality contrasts with the more "analytic" or "conceptual" mode of thinking associated with literacy. This contrast between analytic and correlative thinking is precisely the language I have used to distinguish the thought processes that characterize a Western worldview, dominated as it is by dualistic metaphysics, and the correlativity that features so prominently in the articulation of the traditional Chinese worldview. One immediate signal of this contrast between the dominant Western worldview and its Chinese counterpart is the vocabulary of philosophic reflection. The inventory of dualistic categories pervasive in Western philosophy such as reality/appearance, God/world, reason/experience, mind/body, form/matter, knowledge/opinion, object/subject, and so on, tends to suggest an ontological disparity and independence as a condition of the opposition between them. God is more real than and stands independent of his created world. Chinese philosophy, on the other hand, appeals to the correlative language of heaven 天/earth 地, yin 陰/yang 陽, thing (t'i 體)/function (yung 用), pattern (li 理)/energy (ch'i 氣), guest 客/host 主, husband 夫/wife 婦, ruler 君/subject 臣, father 父/son 子, where the opposites are complementary and mutually entailing. Once again, the correlativity implicit in the Anglo-Saxon oral tradition and its worldview resonates comfortably with the correlativity that is pervasive in the basic vocabulary of Chinese philosophy.

Finally, there are ways in which the Anglo-Saxon language works that make it particularly adaptable for capturing linguistic concerns important to Chinese. Old English is more concrete than are Latin derivations: "to grasp" evokes an image more readily than "to comprehend"; "cow" is more immediately present to the mind than "beef." This same evocative concreteness and concern to focus images is an often noted feature of the Chinese language. But the commonality does not stop here. An important feature of the Anglo-Saxon language that it owes to its teutonic roots is kenning: the construction of compounds or even phrases by juxtaposing words and images. For example, the ocean is the "whale's-bath," the "foaming-fields," or the "sea-street"; the boat is the "sea-wood," the "wave-courser," or the "broad-bosomed"; the king is the "leader-of-hosts," the "giver-of-rings," the "protector-of-earls" or the "heroes-treasure-keeper." These polynomial constructions do the work of abstraction by conjuring one image out of two or more. In this process of kenning, sound was not irrelevant. Often visual, imagistic clarity would be sacrificed in some degree in order to achieve an aural effect. This capacity for kenning—the creation of new meanings by juxtaposing and compounding concrete metaphors—enables the language to express the abstractions of science, theology, and philosophy while maintaining the vividness and vitality of the immediate image. Where there was a need for Old English to import a new idea, rather than appropriating a new word from the foreign language, it would frequently exercise this option of adapting its own resources. The capacity of Old English for kenning is reminiscent of the way in which the pre-Buddhist Chinese language functioned on demand to generate its abstractions, to maintain the focus of its concrete images, and to appropriate ideas from foreign sources.

Ways of thinking and living are sedimented into the languages that speak the world. A failure to be sufficiently cognizant of this linguistic baggage can easily lead to cultural reductionism. On the other hand, an awareness of how languages are rich with historical and cultural allusions is a precondition for the most fruitful kind of cross-cultural conversation.

NOTES

1. Jacques Gernet, *China and the Christian Impact* (Cambridge: Cambridge University Press, 1985), 3–4.

2. The examples of such a usage are many and varied: a Chinese puzzle (an intricate maze), Chinese revenge (doing a mischief to oneself to spite another), a Chinese flush in poker (a hand with no discernable sequence or pattern), a Chinese screwdriver (Australian slang for a "hammer"), and the ever popular Chinese fire drill (a college prank: stopped at a traffic signal, students leap from an automobile, run around in circles, and then as the light changes, they reenter the automobile in an utterly different order, much to the perplexity of other motorists).

3. See the introduction to D. E. Mungello's *Curious Land: Jesuit Accommodation and the Origins of Sinology* (Honolulu: University of Hawaii Press, 1985) for

a discussion of the "curious" (L. *curiosus*) inquiry of the seventeenth-century intellectuals.

4. Jacques Gernet, *China and the Christian Impact*, 210.

5. Ibid., 204.

6. See my "Knowing as Imaging: Prolegomena to a Confucian Epistemology," in *Culture and Modernity: The Authority of the Past*, ed. Eliot Deutsch (Honolulu: University of Hawaii Press, 1991).

7. The sources for this comparison are *Tao Te Ching*, trans. D. C. Lau, rev. ed. (Hong Kong: The Chinese University Press, 1989), pt. 2, 22–29; and Hsiao Kung-chuan, *A History of Chinese Political Thought*, trans. F. W. Mote, vol. 1 (Princeton: Princeton University Press, 1979), 287.

8. Friedrich Nietzsche, *Beyond Good and Evil*, trans. Walter Kaufmann (New York: Vintage, 1966), 20.

9. Ibid., 48.

10. See Albert C. Baugh and Thomas Cable, *A History of the English Language*, 3rd ed. (Englewood Cliffs: Prentice-Hall, 1978).

11. I am alluding here to the Anglo-Saxon poem, "The Dream of the Rood" (anonymous), one of the finest of a rather large number of religious poems in Old English.

12. This discussion is a summary of Walter J. Ong, *Orality and Literacy: The Technology of the Word* (London: Methuen, 1982), especially Chapter 3.

chapter three

THE CONTINUITY OF BEING:
CHINESE VISIONS OF NATURE

Tu Wei-Ming

Editor's note: Tu Wei-ming describes Chinese cosmogony as dynamic and immanent, precluding the Judeo-Christian dualistic view that differentiates between spirit/God and matter. Noting that the Chinese worldview is shared by many peoples throughout the world, Tu defines the concept of *ch'i* as the "vital force" that infuses the spontaneously self-generating and constantly transforming world. *Ch'i* energizes a world that is whole, dynamic, organic, transformative, and natural. The place of humanity is continuous within the dynamic natural world.

THE CHINESE BELIEF in the continuity of being, a basic motif in Chinese ontology, has far-reaching implications in Chinese philosophy, religion, epistemology, aesthetics, and ethics. F. W. Mote comments that

> The basic point which outsiders have found so hard to detect is that the Chinese, among all peoples ancient and recent, primitive and modern, are apparently unique in having no creation myth; that is, they have regarded the world and man as uncreated, as constituting the central features of a spontaneously self-generating cosmos having no creator, god, ultimate cause, or will external to itself.[1]

This strong assertion has understandably generated controversy among sinologists. Mote has identified a distinctive feature of the Chinese mode of thought. In his words, "the genuine Chinese cosmogony is that of organismic process, meaning that all of the parts of the entire cosmos belong to one organic whole and that they all interact as participants in one spontaneously self-generating life process."[2]

However, despite Mote's insightfulness in singling out this particular dimension of Chinese cosmogony for focused investigation, his characterization of its uniqueness is problematic. For one thing, the apparent lack of a creation myth in Chinese cultural history is predicated on a more fundamental assumption about reality; namely, that all modalities of being are organically connected. Ancient Chinese thinkers were intensely interested in the creation of the world. Some of them, notably the Taoists, even speculated on the creator (*tsao-wu che*) and the process by which the universe came into being.[3] Presumably, indigenous creation myths existed, although the written records transmitted by even the most culturally sophisticated historians do not contain enough information to reconstruct them.[4] The real issue is not the presence or absence of creation myths, but the underlying assumption of the cosmos: whether it is continuous or discontinuous with its creator. Suppose the cosmos as we know it was created by a Big Bang; the ancient Chinese thinkers would have no problem with this theory. What they would not have accepted was a further claim that there was an external intelligence, beyond human comprehension, who willed that it be so. Of course, the Chinese are not unique in this regard. Many peoples, ancient and recent, primitive and modern, would feel uncomfortable with the idea of a willful God who created the world out of nothing. It was not a creation myth as such but the Judeo-Christian version of it that is absent in Chinese mythology. But the Chinese, like numerous peoples throughout human history, subscribe to the continuity of being as self-evidently true.[5]

An obvious consequence of this basic belief is the all-embracing nature of the so-called spontaneously self-generating life process. Strictly speaking, it is not because the Chinese have no idea of God external to the created cosmos that they have no choice but to accept the cosmogony as an organismic process. Rather, it is precisely because they perceive the cosmos as the unfolding of continuous creativity that it cannot entertain "conceptions of creation *ex nihilo* by the hand of God, or through the will of God, and all other such mechanistic, teleological, and theistic cosmologies."[6] The Chinese commitment to the continuity of being, rather than the absence of a creation myth, prompts them to see nature as "the all-enfolding harmony of impersonal cosmic functions."[7]

The Chinese model of the world, "a decidedly psychophysical structure" in the Jungian sense,[8] is characterized by Joseph Needham as "an ordered harmony of wills without an ordainer."[9] What Needham describes as the organismic Chinese cosmos consists of dynamic energy fields rather than static matter-like entities. Indeed, the dichotomy of spirit and matter is not at all applicable to this psychophysical structure. The most basic stuff that makes the cosmos is neither solely spiritual nor material but both. It is a vital force. This vital force must not be conceived of either as disembodied spirit or as pure matter.[10] Wing-tsit Chan, in his influential *Source Book of Chinese Philosophy*, notes that the distinction between energy and matter is not made in Chinese philosophy. He further notes that H. H. Dubs's rendering of the indigenous term for this basic stuff, *ch'i*, as "matter-energy" is "essentially sound but awkward and lacks an adjective form."[11] Although Chan translates *ch'i* as "material force," he cautions that since *ch'i*, before the advent of Neo-Confucianism in the eleventh century, originally "denotes the pyschophysiological power associated with blood and breath," it should be rendered as "vital force" or "vital power."[12]

The unusual difficulty in making *ch'i* intelligible in modern Western philosophy suggests that the underlying Chinese metaphysical assumption is significantly different from the Cartesian dichotomy between spirit and matter. However, it would be misleading to categorize the Chinese mode of thinking as a sort of pre-Cartesian naïveté lacking differentiation between mind and body and, by implication, between subject and object. Analytically, Chinese thinkers have clearly distinguished spirit from matter. They fully recognize that spirit is not reducible to matter, that spirit is of more enduring value than matter. There are, of course, notable exceptions. But these so-called materialist thinkers are not only rare but also too few and far between to constitute a noticeable tradition in Chinese philosophy. Recent attempts to reconstruct the genealogy of materialist thinkers in China have been painful and, in some cases, far-fetched.[13] Indeed, to characterize the two great Confucian thinkers, Chang Tsai (1020–1077) and Wang Fu-chih (1619–1692), as paradigmatic examples of Chinese materialism is predicated on the false assumption that *ch'i* is materialistic. Both of them did subscribe to what may be called philosophy of *ch'i* as a critique of speculative thought, but, to them, *ch'i* was not simply matter but vital force endowed with all-pervasive spirituality.[14]

The continuous presence in Chinese philosophy of the idea of *ch'i* as a way of conceptualizing the basic structure and function of the cosmos, despite the availability of symbolic resources to make an analytical distinction between spirit and matter, signifies a conscious refusal to abandon a mode of thought that synthesized spirit and matter as an undifferentiated whole. The loss of analytical clarity is compensated by the reward of imaginative richness. The fruitful ambiguity of *ch'i* allows philosophers to explore realms of being which are inconceivable to people constricted by a Cartesian dichotomy. To be sure, the theory of the different modalities of *ch'i* cannot engender ideas such as the naked object, raw data, or the value-free fact, and this cannot create a world out there, naked, raw, and value-free, for the disinterested scientist to study, analyze, manipulate, and control. *Ch'i*, in short, seems inadequate to provide a philosophical background for the development of empirical science as understood in the positivistic sense. What it does provide, however, is a metaphorical mode of knowing, an epistemological attempt to address the multidimensional nature of reality by comparison, allusion, and suggestion.

Whether it is the metaphorical mode of knowing that directs the Chinese to perceive the cosmos as an organismic process or it is the ontological vision of the continuity of being that informs Chinese epistemology is a highly intriguing question. Our main concern here, however, is to understand how the idea of the undifferentiated *ch'i* serves as a basis for a unified cosmological theory. We want to know in what sense the least intelligent being, such as a rock, and the highest manifestation of spirituality, such as heaven, both consist of *ch'i*. The way the Chinese perceive reality and the sense of reality which defines the Chinese way of seeing the world are equally important in our inquiry, even though we do not intend to specify any causal relationship between them.

The organismic process as a spontaneously self-generating life process exhibits three basic motifs: continuity, wholeness, and dynamism.[15] All modalities of being, from a rock to heaven, are integral parts of a continuum which is often referred to as the "great transformation" (*ta-hua*).[16] Since nothing is outside of this continuum, the chain of being is never broken. A linkage will always be found between any given pair of things in the universe. We may have to probe deeply to find some of the linkages, but they are there to be discovered. These are not figments of our imagination but solid foundations upon which the cosmos and our lived world therein are constructed. *Ch'i*, the psychophysiological stuff, is everywhere. It suffuses even the "great void" (*t'ai-hsu*) which is the source of all beings in Chang Tsai's philosophy.[17] The continuous presence of *ch'i* in all modalities of being makes everything flow together as the unfolding of a single process. Nothing, not even an almighty creator, is external to this process.

This motif of wholeness is directly derived from the idea of continuity as all-encompassing. If the world were created by an intelligence higher than and external to the great transformation, it would, by definition, fall short of a manifestation of holism. Similarly, if the world were merely a partial or distorted manifestation of the Platonic Idea, it would never achieve the perfection of the original reality. On the contrary, if genuine creativity is not the creation of something out of nothing, but a continuous transformation of that which is already there, the world as it now exists is the authentic manifestation of the cosmic process in its all-embracing fullness. Indeed, if the Idea for its own completion entails that it realize itself through the organismic process, the world is in every sense the concrete embodiment of the Idea. Traditional Chinese thinkers, of course, did not philosophize in those terms. They used different conceptual apparatuses to convey their thought. To them, the appropriate metaphor for understanding the universe was biology rather than physics. At issue was not the eternal, static structure but the dynamic process of growth and transformation. To say that the cosmos is a continuum and that all of its components are internally connected is also to say that it is an organismic unity, holistically integrated at each level of complexity.

It is important to note that continuity and wholeness in Chinese cosmological thinking must be accompanied in the third motif, dynamism, lest the idea of organismic unity imply a closed system. While Chinese thinkers are critically aware of the inertia in human culture which may eventually lead to stagnation, they perceive the "course of heaven" (*t'ien-hsing*) as "vigorous" (*chien*) and instruct people to model themselves on the ceaseless vitality of the cosmic process.[18] What they envision in the spontaneously self-generating life process is not only inner connectedness and interdependence but also infinite potential for development. Many historians have remarked that the traditional Chinese notion of cyclic change, like the recurrence of the seasonal pattern, is incompatible with the modern Western idea of progress. To be sure, the traditional Chinese conception of history lacks the idea of unilinear development, such as Marxian modes of production depicting a form of historical inevitability. It is misleading, however, to describe Chinese history as chronicling a number of related events happening in a regularly repeated order.[19] Chinese historiography is not a reflection of a cyclic worldview. The Chinese worldview is neither cyclic nor spiral. It is transformational. The specific curve around which it transforms at a given period of time is indeterminate, however, for numerous human and nonhuman factors are involved in shaping its form and direction.

The organismic life process, which Mote contends is the genuine Chinese cosmogony, is an open system. As there is no temporal beginning to specify, no closure is ever contemplated. The cosmos is forever expanding; the great transformation is unceasing. The idea of unilinear development, in this perspective, is one-sided because it fails to account for the whole range of possibility in which progress constitutes but one of several dominant configurations. By analogy, neither cyclic nor spiral movements can fully depict the varieties of cosmic transformation. Since it is open rather than closed and dynamic rather than static, no geometric design can do justice to its complex morphology.

Earlier, I followed Mote in characterizing the Chinese vision of nature as the "all-enfolding harmony of impersonal cosmic function" and remarked that this particular vision was prompted by the Chinese commitment to the continuity of being. Having discussed the three basic motifs of Chinese cosmology—wholeness, dynamism, and continuity—I can elaborate on Mote's characterization by discussing some of its implications. The idea of all-enfolding harmony involves two interrelated meanings. It means that nature is all inclusive, the spontaneously self-generating life process which excludes nothing. The Taoist idea of tzu-jan ("self-so"),[20] which is used in modern Chinese to translate the English word nature, aptly captures this spirit. To say that self-so is all-inclusive is to posit a nondiscriminatory and nonjudgmental position, to allow all modalities of being to display themselves as they are. This is possible, however, only if competitiveness, domination, and aggression are thoroughly transformed. Thus, all-enfolding harmony also means that internal resonance underlies the order of things in the universe. Despite conflict and tension, which are like waves of the ocean, the deep structure of nature is always tranquil. The great transformation of which nature is the concrete manifestation is the result of concord rather than discord and convergence rather than divergence.

This vision of nature may suggest an unbridled romantic assertion about peace and love, the opposite of what Charles Darwin realistically portrayed as the rules of nature. Chinese thinkers, however, did not take the all-enfolding harmony to be the original naïveté of the innocent. Nor did they take it to be an idealist utopia attainable in a distant future. They were acutely aware that the world we live in, far from being the "great unity" (ta-t'ung) recommended in the *Evolution of the Rites*,[21] is laden with disruptive forces including humanly caused calamities and natural catastrophes. They also knew well that history is littered with internecine warfare, oppression, injustice, and numerous other forms of cruelty. It was not naïve romanticism that prompted them to assert that harmony is a defining characteristic of the organismic process. They believed that it is an accurate description of what the cosmos really is and how it actually works.

One advantage of rendering *ch'i* as "vital force," bearing in mind its original association with blood and breath, is its emphasis on the life process. To Chinese thinkers, nature is vital force in display. It is continuous, holistic, and dynamic. Yet, in an attempt to understand the blood and breath of nature's vitality, Chinese thinkers discovered that its enduring pattern is union rather than disunion, integration rather than disintegration, and synthesis rather than separation. The eternal flow of nature is characterized by the concord and convergence of numerous streams of vital force. It is in this sense that the organismic process is considered harmonious.

Chang Tsai, in his celebrated metaphysical treatise, "Correcting Youthful Ignorance," defines the cosmos as the "Great Harmony."

> The Great Harmony is called the Tao. It embraces the nature which underlies all counter processes of floating and sinking, rising and falling, and motion and rest. It is the origin of the process of fusion and intermingling, of overcoming and being overcome, and of expansion and contraction. At the commencement, these processes are incipient, subtle, obscure, easy, and simple, but at the end they are extensive, great, strong and firm. It is *ch'ien* ("heaven") that begins with the knowledge of Change, and *k'un* ("earth") that models after simplicity. That which is dispersed, differentiated, and discernible in form becomes *ch'i*, and that which is pure, penetrating, and not discernible in form becomes spirit. Unless the whole universe is in the process of fusion and intermingling like fleeting forces moving in all directions, it may not be called "Great Harmony."[22]

In his vision, nature is the result of the fusion and intermingling of the vital forces that assume tangible forms. Mountains, rivers, rocks, trees, animals, and human beings are all modalities of energy-matter, symbolizing that the creative transformation of the Tao is forever present. Needham's idea of the Chinese cosmos as an ordered harmony of wills without an ordainer is, however, not entirely appropriate. Wills, no matter how broadly defined, do not feature prominently here. The idea that heaven and earth complete the transformation with no mind of their own clearly indicates that the harmonious state of the organismic process is not achieved by ordering divergent wills.[23] Harmony will be attained through spontaneity. In what sense is this what Mote calls "impersonal cosmic function"? Let us return to Chang Tsai's metaphysical treatise.

> Ch'i moves and flows in all directions and in all manners. Its two elements [yin and yang] unite and give rise to the concrete. Thus the multiplicity of things and human beings is produced. In their ceaseless successions of two elements of yin and yang constitute the great principles of the universe.[24]

This inner logic of ch'i, which is singularly responsible for the production of the myriad things, leads to a naturalistic description of the impersonal cosmic function. Wang Fu-chi, who developed Chang Tsai's metaphysics of ch'i with great persuasive power, continues with this line of thinking.

> The fact that the things of the world, whether rivers or mountains, plants or animals, those with or without intelligence, and those yielding blossoms or bearing fruits, provide beneficial support for all things is the result of the natural influence of the moving power of ch'i. It fills the universe. And as it completely provides for the flourish and transformation of all things, it is all the more spatially unrestricted. As it is not spatially restricted, it operates in time and proceeds with time. From morning to evening, from spring to summer, and from the present tracing back to the past, there is no time at which it does not operate, and there is no time at which it does not produce. Consequently, as one sprout bursts forth it becomes a tree with a thousand big branches, and as an egg evolves, it progressively becomes a fish capable of swallowing a ship. . . .[25]

The underlying message, however, is not the impersonality of the cosmic function, even though the idea of the moving power of ch'i indicates that no anthropomorphic god, animal, or object is really behind the great transformation. The naturalness of the cosmic function, despite human wishes and desires, is impersonal but not inhuman. It is impartial to all modalities of being and not merely anthropocentric. We humans, therefore, do not find the impersonal cosmic function cold, alien, or distant, although we know that it is, by and large, indifferent to and disinterested in our private thoughts and whims. Actually, we are an integral part of this function; we are ourselves the result of this moving power of ch'i. Like mountains and rivers, we are legitimate beings in this great transformation. The opening lines in Chang Tsai's Western Inscription are not only his article of faith but also his ontological view of the human.

> Heaven is my father and earth is my mother, and even such a small being as I finds an intimate place in their midst. Therefore, that which fills the universe I regard as my body and that which directs the universe I regard as my nature. All people are my brothers and sisters, and all things are my companions.[26]

The sense of intimacy with which Chang Tsai, as a single person, relates himself to the universe as a whole reflects his profound awareness of moral ecology. Humanity is the respectful son or daughter of the cosmic process. This humanistic vision is distinctively Confucian in character. It contrasts sharply with the Taoist idea of noninterference on the one hand and the Buddhist concept of detachment on the other. Yet the notion of humanity as forming one body with the universe has been so widely accepted by the Chinese, in popular as well as elite culture, that it can very well be characterized as a general Chinese worldview.

Forming one body with the universe can literally mean that since all modalities of being are made of *ch'i*, human life is part of a continuous flow of the blood and breath that constitutes the cosmic process. Human beings are thus organically connected with rocks, trees, and animals. Understandably, the interplay and interchange between discrete species feature prominently in Chinese literature, notably popular novels. The monkey in the *Journey to the West* came into being by metamorphosis from an agate;[27] the hero in the *Dream of the Red Chamber* or the *Story of the Stone*, Pao-yu, is said to have been transformed from a piece of precious jade;[28] and the heroine of the *Romance of the White Snake* has not completely succeeded in transfiguring herself into a beautiful woman.[29] These are well-known stories. They have evoked strong sympathetic responses from Chinese audiences young and old for centuries, not merely as fantasies but as great human drama. It is not at all difficult for the Chinese to imagine that an agate or a piece of jade can have enough potential spirituality to transform itself into a human being. Part of the pathos of the White Snake lies in her inability to fight against the spell cast by a ruthless monk so that she can retain her human form and be united with her lover. The fascinating element in this romance is that she manages to acquire the power to transfigure herself into a woman through several hundred years of self-cultivation.

Presumably, from the cosmic vantage point, nothing is totally fixed. It need not be forever the identity it now assumes. In the perceptive eye of the Chinese painter Tao Chi (1641–1717), mountains flow like rivers. The proper way of looking at mountains, for him, is to see them as ocean waves frozen in time.[30] By the same token, rocks are not static objects but dynamic processes with their particular configuration of the energy-matter. It may not be far-fetched to suggest that, with this vision of nature, we can actually talk about the different degrees of spirituality of rocks. Agate is certainly more spiritual than an ordinary hard stone and perhaps jade is more spiritual than agate. Jade is honored as the "finest essence of mountain and river" (*shan-ch'uan ching-ying*).[31] By analogy, we can also talk about degrees of spirituality in the entire chain of being. Rocks, trees, animals, human, and gods represent different levels of spirituality based on the varying compositions of *ch'i*. However, despite the principle of differentiation, all modalities of being are organically connected. They are integral parts of a continuous process of cosmic transformation. It is in this metaphysical sense that "all things are my companions."

The uniqueness of being human cannot be explained in terms of a pre-conceived design by a creator. Human beings, like all other beings, are the results of the integration of the two basic vital forces of yin and yang. Chou Tun-i (1017–1073) says, "The interaction of these two *ch'i* engenders and transforms the myriad things. The myriad things produce and reproduce, resulting in an unending transformation."[32] In a strict sense, then, human beings are not the rulers of creation; if they intend to become guardians of the universe, they must earn this distinction through self-cultivation. There is no preordained reason for them to think otherwise. Nevertheless, the human being—in the Chinese sense of *jen* which is gender neutral—is unique. Chou Tun-i offers the following explanation:

> It is man alone who receives [the Five Agents] in their highest excellence, and therefore he is most intelligent. His physical form appears, and his spirit develops consciousness. The five moral principles of his nature (humanity, rightness, propriety, wisdom, and faithfulness) are aroused by, and react to, the external world and engage in activity; good and evil are distinguished; and human affairs take place.[33]

The theory of the Five Agents of the Five Phases (*wu-hsing*) need not concern us here. Since Chou makes it clear that "by the transformation of yang and its union with yin, the Five Agents of Water, Fire, Wood, Metal, and Earth arise" and that since "the Five Agents constitute a system of yin and yang,"[34] they can be conceived as specific forms of *ch'i*.

That humankind receives *ch'i* in its highest excellence is not only manifested in intelligence but also in sensitivity. The idea that humans are the most sentient beings in the universe features prominently in Chinese thought. A vivid description of human sensitivity is found in the "recorded sayings" (*yü-lu*) of Ch'eng Hao (1032–1085).

> A book on medicine describes paralyses of the four limbs as absence of humanity (*pu-jen*). This is an excellent description. The man of humanity regards heaven and earth and all things as one body. To him there is nothing that is not himself. Since he has recognized all things as himself, can there be any limit to his humanity? If things are not part of the self, naturally they have nothing to do with it. As in the case of paralysis of the four limbs, the vital force (*ch'i*) no longer penetrates them, and therefore they are no longer parts of the self.[35]

The idea of forming one body with the universe is predicated on the assumption that since all modalities of being are made of *ch'i*, all things cosmologically share the same consanguinity with us and are thus our companions. This vision enabled an original thinker of the Ming Dynasty, Wang Ken

(1483–1540), to remark that if we came into being through transformation (*hua-sheng*), then heaven and earth are our father and mother to us; if we came into being through reproduction (*hsing-sheng*), then our father and mother are heaven and earth to us.[36] The image of the human that emerges here, far from being the lord of creation, is the filial son and daughter of the universe. Filial piety connotes a profound feeling, and all-pervasive care for the world around us.

This literal meaning of forming one body with the universe must be augmented by a metaphorical reading of the same text. It is true that the body clearly conveys the sense *ch'i* as the blood and breath of the vital force that underlies all beings. The uniqueness of being human, however, is not simply that we are made of the same psychophysiological stuff that rocks, trees, and animals are also made of. It is our consciousness of being human that enables and impels us to probe the transcendental anchorage of our nature. Surely, the motif of the continuity of being prevents us from positing a creator totally external to the cosmic organismic process, but what is the relationship between human nature and heaven which serves as the source of all things? Indeed, how are we to understand the ontological assertion in the first chapter of the *Doctrine of the Mean* that our nature is decreed by heaven?[37] Is the Mandate of Heaven a one-time operation or a continuous presence? Wang Fu-chih's general response to these questions is suggestive.

> By nature is meant the principle of growth. As one daily grows, one daily achieves completion. Thus by the Mandate of Heaven is not meant that heaven gives the decree (*ming*, mandate) only at the moment of one's birth. . . . In the production of things by heaven, the process of transformation never ceases.[38]

In the metaphorical sense, then, forming one body with the universe requires continuous effort to grow and to refine oneself. We can embody the whole universe in our sensitivity because we have enlarged and deepened our feeling and care to the fullest extent. However, there is no guarantee at the symbolic nor the experiential level that the universe is automatically embodied in us. Unless we see to it that the Mandate of Heaven is fully realized in our nature, we may not live up to the expectation that "all things are complete in us."[39] Wang Fu-chih's refusal to follow a purely naturalistic line of thinking on this is evident in the following observation: "The profound person acts naturally as if nothing happens, but . . . he acts so as to make the best choices and remain firm in holding to the Mean."[40] To act naturally without letting things take their own course means, in Neo-Confucian terminology, to follow the "heavenly principle" (*t'ien-li*) without being overcome by "selfish desires" (*ssu-yü*).[41] Selfish desires are forms of self-centeredness that belittle the authentic human capacity to take part in the transformative process of heaven and earth. In commenting on the *Book of Changes*, Ch'eng Hao observes:

The most impressive aspect of things is their spirit of life. This is what is meant by origination being the chief quality of goodness. Man and heaven and earth are one thing. Why should man purposely belittle himself?[42]

Forming a trinity with heaven and earth, which is tantamount to forming one body with the myriad things, enjoins us from applying the subject-object dichotomy to nature. To see nature as an external object out there is to create an artificial barrier which obstructs our true vision and undermines our human capacity to experience nature from within. The internal resonance of the vital forces is such that the mind, as the most refined and subtle *ch'i* of the human body, is constantly in sympathetic accord with the myriad things in nature. The function of "affect and response" (*kan-ying*) characterizes nature as a great harmony and so informs the mind.[43] The mind forms a union with nature by extending itself metonymically. Its aesthetic appreciation of nature is neither an appropriation of the object by the subject nor an imposition of the subject on the object, but the merging of the self into an expanded reality through transformation and participation. This creative process, in Jakobson's terminology, is "contiguous," because rupture between us and nature never occurs.[44]

Chuang Tzu recommends that we listen with our minds rather than with our ears; with *ch'i* rather than with our minds.[45] If listening with our minds involves consciousness unaffected by sensory perceptions, what does listening to *ch'i* entail? Could it mean that we are so much a part of the internal resonance of the vital forces themselves that we can listen to the sound of nature or, in Chuang Tzu's expression, the "music of heaven" (*t'ien-lai*)[46] as our inner voice? Or could it mean that the all-embracing *ch'i* enables the total transposition of humankind and nature? As a result, the aesthetic delight that one experiences is no longer the private sensation of the individual but the "harmonious blending of inner feelings and outer scenes"[47] as the traditional Chinese artist would have it. It seems that in either case we do not detach ourselves from nature and study it in a disinterested manner. What we do is to suspend not only our sensory perceptions but also our conceptual apparatus so that we can embody nature in our sensitivity and allow nature to embrace us in its affinity.

I must caution, however, that the aesthetic experience of mutuality and immediacy with nature is often the result of strenuous and continual effort at self-cultivation. Despite our superior intelligence, we do not have privileged access to the great harmony. As social and cultural beings, we can never get outside ourselves to study nature from neutral ground. The process of returning to nature involves unlearning and forgetting as well as remembering. The precondition for us to participate in the internal resonance of the vital forces in nature is our own inner transformation. Unless we can first harmonize our own feelings and thoughts, we are not prepared for nature, let alone for an "interflow with the spirit of Heaven and Earth." It is true that we are consanguineous with nature. But as humans, we must make ourselves worthy of such a relationship.

NOTES

1. Frederick W. Mote, *Intellectual Foundations of China* (New York: Alfred A. Knopf, 1971), 17–18.

2. Ibid., 19.

3. For a thought-provoking discussion on this issue, see N. J. Girardot, *Myth and Meaning in Early Taoism* (Berkeley: University of California Press, 1983), 275–310.

4. For a suggestive methodological essay, see William G. Boltz, "Kung Kung and the Flood: Reverse Euphemerism in the *Yao Tien*," *Toung Pao* 67 (1981): 141–53. Professor Boltz's effort to reconstruct the Kung Kung myth indicates the possibility of an indigenous creation myth.

5. Tu Wei-ming, "Shih-t'an Chung-kuo che-hsüeh chung te san-ko chi-tiao" [A preliminary discussion on the three basic motifs in Chinese philosophy], *Chung-kuo che-hsüeh shih yen-chiu* [Studies on the history of Chinese philosophy] (Peking: Society for the Study of the History of Chinese Philosophy) 2 (March 1981): 19–21.

6. Mote, *Intellectual Foundations of China*, 20.

7. Ibid.

8. See Jung's Foreword to the *I Ching (Book of Changes)*, translated into English by Cary F. Baynes from the German translation of Richard Wilhelm, Bollingen Series, vol. 19 (Princeton: Princeton University Press, 1967), xxiv.

9. Needham's full statement reads as follows: "It was an ordered harmony of wills without an ordainer; it was like the spontaneous yet ordered, in the sense of patterned, movements of dancers in a country dance of figures, none of whom are bound by law to do what they do, nor yet pushed by others coming behind, but cooperate in a voluntary harmony of wills." See Joseph Needham and Wang Ling, *Science and Civilization in China*, vol. 2 (Cambridge: Cambridge University Press, 1969), 287.

10. Actually, the dichotomy of spirit and matter does not feature prominently in Chinese thought; see Tu, *Chung-kuo che-shüeh shih yen-chiu*, 21–22.

11. Wing-tsit Chan, trans. and comp., *Source Book in Chinese Philosophy* (Princeton: Princeton University Press, 1969), 784.

12. Ibid.

13. For a notable exception to this general interpretive situation in the People's Republic of China, see Chang Tai-nien, *Chung-kuo che-hsüeh fa-wei* [Exploring some of the delicate issues in Chinese philosophy] (T'ai-yuan, Shansi: People's Publishing Co., 1981), 11–38, 275–306.

14. For a general discussion on this vital issue from a medical viewpoint, see Manfred Porkert, *The Theoretical Foundations of Chinese Medicine: Systems of Correspondence* (Cambridge: MIT Press, 1974).

15. Tu, "Shih-t'an Chung-kuo che-hsüeh," 19–24.

16. A paradigmatic discussion of this is to be found in the *Commentaries on the Book of Changes*. See Wing-tsit Chan, *Source Book in Chinese Philosophy*, 264.

17. See Chang Tsai's "Correcting Youthful Ignorance," in Wing-tsit Chan, *Source Book in Chinese Philosophy*, 501.

18. For this reference in the *Chou I*, see *A Concordance to Yi Ching*, Harvard-Yenching Institute Sinological Index Series Supplement No. 10 (reprint; Taipei: Chinese Materials and Research Aids Service Center, Inc., 1966), 1/1.

19. The idea of the "dynastic cycle" may give one the impression that Chinese history is nondevelopmental. See Edwin O. Reischauer and John K. Fairbank, *East Asia: The Great Tradition* (Boston: Houghton Mifflin, 1960), 114–18.

20. Chuang Tzu, chap. 7. See the Harvard-Yenching Index on the *Chuang Tzu*, 20/7/11.

21. See William T. de Bary, Wing-tsit Chan, and Burton Watson, comps., *Sources of Chinese Tradition* (New York: Columbia University, 1960), 191–92.

22. Wing-tsit Chan, *Source Book on Chinese Philosophy*, 500–01.

23. Ibid., 262–66. This idea underlies the philosophy of change.

24. Ibid., sec. 14, 505. In this translation, *ch'i* is rendered "material force." The words *yin* and *yang* in brackets are added by me.

25. Ibid., 698–99.

26. Ibid., 496.

27. Wu Ch'eng-en, *Hsi yu chi*, trans. Anthony C. Yu as *Journey to the West*, 4 vols. (Chicago: University of Chicago Press, 1977), 1:67–78.

28. Ts'ao Hsüeh-ch'in (Cao Xuequin), *Hung-lou meng* [Dream of the Red Chamber], trans. David Hawkes as *The Story of the Stone*, 5 vols (Middlesex, England: Penguin Books, 1973), 1:47–49.

29. For two useful discussions on the story, see Fu Hsi-hua, *Pai-she-chuan chi* [An anthology of the White Snake story] (Shanghai: Shanghai Publishing Co., 1955), and P'an Chiang-tung, *Pai-she ku-shih yen-chiu* [A study of the White Snake story] (Taipei: Students' Publishers, 1981).

30. P. Ryckmans, "Les propos sur la peinture de Shi Tao traduction et commentaire," *Arst Asiatique* 14 (1966): 123–24.

31. Teng Shu-p'in, "Shang-ch'uan ching-ying-yü te i-shu" [The finest essence of mountain and river—the art of jade], in the *Chung-kuo wen-hua hsin-lun*

[New views on Chinese culture] (Taipei: Lien-ching, 1983), Section on Arts, 253–304.

32. Wing-tsit Chan, *Source Book in Chinese Philosophy*, 463. This translation renders *ch'i* as "material force."

33. Ibid.

34. Ibid.

35. Ibid., 530.

36. Wang Ken, "Yü Nan-tu chu-yu" [Letters to friends of Nan-tu], in *Wang Hsin-chai hsien-sheng ch'üan-chi* [The complete works of Wang Ken] (1507 edition, Harvard-Yenching Library), 4.16b.

37. Wing-tsit Chan, *Source Book in Chinese Philosophy*, 98.

38. Ibid., 699.

39. Menicus, 7A4.

40. Wing-tsit Chan, *Source Book in Chinese Philosophy*, 699–700.

41. For example, in Chu Hsi's discussion of moral cultivation, the Heavenly Principle is clearly contrasted with selfish desires. See Wing-tsit Chan, *Source Book in Chinese Philosophy*, 605–06.

42. Ibid., 539.

43. For a suggestive essay on this, see R. G. H. Siu, *Ch'i: A Neo-Taoist Approach to Life* (Cambridge: MIT Press, 1974).

44. Roman Jakobson, "Two Aspects of Language and Two Types of Aphasic Disturbances." In Roman Jakobson and Morris Halle, *Fundamentals of Language* (Gravenhage: Mouton, 1956), 55–82. I am grateful to Professor Yu-kung Kao for this reference.

45. *Chang Tzu*, chap. 4. The precise quotation can be found in *Chuang Tzu ying-te* (Peking: Harvard-Yenching Institute, 1947), 9/4/27.

46. *Chang Tzu*, *cap.* 2 an *Chuang Tzu ying-te*, 3/2/8.

47. For a systematic discussion of this, see Yu-kung Kao and Kang-i Sun Chang, "Chinese 'Lyric Criticism' in the Six Dynasties," American Council of Learned Societies Conference on Theories of the Arts in China (June 1979), included in *Theories of the Arts in China*, eds. Susan Bush and Christian Murck (Princeton: Princeton University Press, 1983).

chapter four

THE CENTRAL TRADITION IN TRADITIONAL SOCIETY

Wilt Idema and Lloyd Haft

Editor's note: Idema and Haft explain that *dao*, the universal pattern or ordering principle, is revealed through the on-going process of historical existence both in nature and also in human society. The central tradition of Confucian thought describes society as an expression of *dao*, defining *de* as virtue practiced within the hierarchical ordering of society. The practice of literature is an important act of self-cultivation within this tradition, affirming the typical, rather than the unique, since it expresses order and virtue. The literati were models of self-cultivation; the civil examinations demonstrated the place of the literati within the orderly social system.

THE WAY

THE BIBLE BEGINS with the creation of the world. As a consequence, in traditional Western thought the world of time and space is assumed to have been created by an eternal God, and a clear division is felt to exist between earthly and heavenly realms. The earth is associated with whatever is transitory, impermanent, imperfect, bodily—and sinful. Heaven is the sphere of the eternal, permanent, perfect, spiritual, and holy.

Traditional Chinese thought has no place for the idea of a creation. What exists has always existed and shall always do so. Accordingly, there is no concept of necessary "development" or "improvement" or "correction" of the creation through such means as a Fall, the birth of a Savior, a Last Judgment. Nor, on the other hand, is the existent world taken to be hopelessly engaged in continual degeneration. Chinese thought did not find it necessary to look outside this world for a First Cause. In the Chinese view there is no fundamental dualism: gods and demons belong to the same continuum as humans and animals; they obey laws that are similar or parallel to those governing the thoughts and actions of human beings. They are not denizens of a radically other or higher world unknowable in principle by men.

To be sure, there do exist Chinese creation myths, such as that of Pangu, out of whose body the world was supposed to have been formed. But these ideas are peripheral to the Central Tradition, functioning mainly as occasional sources of poetic imagery. And in the absence of any strong concept of a Creator, the traditional Chinese writer does not assume the role or pose of a god-like "creator" in his own right, as many Western authors have done. The Chinese writer does not have the pretension of creating a world of words out of nothing. Rather, he weaves or reworks given, existing words and ideas into a new text.

Since all that exists is regarded as constituting a single, integrated whole, there is no external realm or dimension in which supposedly higher truth can be sought. In the Chinese Central Tradition, an ordering principle is inherent in all that exists. It is not, as in some Western philosophies, a sort of inferior shadow or distortion of an Idea; nor is it an imperfectly glimpsed sign, symbol, or allegory of something else. In Chinese thought, although persons, things, or events are often regarded as exemplary or typical, they are never seen as mere reflections of supposedly transcendental realities.

Things are as they are simply because that is the way they are. The inherent principle of order, common to all that exists, is called the Way (*dao*). The way is not some sort of law or pattern that any higher power imposed on what exists. And since the Way is not so foreign to everyday human reality as to be past man's finding it out, it was never necessary for the Way to be revealed either by a God or by prophets. The Way reveals itself in the ongoing process of historical existence, and human beings who apply themselves to discovering the pattern or recurrent regularities in that process are perfectly able to do so.

The present is understandable as the instance of a pattern only if it can be interpreted as the recurrence of a similar situation in the past. Since it is vitally important to be able to compare present and past, very great value is attached to the writing of history. Written history makes the present meaningful and "workable." In all forms of Chinese literature, historical precedent is what is most authoritative. A given situation is not described in terms of myths, gods, or fictive abstractions, but in terms of concrete historical examples. Only what is typical has value. The unique, the individual, is a curiosity without meaning: a freak. The Way is knowable to man thanks to the accumulation of experience: Shennong (the Divine Husbandman), one of China's emperors in predynastic times, is said to have discovered the characteristics of the various plants by tasting them himself.

In Chinese literature there are no texts, like the Bible or the Koran, which enjoy the unique status of being considered the word of God. The Chinese writer did not aspire to prophetic stature, nor did he appeal to a Muse to inspire him. However exceptional the understanding of the Way attained by Confucius, or by his great model, the duke of Zhou, these great figures were and remained of human proportions. The Way is present not only in the physical world of nature—where it expresses itself in the alternation of the seasons and in the growth cycle of plants and animals—but also and pre-eminently in the life of human society. As part of the Way that inheres in all that exists, there is also a Way in society: a normal system of mutual relations between humans. It implies loyalty of the subject to the ruler, obedience of children to their parents, mutual reliability between friends, and so on. Ethical rules and the norms of morality are regarded as no more than the explicit for-mulation of natural tendencies that are in all persons from birth. There is only one Way, and for every relationship or situation that can develop, there is only one correct procedure. Every deviation from the one correct Way is incorrect and should be avoided.

There is, however, no such thing as an anti-Way, actively operating to seduce mankind into error. There is no such thing as a struggle between a saving Redeemer and a tempting Devil, between Light and Darkness, or between Good and Evil. Whatever deviates from the straight Way is crooked, deformed, heterodox. Crimes and misdeeds are seen as the result of defective understanding—a sort of evil arising from stupidity, caused by the confusing influence of desires. There is no antagonism between body and soul or spirit; desires are normal, but must be kept under control.

As long as all people conduct themselves in accordance with the one correct and normal Way, order (*zhi*) will prevail in society. Otherwise disor-der (*luan*) will result. The Central Tradition is acutely aware of how precari-ous and fragile a thing an orderly society is. People easily let themselves be seduced into forgetting morality in search of their own private aims, thereby obscuring the "difference between human beings and wild beasts." Chinese thinkers were strongly preoccupied with the horrors of misused and arbitrary power, of violence and of war. For them these things were Hell enough. Dis-order and anarchy were anathema, while order, rare as it was, seemed to them a Heaven on earth. Blessedness, for Chinese thinkers, is not a condition to be hoped for in a hereafter, but in life on earth in a well-ordered society. There is no Paradise other than what is brought about here and now by man on earth.

Order and disorder in society are so important that they actually have influence on all that exists. When disorder prevails in society, rains can be expected to fall out of season, crops to fail, and famines and natural cata-strophes to follow. When there is order in society, nature also flows along lines of regularity, making prosperity and happiness possible. Heaven and earth themselves are an accurate barometer of social processes.

Not surprisingly, the question of paramount interest to early Chinese philosophers was how to establish order in a disorderly world, and this same question remained the principal preoccupation of the Central Tradition down through the centuries. Students of comparative religion have sometimes described religion as an approach to issues of ultimate concern. The West has tended to contrast religion, as a field of the high and the pure, with worldly and "impure" matters like politics. Indeed, it has often been thought improper for the church to become involved in politics. In China, however, the ordering of society—that is, politics—was itself the issue of ultimate concern. Religion, as the quest for personal enlightenment, physical immortality, or eternal bliss, was, from the viewpoint of the Central Tradition, a private affair at best—which could easily degenerate into antisocial behavior. Owing to the concrete, this-worldly attitude of the Central Tradition, much Chinese literature strikes a first-time Western reader as rather superficial. On the other hand, tangible problems were treated with a seriousness that has sometimes been lacking in Western literature. Rather than speculating on how many angels could sit on the point of a needle, Chinese writers preferred to calculate how much seed refugees needed in order to make a new start as farmers. In high Chinese literature, at least, this seriousness resulted in a striking lack of humor.

Of course, even within the Central Tradition, there was more than one style of thinking about the Way. The older Confucianism always held that the Way, as present in society, is good, and that it can be known and formulated by man—for example, in the *li* (the rules for correct behavior, etiquette, and ceremonial). In the philosophical Taoism of the *Laozi* and *Zhuangzi*, by contrast, it is often stated that the Way in its totality can only be experienced through mystical contemplation; it cannot be formulated in words. These Taoist texts also describe the Way as amoral: as the foundation of all that exists, the Way is in the nature of an abstract principle and does not concern itself with the fate of individual humans. Numerous passages in *Zhuangzi* ridicule the Confucians and their constant striving to combat disorder by formulating norms for behavior.

Nevertheless, there is no fundamental antagonism between the two schools: both agree that there is one true Way and that order prevails if man lives in accordance with it. So it was possible for third-century Confucianism (Neo-Taoism) to gloss over the most obvious differences by asserting that the Way, inherent in all things, is to be experienced in its totality through mystical contemplation; it is one *and* moral. The Way as a whole expresses itself in the primary, complementary aspects of rest and movement, most clearly expressed in the undistorted forms of nature: rocks and streams, mountains and rivers. Starting in the third and fourth centuries A.D., nature mysticism, in which the contemplating spirit merges with the contemplated landscape and attains union with the Way, became an important element in Chinese literature and painting. Of philosophical schools, only Legalism (third century B.C.) challenged the idea of a single unchanging Way, claiming that each historical period has its own specific qualities and requires equally specific reactions and behaviors from man. But this iconoclastic view had no lasting influence and has always been decried as the ultimate heresy.

THE RULER AND HIS VIRTUE

All ancient Chinese philosophical schools (including Legalism) agreed that the primary responsibility for ensuring the propagation and observance of the Way and for bringing about an ordered and properly hierarchical society, rests with the ruler—the king or emperor. This remained one of the most fundamental axioms of the Central Tradition. The idea of society as a republic or an association of equal citizens was entirely foreign to Chinese thought, and Chinese history is entirely without examples of any such thing. It went without saying that the structure of society should be hierarchical; Chinese thinkers could conceive of a leaderless society as resulting only in total anarchy, the war of all against all. The self-evident nature of the hierarchical order of society in Chinese thought has been linked by some scholars to the universal practice of ancestor worship in Chinese culture, as ancestor worship insists on the subordination of the younger to the older.

The ideal situation is for human society to be united under a single ruler, whose power extends to the entire world. The ruler should fulfill his awesome responsibility by being a living exemplar of the Way, spontaneously displaying the behavior and speech appropriate to every context. His exemplary behavior toward his subordinates will induce similarly correct behavior in them; their own subordinates will then be likewise inspired, and so on, so that eventually all levels of society will function harmoniously and the whole world will be brought into a condition of order.

If the ruler succeeds in inspiring the appropriate behavior in his subjects, he is said to have *de*—a word which has been variously translated as virtue, force, *virtu*, and *mana*. The greater his virtue or *de*, the greater the social and cosmic order that will radiate outward from his court, permeating society and cosmos. The ruler is personally responsible for natural catastrophes; Chinese censors did not hesitate to attribute droughts or floods to culpable private behavior on the part of the emperor.

The ideally perfect ruler is said to "do nothing" (*wu wei*—no doing, nothing to attain). In other words he fulfills his ritual responsibilities, such as performing the yearly sacrifices to Heaven and Earth, but does not need to take more concrete steps to interfere in the course of events. The reason is that his *de* exerts such strong influence that all members of society automatically comport themselves in ways appropriate to their positions; there is no need for explicit correction. He is like the Pole Star, which remains stationary while the other stars turn in their orbits around it. Forcefulness in a ruler is laudable only as long as order is still to be established. Resort to force of arms is a sign of weakness. In practice, of course, war has played a prominent role in China's history, but at least in theory the Central Tradition has always regarded military matters as a necessary evil. Though soldiers were to be duly rewarded for their services, the Chinese Central Tradition has never known the romantic idealization of warfare that was a feature, for example, of Western chivalric culture. Narrative celebration of martial prowess developed in China only as a form of oral literature, subsequently having some influence on trivial literature (novels, the drama). But the deeds and words of the ruler, being important on a cosmic scale, were matters of intense interest at all levels of society. Historiography centered on the chronicles of the successive rulers, and the lives of the emperors continued to be a favorite subject of both high and trivial literature.

The ruler's responsibility for the world's well-being is unlimited. Aided by the apparatus of government, the ruler is to see that in every situation, every person shall think, act, and speak correctly. No distinction is made between state and society. In contradistinction to the West, where limitation of the powers of government was formulated in legal terms from an early date, in China there were in principle no limits to the legitimate scope of governmental authority: the individual had no rights vis-a-vis the government.

In practice, the government lacked the technical means to enforce its will directly on more than a few specific sectors of social life. Nevertheless, the government regarded itself as obliged and entitled to intervene wherever it deemed necessary. The citizen had no right to resist this influence, which presented itself in terms of paternalistic instruction and benevolent guidance. There was no division between the individual's rights and those of society (as represented by the government). Nor was there an equivalent of the Western distinction of church and state, whereby individuals, in certain matters of conscience, might claim to be under a different jurisdiction than that of the temporal authority. The Chinese government, for example, not only regulated concrete facets of the life of Buddhist monks but also intervened in matters of doctrine. In sum, the ruler united in his person the highest spiritual and worldly authority—which the Chinese tradition did not regard as separable—over the wide realm referred to as "all-under-Heaven."

THE BUREAUCRATIC CAREER

The life of an individual, especially a gentleman, acquires its value from the contribution the person makes to the ruler's sacred enterprise of ordering the world. It is potentially within every person's power to exude civilizing influence; one's *de* can have a positive effect within one's own milieu. This effect is predominantly on one's inferiors, but superiors are also susceptible to it. The higher a person's position in society, the more far-reaching the influence of that person's virtue. The greatest influence of all is exercised by those who fill posts in the government bureaucracy. Within government circles, in turn, it is those of the highest rank whose *de* is potentially the most widely efficacious. And the very greatest potential resides with those who serve at the ruler's side. A career in government service is the most noble calling possible for man. It also represents the only realistic chance of immortality, in the form of the lasting fame which one can acquire for the meritorious role one plays in the sacred work of ordering all-under-Heaven.

Though a career in government was extremely lucrative, the thought of financial gain was supposed to play no role in one's motivation. Only when severe poverty made it impossible to care appropriately for one's parents was it allowable to seek a modest government post specifically for the emolument.

Of all the gentlemen in the realm, the ruler is expected to select the most virtuous to be his helpers. Some are to fill specialized posts in the capital; others will represent the emperor in outlying areas. During the reign of a good ruler it is considered shameful to live in poverty because one has failed to be selected for a post. Ideally, one's rank in the bureaucracy is supposed to be proportional to one's *de*, and it is on grounds of their virtue that the ruler promotes his subordinates. In choosing his gentleman-helpers and evaluating their performance in office, the ruler and his representatives are supposed to attend only to their capacities or lack thereof; personal feelings or family ties are to be irrelevant. Whether the ruler appoints men as vassals or as bureaucratic office holders, the principles are the same. In choosing successors, the perfect rulers of antiquity bypassed even their own sons, giving preference instead to the most capable administrators. Appointment to office and promotion from one office to another are both taken as proofs of one's virtue. It is the most natural thing in the world for the holder of a high rank to regard his status as indicative of both his own virtue and that of the ruler; the countless self-satisfied eulogies were undoubtedly meant in all sincerity.

Since a career in government is to be the highest calling of man, there can be no greater evil than the presence of slanderers and flatterers who becloud the ruler's judgment. Speaking ill of others merely to better their own position, they keep the ruler ignorant of the qualities of those whom they slander. Good men fail to gain the appointments they deserve, play no part in the sacred work of ordering the empire, and are deprived of their chance at eternal fame. In theory, a perfect ruler will naturally see through the machinations of such schemers and punish them severely. Alas, not every ruler is perfect.

One of the oldest Chinese poems is the plaint of a dismissed administrator, who has been victimized by slanderers, unjustly banished from court, and thereby evicted from the sphere of blessedness. This plaint—the "Lisao" (Encountering sorrows) attributed to Qu Yuan (ca. 339–ca. 278 B.C.) and included in the *Chuci* (Songs of Chu)—makes heavy use of the erotic imagery of the shaman songs that were current in Chu. The ruler is presented, among other things, as the passionately desired but unattainable loved one; the mis-understood administrator appears in the role of the eager suitor. The plaint of the insufficiently appreciated gentleman persisted as a central theme in traditional Chinese poetry.

If it is shameful not to serve during a good ruler's reign, it is equally shameful to be in office under a bad ruler. Since a ruler will seldom be ideally perfect, even if his errors are many and serious, a gentleman should be ready and willing to serve under him as long as there is hope that he may mend his ways. If the gentleman becomes aware of abuses in the functioning of the empire, he is to report them immediately. He is not to hesitate to censure the ruler, preferably indirectly, but if necessary in strong language, even at the risk of putting his own life in jeopardy. Only after all attempts to reform the ruler have failed, and the ruler has revealed himself as thoroughly and hopelessly corrupt, must one give up one's post, or refuse a new one if offered. Such refusal in itself amounts to a denunciation of the regime, an impeachment of the sovereign. It also implies criticism of all those who do remain in office, suggesting that they are but evil flatterers, lacking in virtue, motivated only by the lust for money and fame. It is a condemnation of contemporary politi-cal activity as nothing but a vulgar power struggle.

Such a decision is not to be taken lightly. In the interest of maintaining one's moral integrity, one is deliberately excluding oneself from participation in the work of blessedness and from the hope of eternal eminence. Con-sidering the weighty implications and consequences, it may be advisable to disguise one's true motives by pleading one's own lack of talent, one's unsuit-ability for service—yet in itself, such modesty is a sign of virtue.

A gentleman who has withdrawn from government service is supposed to apply himself to the improvement of his own *de*—for example, through study or contemplation—and to wait for better times. Meanwhile, he is only too aware of the irreversible passage of time and the shortness of his own life. No matter how charming or enjoyable the retired life of the "hermit" may be, or how idyllically it is often portrayed in literature and the arts, it remains a last-ditch measure. The true vocation of the gentleman is a career in government.

THE STUDY OF LITERATURE

One prepares for a career in government by study, which is a never-ending process of self-cultivation. The goal of study is not the amassing of knowledge but the perfection of behavior. Through education man can be brought to full knowledge of the Way, so that in every situation that can arise in society he will spontaneously exhibit the correct behavior and speech. Though the norms are innate, man needs practice if he is to react normally at all times. The human mind is often compared to a (bronze) mirror, which must be polished until it reflects all phenomena completely and without distortion, allowing man to act entirely in accord with the moral situation. Mental growth is not a goal in itself. It becomes valuable only when it is substantiated in social relations. In principle, action does not have to be preceded by a weighing of alternatives, since in every situation there is but one correct action. Hesitation is a symptom of imperfection. A person's value does not depend on the heights or depths of his subjective experience or psychological processes, but on the way in which he fulfills his social role as father, son, friend, bureaucrat, and so on. Virtue is evident in deeds and words; one is judged on the basis of one's comportment.

Chinese biographers are not much interested in the supposed man behind the public figure. They nearly always confine themselves to a survey of the main events in the person's public life (especially the bureaucratic career); the comportment is sketched in a few bold strokes by citing typical acts and characteristic quotes. No attention is given to private life or inner experience.

Study is to be carried out on the basis of literature, and under the direction of a teacher. The Chinese teacher does not merely instruct his pupil in matters of knowledge or skills, but more importantly he guides the pupil in his continual rehearsal of self-perfection. The true teacher is an exemplar who does not merely expound the Way, but actually reveals it in his living.

Literature, upon which study is based, consists of writings that record the deeds and words of the holy rulers and their wise advisors—the formulations of the Way. Needless to say, within the body of literature, the highest importance attaches to those writings which record the deeds and words of the *holiest* rulers and the *wisest* advisors of antiquity. These are known as "The Classics" (*jing*, literally "warp of the fabric"). There is, however, no absolute boundary between these writings and those which embody the deeds and texts of rulers and dignitaries of later ages. As time goes on, the body of literature to be studied grows larger. By continually immersing himself in the words and deeds of those who embodied the Way, the student tries to assimilate himself to their ways of thinking and doing so that his behavior in comparable situations will be similar.

THE PRACTICE OF LITERATURE

The practice of literature—the writing of texts—is an aspect of behavior. In fact, it is the behavior! To write a text is to formulate the situations in which one finds oneself: the correct formulation of the correct perception, which must inevitably lead to the correct actions. To write a text is to put into words the feelings that a given situation calls up. Chinese literature testifies: the prose is historical or argumentative, and the poetry is lyrical. But the Chinese writer certainly does not, like the Dutch art-for-art's-sake poet Willem Kloos, strive for "the very most individual expression of the very most individual emotion." His goal is to formulate correctly the spontaneously normal feelings in a given situation in which such formulation is necessary or desirable. He is confident that the formulation of those feelings will evoke similar feelings in the hearer or reader. The traditional Chinese literary critic, naturally enough, uses one and the same term for the aspect of reality under consideration (the "subject"), the inner state of the writer, the style of his work, and the reader's response.

The literature of traditional China can be described as a sort of mathematics of society. Every situation permits but one moral evaluation. With regard to any matter whatsoever, the writer's standpoint and the feelings he experiences are supposed to be entirely appropriate to the situation. The formulation of his own judgment then coincides exactly with the description of the situation; and this formulation, being the correct interpretation, shall be utterly convincing. The writer's activity can be compared to that of a scientist: the scientist applies to a given process a specific mathematical formula which is both an adequate description of the process and a demonstration of the scientist's understanding of that process. Once the scientist has come up with the proper formula, it is entirely reasonable that he should rely on it for practical applications, and the elegant concision of the formula, recognizable as correct by others having the necessary expertise, wins confidence in its reliability.

A text is an act, a deed. The traditional Chinese reader approaches a text as both the description of a situation and an expression of the character of the author. Though he may well admire the internal structure of the text aesthetically, the text is never divorced from its referential and expressive functions. Also, the reader makes no distinction between the persona assumed by the writer in the text and the writer's actual personality. The "I" in the text is taken to refer to the writer himself.

THE STATE EXAMINATION

Since texts are regarded as directly revealing the character of their authors, the ruler can choose his administrators on the basis of texts they have produced—in practice, of written examinations. Once examinations have become institutionalized as the royal road to the coveted blessedness of a career in government, skill in writing and the mastery of existing literature take on an added aura of importance in society. The study of literature becomes more than just the pursuit of wisdom: it is the way to get rich. Before long the examinations become a mechanical formality, and the students devote their attention primarily to the types of text they will need to know to pass. Being the supreme embodiment of the belief that the text reveals the virtue of its writer, the examinations incited frequent travesty of that principle. Texts were often little more than impersonal demonstrations of technical ability and were criticized accordingly. Nevertheless, the idea that literary merit cannot exist in the absence of moral virtue has remained pervasive.

Notwithstanding frequent criticism of the examinations as overly formalistic, in one form or another they continued in use until the twentieth century. The traditional admiration for literary talent (*cai*) never diminished; the ability to improvise well on a given subject was especially prized and became itself a well-loved theme treated in countless literary anecdotes, plays, and fiction.

Despite the very high prestige it enjoyed in society, being a writer or a poet was never a goal in itself. To be famous only as a poet was to have failed as a responsible member of society. A great writing talent finds its crowning glory in a bureaucratic career: literature, after all, is practiced as a way of attaining virtue. High administrators, and the ruler himself, should also be the best writers. Writers and poets are not bohemians. Far from regarding themselves as at odds with society, they are actually the ideal types within society. The writer is a government official or hopes to become one. The modern Western reader is surprised if an ordinary well-behaved citizen, not even to mention a high executive, turns out to be a great writer. The traditional Chinese point of view reverses these terms: how is it possible that such a great poet as Li Bai (701–762) failed to attain prominence in government?

LITERATURE AND GENDER IN CHINA

By now it must have become abundantly clear that most authors in traditional China were men. Moreover they wrote for other men about the affairs of men. The ability to read and write was a precondition for a successful official career, and the act of writing was an act of participation in public life. In traditional Chinese society, the elite maintained strict separation of the sexes. While their menfolk pursued careers in society, in schools, and in the bureaucracy, the women of the aristocracy and of the gentry lived their lives secluded in the inner quarters. Before marriage a woman was expected to obey her father; following her marriage and entrance into a different family she was to obey her husband; upon the husband's death she was to obey the eldest son. Ideally, even a young widow was not supposed to remarry.

In the hierarchical order of society, women were subordinated to men at every level. While there was little explicit opposition to literacy for women as such, many men expressed concern that wide reading might well make women dissatisfied with their societal role. The very act of a woman's writing—let alone the desire to see her writings published!—was seen by many men as an unbecoming transgression of the limits imposed upon her. "For a woman, to have no talent is a virtue" was a proverb current in the Ming (1368–1644) and Qing (1644–1911). It is perhaps no accident that Li

Qinghzao (1084–ca. 1151), the only woman poet to achieve status fully equal to male poets', lived at a moment in history when on the one hand books had become widely available (she has left us a detailed description of the rise and fall of her and her husband's library), while on the other hand the increasing strictness of the Neo-Confucianist rules for personal behavior had not yet become institutionalized. Outside the home the only classes of educated women men encountered were courtesans and nuns. As courtesans were trained to entertain men by their wit and skills, many were literate and able to versify. Some were actually famous for their verse. Nuns needed literacy in order to be able to recite the scriptures.

Women with an inclination to write encountered another difficulty: tra-ditional literature offered scarcely a single form or genre that fitted their cir-cumstances, as the forms and subject matter of literature were determined by the social life of men. There existed a limited body of writings, usually by women, concerning the duties and tasks of women, but these urged against any literary ambition and hardly provided models for emulation. The earliest of these tracts is the *Nüjie* (Rules for women), written by the learned woman historian Ban Zhao (ca. 48–ca. 116), who ended her life as a teacher of women in the emperor's seraglio. Whenever literacy for women was defended, one of the most-heard arguments was that reading these texts on ritual and personal behavior would teach women their place. The impossibility of a woman's pur-suing a higher education and venturing out into the world of men was dra-matized in the very old and perennially popular story of Liang Shanbo and Zhu Yingtai. Zhu Yingtai insists on leaving her parents' home in order to study, and her parents eventually allow her to do so dressed as a boy. While study-ing, she falls in love with a fellow student, Liang Shanbo, who does not suspect she is a girl. Zhu Yingtai urges him to visit her parents and ask for the hand of "her sister"—i.e., herself—in marriage. When she herself returns home, she discovers that her parents have already promised her in marriage to someone else. When Liang Shanbo visits the Zhus, his request is denied, and soon afterward he dies. Zhu Yingtai requests that her wedding procession pass by his grave. The grave opens up and she jumps into it, after which it closes and a pair of butterflies are seen fluttering about.

Only a few subgenres of literature were more hospitable to women. Men often affected the persona of a lady pining in her boudoir, lamenting the absence and faithfulness of her lover but utterly devoted and loyal to him. The figure of the woman abandoned by her lover was an analogue of the offi-cial neglected by his emperor, and the use of the persona of a woman empha-sized the humility of the author toward his prospective patron. Many women wrote boudoir laments using the settings and vocabulary developed in this tradition. Li Qingzhao is a case in point. She and other women poets infused their poems with a poignancy and authenticity all their own; some went further and (though very rarely until the end of the nineteenth century) questioned the social rules that excluded them from full and meaningful participation in literary life and contemporary politics. Another genre of writing popular among women under the last dynasty was the *tanci* ("songs for picking"), long and involved narrative ballads in prosimetric form. One of the earliest preserved works in this genre by a woman relates the tale of a girl who, dressed as a boy, succeeds in the highest examinations and achieves the highest position in the bureaucracy.

Most authors in traditional China, whether male or female, accepted the hierarchical structure of society and the separation of the sexes as self-evident and unquestionable. Tales of women eloping with exceptional students who later pursue brilliant careers were probably not written or read as attacks on conventional gender roles, but rather as affirmations of the exceptional qualities of the male heroes. Traditional Chinese literature, both high and low, reflects male fantasies, male fears, and a male view of society and culture. While sex was never considered sinful, and marriage was regarded as the only normal condition of adult men and women, traditional physiology taught that a man possessed a strictly limited amount of vital force, which he might easily squander by overindulging in sex. He might even be robbed of his precious vital force by immoral women, fox spirits, female ghosts, or demons. Many visions of women in male writings reflect the same male anxieties found in other cultures. Typically, women are either glorified as self-sacrificing wives and mothers or vilified as insatiable temptresses. The more male society insisted upon the rigid application of the rules governing separation of the sexes, the stronger the fear of the dangerous woman seemed to become. On the one hand, stories of female suicides and virtuous courtesans abound. On the other hand, the figure of the female swordfighter becomes more and more prominent, perhaps reflecting an archetypical castration anxiety.

Not all male authors were completely blind to the injustices involved in the subordination of women. One way in which male authors in later centuries addressed these issues was through sex-role reversal, setting their stories in some mythical country where women, rather than men, have more than one spouse, and where the men are subjected to such painful practices as footbinding. Eighteenth- and nineteenth-century authors also show a distinct interest in the theme of the effeminate man and the masculine woman, and at least one lengthy novel describes a colorful assortment of homosexual relations. The first to question fundamentally the position of women in society were the reformers of the last years of the nineteenth century; yet their persistent male perspective is betrayed by the fact that they wanted society to produce healthier and better-educated mothers, who would raise stronger and more intelligent offspring. The first decade of the twentieth century saw the appearance of the first Chinese feminist, Qiu Jin (1875–1907), who dressed as a man, went to Japan for study, and insisted on full equality and economic independence for women.

All in all, whereas many other aspects of traditional culture have been swept away by the reforms and revolutions of the twentieth century, traditional ideas of gender have proven extremely resistant to change. Despite undeniable improvements in the position of women in Chinese society, equality of the sexes and female rights are still often seen as a gift bestowed on women by the government or the Party, rather than as their birthright.

chapter five

WOMAN, MORAL VIRTUE, AND LITERARY TEXT

Wendy Larson

Editor's note: In this essay, excerpted from a longer study, Wendy Larson considers *cai* and *de* as oppositional and gendered concepts of literary skill and virtue. Because *cai* is a public practice of literary statesmen, *de* discourages literary expression for women, whose virtue is traditionally practiced within a private sphere. This opposition has traditionally served to hinder women writers, and has also been greatly influential in the modern period. For modern writers who find fault with Chinese social tradition, the gendered concepts of *de* and *cai* have been specific locuses of criticism.

As a state-identified being, the self of the male citizen is fully unfolded and made complete. The state is the arena that calls upon and sustains the individual's commitment to universal ethical life, satisfying expansive yearnings through the opportunity to sacrifice "on behalf of the individuality of the state." . . . To preserve the larger civic body, which must be "as one," particular bodies must be sacrificed.

Jean Bethke Elshtain, "Sovereignty, Identity, and Sacrifice"

DURING THE QING DYNASTY, when literati engaged in an extended debate about textual training for girls, Yuan Mei elicited angry denunciations for his heterodox views on gender and literary talent and his poetry school that accepted girl students. The issue of textual training for girls became more pressing when missionaries set up schools for girls, and when Chinese intellectuals published controversial translations and books on education for girls. It was within the context of the national humiliation caused by the Opium Wars that the intelligentsia learned that the victors, previously dismissed as barbarians but quickly reappraised as they wrestled the mantle of civilization away from China, *seemed* to live by a set of gender meanings that allowed women not only a different social role, but also access to the entirety of national learning.

By the early twentieth century, when nation-states were forming all over the world, Chinese social critics working on the "problem of women" (*funü wenti*) often fixed on issues that recognized a certain historical background: in premodern Chinese traditions, *de* (moral virtue) functioned as a female sphere of knowledge and self-presentation against *cai* (literary talent), a transcendent male sphere of knowledge and self-presentation that included complex issues of education and learning.[1] Whereas some aspects of the *de/cai* relationship were restricted to elite culture, many extended into society at large. The combination of two discursive categories, that of *woman* and *literature*, in the practice of women's writing (*nüxing wenxue, nüzi wenxue*, or *funü wenxue*) transgressed both the sphere of *de* and that of *cai*, and became a radical modern alternative, promoted by a number of reformist critics.[2] Reformers presented woman/literature as "modern" and attacked woman/morality as a remnant of the past. However, the issue was hotly contested precisely because the traditionally sanctioned contradiction between (feminine) moral virtue and (masculine) literary talent came to the surface in the idea and work of the woman writer.

The reformist's promotion of women writers and women's literature should be viewed as a promotion of modernity, with its typical dissatisfaction with a past that can only be set right with new cultural practices. Yet it was not only that. The modern gaze, which looked back and found fault with the past, focused on the specifically Chinese social traditions of *de* and *cai*, which carried gendered meanings that had the potential to extend their influence into modern life.

DE AND CAI: MORAL VIRTUE VERSUS LITERARY SKILL

And, while it is not true that none of the virtuous and model ladies of China are literate and cultivated, still, the best of them are immersed in poetry, content with brush and ink [rather than useful skills and moral principles]. Words about sighing over old age and lamenting sorrow fill the women's quarters; phrases about spring flowers and the autumn moon abound in ink on paper. And the poorest are buried in stories from fiction and popular rhymes. Their fathers and elder brothers have failed to guide them according to their inclinations. On the contrary, they consider these [literary pursuits] useless and prohibit them. . . . Let us rescue 200,000,000 prisoners from the dungeons, eradicate the foul and absurd customs of more than 2,000 years, propagate the Way of the Sage, and restore our great utopian commonwealth [*Ta-t'ung*]. Alas, China, do not impoverish yourself by stopping up talents and stifling intelligence!

Kang Tongwei, "On the Advantages and
Disadvantages of Educating Women"[3]

In an article on women and literary talent during the Qing, Liu Yongcong invokes the saying that "Moral virtue is superior to literary skill" (*de zhong yu cai*) to explicate the meaning of *cai* for women. Through numerous references, Liu argues that although *cai* sometimes referred to general skill, it usually meant literary talent or *wencai*. The gist of Liu's research is to show that for both women and men, *cai* was often considered a liability that could result in poverty, misfortune, or early death—thus the opposition between *cai* and *ming* (life)—but for women, *cai* was an especially dangerous quality and something to be avoided. *De* was definitely preferred. Thus, in *Fushen liuji* (*Six chapters of a floating life*) by Shen Fu (1763–1807), the early death of Shen's wife, Chen Yun (1763–1803), became an example of what could happen to women with excessive literary talent. Chen's death also elicited criticisms of excessive emotion between husband and wife and highlighted the conflict between *cai* and *de* for women. *Cai* was valued, but it entailed a sacrifice, especially when women aspired to it. To show that the concept of *cai* was only with difficulty associated with women, yet that this view at the same time was contested, Liu quotes *Cainü shuo* (*On talented women*) of Chen Zhaolun (1700–1771): "It is commonly said that women should not gain fame from literary talent, and those who do gain fame from literary talent will often suffer misfortune. I hardly think so. On its own, fortune is not easy to gain, and hard to hold."

The ability of *de* to suppress and fight against *cai* in women is brought out in Liu's quote from Ye Huang, who claimed that women with *cai* became melancholy and pathetic, and would, if their *cai* was further developed, sink into melancholic oblivion; thus "it is necessary to suppress *cai* with *de*" (*gu cai bi zhen zhi yi de*).[4]

Other scholars who have considered women's culture from late Ming to mid-Qing times, have focused on the meaning of the woman's voice in poetry and the way in which it subverted or appropriated the dominant discourse, turning it toward new ends.[5] Late eighteenth-century polemics on the correct interpretation of classical texts grew into discussions on the meaning of writing, and approached another, more general topic: the relationship between the proper woman and proper writing. Although it may have originated much earlier, by the late Ming the saying that lack of literary talent was a virtue for women (*nüzi wucai bian shi de*) became widely quoted. This oppositional situating of literary talent or *cai* and moral virtue or *de* continued through the Qing up into the twentieth century.[6]

Part of the difficulty in associating virtue with talent was in the public nature of talent. The practice of *cai* could result in the dissemination of texts and, in that sense, *cai* allowed its practitioners to go out, thus crossing the boundary of the the inner/outer dichotomy that stipulated structured social interactions between women and men and separate spheres for men and women in architectural arrangements, clothing, education, and family relationships. In the story of the woman poet Xiaoqing, Ellen Widmer shows how celebrity became a problem for a woman, bringing dishonor and misfortune onto herself and her family.[7] Susan Mann traces how Zhang Xuecheng's famous attack on Yuan Mei, *Fuxue* (*Women's learning*), used the public nature of literary display to invert the meaning of talent. Zhang claimed that because men were overly ambitious for fame (*ming*), their talent was corrupt and the *dao* of their writing was inauthentic. Women, on the other hand, were not caught up in the game of public honors and thus expressed a purer and more lofty meaning. Zhang claimed that

> wherever official honors are proffered, the wise and the talented will vie for them. In that sense, the scholar pursues learning for the same reason that the farmer tills his fields, and there is nothing at all unusual about it. But a woman's writing is not her vocation, and so when a woman happens to excel as a result of her own natural endowment, she need not compete over style, nor be stirred by the promise of fame and reputation.

Zhang blamed the decline of women's literary culture on the creation of the Palace Music School (*jiaofang si*) during the Tang, when "women were transformed from literary subjects into objects of male desire."[8]

In her discussion of the "female voice" in poetry, Maureen Robertson finds in poems written by men the voyeuristic eye and the presentation of sexualized and romanticized suffering, narcissism in women, and fetishized boudoir furniture, clothing, and objects. These "literati-feminine" voices also can be found in the poems of women writing during the Tang, such as the three major poets Li Jilan, Yu Xuanji, and Xue Tao. Robertson argues that during the late Ming and Qing, women poets utilized various strategies to negotiate with this apparently feminine yet masculinized, or male-feminine language, including rewriting image codes, neutralizing the gaze within the boudoir, marking new topical territory, and shifting the voice in friendship poetry addressed to women.[9] Martin W. Huang also has written about the conventional use of female figures to "project a male literati author's anxieties," a practice that constructed an analogy of marginality between deserted wives and the literati. Thus, just like a wife or concubine "who had to vie with other wives/concubines for her husband's favor, a minister had to compete with other ministers for the emperor's favor." Because of this concubine complex, poets often adopted a feminine voice and created a literary tradition of politio-erotic lyricism.[10]

The question of women's education and its ability to establish *cai* or *de* as the underlying theory of women's existence is taken up by Dorothy Ko, who points out that the debate on women's virtue and talent intensified exactly at the time when more and more women were becoming educated and transgressing the boundaries between inner and outer. Ko argues that the opposition between *cai* and *de* was only one vision of women's education. A new theory, emerging through mother-daughter relationships in the inner quarters, viewed *cai* and *de* as mutually reinforcing, and produced a literary practice that differed from the prevailing logic:

> In real life, the inner-outer boundary was constantly being trespassed or redrawn. Women's education was a powerful impetus to such negotiations between domestic and public space, or between male and female domains. It is no accident that the rationale for and contents of women's education were among the most contested issues in seventeenth- and eighteenth-century China. As we shall see, this debate was linked to efforts to redefine womanhood, or a woman's natural calling.

Yet even if the meaning of the public presentation of women's literary writing was changing, there were still many references to families burning manuscripts written by women (because writing was not a woman's calling); indeed manuscripts were often inscribed with the words "rescued from fire" as a reference to their unsuitability for publication.[11] Whereas writing for self-amusement or to alleviate grief was more acceptable (but still dangerous in its ability to distract women from household chores), public writing was less so.

Recently, Dorothy Ko has continued to investigate the meaning and practice of writing, specifically as performed in the seventeenth century by Jiangnan wives and daughters of scholar-official families. While Ko cites many examples of women writing and emerging publicly as writers, she emphasizes how this in fact reinforced the Confucian doctrine of separate spheres, and comments that the times were changing so rapidly that it is difficult to assess the influence of these writing opportunities on women. Because Ko is arguing against a notion of the women's world as "cloistered, monochromatic, or repetitive," she emphasizes the "positive image of the woman writer" that emerged from the urban world of reading and writing where, she believes, gender boundaries were blurred. Part of this image came from the elevation of feminine characteristics, such as serenity, as the basis of true and pure poetry. At the same time, however, Ko believes that the woman writer's positive image is difficult to interpret:

> From hindsight, the impact of the urban print culture can only be described as a paradox. On an individual level, some women gained parity with men in the world of learning and literature; the opposite is true on a systemic level, where the promotion of the woman writer served only to reinforce the prevalent premise of gender distinctions. . . . The rise of the woman reader-writer, in other words, was a sign largely of the strength of the Confucian gender system, not its demise. The educated woman brought her new cultural resources to the service of her supposed natural duties of motherhood and moral guardianship. With the support and promotion of the new woman as erudite mother and teacher, the underpinnings of the gender system became even more solid than before.[12]

Although Ko's work provides some evidence to show that within a limited environment, constrained by place and class, some aspects of the *cai/de* opposition may have been changing or may not have been absolute to begin with, her work as a whole supports my argument: through the Ming and into the Qing, and right up to the modern period, the concepts of *cai* and *de* contained, as theory and practice, gendered and counter meanings.

The contradictory meanings of *de* and *cai* continued into the twentieth century, where they interacted with gender ideas that developed through China's increasing contact with Japan and the West. In one of the earliest systematic twentieth-century expositions on male-female equality, Jin Yi's *Nüjie zhong (Bell of women's world)* in 1903, the author pointed out that the so-called deficiencies of women all resulted from their lack of study, which prevented them from producing *cai*, and from their lack of social interaction, which disallowed them from engaging in appropriate activities. Jin Yi blamed the historical loss of the nation (*wangguo*) on the Chinese and their customs, including the doctrine of male and female separation. Jin Yi criticized the physical nature of the definition of women, including footbinding, make-up and decoration, and elaborate hair styles, all of which sapped female energy and wasted time, advocated equality for women and men, and encouraged women to go abroad to Europe and America to study.[13] Another example of a critique that implicitly recognized the physical nature of gender ideology as applied through ideals of self-sacrifice was that of Qiu Jin, who in her newspaper *Zhongguo nübao*, encouraged women to dedicate their bodies to revolution and promoted natural feet, freedom in marriage, women's education and independence, women's militia, and women's physical education, and attacked the standard of morality applied to women. . . .

The contemporary scholars Meng Yue and Dai Jinhua analyse literature as a masculinist discourse even more powerful than the law in its ability to create and transmit an oppressive discourse of woman. The textual focus on female beauty in traditional literature is a good example of how literati constructed female images to express and concoct their own desire—not sexual desire strictly speaking, but the desire to objectify and possess women, and the simple right to desire. What is shocking about this tradition, according to Meng and Dai, was its consistency over hundreds and even thousands of years. Symbolic of literature's ability to construct a beautiful yet oppressive image was the transformation of the female foot; after passing through literary reconstruction, the deformed physical foot was lost and what appeared and reappeared was the magically evocative "golden lotus" and the "lotus step." Meng and Dai identify traditional literature, and more broadly textual work, as a central discursive technique by which men manipulated and imaged women in order to give materiality to men's own subjective construction. Thus the participation of women as literary producers in this tradition could not easily be sanctioned.[14]

In short, in the early twentieth century and before, the conceptual categories of *woman* and *literature* were to some degree oppositional, a situation based on perceived moral content (*de*) of *woman*—physical, concrete, and

self-sacrificing—that was not in tune with the talent (*cai*) implied in literature—abstract, transcendent, and self-promoting. This configuration was produced historically, in references and discussions in numerous texts, and
entered the common sensibility in various customs and in simple phrases such
as *nüzi wucai bian shi de*.[15] Female morality contained a starkly physical aspect:
the demand that in daily life, women enact, embody, and perform morality
through physical ordeal. Furthermore, the female body, which writers had
traditionally portrayed in many literary guises (the eroticized denizen of the
boudoir, the self-sacrificing female martyr, etc.), became central to the
redefinition of the modern woman/literature paradigm. A hotly disputed and
symbolic aspect of female bodily practice, both in traditional and modern
times, was the requirement of chastity.

THE QUESTION OF CHASTITY

Chastity required that a woman be a virgin before marriage, have sexual relations only with her husband during marriage, and not remarry or have sexual
relations should her husband die or leave her. In many times and places, a
woman who lost her chastity through rape could be criticized for not com-
mitting suicide out of shame, or, as in the case of Xiang Lin's wife in Lu Xun's
Zhufu (*The new year's sacrifice*), could be assumed to have survived because
she did not put up enough resistance. In either case, the result could be the
humiliation of the woman and her family. Because chastity, unlike other physical performances of virtue, was theorized as solely applicable to women, it is
an excellent prism for separating the various meanings of embodied female
virtue and analyzing the relationship between this traditional *de* and modern
ideologies of writing.

In her study of female virtue, Katherine Carlitz writes that although the
main topics common to the *Lienü zhuan* (*Biographies of notable women*) can be
found in Han dynasty texts, by the Ming, the "cultural vocabulary" had
changed, foregrounding the husband-wife relationship and emphasizing its
correspondence to the ruler-minister relationship. The central evidence of
this shift is that whereas

> in the Han *Biographies of Notable Women* a small number of strong-minded wives
> die to bring errant husbands to their senses, by the time Ming scholars wrote up
> the Yuan dynastic history, half the widows eulogized had committed suicide upon
> the death of their husbands.

This emphasis on the female body's physical effacement in the name of moral
virtue was also accompanied by an increase in reports with

> lurid detail: a filial daughter eats the maggots infesting her mother-in-law's bed;
> a faithful widow avoids remarriage by tattooing "fidelity" (*jie*) all down her arms;
> another keeps for forty years a handkerchief soaked in the blood her husband

coughed up when he died. . . . Debauched mothers-in-law drive their pure daughters-in-law to suicide; good daughters-in-law not only make soup of their own flesh to feed their mothers-in-law, as filial sons had always done; they also breastfeed them.[16]

In emphasizing the ordeal that virtue had become by Ming times, Carlitz shows how *de* was not solely a state of mind, a theory, or a way of speaking, but a physical practice that demanded the mutilation and possible effacement of the body. The trials that a woman had to endure to preserve a threatened chastity included disembowelment, dismemberment, and ultimately suicide.[17]

One of Carlitz's main points is that "the social organization of art—and the increasing skill of the illustrators—affected the way women's virtue was imagined." Carlitz points out that pictures depicting virtuous women undergoing physical ordeals became increasingly beautiful, sentimental, and delicate as the Ming progressed. Because illustrations were becoming more common in fiction and drama, the morality texts for women were "assimilated to the traditions of entertainment and connoisseurship."[18] Thus the fine books produced to recognize female virtue, complete with lists of donors, were used to boost the prestige of a family and were also transformed into artifacts in the connoisseurship of women. The images of virtuous women, produced in books and thus intertwined with the textualized traditions of literature, established an oppositional yet complex gendered connection between writing and female moral virtue. Writing either idealized women's physical sufferings in a masculinist discourse of connoisseurship, or promoted their bodily effacement through moralistic tales.

The tension between a textual system that supported and extended itself as overwhelmingly masculine and *de* as overwhelmingly feminine was also evident outside literary pursuits. C. Fred Blake finds the sacrifice and duty exemplary of feminine virtue to be the ideological underpinning of footbinding, which he connects to writing. In an example that provocatively puts into a parallel relationship the footbinding of women with writing for men, Blake notes that in Henan, a girl having her feet bound may receive from her mother a writing brush, a "powerful symbol of masculinity and the world of civil affairs"; once the girl's feet were formed into a brushlike shape, she could give the shoe pattern to "the man in her life to use as a bookmark and an antidote against bookworms." Blake further comments that footbinding "put women's embodiment of virtue (*de*) on par with the 'power of virtue' implied in male 'talent' (*cai*)—and, most important, it made the 'power of virtue' entirely feminine." Thus elite females and males experience self-realization, or "becoming their respective bodies in relationship to others," quite differently; the boy's self "focused on the locutionary and literary power of the word," while the girl's self-realization "required her not merely to become, but to 'overcome her body' by restricting the space it filled."[19]

When Blake comments that the power of virtue has become feminine, he shows how women's lack of official and public access to *cai* made *de* more concentrated as a feminine practice. Footbinding was the gendered practice that for girls corresponded to immersion into texts for boys, because the "age when girls started to have their feet bound coincided with the age when boys moved out of the women's quarters to enroll in lineage schools or begin instruction with private tutors."[20] The implements used in footbinding were those used in the women's world—nail clippers, needle and thread, and scissors—and were items that were associated with women's traditional work.

In an even more direct tie between the textualized literary tradition and women's virtue, T'ien Ju-k'ang discovers that in Chinese economic and cultural centers during the Ming and Qing dynasties, there was a positive correlation between the numbers of female suicides and the number of *juren*, or diploma holders for the lower levels of the examination.[21] Although T'ien interprets these findings to indicate a relationship between "females' destruction of their own life and the wounded feelings of males" who could not progress to the higher degrees, they also indicate the association between female suicide and the construction of a textual tradition by lower degree holders. T'ien points out that the cult of female chastity gained momentum during the Qing dynasty and early on was promoted by famous scholars such as Gu Yanwu and Huang Zongxi. T'ien's work demonstrates how the process of petitioning for the rewarding of virtuous women, which was consolidated during the Ming, made scholars' services indispensable. T'ien believes that the formalization of the tradition in moralistic exegeses promoted and encouraged the practice. He concludes that "without the existence of frustrated scholars, the cult of female marital fidelity would not have developed to the great extent that it did."[22]

In his research on chastity in the Qing dynasty, Matthew H. Sommer shows how without adequate property, a widow had little chance of remaining chaste. If a widow were a member of the propertied elite, however, her chastity—her ability to avoid penetration by a man—was so important that it bestowed upon her a "right" belonging to few Chinese women: the right to resist marriage. Sommer notes that in 1803, when former guidelines were relaxed, a woman could qualify for the status of a martyr even if she had been penetrated, showing how the meaning of chastity changed. What was once simply an objective fact became an issue of intent and its purity.[23] From my point of view, this development also indicates that chastity became more of an abstract female quality rather than an act or behavior; women's chastity, in other words, was increasingly naturalized. By the early twentieth century, You Guifen's claim that it was "the natural disposition of women to be chaste" made perfect sense.[24] . . .

To many May Fourth writers, Western humanism, with its focus on individual rights and privileges, seemed an exceptionally useful weapon in the fight against Confucian practices.[25] Advocates of women's rights found it particularly potent in fighting the neo-Confucian demarcation of separate inside/outside realms that barred women from acting outside the household.[26] In his article "Nüren ren'ge wenti" (The problem of women's personality/character), Ye Shaojun compared the terms *nüren* (woman) and *ren* (person) to expose the large, oppressive discrepencies between the social and personal implications of the two terms.[27] Ye's main question was that of *ren'ge*, which women, if they indeed are *ren*, should possess. Ye defined *ren'ge* as

> a type of spirit that an individual within a group should have. In other words, it is the kind of spirit that will let one be an independent and complete part of a group. In order to be independent, one must allow one's abilities to develop fully; in order to be complete, one cannot blindly follow, but must love the truth. These are the conditions necessary to realize *ren'ge*.[28]

Ren'ge was both abstract and concrete; it was what allowed the individual to maintain his or her identity separate from the group, yet it was this independence that made the group function better. Ye framed the question in reference to individual essence, arguing that although women were part of the mass of humanity and thus should have *ren'ge*, they traditionally had neither independence nor completeness, and therefore, with a few recent exceptions of highly educated and progressive individuals, they did not possessed *ren'ge*.

A crucial term in Ye's delineation of *ren'ge* is *rensheng guan*, life-view. Ye argued that because women had been confined to the household, not allowed to participate in outside affairs or thought, and denied opportunities to study and to speak publicly, they did not have a distinctive view of life and thus their "love for truth" gradually faded. Women's "innate" characteristics, here blamed on the seclusion of women dictated by the Confucian notion of separate spheres, are highly negative in Ye's view. What he constructed as a distinctly human quality, the love of truth that results from independent thought, was denied to women, who were defined either as "someone else's person" (wife, mother, daughter), or as a machine that men could manipulate (buy, sell, exchange) at will.

Since Ye identified childbirth as the physical reality that anchored masculine ideologies of oppression, he suggested that childbirth be reconstructed as a sacred service to society at large rather than to men and implicitly, to family and the cult of ancestry. Society, then, must repay this service by extending to women all the privileges that conferred *ren'ge* rather than turning women into servants. Ye ended his essay by advocating change for the benefit of the entire group. Thus, underlying his humanistic approach was a focus on the health of the nation. Women would bear children not to carry on the male line, but for the good of society, a reconfiguration that would break kinship bonds and establish women as equal partners in the production of modern society. Ye believed that the destruction of the Chinese family system, with its ancestor worship and parental control, was necessary for women to gain *ren'ge*; practices of moral virtue, enveloped within the family structure, were what prevented women from becoming whole persons.

The awarding of official honors to chaste and virtuous women continued well into the twentieth century. In 1917, the Republican government established criteria for determining eligibility for a presidential commendation. A woman could be honored for "being a good wife and mother, for twenty years of virtuous widowhood, for not remarrying after her fiancee's death, and for resisting or atoning for rape by suicide."[29] Chastity, then, was an officially and personally performed aspect of femininity sanctioned throughout society by award and recognition.

The value of chastity—the most feminine and symbolic part of women's virtue—was quite different than that of literary skill for men. Chastity was profoundly physical: it demanded foregrounding of the female body and its function, space, position, and role. Its meanings invaded all aspects of a women's bodily existence, including her relationships with kin and non-kin; her sense of her body in terms of sexuality, appearance, and demeanor, and her every behavior. As an ontology, chastity had personal, familial, and national significance. In this sense it possessed, for women, a metaphorical meaning that was also unchanging in content—self-sacrifice and service through physical ordeal—and thus constantly functioned as a belief and practice rather than a means of analysis, thought, or critique. Literary skill, however, was only partially an ontology, to the extent that one aspect of the traditional discourse of texts and literati was a kind of self-development (*xiushen*)—but even more importantly was an intellectual discourse that contained a variable content.[30] In literature, topics changed and styles were numerous.

A practitioner could express himself and his intellectual acumen through these changing topics and styles and through various literary outlets. Thus those whose self-realization came through textual practices had access to the transcendent values of society and nation, and at the same time their writing could create, critique, and re-create not only themselves but also society and nation.

By the twentieth century, the doctrines of separate spheres, of female chastity, and of women's unsuitability for the public roles of writer and critic had long been under attack, but as we have seen, they retained considerable power in official life, where awards were given and educational goals set, in intellectual debate, and in daily life, where traditional ideologies merged with the new modern ideals. In the 1920s, women were writing and becoming known as writers, and their work was published in an increasingly supportive critical environment. Yet the constitution of writing as transcendent and male, and of woman as concrete, limited, and full of being, persisted in their work. Women writers problematized the female body, drafting characters for whom the body was an obstacle that demanded extraordinary solutions, such as excessive illness, effacement in suicide, or death. The relationship of a woman to other women and men, particularly in the bodily and emotional aspects of love and sexuality, were primary topics, because these physical relationships, and even women's relationship to their own bodies, produced different meanings for women and men.

NOTES

1. Here the term *self* refers not to the deep, psychologized interior of the mind developed in the West, but to the cultural and historical view of personhood characterized by a person's relations with others, situation in the physical and social space, and acts and behaviors of daily life.

2. Ellen Widmer, "Xiaoqing's Literary Legacy and the Place of the Woman Writer in Late Imperial China," *Late Imperial China: Special Issue: Poetry and Women's Culture in Late Imperial China* 13, no. 1 (June 1992): 112, argues that the concept of "woman writer" was common by the late sixteenth century. However, because of the difficulty of printing and disseminating work and because of well-known and oft-repeated strictures against women writing, few authors set out to establish themselves as "woman writers."

3. See K'ang Tung-wei (Kang Tongwei), "On the Advantages and Disadvantages of Educating Women," in J. Mason Gentzler, ed., *Changing China: Readings in the History of China from the Opium War to the Present* (New York: Praeger, 1977), 97–100. All bracketed words are in the English translation.

4. Liu believes that basically the notion that *cai* brings misfortune is equivalent for women and for men, and even for men, virtue is thought to be superior to *cai*. However, we can see that throughout the Ming and Qing, women became part of a system that rewarded virtue as an extremely physical and immediate daily life sacrifice, but did not often demand men's virtue. Men were called upon to be virtuous when a woman was not available to take care of the man's parents, or when one dynasty was replaced by another and as a loyalist, a man must declare his allegiance to the fallen power, even when that act endangered him and his relatives. See Liu Yongcong, "Qingchu sichao nüxing cai ming guan guankui" (A glance at views on women's talent and fate during four Qing dynasty reigns), in Bao Jialin, *Zhongguo funüshi lunji sanji* (Materials on the history of Chinese women), vol. 3 (Taipei: Daoxiang chubanshe, 1988), 29–40, 122, 124–28, 127, 134–35, 136, 142.

5. See *Late Imperial China: Special Issue: Poetry and Women's Culture in Late Imperial China* 13, no. 1 (June 1992): 1–172.

6. The authors in this special issue of *Late Imperial China* disagree on the history and influence of this saying, oft quoted in the early twentieth century. Susan Mann,

"'Fuxue' (Women's Learning) by Zhang Xuecheng (1738–1801): China's First History of Women's Culture," *Late Imperial China: Special Issue: Poetry and Women's Culture in Late Imperial China* 13, no. 1 (June 1992): 54, argues that the saying was, by the eighteenth century, out of fashion, but according to Ellen Widmer, "Xiaoqing's Literary Legacy and the Place of the Woman Writer in Late Imperial China," *Late Imperial China: Special Issue: Poetry and Women's Culture in Late Imperial China* 13, no. 1 (June 1992): 112, the phrase was used against talented women throughout the Ming and Qing.

7. Ellen Widmer, 132.

8. Susan Mann, 44–45, 47.

9. Maureen Robertson, "Voicing the Feminine: Construction of the Gendered Subject in Lyric Poetry by Women of Medieval and Late Imperial China," *Late Imperial China: Special Issue: Poetry and Women's Culture in Late Imperial China* 13, no. 1 (June 1992): 69, 82.

10. Martin W. Huang, *Literati and Self-Representation: Autobiographical Sensibility in the Eighteenth-Century Chinese Novel* (Stanford: Stanford University Press, 1995), 78–81.

11. Dorothy Ko, "Pursuing Talent and Virtue: Education and Women's Culture in Seventeenth-and Eighteenth-Century China," *Late Imperial China: Special Issue: Poetry and Women's Culture in Late Imperial China* 13, no. 1 (June 1992): 9, 4, 18–19, notes that wariness about women writing "can be gleaned from the glut of remarks found in Ming-Qing records of a sister or a neighbor who wrote for divertissement but would burn her manuscript afterward, saying that poetry or writing was not a woman's calling" (9). See also Joanna F. Handlin, "Lu K'un's New Audience: The Influence of Women's Literacy on Sixteenth-Century Thought" in Margery Wolf and Roxane Witke, eds., *Women in Chinese Society* (Stanford: Stanford University Press, 1975), 13–38.

12. Dorothy Ko, *Teachers of the Inner Chambers: Women and Culture in Seventeenth-Century China* (Stanford: Stanford University Press, 1994), 65, 15, 51, 62, 66–67.

13. See Bao Jialin, "Xinhai geming shiqi de funü sixiang" (Women's thought in the *xinhai* revolution) in Bao Jialin, *Zhongguo funüshi lunji* (Materials on the history of Chinese women) (Taipei: Daoxiang chubanshe, 1988), 276–79. Bao speculates that Jin Yi was Jin Tianfan of Jiangsu, who had set up Minghua Girls School and contributed financial support to Zou Rong for the publication of *Geming jun* (Revolutionary soldier). See also Jin Yi, "Nüzi shijie' fakan ci" (Foreword to the *Women's World*) in *Zhonghua quanguo funü lianhehui*, 1981: 289–90.

14. Meng Yue and Dai Jinhua, *Fuchu lishi dibiao* (Floating out from the surface of history) in Li Xiaojiang, gen. ed., *Funü yanjiu zongshu* (Collection of research on women) (Henan: Henan renmin chubanshe, 1989), 15–16.

15. See also Editors, "Nüzi wucai bian shi de bo" (Rebuttal of [the idea that] for women lack of literary talent is a virtue), *Zhongguo xin nüjie zazhi* (Journal of the new Chinese women's world) 3 (Apr): 277–79, which argues that faced with the onslaught of imperialism, both women and men need *cai*.

16. Katherine Carlitz, "The Social Uses of Female Virtue," *Late Imperial China* 12, no. 2 (Dec.): 121–22.

17. See also Jennifer Holmgren "Widow Chastity in the Northern Dynasties: The Lieh-nü Biographies in the Wei-shu" (1981), 183, and Margery Wolfe, "Women and Suicide in China" in Margery Wolf and Roxane Witke, eds., *Women in Chinese Society*, 111–42. Holmgren investigates the relationship between the two ideas of widow chastity and service to the husbands' parents, and also traces the history of self-mutilation "as an acceptable way of concluding the agreement between a widow and her family that she would abide by the rules of chaste conduct."

18. Carlitz, 121, 127.

19. C. Fred Blake, "Footbinding in Neo-Confucian China and the Appropriation of Female Labor," *Signs: Journal of Women in Culture and Society* 19, no., 3 (Spring 1994): 681 and 681n. 5.

20. Ko, *Teachers of the Inner Chambers*, 149.

21. See also Bettine Birge, "Chu Hsi and Women's Education," in William Theodore de Bary and John W. Chaffee, eds., *Neo-Confucian Education: The Formative Stage* (Berkeley: University of California Press, 1989), 337n. 50. Birge notes several Song dynasty references to cutting of the flesh by women to illustrate filial piety. Also, although there were no prescriptions against women learning to read and write in the Song, whereas Zhu Xi's *Elementary Learning* (*Xiaoxue*) notes that after the age of ten boys were supposed to be tutored in writing and arithmetic, it is silent on the literacy of girls (p. 353).

22. T'ien Ju-k'ang, *Male Anxiety and Female Chastity: A Comparative Study of Chinese Ethical Values in Ming-Ch'ing Times* (Leiden: E. J. Brill, 1988), 145, 126, 102. Patricia Buckley Ebrey, *The Inner Quarters: Marriage and the Lives of Chinese Women in the Song Period* (Berkeley: University of California Press, 1993) finds that although the notion of separation of sexes was well established during the Song, female chastity was not always observed, and well-known literati promoted reading skills for women as long as they did not extend their interest in literary matters beyond the household. She speculates that footbinding developed during the Song in part because the model for masculinity had shifted from emphasis on the ability to ride a horse or hunt to the ideals of the literati, who were "elegant, bookish, contemplative, or artistic, but did not need to be strong, quick, or physically dominating" (33). Thus, because the Song ideal male was a refined, subdued character, "he might seem effeminate unless women could be made even more delicate, reticent, and stationary" (41).

23. Matthew H. Sommer, "The Uses of Chastity: Sex, Law, and the Property of Widows in Qing China," *Late Imperial China* 17, no. 2 (Dec. 1996): 86, 81n. 6.

24. You Guifen, "Lun nüzi jiayu dang zhuzhong daode" (On the need for women's education to emphasize morality), *Funü zazhi* 1, no. 6 (June 1915): 8.

25. For an example of western humanism applied to feminism in China, see Luo Jialun, "Funü jiefang" (Women's liberation), *Xinchao* 2, no. 1 (Oct. 1919): 1–21.

26. For example, in his article "Nannü shejiao gongkai wenti guanjian" (Views on freedom of social intercourse between men and women), *Zhonghua quanguo funü lianhehui* 1981: 181–84, published in 1920, Shen Yanbing (Mao Dun) refers to the book *Love and Marriage* by Ellen Karolina Sophia Key (1849–1926). Bing Wen, "Hunyin ziyou" (Freedom of marriage), *Zhonghua quanguo funü lianhehui*, 1981: 233–35, also published in 1920, refers to *Outlook from a New Standpoint* by Ernest Belfort Bax (1854–1926). In his "Jiating gaizhi de yanjiu" (Research on the change of the family system) in *Zhonghua quanguo funü lianhehui* 1981: 246–56, published in 1921, Mao Dun refers to the work of several foreign scholars, including Edward Carpenter (1844–1929), August Bebel (1840–1930), Herbert George Wells (1866–1946), Walter Lionel George (1882–1926), Ellen Key, and Charlotte Perkins Gilman (1860–1935).

27. I have translated *ren'ge* as personality/character because neither word by itself seems to represent adequately the term as Ye used it. Ye's discussion of *ren'ge* implies independence, vision, completeness, and activity (as opposed to passivity).

28. Ye Shaojun, "Nüren ren'ge wenti" (The problem of women's personality/character), *Xinchao*, 1, no. 2 (February, 1919). Reprinted in *Zhonghua quanguo funü lianhehui* 1981: 124.

29. Sally Borthwick, "Changing Concepts of the Role of Women from the Late Qing to the May Fourth Period" in David Pong and Edmund S. K. Fung, eds., *Ideal and Reality: Social and Political Change in Modern China, 1860–1949* (New York: University Press of America, 1985), 82.

30. Under the onslaught of antitextual ideologies in the twentieth century, the literary discourse as ontology lost authority and became ambivalent. See Wendy Larson, *Literary Authority and the Chinese Writer: Ambivalence and Autobiography* (Durham: Duke University Press, 1991).

chapter six

OMEN OF THE WORLD: MEANING IN THE CHINESE LYRIC

Stephen Owen

Editor's note: Owen describes lyric poetry in the great poetic tradition of the Tang dynasty, as revealing immanence: that is, as expressing the inherent aesthetic pattern of the world through the poet's particular experience. Whereas in Western lyric poetry, the physical metaphorically reveals transcendent meaning, or truth, Chinese occasional poetry describes a real experience that correlates to, rather than symbolizes, the cosmic order (*wen*). Debating probable Western objections to Chinese aesthetics, Owen elucidates the philosophical foundations of Chinese culture and thus demonstrates the importance of reading Chinese poetry as a practice of Chinese aesthetic sensibilities.

Poetry is the displaced prophetic vocation.

Ernst Bloch

If so, then Chinese poetry is the displaced vocation of the diviner.

PROPHECY ARISES from inner vision, private but ordained by its own laws to be shared; for sharing, the common words of the world are needed, though they are stubborn words that always threaten to fail the brightness of vision. But the inborn gift of divination depends upon the immanence of truth in this physical world: it is visible to all who look for it and who know how to look; this is outer vision and the words of the physical world will do. The diviner observes and reflects:

> Slender grasses, breeze faint on the shore,
> Here, the looming mast, the lone night boat.
> Stars hang down on the breadth of the plain,
> The moon gushes in the great river's current.
> My name shall not be known from my writing;
> Sick, growing old, I must yield up my post.
> Wind-tossed, fluttering—what is my likeness?
> In Heaven and Earth, a single gull of the sands.

Tu Fu 杜甫 (712–770) "Writes of what he feels, traveling by night" 旅夜書懷.[1]
The title, given for the reader's sake, frames the poem with an occasion and
tells what "kind" of statements are made in the poem: Tu Fu's lines are *huai*
懷, "what he feels," or more precisely, what is on his mind with concern and
strong feeling. The *huai* may be something perceived, something thought,
something felt: the scene drawn in the first two couplets is no less *huai* than the
reflections in the third couplet. The simile of the last couplet is also *huai*, something *he feels*; it is presented not as a device of poetry but as the act of a living
mind—discovering an analogue for the self.

Tu Fu's words might be a special kind of diary entry, differing from
common diary in their intensity and immediacy, in their presentation of an
experience as occurring at that very moment. Like diary, the poem promises
a record of historical experience: the exact time, the exact place, the exact
conjunction of circumstances may be lost beyond recovery, but the reader
trusts their historical reality and depends upon it. The greatness of the poem
emerges not through poetic invention but through the happy chance of this
poet meeting this moment and this scene.

Another poet stands on Westminster Bridge at dawn on September 3,
1802, and looks at London:

> Earth has not anything to show more fair:
> Dull would he be of soul who could pass by
> A sight so touching in its majesty:
> This City now doth, like a garment wear
> The beauty of the morning; silent, bare,
> Ships, towers, domes, theaters, and temples lie
> Open unto the fields and to the sky;
> All bright and glittering in the smokeless air.
> ....[2]

Wordsworth's title precisely locates the time and place. We could go back to
old maps and engravings, we could guess which dome and which temple might
have been seen then from Westminster Bridge, we might check old almanacs
for dawn's hour and minute, exhume shipping records to estimate the number
of ships lying at anchor that day and position their masts in the field of vision.
But even the most passionate antiquarian will know that this interest in
circumstance is not essential to the poem. It does not matter whether
Wordsworth saw the scene, vaguely remembered it, or constructed it from his
imagination. The words of the poem are not directed to a historical London
in its infinite particularity; the words lead you to something else, to some significance in which the number of vessels on the Thames is utterly irrelevant.
That significance is elusive, its fullness eternally out of reach, as open as
the city itself. We can try to lock up that elusive significance in a hundred
ways: we can say it is "nature making all natural," or "the epiphany of soli-

tary vision," or "a reactionary revulsion against the new industrial and urban society." The ways in which we name the poem's significance may be gross or fine, certainly true or hardly likely; the text points to a plenitude of potential significance, but it does not point to London, at dawn, September 3, 1802.

Texts lie open to the inclinations of their readers. Significance is granted in reading; and readers, unlike poets, are made, not born. Though the learned rules of reading differ from age to age, from school to school, certain fundamental assumptions unify all diversity and place boundaries on change and variation. Such unities define a literary tradition. The canons of Western literary education hammer home the first lesson again and again:

> . . . the nature of literature emerges most clearly under the referential aspects. The center of the literary art is obviously found in the traditional genres of the lyric, the epic, the drama. In all of them the reference is to a world of fiction, of imagination. The statements in a novel, in a poem, or in a drama are not literally true; they are not logical propositions. . . . Even in the subjective lyric, the "I" of the poet is a fictional, dramatic "I."[3]

Which is another way of saying, with Sidney, "Now for the poet, he nothing affirms, and therefore never lieth."

It matters not at all whether Wordsworth ever actually stood on Westminster Bridge on September 3, 1802, and gazed at the city of London. It is only a fiction—this lyric "I" which pretends to report what it perceives. The reader assumes that the poet's historical "I" makes use of the lyric "I," and that his visions, real or pretended, become poetry only for the sake of some other ends. The city "doth like a garment wear / The beauty of the morning": the comparison occurs on the level of the poetic art with its many mysterious motives; the comparison is not taken as an action in the mind of the historical poet, standing on the bridge. The reader is taught to ignore Wordsworth's precise instructions: dawn, September 3, 1802, Westminster Bridge.

We have two different ways of reading poetry. For the reader of Wordsworth, all is metaphor and fiction; the referential instructions to regard place and moment are an embarrassment, an unwanted intrusion. Literary language is supposed to be fundamentally different from the language of diary and empirical observation: its words mean Something Else, something hidden, richer, infinitely more satisfying.

In Tu Fu's poem, the assumptions through which significance grows are different, and potent consequences follow from those initial differences, which at first seem so slight. The differences shape two fiercely distinct concepts of the nature of literature and its place in the human and natural universe. For Tu Fu's reader the poem is not a fiction: it is a unique, factual account of an experience in historical time, a human consciousness encountering, interpreting, and responding to the world. And in his own turn the reader, at some later historical moment, encounters, interprets, and responds to the poem.

Consider two versions of metaphor: "The poet is a gull between Heaven and Earth"; "It seemed to me I was like a gull between Heaven and Earth." Between these two statements is the center of the difference between two traditions of poetry and reading. The first statement is not true: it is a metaphorical fiction and asks you to consider how the poet might be like a gull. The second statement may be literally true; it also asks you to consider the relation between poet and gull, but it asks for the sake of what the comparison reveals about *the state of mind of the poet*, the direction of his attention, his desire to know himself, to find one like himself, to share his condition with another.

The distinction extends beyond obvious metaphors. One poet perceives "ships, towers, domes, theaters, and temples"; the other poet, "slender grasses, breeze faint on the shore." We assume that Wordsworth is not simply naming what he saw; the items of the scene are listed for some purpose; we look beyond the mediating scenes for ends and artistic motives which we must intuit or guess—perhaps to show how in the silence of the vista all works are joined in harmony, the sacred and secular, the mercantile, military, and artistic? perhaps to give concrete particularity to a panorama, not a bland "everything" but "this, this, and this"? perhaps to indicate the naturalization of human constructs when bare of the humans who made them and consider them only for their use? Though the precise purpose must remain forever uncertain, we accept with certainty that the fusion of significance and word-scene occurs on the level of art. But for the other poet, we presume instead that the "slender grasses, breeze faint on the shore" is indeed simply what he has seen, or more precisely, what has drawn his attention: the enumeration in the poem indicates some meaningful pattern which is both present in the world at that moment and of special interest to the poet's mind. For Wordsworth's reader, the poem (and sometimes even the world itself) is a created set of hermetic signs. For Tu Fu's reader, meaning is subtly infused in the particular forms of the world perceived and uncertain, perhaps, even to the poet; the poem raises up portentous forms, and in doing so, it tells you about both the world and the inner concerns of the poet.

細	草	微	風	岸
fine/thin	grass/plants	faint	wind	shore
危	檣	獨	夜	舟
high/precarious	mast	alone/lone	night	boat

Slender grasses, breeze faint on the shore,
Here the looming mast, the lone night boat.

He travels on by boat that night; the moonlight outlines roughly the shapes of the scene, but the finer forms in the night landscape are hidden in darkness. How then, we wonder, can he make out those slender blades of grass and thin tendrils of plants, 細草, swaying on the shore? And this faint breeze he may feel on the water—how can he know its effects on the bank? The two parts of the line need one another: they act upon each other according to the laws of the empirical universe, and in their interaction a relation is known—the hidden image of thin grasses bending in the breeze. The movement of the slender blades, of only the slender blades, shows a breeze and only the faintest breeze. Or the faint breeze on the shore will, he knows, move the grasses, but only the slender blades, unseen.

The mast looms, above him, *wei* 危, its shape "high" and "precarious," threatening fall. There is an instability in it that conveys uneasiness, as it sways with the rocking movement of the boat. His eyes, moving from thing to thing, follow a mutation of forms: the tiny, bending blades of grass recur transformed in the mast that sways menacingly above him. And the watcher's perspective defines his size—immense and secure as he looked out to guess about the tiniest shapes in the darkness, then suddenly small as the shape reappears, rocking above him.

In the recurrence of forms comes an intuitive sense of differences and oppositions: out there, the many; here, the one. There, the stable shore; here, the world water and flux. There, the supple, the bending but firmly rooted; here, the rigid and precariously swaying. There, tininess and insignificance; here, true magnitude. The oppositions are portentous; they echo in correlative frames of reference: flux and endless movement, set against stability and rootedness; one who travels on alone, set against others living in security; endangered uprightness, great stature, and nobility, set against the pliant, the lesser, the common. No assertions are made; no contradictions are excluded; a pattern is rising up.

This is a moment's work in the good reader's mind. He grasps the fullness of the oppositions, senses their importance to Tu Fu, and sees their horizon of significance extend outward. In the pattern of this brief scene correlatives echo in the poet's life, in the order of the universe, in the moral order, in the social order, in the order of literature where the "breeze," *feng* 風, is "song," *feng,* the moral power of one whose "influence," *feng,* makes the "many" bow low to it.

The natural cosmos, of which the historical empire was the institutional reflection, was a system of processes, things, and relations. Between systems, correlations were made by a principle which might be called analogy, if analogy did not presume some fundamental difference. The most apposite term in Chinese is *lei* 類, "natural category": these correlations of pattern were not made by a willful act of analogy but rather occurred because their elements were, in essential ways, "of the same kind."[4]

The term which situates literature in this orderly cosmos is *wen* 文; in its most general sense, *wen* is "pattern," in which aesthetic value and significance are conjoined.[5] *Wen* is "literature" and sometimes, "writing" itself; *wen* is to be "cultivated," to have the grace, restraint, and sensibility of education; *wen* is the civil aspect of society, as opposed to the military. The great king Wu of the Chou embodies the virtue, "mighty (*wen*), not in his wrath of force of arms but in the civilizing force of culture.[6] A person who aspires to be *wen* will unite the semantic meanderings of the word: becoming *accomplished* through education, he may serve the government in a *civil* post, his capacity for such a position having been examined by a public test of his *writing*; he finds himself naturally drawn to *literature in which the "aesthetic pattern"* (*wen*) of the universe becomes manifest. Liu Hsieh 劉勰 (465–522) writes of *wen*:

> Great is the fulfilled power of aesthetic pattern, for it appeared along with the generation of Heaven and Earth. All color derives from a blending of the Dark of Heaven and Earth's Yellow; by the circularity of Heaven and Earth's square-ness all shapes are differentiated. The successive disks of sun and moon are sus-pended configurations that make the heavens lovely, while the luminous intricacy of hills and streams unfold forms that order the earth. We might say that this is the aesthetic pattern of Natural Process [Tao]. Above we may contemplate radiant brilliance; below we examine the latent sectioning; and in these we find the fixed positions of high and low. Thus the two basic Principles appear.
>
> Man, endowed with the spark of spiritual nature, is added to these to form the Great Triad. Man is the flower of the Elements and the mind of Heaven and Earth. With mind, language appears, and in language, aesthetic pattern becomes manifest. This is an inherent character of Natural Process.
>
> Yet when we go on to consider all the multiple categories of things, we find that everything, animal and vegetable, possesses aesthetic patterning. Dragon and phoenix show auspicious events in the brilliance of their design; the tiger by his brightness, the leopard by the tended lushness of his spots ever indicate a magnificence of manner. In the plastic forms and colors of the clouds, there is something which goes beyond the greatest subtlety of the master painter; nothing in the flowered splendor of the vegetation need yield to the most wondrous craft of the embroiderer. In no way are these things adorned from without; they are the way they are by their very natures. And when the vents of the forests form their lingering echoes, they are as much in harmony as the music of pipes or strings; or when tones are stirred by the stones of a brook, they blend as per-fectly as chimes and bells. With any form, there appears manifest sectioning [*chang* 章]; with sound emitted, there appears aesthetic pattern [*wen* 文; together, these terms constitute *wen-chang*, a "literary piece" or "literature"]. If such things, unaware, possess the radiance of many colors swelling within, how can this human vessel of mind lack its own aesthetic pattern?[7]

Wen, aesthetic pattern, is the outward manifestation of some latent order. From the primal configurations of Heaven and Earth down to the animals and plants, each class of phenomena manifests *wen* appropriate to its own kind. In the human, *wen*'s outwardness does not appear on the physical body (which is, all in all, rather plain in comparison to nature's gaudier displays); *wen* is here manifest through the essential human characteristic, "mind" (*hsin* 心), "mind" as the seat of consciousness, thought, and emotion). The outward, manifest form of the activities of "mind" is "writing," *wen*—or in its essential form, "literature," *wen*. (A distinction can be made between "writing" and "literature" by compounding *wen* with another character, but alone, *wen* comprehends both.) As "the mind of Heaven and Earth" 天地之心, the human is the only creature with reflective consciousness, but the phrase also suggests that man serves the function of "mind" in the cosmic "body." All phenomena have an inherent tendency to become manifest in *wen*, and their manifestation is for the sake of being known and felt; only the human mind is capable of itself knowing and feeling, and of that process, literature is the outward manifest form. Literature thus stands as the entelechy, the fully realized form, of a universal process of manifestation.

In the passage above from the opening chapter of Liu Hsieh's general survey of the literary art, literature is granted a special privilege over the visual arts.[8] In failing to attain the degree of intricacy and complexity of visible nature, the visual arts are set in a mimetic relation to nature (whether the painter or embroiderer is in fact trying to imitate nature is less significant than the judgment of their work by the criterion of its approximation to nature's intricacy).[9] Insofar as the visual arts merely imitate nature's *wen*, they are subject to the Platonic critique of art as a secondary (or tertiary) phenomenon. But in this formulation literature is not truly mimetic: rather it is the final stage in a process of manifestation; and the writer, instead of "representing" the outer world, is in fact only the medium for this last phase of the world's coming-to-be.

Not only does a particular instance of literature emerge naturally from the conjunction of a particular aspect of the world and a particular human consciousness, the written language (*wen*), in which the conjunction becomes manifest, is itself natural. Directly after the passage quoted above, Liu Hsieh traces the origins of writing: its primary forms are the trigrams and hexagrams of the *Book of Changes*, the most basic schematizations of pattern. Writing is not constituted of arbitrary signs, created by historical evolution or divine authority; writing appears from observing the world.

Concepts of imitation, representation, or even expression can never entirely free literature from its status as a secondary phenomenon, later and less than some "original" (in the case of expression, the "original" is a state of mind). Western theories of literature are the children of the Platonic critique, and though they rebel and marry into less tainted lines, they cannot escape their ancestry. If the "originals" belong to this sensible world, the deficiencies and deviations of the imitation are all too apparent. To escape the foredoomed failure, a most ingenious revision was devised: the "original" was displaced out of this world and became a hidden Something Else to which the poem gives unique access. By this strange inversion, the "original" significance becomes epistemologically contingent on the secondary representation. The history of Western literary thought develops in a melancholy competition between determining representation and a determining but hidden "original" content. Each lineage takes its turn in partial dominance. And our art of reading is founded upon these shifting ratios in the power of word versus the "truth beyond language."

But if literature (*wen*) is the entelechy of a previously unrealized pattern, and if the written word (*wen*) is not a sign but a schematization, then there can be no competition for dominance. Each level of *wen*, that of the world and that of the poem, is valid only in its own correlative realm; and the poem, the final outward form, is a stage of fullness.

The process of manifestation must begin in the external world, which has priority without primacy. As latent pattern follows its innate disposition to become manifest, passing from world to mind to literature, a theory of sympathetic resonance is involved. Again Liu Hsieh:

Springs and autumns follow on in succession, with the brooding gloom of dark Yin and the easeful brightness of Yang. And as the bright countenances of physical things are impelled in their cycles, so the affective capability of mind [*hsin*] too is shaken. When the Yang force sprouts in the darkness of the twelfth month, the black ant scurries to its hole; and when the Yin begins to coalesce, the mantis feasts. It touches the responses of even the tiniest insects: the four seasons impel things deeply. . . . All the bright countenances of things call to one another, and how amid all this may man find stillness?

When spring appears with the incoming year, feelings of delight and ease spread; in the billowing luxuriousness of early summer, the mind too swells with happiness. And when autumn's skies are high and the animating air takes on a chill clarity, our thoughts, sunken in the darkness of Yin, touch on far things; then frost and snow spread over limitless space, and brooding deepens, grim and stern. The year has its physical things, and these things have their countenances; by these things our emotions are shifted, and from emotions language comes. The fall of a solitary leaf finds its place in our understanding [and we know that autumn is coming]; in the voices of insects we find something capable of drawing forth the mind. And how much stronger than these merely partial evidences would be cool winds and a bright moon, together on the same night; or radiant sunlight and spring groves in the same morning? When poets are stirred by physical things, the categorical associations are endless. They forget themselves in their wanderings through the configurations of phenomena, even to their limit, and with deep seriousness they sing out the minutiae of what they see and hear. They sketch the animate spirit and delineate outward appearance, as they themselves are rolled round and round with the course of things; they apply the right palate of colors, match correlate sounds, and linger on about things with their minds.[10]

Though rational and conscious of the world, the human is also a part of the natural world, linked to it by those same patterns of resonance that impel all creatures in their cycles. Liu Hsieh here speaks primarily of the cyclical dimensions of resonance and the gross patterns of seasonal change, but the same resonance will emanate from the finer and more subtle aspects of the "bright countenances of physical things"—the interaction between a blade of grass and the breeze, the opposition of the flux of the river and shore's stability. The mind of the poet is "rolled round and round with the course of things": he is both in the physical world and at the same time aware of being caught up in it. The poet is the passive scientist of the natural order through whom its empirical principles are made manifest.

Being of the world's stuff, we not only share in its fluctuations, we also know its sequences and replications. Liu Hsieh speaks also of the capacity for categorical association: each thing and event of the world is the fragment of a coherent whole, and knowledge of the whole unfolds out of the fragment. To see a single leaf fall is to know autumn; to know autumn is to know its correlatives in the cycle of human life, in the dynastic cycle, in all domains of reference. To see a single blade of grass bending is to know a faint breeze; to feel a faint breeze is to know that the thin blades of grass are bending. Association is endless: it spreads horizontally, filling in the relations between things in the scene at hand; it rises in vertical resonance through correlative frames of reference. This process lingers after the words of the text are over: "When the bright countenances of physical things are gone, the response still lingers on—this is perfect understanding."[11]

Liu Hsieh's "lingering response" became an enduring theme of Chinese literary theory, richly varied and elaborated in later ages: at its best, poetry continues after the text. The text, the entelechy of one process, is only the beginning of another living process in the mind of the reader.

星	垂	平	野	闊
stars	hang	level	wilderness	broad
月	湧	大	江	流
moon	gush/bubble	great	river	flow

Stars hang down on the breadth of the plain,
The moon gushes in the great river's current.

Space grows, and with its increase, the viewer's dimensions shrink; the eye runs from the slender blades of grass, unseen, up to the looming mast, then out and up further, to the full breadth and height of the night scene. There the eye meets repetition of the pattern observed on earth: grasses firmly rooted and stars securely hung, tending downward as the blades of grass are bent down. Many stars securely tied; one moon fallen, fallen as a reflection in the river where its light is cast about and shattered by the waves. The tiny entities rooted below and those strung above are set against one mast waving precariously over the water, then one moon fallen down, into the water. One great light is at the mercy of the fluid shapings of the river's surface, shattered; many lesser lights remain secure and whole.

The first line of the couplet is composed of two unsubordinated segments; set together, the segments act upon one another and intrude upon the poet's and reader's mind. The two lines of the first couplet form parallels and oppositions, generating ever more associations, increasingly complex relations. Then we have two couplets, matching one set of oppositions by a correlative set of oppositions, defining change and entering a wider frame of reference.

The oppositions becoming manifest in the world find resonance in the mind of the solitary poet, traveling by night on the river; they fix his attention and echo his insecurity, his constant movement, his sense of isolation, his pride in his uniqueness and superiority. But at the same time that he feels the resonance with the great, endangered "ones" of the riverscape, his own dimensions are shrinking in the widening scope of his vision, and he becomes a smaller and smaller point in the immensity of the night scene.

We begin with "things" set side by side to act upon one another; the repetition of certain patterns of opposition makes those patterns manifest, visible to both the poet and the reader. We may read this process as an omen which the outer world offers; we may understand it as the poet's compulsion to notice, the scar of his private pain. In either case,

伊茲文之為用　　固眾理之所因

The true function of literature/*wen* is to be the means by which all inherent order may come through.[12]

Literature is a gate for the latent and inarticulate to become manifest. The poem is not simply the manifest state of the world's inherent order; its movement is the process of that order *becoming* manifest.

The oppositions in the physical scene may set up resonances in the realm of the poet's life:

名	豈	文　章	著
name/fame	how	literary writings	manifest?
官	應	老　病	休
office	surely must	old　sick	quit

My name shall not be known from my writing,
Sick, growing old, I must yield up my post.

As before, one confronts many; here it seeks recognition; the separation cannot be overcome and a greater falling away threatens. The present does not know me; the future will not remember me; I must yield up even my minor post. There will be no place for me either in literature or in history, which together are the collective recognition and memory of our civilization. A precariously swaying mast, a fallen moon, a forgotten poet—all are things that rest upon the river and are subject to its flux.

But a poem is an act of making manifest what is overlooked, lost, hidden; and this poem, through which the poet becomes aware of his isolation and a falling away from others, makes that very truth manifest to others. The literary work

> Passes thousands of miles, no impediment,
> 恢萬裏而無閡
> Spans a million years, a way across them;
> 通億載而為津
> Hands down models to coming generations,
> 俯貽則於來葉
> Gives us images to consider from men past.[13]
> 仰觀象乎古人

A poem is the manifest form of the mind's activities, and this manifestation is, in its turn, directed to other minds. Tu Fu's poem strikes out at the barrier between others and the self which is falling away from them: in its genesis the poem strives to overcome the very order of the world it perceives. The poem begins with the private and particular and moves to things manifest and shared.

飄	飄	何	所	似
fluttering	wind-tossed	what	be resembled to	
天	地	一	沙	鷗
Heaven	Earth	one	sand	gull

> Wind-tossed and fluttering—what is my likeness?
> In Heaven and Earth, a single gull of the sands.

After observing a series of *correlatives* for the self, the poet makes a true *analogy* in the simile of the gull. Metaphor (or simile) is not essential to a poetry that writes what the poet sees, thinks, and feels; the metaphor is no more than one action of the mind among others. But in this particular poem the formation of a simile is a resolution and escape from the oppressive repetition of the pattern noticed everywhere in the visible world—one separated from many. The very form of a simile admits the possibility of essential likeness in things which are different: there is something that may be shared across the barriers of identity. Simile makes kinship possible, and in the gull the poet finds true kin.

Here is the bird which both is and is not the man. As a human is the third term joined with Heaven and Earth in the Great Triad, so this creature is also the third, belonging neither to the heavens, where the stars hang securely, nor to the earth, where the grasses are firmly rooted; it is a creature of the river, a creature moving from element to element, forever in-between. Like the slender blades of grass, the bird is tossed by the winds; yet it does not bend; it soars with or against the wind, frail and unattached but somehow resilient. The immensity of the perspective—Heaven and Earth—diminishes the small creature to a tininess, but its solitary dominion over the vast emptiness (Heaven, Earth, and one bird) grants it a unique interest and importance. The poet has stopped his outward gaze into the world to read the omens of one separated from the many; the many have disappeared, and all that remains is the poet confronting his parallel identity.

DIGRESSION: COUNTERSTATEMENT EXPOSING THE MOTIVES OF THE CORRELATIVE COSMOS

The world has no inherent order of correlatives and transformations. The illusion of such order is no more than the projection of a human mind. And in the human mind no system of order is innate; systems of order are learned and taught; neither of those processes is disinterested. Behind every system of ordering the world lie the potent motivations of economic and social realities. Furthermore, when these true motivations are kept carefully concealed, we know that the powers which sponsor the system cannot bear the exposure of its motivations.

There is a complicity between Chinese classical literature and the imperial system. The complicity is obvious in the public face of that literature, speaking for the imperial system and supported by it. But the values of the unified empire are no less present in ostensibly private poetry and prose. Consider the T'ang Dynasty (618–907), the period which most later readers saw as the height of classical poetry: during the T'ang, poetry was composed and read only by a small segment of imperial society. Poetry did not even belong to an entire class—only to those propertied families that had some tie to the central government. And even in that small minority of a single class, poetry presents us with neither a full nor even an adequate picture of their lives and experiences: poetry portrays them in only one attitude, their faces turned toward the central government. It is a poetry that promises to make experience manifest, but in fact it speaks only for the approval of the ruling powers. The force of their approval shapes poetry into no more than an instrument of the central government in its eternal struggle with local interests.

There is no question that the great efflorescence of poetry in the eighth century was linked to its introduction into the chin-shih examination. Only afterwards did poetry spread to a truly broad range of social occasions and private situations. Poetry's dominant public modes were petition and apology—seeking office or explaining the motives and reasons for being out of office in terms acceptable to the central government. Poetry's dominant "private" mode was self-definition—obsessively trying to place the self in the orderly imperial cosmos.

Expose poetry even more harshly: a poem was a symbolic act of loyalty to the central government. For this reason and for this reason alone, the composition of poetry was used as a means to quality prospective officials in the *chin-shih* examination. This is a *most* peculiar way to choose civil servants; qualification for public service should reasonably demand some test of administrative competence, intelligence, or experience. If skill in poetic composition to a set topic qualified a person to serve, then there must have been something in that ability which answered the government's needs more perfectly than competence, intelligence, or experience. If the poem in no way proved the candidate's capacity to serve the people, then perhaps it proved something in the other direction—concerning the candidate's adherence and loyalty to the central government.

Qualification by such an elaborate act of literary obeisance must imply a potent sense of threat and concern for the candidate's loyalty. Who is put to this peculiar test? For those whose family interests are already inextricably bound up with those of the ruling dynasty, service is open by hereditary privilege and other means of recommendation. The examination in poetry is used primarily to draw outsiders—sons of collateral branches of great families, sons of lower provincial officials, sons of independent propertied families—into the imperial system. For such candidates with independent family interests, some proof might be required to show that they possessed or could adopt the point of view of the central government and could conceive of the world in its authorized terms.

Within the highly circumscribed rhetorical moves of examination verse are found the formal embodiments of the imperial ideology—the politically legitimate sentiments, the attention to only the authorized aspects of the outer world, the parallelism and rules of rhetorical amplification which teach that all objects and events belong in a system of received relations. In other poetry the rigid rules of examination verse seem to be relaxed, but this liberation is only illusory: beneath the surface all the proprieties are either observed or denied in acceptable ways. Poetry becomes an extension of the Confucian doctrine of *cheng-ming* 正名, "calling things by their 'proper' names": it gives politically acceptable words by which to comprehend and express the darker motions of the human spirit.

A poem does not simply say "I am loyal"; such a statement too-openly acknowledges the dangerous alternative. Instead, the poem demonstrates a thorough assimilation of the correlative cosmology on which the government's authority, even its justification to exist, is founded. The imperial ideology appears in poetry in many guises. Most obvious are the inviolable taboos that surround the domain of poetic discourse. All such taboos involve interests which might conflict with those of the central government—ties of family and clan, sexual passion, personal hatreds, private economic interests. Such dangerous interests existed; rather, it is inconceivable that they did not exist, even though they appear only in fragmentary hints through the filter of T'ang writing. To neutralize the power of those interests, the government sponsored in poetry and prose a set of substitutions, of alternative intellectual terms in which to understand disruptive desires. One who could use these authorized terms, who could use them as if they inhered naturally in the world, proved himself capable of transcending dangerous private interests and was thus qualified to serve the state.

Begin with poetry expressing "private" values, where the need for a sub-missive acknowledgement of the government's authority is most acute. Why is there so much poetry of "reclusion" in the T'ang? Why did the government and its high officials look so fondly on "recluses"? Reclusion is a theme in poetry and prose, constituted of a set of terms, values, and images; these frame a certain attitude and life situation which roughly corresponds to Western "reclusion." But is the concept of reclusion consonant with the historical realities to which the term is applied?

An official under the pressure of work or attacked by enemies may long for "reclusion." A "recluse" may present himself in the capital and form social connections in hopes of being recruited for service.

Dismissed from office or failing to gain office, a poet may extol a life of "reclusion." In addition there were a handful of sincere misanthropes who wanted nothing to do with human society; a few of those even wrote some poetry: to such the term "reclusion" properly applies. But between contented service in public office and misanthropy lies a vast range of situations and attitudes. Poetry admits only an "either/or" (the desire to serve or the desire to avoid human society); it overlooks that vast intermediate range, and the oversight is a good indication of the kinds of social ties which the sponsor-ing powers did not want considered.

The language of reclusion was applied to any period in a person's life when that person was not directly involved in the central government. This included all forms of life as a private citizen—living off the income of family estates and property, travels to do business for the family, etc. To name such normal activities "reclusion" was to set them in a negative relation to state service; "reclusion" transformed all motives for not serving the state into a purely personal inclination, and it severed any significant connection with local economic and political interests. The authorized theme of "reclusion" effectively kept a person from affirming the priority of any social organization other than the central government. In the poetic ideology there were only two situations a person could conceivably desire—to serve the central gov-ernment or to live as a "recluse," a private alternative to state service in which one found "peace of mind."

For other interests and passions, too, the poet must resort to silence or to trivializing substitutions. For sexual passion, substitute a bland sensuality, as in observing dancing girls at a party. If, as seems to be the case in the poetry of Li Shang-yin, the passion is overwhelming, cloak it so hermetically that it can be taken as political allegory. For the bitter hatred of private feuds, substitute "slander," acknowledging the subordination of both enemies to a higher (though easily misled) authority. The language is Statethink, new words to emasculate all threats to the central order.

But these are only words; the state's complicity in the poetic cosmos goes still deeper. The intellectual system which gives meaning to the world is reinforced and supported by the central government. Private interests, family interests, and local interests always constituted the primary threat to the central government, the greatest potential source of conflicting loyalties. Such threats may be met more or less successfully, but they never disappear. To subordinate local and family loyalty to loyalty to the central government requires a faith in hierarchical correlatives, not as a mere poetic device but as an inherent structure of the universe: my loyalty to the emperor is the correlative of my loyalty to clan and father, but on a higher level. The legitimacy of this simple analogical operation rests on the universal and absolute validity of correlation as the structural principle of the cosmos. Correlative links cannot be seen to come simply from the state's needs: they must be *believed*. As a symbolic act of loyalty to the state, the poem affirms this principle of order and makes it manifest. The parallel couplet, the structured description of a landscape, the presumption of meaning incarnate in the world—all these formal patterns and conventions of figuration carry the secret message, "I believe in the universal and eternal validity of the cosmic-imperial system."

Someone asked me about this.

I said: This is nothing more than an unkind context, attempting to diminish poetry by "exposing" its "true" motives. Our affection for poetry is not so fragile that it can be turned to contempt by the sly rhetoric of exposure. But if we look behind the rhetorical posture, there are principles here with which we may agree: one function of poetry is indeed *hua* 化, "to transform and civilize," 變其視聽 "to change the way people see and hear things."[14] If we choose to look to the relation between a literature and its society, we can hardly be surprised to discover that they support each other. If we choose to construe that mutual support as literature reinforcing the values of a society, we will find that too. But to "expose" that relation creates the illusion that it is the sole determinate force in what is, in fact, an open and complex interaction between a literature and its society. The parts of a civilization are a living whole: even an art that promises autonomy and independence of social motives serves a social need for some realm of experience apparently free of social motive, and thus finds itself impelled by a negative social motive.

Someone asked: Is it true that Chinese poetry avoids all social and private interests that conflict with the interests of the central government?

I said: In general, yes. But the significance is more complex than the interlocutor of the Digression allows. Consider, for example, a poem thanking a semi-independent military satrap for his patronage: the warlord will be lauded as the staunchest upholder of the imperial throne. A poem in which the "recluse" returns to the georgic bliss of his farm probably conceals shrewd land transactions, the appointment of a third cousin as overseer, and a strict watch kept on lazy fieldhands. Poetry does indeed tend to reduce a wide range of circumstance to an "either/or" of reclusion or state service. However, the true question is whether the "either/or" served the interests of the state by silencing alternatives or whether all finer distinctions simply faded before the larger opposition that was of paramount concern to the civilization as a whole— social responsibility or freedom from it.

It is impossible to say whether the state justified itself by the correlative cosmology implicit in poetry or whether the state was itself shaped by the cosmological model, received from the past. The model was received, learned with the written language; and when someone wanted to speak of justifiable social responsibility, the terms of the imperial state were the only terms available. Thus to praise one's military patron as the most loyal servitor of the imperial throne (rather than as "the toughest warrior east of Lo-yang") might be less an act of support for the central government than an appeal to the only values which could comprehend service to a warlord. To speak of serene reclusion in the canny management of the family estate may be no more than recovering from the experience what is comprehensible and valuable. Can we truly say that the state demands its servants to express their experiences in terms of those values? Can an institution, independent of the people who fill it, be said to possess such precise, Machiavellian instincts? We should not underestimate the productive power of an intellectual tradition to shape both institutions and individual values through the terms it provides.

Someone asked: By constantly linking individual, particular experience to larger patterns of order, doesn't poetry strip experience of its intensity? Even if this process does not come from the state's desire to erase dangerous private passions, isn't it still frighteningly Apollonian? Framed by the magnitude of the cosmic order, all joy, rage, and passion mellow into ephemeral manifestations of immutable pattern. Where are the flytings and harsh satires of Western poetry, the poems of passion, the devotional poems, the ecstatic drinking poems?

I said: I could answer you with a series if Li's—Li Po, Li Ho, and Li Shangyin. I could quote you dozens and dozens of examples to show you that such poetry does indeed exist. But in general, you are correct: there is a pervasive moderation, and where there is no moderation, there is repression—some things must not be said. But consider—the peculiar intensities of experience will never leave the human species: they were known by the poets and will be known by the readers of the poets. More important, the readers know that the poets themselves knew those intensities. In the best poetry the readers do not see mere mellowness but the winning of a mellowness out of frenzy; they see not only the surface of a repression but the power of the danger that called for such repression. Everywhere you are disturbed by the discontinuity between chaotic humanity and poetry's order and values. Your error is in seeing only the order and values, as if the poem were merely a textbook of ethics, government, or cosmic science. The poem is not mere order and value; it is a strenuous process of discovering and asserting order and value. The poem lies in the space between the chaotic and inarticulate realities of human experience and a hard-won ordering.

BACK FROM THE DIGRESSION: PROPOSITIONS

1. In the Chinese literary tradition, a poem is usually presumed to be non-fictional: its statements are taken as strictly true. Meaning is not discovered by a metaphorical operation in which the words of the text point to Something Else. Instead, the empirical world signifies for the poet, and the poem makes that event manifest.
2. Significance can appear in the forms of the sensible world through the presumption of a correlative structure of the universe. This presumption does not belong to literature alone, but rather it is central to the entire intellectual tradition, including the state.
3. Significance and pattern are latent in the world. The poet's consciousness and the poem are means by which latent significance and pattern become manifest.
4. The crossing of analogical levels is based on the principle of sympathetic resonance and categorical association. These are conceived as a process, one which, at its best, outlasts the reading of the text.
5. Although the poet sometimes interprets the significance of a scene explicitly, more often he simply orders the patterns of his experience and responds to it, leaving to the reader the greater part of the process of association.

Tu Fu		Facing the Snow		對雪[15]
戰	哭	多	新	鬼
battle	weep	many	new	ghosts
愁	吟	獨	老	翁
sad/sorrow	recite/groan	lone	old	aged man
亂	雲	低	薄	暮
disorderly/rebel	clouds	lower		sundown
急	雪	舞	迴	風

urgent/swift	snow	dance		whirlwind
飄	棄	尊	無	綠
ladle	cast aside	cup	is no	dark green
爐	存	火	似	紅
brazier	endure	fire	resemble	red
數	州	消	息	斷
several	prefectures	news	cut off	
愁	坐	正	書	空
sad	sit	just now	write words	emptiness

Weeping of battle, many fresh ghosts,
Sadly chanting a poem, a lone old man.
Riotous clouds lower in sunset,
Swift, urgent snow dances in whirlwinds.
The dipper tossed aside, no rich color in the cup,
The brazier lasts on, its fire seems a red.
From several provinces news has been cut off—
I sit in sorrow just now tracing words in the air.

The time was the winter of 756. The northeastern armies under the command of the Sogdian general An Lu-shan had revolted against imperial authority and marched on the capital. The emperor Hsüan-tsung fled to the west, and Tu Fu was trapped in the fallen capital, unable to make his way through enemy lines to reach T'ang forces. On November 17, the flower of the imperial army, under the inept command of the minister Fang Kuan, had tried to stop the advance of the rebel armies at Ch'en-t'ao, west of the capital, and had been disastrously defeated. The remnants of those forces rallied and joined with fresh imperial reserves to meet the rebels again a few days later at Ch'ing-fan, where the loyalists were again put to rout. In the winter of the year, with loyalist fortunes at low ebb, Tu Fu, still trapped in the capital, sat facing the snow.

"Weeping of battle, many fresh ghosts, / Sadly chanting a poem, a lone old man"—English forces us to make choices here, to limit and exclude some of the possibilities left open in the Chinese text: in the undefined relation between "weeping" and "battle," the perplexing "of" helps us defer comprehension. We do not know if this weeping is for all battles, or for the battles that have been fought this past year, or for this last, most recent battle. Nor do we know who is weeping—the ghosts, the poet, or people in general, weeping for recent ghosts. And the Chinese text generously admits possibilities which are lost in even the vaguest translation—a transitive weeping in which this battle brings the newly dead to tears, as sorrow drives the old man to compose. Amid this uncertainty of events with indeterminate contexts, the rules of punctuation ask that we lift the comma from its steadfast, imaginary line at the bottom of words and flatten it to hold the two halves of the line

apart: weeping of battle—many fresh ghosts. Weeping there is, and weeping
is to be expected—so many recent dead to stir tears in their comrades, both
those left living and the "old ghosts," fallen in earlier battles—recent dead
who bring tears to their families in the capital and drive the poet to weep and
write of their weeping. It is a general weeping, a "battle-weeping," *chan-k'u*
戰哭, two terms set side by side to show us that battle and weeping come
together in too many ways.

What makes them weep most—that there was a battle, that so many have
fallen, that the battle was lost? Out of the battle have come "many fresh
ghosts," weeping themselves and wept for by all. A "fresh ghost" is a "new
ghost," *hsin-kuei* 新鬼, and though all ghosts must at some time be "new," they
are best made from old bodies and not from the bodies of young men, "youth
of the best families whose blood is the water in the marshes of Ch'en-t'ao."[16]

The poet sits staring out the window towards the west at sunset, facing
the snow: where in the scene are these new dead? Does he simply assume their
presence, out there beyond his field of vision on the fields of Ch'en-t'ao and
Ch'ing-fan? Does he seem to hear them weeping in the winds of the growing
storm? Or perhaps, just perhaps, does he see them here too, as shapes in the
whirling snow?

He makes a poem, an old man lamenting the young: one alive and alone
inside, many youthful dead out there. He repeats his oldness—an "old, aged
man," *lao-weng* 老翁—as though emphasizing the incongruity: the young
should be lamenting the old, many should lament a single death—it should
not be like this.

The title gives a pattern of opposition, "Facing the Snow": something out
there and a self in here confronting the outer world. The first couplet allows
one line to each term of the opposition: out there are the dead; in here, the
old poet reciting his poem. The second and third couplets develop one term
each: the second couplet considers the snow scene; the third couplet looks in
to the objects of the room. Then in the final couplet, inside and outside draw
closer together for the last confrontation at the impermeable barrier on which
the poet writes his invisible message.

Out there, "riotous clouds lower in sunset"—*luan* 亂 clouds, "riotous,"
"rebellious," "disorderly" clouds, as though in the tumult of cloud were appearing configurations of the empire's fate and the vague shapes of physical battle.
But only perhaps this is so, as perhaps there are ghosts in the snow. The clouds
are not metaphors, not symbols, but what is seen out there in the sunset; they
pour snow in front of the poet's window, and if they seem metaphorical or
symbolic, it is just a hint of delusion in the poet's mind, so shaken by "weeping
of battle." Down these clouds come in the west, from out where Ch'en-t'ao
and Ch'ing-fan lie, darkening still more this scene already darkening with
evening—clouds closing off the horizon, closing off the vista, enclosing a poet
already enclosed in his room, facing the snow.

What kind of snow is falling?—*chi* 急 snow, a "swift and urgent" snow that moves with the "alarums" 急 of war, with the "hard-pressed" 急 advance of levies to the front; troops moving hastily, snow driven whirling in the wind—the hidden pattern of battle and dissolution. It is coming toward him: from the battlefields out beyond the horizon, to the tumult of cloud pressing down at the horizon, to the frenzied swirls of wind-driven snow before the window, disintegration and disorder are closing in upon the poet, advancing on the barrier across which he faces the snow.

It is the darkness of winter and winter's cold, the lowest point in the cycle of the seasons, when black Yin is dominant and mastered Yang flickers in the center, like a red fire in the brazier in the darkening night. It is the coldest time of the year, when men inside facing the snow need the warmth of wine and the forgetfulness of sorrow it brings. The wine is gone, the ladle cast aside, the purplish green lees are drained from the goblet. Something is gone; something endures: nothing is left of wine's forgetfulness, but some of its warmth remains in the fire of the brazier, a tiny spot of heat and color at the very center of the night.

All things converge upon this point of light. Here the poet is, and here, the barrier across which the poet faces the snow. This is the interface between darkness and light, between cold and warmth, between the bright red color of coming spring flowers and the grappling of black and white, Yin and Yang, in the night snow. Here is the point where the observing self meets the disintegrating world outside. Nothing comes in through the barrier: news is cut off, no communication, fragments of the empire fall away. And nothing goes out over the barrier: no way to find out what is happening there, no way to send a message of counsel to our armies—"hold on, wait till next year, don't be in a hurry."[17] This is not the season for action; the light is still small now. Spring and the next year promise change of fortunes, the light's dominion: "wait till next year."

There is a structural interface in the poem as well, an interface across which the poet looks out on the world and speaks to it. The thematic opposition in the poem between "inside" and "outside" corresponds to the essential structure of the Chinese lyric. So many poems were built upon the movement between exterior "world" and interior "response" that in later poetics it came to define the largest structural subclass of the Chinese lyric. The "lone old man" of the first couplet is the self seen as object, belonging to the outer world; the gesture of the last line is the true, first-person response to the experience of the preceding lines. The moving focus of the poem— from the horizon, to the window, to the room, to within the poet—belongs to a more general poetic process of internalizing. The response in "Facing the Snow" is problematic, speaking to the structure of the lyric as well as to the disintegration of cosmos and empire: it is an intense gesture of response which fails, which does not "come out" to cross the boundaries and touch the world.

We cannot read the message he writes: we read only the intensity with which the message is given.

Watching from outside, we know the emotion but not the content that the emotion fills. If the poem is an act of setting the self in relation to the world, then it will be the emotions, the most emphatically interior aspect of the self, which represent inner life. The movement from outer world to emotion defines the vector toward manifest, articulate meaning in the lyric. The poet perceives meaning latent in the world but usually suppresses direct interpretation of it. Instead, he makes his comprehension internal by "responding" to the external truth he sees. That act of suppression is the rule of enigma: like the unreadable message written in air, enigma generates the energy of concealment which asks the reader to understand the poem. We readers perceive what he perceives; we know what he feels; between those two certainties, we try to penetrate the barrier of the self and know what he knows. As in the metaphorical mode of Western reading, manifest under-standing is a goal that is eternally deferred: it lies at the end of an endless process of association and correlation that occurs in the reader's mind.

Response, which makes the significance of what has been perceived inter-nal to the poet, also engages a principle of sympathetic resonance in the reader. "Being stirred," *kan* 感, comes from reading, reciting, and hearing poetry: we readers also belong in that universe whose seasons touch the things of the world and the minds of poets. As we move toward articulate meaning, sympathetic resonance promises us that we will feel what the poet feels: the significance of experience will be internal and not a mere object of reflection. As we are drawn to learning "what" a manifest experience means, we are to instinctively be aware of "how" it means.

FURTHER DIGRESSION: COUNTERSTATEMENT ON SELF-DRAMATIZATION

It is an illusion, of course. To assume that the poem embodies an experience of the world in historical time is a charming illusion, but an illusion never-theless. The truth is well known and firm in our certainty: when the poet's self writes of an experience, that self is already distant from the experience. For this always later, retrospective self, the self of the creative artist, the expe-rience of which he writes is irrevocably past. He has been changed by it; he is different from what he was while he was "in" the experience.

The act of writing a poem is no innocent and spontaneous production of a correlative for experience. The writing has its own ends, which lie entirely outside the experience. A poem is directed to a reader: words must be given form according to the laws of literature and representation, not according to the laws of the physical universe. Poets write couplets; nature does not. The poem is—unfortunately, but necessarily—an artificed construct. The poems we have read are distinguished by being artifacts which aspire to cast the *illusion* of immediate experience of the world.

These poems are carefully staged little dramas in which the stage surrounds not a group of actors but the consciousness of one actor. It is an interior drama which, in a remarkable way, offers you the best seat in the actor's mind. You may see what the actor sees, hear what the actor hears, perhaps even be brought to feel some semblance of the emotions which the actor evokes—but such artistic successes do not change the truth that the actor is no more than an actor, a simulacrum and not a person inhabiting a living world. You are the audience within; but outside both the actor and your field of vision stands the stage director, our poet, manipulating this simulacrum of an anterior self: "Look now on the horizon, now at the snow before your window, now at the ladle cast down—that's a nice touch!" It is a great and very special kind of drama, but the only difference between this and Western drama lies in the peculiar demand that the audience believe that the drama's actions are real and occurring right now. It is quite possible that something similar to the events of the poem did indeed once happen; but this matters not at all—the poem is a "reenactment," carefully staged and from a distance.

Someone asked me about this.

I said: I expected it—he always thinks of things like this. But I hope you realize that he has it all backwards. The creative artist is a charming illusion, obsessively bringing forth experiences time and again, while defensively disguising them and pretending to be in full control of his "creations." Nevertheless, both truths about the "real" status of the poet are irrelevant. Our interest lies in how the poem is to be taken, not in whether the way the reader takes it is an accurate or adequate reflection of the poetic act.

But so as not to seem evasive, I'll try to respond on the level to which our contentious interlocutor wishes to speak—the creative act itself. Even here his arguments about self-dramatization are not a true critique. No claim is made that the poem is identical to the original experience; it is simply an organic correlative for it. The interlocutor would focus our attention on the productive mechanics of a poem; he locates the essentially "poetic" in the distance between the creating self and the prior historical self that had the experience. This Wordsworthian problem is central only if you grant it centrality: it was not central in the Chinese theoretical tradition, nor must it necessarily be so in a theory of poetry.

Someone answered: Always appealing to "correlation" is too easy an escape from these problems. There are serious implications in that bit of "productive mechanics." If the correlative theory were true, then the identity of the poem would be determined by the identity of the original experience. But a poet can make a vast number of poems from any given experience. I can accept that the poet may in good faith try to recreate what he *believes* to have been the original experience, but what determines the verbal form of the poem, the power of making and choice, lies in the creative poet and not in the experience.

I said: Again you force me to argue not how the poem is to be taken but how it actually is; so be it. First, I am by no means convinced that a "vast number" of poems can come from a given experience. The ability to create a variety of different versions of one experience implies that the poet is willfully *asserting* his distance from the experience, showing his power to manipulate and transform. In such a case, the poem is not about the ostensible experience at all but rather about the poet's capacity for invention. That is an interesting enough topic in itself, but it grows wearisome after a while.

But just suppose—and I am by no means convinced of it—that a "vast number" of poems can indeed come from one experience without a willful display on the poet's part of his power to manipulate. You have invoked a simple causal paradigm—one effect for one cause, one poem for one experience. I certainly never offered this model. If by "experience" you mean the historical whole, then a number of patterns of attention and response could quite naturally grow out of it, as two or more trunks can grow out of one root. However, we would, in such poems, sense the shared ground very strongly. On the other hand, if by "experience" you mean the exact elements perceived and felt in the poem, then I cannot see how more than one poem could be written of them, for these elements are the poem.

Someone replied: Now we have tree metaphors—it is very difficult to be convinced by an argument based on tree metaphors. You are either exceptionally obtuse or stubborn. You either cannot or refuse to recognize the power of literature to shape an originating experience. How can you account for revision?

I answered: I am both obtuse and stubborn; I cannot understand these mysterious processes you speak of, unless you mean that when pre-articulate experience emerges as a poem, it becomes articulate and has the characteristics of language . . .

Someone muttered: I don't like the way this is turning out.

I continued: . . . in which case the subtlety of your observation astounds me. You seem to want to compare the seed and the tree that grows from it, saying "Look—one ceases to be when the other exists; one has branches, bark, and leaves, but the other has none!" The comparison can be made, but it is less interesting than the fact that one grew from the other, and that each belongs to a different stage, each stage having characteristics and a mode of being appropriate to it.

When you try to catch me up on revision, I can see the hidden presumptions of Western rhetoric in your argument—that there is some articulate "content" which is shaped into a literary form for certain ends, of persuasion or art. I cannot agree with this: the written poem is a version of nothing else but the not-yet-written poem. You make revision the clear evidence of artistic manipulation—a peculiar thought! I think of revision as the mark of dissatisfaction: it occurs only when the poet senses something is wrong with the poem, that it is in some way inadequate. Revision is not gratuitous manipulation: the poet returns to the text for the sake of something, and I would suggest that "something" is adequate correlation. A historical distance does lie, as you noted, between the writing poet and the experiencing self: that distance is the time in which the poem "becomes."

Someone muttered: It is impossible to hold an intelligent discussion with a person who uses tree metaphors. . . .

The world is a vast, fluctuating omenscape, and the poet is the omen-reader of the world. As portents and prodigies appear to the government, revealing the conditions of society, so the omen of the world is the true configuration of the present perceived by the poet. These omens are not prophecies (though one who knows the world's cycles may be able to read something of the future in them). They are latent marks of the governing structure of the present.

The turbulent phonetic migrations of Indo-European languages, with their hordes of prefixes, suffixes, and sound mutations, permit the uncontrolled proliferation of semantic entities which too quickly forget their ancestry. Unless the scholar reminds us, we do not take note of "literature's" link to the "letter." But the more retentive process of compound formation in Chinese allows the creation of new semantic units, in which are embedded the older, one-syllable forms that have too many meanings. The term for "literature" in Chinese may be *wen-hsüeh* 文學 or *wen-chang* 文章, but it is also their moiety, *wen*, the "written word."

In traditional Chinese thought we often find the same etymological impulse which leads the Western scholar to remember "letter" in "literature." To think of the origins of literature (*wen*), we think of the origins of writing (*wen*). These origins were ultimately traced to the trigrams and hexagrams of the *Book of Changes*. Here in the disposition of broken and solid lines, the most basic situations of change are schematized. Out of these primal marks evolved all the finer distinctions of the written word.

It all began by observing the tracks made by birds: all things and events have schematic impressions. The marks of *wen* are not "signs" but outlines and impressions, evidences of what lies outside of language. In the first chapter of the *Wen-hsin tiao-lung* 文心雕龍 Liu Hsieh locates the source of human *wen* in the "Configurations" or "Images" 象 of the *Book of Changes*.[18] Under each hexagram in the *Book of Changes* there is a section entitled "Image"; but these written passages are not the Images themselves, rather they are the words manifesting the Images. In this difficult concept of Image, we discover the organic link between words, meaning, and the things of the world. The third-century philosopher Wang Pi explained Image thus:

An image is what brings forth concept [意]; language is what makes an image manifest [明]. Nothing accounts for concept as completely as the image, and nothing accounts for the image as completely as language. Language was generated out of image, so that we may consider the image by looking for it in language. The image originated out of the concept, so that we may consider the concept by looking for it in the image.[19]

An Image, such as the dragon for the primal hexagram Ch'ien, is the schematization of the thing—not the dragon you might encounter in the everyday world, but a schematized envisagement of "dragon." This image necessarily mediates between words and meaning; the epistemological process seems to require it. The hexagram Ch'ien embodies a vital power and capacity for transformation, but such "meaning" appears only through the Image of the dragon. We may read words describing the dragon, grasp the image, and come to understand the fullness of Ch'ien's significance. But to attempt to go directly from words to meaning—to talk about Ch'ien as the capacity for transformation—is somehow inadequate for the concept. Image, in turn, appears in *wen*, the marks of the written word. It is image that Tu Fu sees when he "faces the snow," and he helps the image become *wen*.

For the poet, this triad of meaning, image, and word appears upon the ground of a particular experience. Out of the sensible world images appear, fully accounting for some meaning (盡意), and asking to be made manifest (明) in words. Sometimes a poet may even perceive the Images of the hexagrams of the *Book of Changes* in a landscape, as Hsieh Ling-yün 謝靈運 (385–433) does, sailing into exile past Fu-ch'un Isle:

> This night we crossed the pool of Fisherbank,
> 宵濟漁浦潭
> And by dawn have reached the walls of Fu-ch'un,
> 旦及富春郭
> Where Steady Mountain lies far in fog and cloud,
> 定山緬雲霧
> Where Red Pavilion admits no mooring.
> 赤亭無淹泊
> Up against current struck splashing swiftness,
> 逆流觸驚急
> Came to headlands blocking, a tumult of crags.
> 臨圻阻參錯
>
> . . . .
> "Rushing water arrives where it will"—proper to be inured;
> 洊至宜便習
> "Mountains ranged"—important to keep still, to hold on. . . .[20]
> 兼山貴止託

In the landscape around Fu-ch'un, the Images appear, embodying the situation and giving silent counsel to the exile. Out there lies the Image of hexagram twenty-nine, the Gulf 坎: "rushing water arrives (where it will)"; up there is hexagram fifty-two, Stillness 艮, "ranged mountains." For these Images the text of the *Book of Changes* teaches the proper response—endurance, stillness.

But the world is not always so easy to read, not easy for the poet and not easy for his reader. A world in which the fragmented images lead to no recognizable or unifying pattern can be a nightmare. In Tu Fu's poetry there is often such multiplicity in the possibilities of pattern and meaning that their sheer density leaves the world unintelligible and opaque, as though it lacked meaning altogether. Li Shang-yin 李商隱 (813–858) encounters worlds of hermetic and discontinuous fragments which are clues to some mystery that is never revealed. In the fragmentation he finds the correlative of a living disorientation—of dream, of madness, of passion—as he did "At Ch'ung-jang House, in the First Month of the Year" 正月崇讓宅.[21]

密	鎖	重	關	掩	綠	苔
secret	lock	layered	gates	close/cover	green	moss
廊	深	閣	迥	此	徘	徊
(outside) corridors	deep	high chamber	far	this/here	pace-about-anxiously	
先	知	風	起	月	含	暈
beforehand	know	wind's	rising	moon	holds in	halo
尚	自	露	寒	花	未	開
still	of itself	dew	cold	flower	not yet	open
蝙	拂	簾	旌	終	展　轉	
bat	brushes	curtain	sash	at last	toss-and-turn	
鼠	翻	窗	網	小	驚	猜
rat	turns over	window	screen	a little	startle-awake	doubt
背	燈	獨	共	餘	香	語
one's back	to lamp	alone	together-with	remaining	scent	talk
不	覺	猶	歌	夜	起	來
not	aware/awake	still	sing	"Night	Rise up	Come"

Locked away secretly, gate behind gate, closed by green moss,
Passages deep, the chamber far—here pace anxiously.
And know ahead that the wind will rise—halo close about the moon;
The dew still cold, as it should be; the flowers not yet open.
A bat brushes the curtain sash, but at last only toss and turn;
A rat knocks over the window screen—a moment's shock, wondering.
Now all alone, back to the lamp, speak to the fading scent,
And without knowing it, still to be singing "Rise Up Tonight and Come."

One person alone; two might have been together, were together, will be together, at some other place and at some other time—but they are not together now. We guess they are lovers. The occasional title tells us the speaker is the poet and not the persona of a woman (though if the poem were *yüeh-fu,* it might be otherwise). A woman (if it is a woman) is loved, but somewhere else—dead, lost, cloistered behind the tiers of gates.

It is a poem of barriers, of lockings—a series of gates in succession, at once leading to and sealing off something secret, hidden within. The poet speaks of a secret, and he speaks of it secretly: like the gates, the poem tells and hides, points insistently to something while blocking vision. No passage—gates covered with green moss of long time and disuse, a genital architecture that invites and forbids entrance.

Where is the poet?—inside waiting or outside these gates, imagining someone closed within? Is he outside feeling the cold as he stares at the moon and the unopened flowers; is he inside, tossing in his bed, his attention going with every sound to the openings in the room? Why is there this locking, and who lives behind the barriers? Each moment, each scene seems to be charged with portentous significance, but that significance is hidden away, like the person.

Passageways around the outside of the buildings set deep within the layers of wall, leading from room to room and to a far chamber set high. Someone is pacing back and forth, going nowhere—the poet, perhaps, pacing the corridors, perhaps pacing outside the gates, unable to enter, gazing toward the deepest corridors which lead to the far chamber. Linking passageways, a chamber to be entered, with barriers and blockages—crossing over forbidden, frustrated. But the why and the who and the where are all concealed, all part of the mystery. There is no ground of narrative space on which these links and blockages, goals and gestures, can arrange themselves and have meaning.

Set in this dreamlike puzzle of objects and movements, we try to look to the principles of cosmic order, the rules of reading, hoping in that way to piece together the fragments and find some pattern. Look to the halo around the moon; augur in it the coming of the wind, cold now in February, cold to one pacing outside the gates or circling through the outer corridors. And as the dew forms in the depths of the night—a dew which chills the person walking to the very bone—know that it is proper for this season of the year, and know that the buds of the flowers will not have yet opened, as neither the gates nor the mystery have opened.

Make all these connections, do the good reader's work, and learn nothing more than the growing chill of the night, the chill of the dew, and the coming of the wind. It is a cold that belongs to circles—of someone pacing around, thinking of the hard, round knots of the unopened buds, the icy circles of the dew, the circle of the moon with its encircling halo held tight about it, the corridors circling around the outsides of the buildings, set within ring after ring of circling walls.

Then we are in a room, surrounded by walls, anticipating an intrusion, a piercing of the barrier. There are hints, false evidence to interrupt silent desire, to tease you to suppose what is not true—illusions of entrance and someone coming in. The curtain sash stirs, the screen in the window opening falls—only a bat flying past, only a rat scurrying over. Someone is inside this room, tossing and turning, dozing off then startling awake at the least movement, expectant.

Tossing and turning, dozing and waking—could the lines before have been only a dream, a dream of a series of gates and pacing outside on the cold corridors in the February wind? Or were the lines the true events of waking life, but since that time something else occurred—waking or in the dream—which the poem passes over in silence?

There is someone awake now, the lamp at his back (or at her back—in fantasy, in memory, or in a dream), casting his shadow before him as the silent companion of his talking. He speaks to shadow and fading scent, of woman or flower, the faintly lingering evidence that someone was indeed here and now has gone. Somewhere between the frustrated desire and this moment, something has been missed, passed over in silence. Except for this scent, it might have been a dream. The hard, unopened bud has blossomed, and only the fading traces of its scent remain. Again the barriers are in place: whoever it was that he or she did or did not meet, that someone is again back in beyond the barriers, lost.

And amid all this, the words of a song come out unconsciously; emotions unspoken, blocked within, break out, through the locking silence and give the commemoration or invocation "Tonight Rising," "Tonight Rise Up and Come," "Tonight She Rose and Came." The song, hidden emotions becoming manifest, speaks to us with passionate clarity but tells us nothing, offers no key to the mystery.

These illusions, born out of dream and passion, form a world of fragments that haunt the mind. The mind wants to seize them and penetrate the mystery, but it cannot. What has happened and what will happen remain concealed, and the song, the concluding response, manifests only bare desire, with neither the narrative nor the objects upon which the desire can come to rest.

Commentary by an unknown Taoist Master:

Truly great poetry is by nature passive; the essay is correct. The poet's mind moves the course of things and thus the words betray no trace of the axe and hatchet. He rests in the Way, and the poem comes of itself. In the highest craftsmanship there is no craftsmanship; the finest poetry is where there is no Poetry. No making, no forcing, no posing, no forming, the eye meets the world, and a poem emerges—this is Natural Process. Force it and it grows thinner; seek for it and it is gone; form it and it grows warped. Only when spirit, eye, and the writing hand are in perfect accord does the poem avoid becoming entangled in words—only then will the echoes linger in the mind without impediment.

Another, later commentary:

How foolish are the words of the Taoist master! To create the correlative world of poem, the poet must act with the powers of *Continuous Creation*, *Tsao-hua* 造化. As all the myriad things were endowed with shape, so the correlative creation of a poem too must give shape and form. The poet is no passive vessel through which nature speaks; rather he is an equal power in a parallel realm. The vital intricacy of the poem requites the intricate order of Creation. This can be attested by the closing of Han Yü's 韓愈 (768–824) poem on the South Mountains 南山詩:[22]

> Mighty they stand between Heaven and Earth,
> 大哉立天地
> In perfect order like the body's ducts and veins.
> 經紀肖營膝
> Who was it first laid out the origin?
> 厥初孰開張
> Who, in striving and labor, urged it on,
> 僑倪誰勸侑
> Creating in this place the simple and the artful,
> 創茲朴而巧
> Joint efforts enduring long-suffering toil?
> 戮力忍勞疢
> The axe and hatchet must have been used;
> 得非施斧斤
> It could not have been done without spells, incantations.
> 無乃假詛呪
> No traditions survive from that age of Chaos.
> 鴻荒竟無傳
> But the deed was mighty—none can repay it.
> 功大莫酬僦
> I have heard from the priest of the sacrifice
> 嘗聞於祠官
> That the god descends to take the offer's scent;
> 芬苾降歆嗅
> Finely wrought, I have made this poem
> 裴然作歌詩
> So that I too may join in requiting him.
> 惟用贊報摭

EPILOGUE

With Li Shang-yin at Ch'ung-jang House, we are on the border of a fiction: only the thinnest line separates a fiction from delusion and dream. Fictionality may be the center of the Western literary art, but fiction-making is a human event which occurs in historical time. The poetry of dream and imagination is a border realm which pays allegiance to both the domain of fictional poetry and the referential realm of the Chinese *shih*. This dual allegiance helps us to understand some of the distinctive characteristics of the Chinese lyric, the *shih* 詩—the impulse to frame a visionary poem with the statement "I dreamed," "I imagined," "it seemed to me as if . . . ." Metaphors and fictions tend to be revealed as subjective acts. Li Ho has a vision of the unappeased slain as he passes over the ancient battlefield of Ch'ang-p'ing: the demonic interruption is securely located in a sublunary itinerary.

Past these fringes of the *shih* is a true fictional poetry, *yüeh-fu* 樂府, "ballads" (though the term *yüeh-fu* is sometimes applied to nonfictional poetry as well). Here conventional personae and figures from history and legend appear in a mode identical to that of their Western counterparts in poetry. But even here the power of the reading tradition of the *shih* makes the most obtuse readers yearn for some grounding biographical circumstances: the fiction is explained as a willful concealment, masking an experience so dangerous or painful that it cannot appear in the common *shih*. The mode of such reading is topical allegory, in which the surface text is only a veil whose shape is given by the historical body behind it. Fiction-making is neither divine, nor playful, nor natural, nor demanded by the essential hiddenness of Truth— fiction-making is quite the opposite, the defensive mark of pain, fear, and taboo.

NOTES

1. Hiraoka Takeo et al., comps, *Tōdai no shihen* (Kyoto, 1964–1965) [hereafter *Tōdai*], no. 11433; *Chiu-chia chi-chu Tu-shih*, vol. 2 of William Hung, ed. *A Concordance to the Poems of Tu Fu*, Harvard-Yenching Sinological Institute Series, no. 14 (rpt. Taipei, 1966) [hereafter *Chiu-chia*], 27/10, p. 415. Note that in line 7, I read 飄飄 in place of the *Chiu-chia* 飄零. For another extensive and rather different discussion on this poem, see Shuen-fu Lin, *The Transformation of the Chinese Lyric: Chiang K'uei and Southern Sung Tz'u Poetry* (Princeton: Princeton University Press, 1978), 100–06.

2. "Miscellaneous Sonnets" XXXVI, "Composed upon Westminster Bridge, September 3, 1802," William Wordsworth, *Wordsworth Poetical Works*, ed. Thomas Hutchinson, new ed. rev. Ernest de Selincourt, Oxford Standard Authors (Oxford: Oxford University Press, 1978), 214.

3. Rene Wellek and Austin Warren, *The Theory of Literature* (New York: Harcourt, Brace and World, 1956), 25.

4. The correlative structure of traditional Chinese cosmology is a complicated area of study unto itself. Recommended are Joseph Neeham, *Science and Civilisation in China*, vol. 2, *History of Scientific Thought* (Cambridge: Harvard University Press, 1956), and Hellmut Wilhelm, *Heaven, Earth, and Man in The Book of Changes* (Seattle: University of Washington Press, 1977).

5. The semantic range of *wen* is presented most fully in English in James J. Y. Liu, *Chinese Theories of Literature* (Chicago: University of Chicago Press, 1975), 7–9.

6. For example, *Shih* 285. For a discussion of this and related issues, see Wang Ching-hsien, "Towards Defining a Chinese Heroism," *Journal of the American Oriental Society*, 95.1 (1975), 25–35.

7. *Wen-hsin tiao-lung* (*Ssu-pu ts'ung-kan*, ed. [hereafter *SPTK*]), 1.1a–1b.

8. In other texts, music is given its own privilege as the form in which the cosmic order is most perfectly embodied: as in the West, music was associated in early China with cosmic harmony. Note, also, interesting parallels between Liu Hsieh's argument in favor of literature here and Hegel's privileging of literature in the *Philosophy of Fine Art*, III.2, introduction.

9. There were, of course, sophisticated works on the theory of painting, but even in these we find a strong tendency to reject the imitation of merely visible forms.

10. *Wen-hsin tiao-lung* (*SPTK*), 10.1a–2a.

11. Ibid., 10.10b.

12. *Wen fu*, in *Liu-ch'en chu Wen hsüan* (*SPTK*), 17.14a.

13. Ibid., 17.14a–14b.

14. Li O, *Shang Sui Kao-tsu ko wen-hua shu*, in *Ch'üan Sui wen*, 20.8b, in Yen K'o-chün, ed., *Ch'üan shang-ku San-tai Ch'in Han San-kuo Liu-ch'ao wen* (Kuang-ya shu-chü, 1893; rpt. Taipei, 1963).

15. *Tōdai*, no. 10973; *Chiu-chia*, 19/5, 295. For full notes to this poem, see Stephen Owen, *The Great Age of Chinese Poetry: The High T'ang* (New Haven: Yale University Press, 1981), 390–91. In several cases in these essays I have revisited poems discussed in *The Great Age of Chinese Poetry*, and in at least one case I have pointed out many of the same features. I hope that this will not strain the patience of my readers—that they will recognize the difference in the two tours.

16. *Tōdai*, no. 10538; *Chiu-chia*, 2/22, 44–45.

17. *Tōdai*, no. 10539; *Chiu-chia*, 2/23, 45.

18. For a fuller discussion of the Images, see Wilhelm, *Heaven, Earth, and Man*, 190–221.

19. Wang Pi, *Ming Hsiang*, in *Chou Yi lüeh-li*, in *Chou Yi* (*SPTK*), 10.8a.

20. *Liu-ch'en chu Wen hsüan* (*SPTK*), 26.33a–33b.

21. *Tōdai*, no. 29574; *Li-Yi-shan shih-chi* (*SPTK*), 5.21b.

22. *Tōdai*, no. 17790; *Chu Wen-kung chiao Ch'ang-li hsien-sheng chi* (*SPTK*), 1.16a.

chapter seven

THE DISTINCTIVE ART OF CHINESE FICTION

Paul S. Ropp

Editor's note: Ropp describes the distinctive aesthetic qualities of Chinese fiction, especially vernacular fiction, as compared to Western fiction. In Chinese fiction, the Confucian, Daoist, and Buddhist philosophical perspectives do not support the tragic view of life, so important in Western fiction. Instead, Chinese fiction has a strong tradition of optimistic moralism based on community values and perspective.

STORYTELLING IN CHINA probably began in the cave, and it continues to flourish in the late twentieth century. For a civilization as old and continuous as China's, a complete history of fiction would fill many books. My purpose in this chapter is more modest: to suggest the uses and pleasures of reading Chinese fiction in English translation, to give a sense of the distinctive qualities of fiction (especially vernacular fiction) in China as compared with Western fiction, and to review some of the highlights of the Chinese tradition.

There are many ways to try to understand a civilization. No one way is necessarily superior to the others, but certainly one of the most enjoyable ways to explore the riches of Chinese civilization is through its fiction. As a very popular art form in China, fiction can tell us a great deal about the beliefs, values, and customs of ordinary people. In describing the details of daily life Chinese storytellers from at least the fifth century A.D. onward have given us our most extensive sources on the actual texture of Chinese life, what Lionel Trilling once called the "hum and buzz of implication" that we take for granted in our own lives but that gets lost in most formal or official records from the past.

Fiction naturally invites analysis from many different perspectives.[1] Part of its perennial appeal is that it can be read and enjoyed on so many different levels. The highly trained literary theorist might probe a particular work with mind-boggling erudition, but a beginning student can read the same work at a less sophisticated level and still gain a great deal of pleasure and understanding.

Fiction can also be an illuminating vehicle for the comparison of two civilizations. Chinese fiction has not had much influence on Western literature, and until the late nineteenth century the West had little or no impact on Chinese fiction. In part, this separation is what makes Chinese and Western literatures interesting to compare. In such a comparison, we see both universals of human storytelling and evidence that different civilizations with their particular conceptions of human life, social and political organization, moral and religious teachings, and modes of entertainment inevitably shape their fictions to meet their own needs and concerns.

The development of fiction in China and the West offers many striking parallels. In both China and the West fiction has generally been seen to have a dual mission: to entertain and to instruct; and in both cultures these two goals have frequently been in conflict. Until relatively recently (perhaps the eighteenth century in the West and the twentieth century in China) the social status of the practitioners of fiction has been relatively low. Fiction was frequently condemned by philosophers and moralists in both cultures for "leading people astray," "glorifying vile behavior," and "wasting valuable time" that would otherwise be spent, it was assumed, in more uplifting or productive pursuits. (These arguments alone have always assured fiction a ready audience in both cultures!)

Apart from moral attitudes toward fiction, there are also important parallels in the evolution of storytelling forms in China and the West. In both cultures there has been a general development from shorter to longer works, from an earlier emphasis on myths and folktales to a later emphasis on the individual experience and observations of particular authors. As fiction became more sophisticated and self-conscious in both cultures, it also evolved from an earlier tendency to endorse wholeheartedly the society's common values and moved instead to a more ironic stance that questioned or criticized the dominant values of the civilization. Although fiction was to some extent more valued in the West than in China early on, the direction of change in both has been toward a growing appreciation of the serious importance of fiction not just as entertainment but as a way of exploring profound social, moral, philosophical, and psychological questions.

To be slightly more specific and to anticipate the second half of this chapter, it is worth noting the parallel development of the novel in both China and the West. The extended prose narrative that realistically creates a believable world of its own evolved in China from the fourteenth through the eighteenth centuries, slightly anticipating but very closely paralleling the development of the novel in Europe. In both cultures these literary developments seem to accompany the rise of a money economy, urbanization, a growing entertainment industry, and the spread of printing, literacy, and education. In both China and the West the novel was also primarily the work of a highly educated elite writing for educated readers. Most striking are the parallels from the sixteenth through the early nineteenth centuries when the novel in both cultures became increasingly autobiographical and increasingly serious in the exploration of social, moral, and philosophical problems.[2]

In addition to these similarities, there are some important differences between Chinese and Western fiction. Several themes from the other chapters in this volume are especially important in the traditions of Chinese fiction. Among these, I would emphasize the importance of history and historical-mindedness, and relative optimism of the Chinese worldview, the moral humanism of Confucian philosophy, and the relative emphasis from very early in Chinese history on collective behavior and the welfare of the group rather than the individual.

As I already noted, early fiction in China and in the West was assumed to have a moral purpose, but the moral emphasis has generally been stronger, or has survived longer, in the Chinese tradition. Michael Sullivan has remarked on the Chinese tendency to assume that great art is by definition moral.[3] The dominant stated purpose of Chinese storytellers has been to uplift their readers, to reassure them that the universe is friendly, that human life is meaningful, and that human morality above all makes it so. This moralistic humanistic optimism in traditional Chinese fiction (despite exceptions to be noted later) gives it a didactic quality that contemporary Westerners have sometimes criticized as trite at best and dishonest at worst.

It would be a great mistake, however, to assume that Chinese storytellers lacked courage or insight into society because they were optimistic and didactic. We should note that fiction writers had to attract readers somehow; unlike poets and philosophers, storytellers had no captive audience among aspiring scholar-officials. The need to attract and keep a reader's attention cut against the Confucian grain of moralistic optimism. As Tolstoy wrote at the beginning of Anna Karenina, "All happy families are alike; each unhappy family is unhappy in its own way." Virtue is unfortunately boring in its predictability, and evil is fascinating in its sheer variety. For these reasons Chinese storytellers have never stayed wholly within the bounds of respectability. The audience for tales of sex, violence, intrigue, and adventure has been as vast and as eager in China as anywhere else.

The storyteller's most common solution to the conflicting demands of didacticism and attracting an audience was to put a moral gloss on every story and then (as often as not) ignore or contradict the self-proclaimed "message" while trying to make the story as exciting, as funny, or as believable as possible. This pattern is most obvious in traditional Chinese love stories. These stories, particularly the erotic or pornographic ones, invariably pose as moral tales warning readers of the dire consequences of romantic love and unbridled sexual indulgence. Yet the storytellers often take such graphic delight in the love scenes in these stories that they could not possibly have succeeded in their proclaimed goal of encouraging sexual abstinence and debunking romantic love.[4] The point here is not to question the honesty or virtue of the storyteller or his audience, but simply to note how fiction can illustrate the social and moral tensions of a civilization.

Among the important sources of optimism and moral didacticism in Chinese fiction were its origins in the writing of history and what David N. Keightley notes as the profound philosophical optimism of the early Chinese.[5] If the universe is friendly, if it "makes sense" morally, and if human beings have the power to make collective improvements in their lives, the possibilities for a tragic view of life are greatly diminished. Needless to say, there have been tragedies in Chinese literature and more tragedies in Chinese life, but the relative Chinese disinterest in tragic stories is very striking in its contrast with Western traditions from ancient Greece onward. More than anything else, this profound philosophical optimism is what modern Western critics have found objectionable in the Chinese storytelling tradition. But a disinterest in tragedy does not mean that human ignorance, folly, greed, and misery are ignored or glossed over in Chinese fiction. On the contrary, these themes occupy a well-deserved place in Chinese, as in all human, fiction. The task of the Chinese fiction-writer (and the Chinese historian) was to redeem these dark themes from the abyss of despair by "making moral sense" of them.

In Chinese fiction the moralistic and optimistic emphasis of Confucianism was ironically reinforced by the spread of Buddhism and the concepts of reincarnation, karma, and moral retribution. Although Confucian scholars often criticized Buddhism, the religion flourished in China from the second century A.D. onward, and Buddhist views of reincarnation and moral retribution came to be embedded in the popular Chinese worldview. This belief could explain away the most horrible examples of apparent injustice, and thousands of Chinese short stories take as their theme the rewarding of good and punishment of evil in this life or the next (or the one after that).

As a part of their mutual faith in a moral universe, Confucians and Buddhists both saw the primary value of fiction in moral terms. One might even go so far as to suggest that Confucian historiography and Buddhist missionary efforts provided the first great impetus for the development of storytelling in China. Confucian historians developed narrative models that storytellers copied verbatim, and Buddhist missionaries discovered that a good exciting story was a far better lure to religion than the dry explication of a sacred text. Despite their radical disagreement on the meaning of life, Buddhists and Confucians agreed on the moral purpose of fiction and each group affirmed an ethicoreligious order with little room for tragedy or despair.

Confucians and Daoists shared a faith in harmony, balance, and a cyclical view of reality that also worked against the development of tragedy. Confucians urged moderation in all things, and Daoists argued that all situations and qualities contain the seeds of their opposite. Extreme power leads to defeat, extreme wealth to poverty, and any one virtue, if carried to extremes, becomes a vice. In this view (shared by Confucians and Daoists alike) a hero is by definition moderate. Thus, in contrast to the typical Greek tragic hero, the Chinese hero is not likely to be destroyed by a noble impulse carried too far. A faith in the cyclical nature of life also helps to rob death of its sting. When the philosopher Zhuangzi surprised his friends by singing cheerfully after the death of his wife, he responded by defining death as a natural part of life, not something to be feared or mourned. For Confucians death brings sadness—the sadness of parting—but not terror or pity, the stuff of Greek tragedy.

Another factor that worked against a tragic view of life in China was its emphasis on the society or the collectivity rather than the individual. This collective emphasis with its bureaucratic overtones may seem inhibiting and confining to contemporary Westerners, but it was a source of great social strength and stability in Chinese civilization. If an individual is defined solely in individual terms, the opportunities for tragedy are unlimited, but where individuals are defined by their social function and their ties to society, the possibility of tragedy quickly recedes. An individual might die a horrible death, but in the Chinese view an individual's death is understood less as the fate of an individual soul and more as an event in the ongoing stream of humanity. If a good person suffers in justice and dies for a lost cause, it is not to be seen as a terrible tragedy. The very praise of the storyteller or historian affirms and perpetuates the values of society and thus redeems the tragedy.

The greater emphasis on the group rather than the individual in early China is also evident in another way in Chinese fiction. In general (some exceptions are examined later) early Chinese storytellers were more interested in plot and incident than in psychological description. I should note that the "psychological novel" with its detailed exploration of individual consciousness is a relatively recent phenomenon even in the West. But placing Western and Chinese traditions side by side, we see more emphasis on individual psychology in the West, at least from the sixteenth century onward. Chinese storytellers tended to take a longer-range view than their Western counterparts and to focus on the broad canvas of human society (which of course has its own charms, as in a Chinese handscroll or a Brueghel painting).

The relative inattention to individual psychology in much Chinese fiction is partly a matter of perspective, for in the grand totality of the universe, the individual human psyche may not amount to much. Chinese thinkers (including storytellers) have generally viewed human nature as very malleable and as heavily influenced by the larger society. By contrast, Westerners have tended to view the individual as morally and socially autonomous, with the power to shape his or her own destiny. A traditional Chinese critic might well respond to the Western approach by saying that so much attention to individual psychology trivializes and distorts reality by ignoring the more important factors of social pressures and role expectations and by being too concerned with the "short run" rather than with the more significant long-term development of a whole society.

One final comparison of Chinese and Western approaches to literature illustrates another recurrent theme: what may appear to modern Westerners as defective Chinese literary technique often reflects deep differences in worldview. Western readers have sometimes criticized Chinese fiction for its lack of coherence in plot development, its highly episodic quality, and its general looseness in structure. Andrew Plaks has made two astute observations regarding these criticisms: first, the holistic and organismic Chinese worldview, which sees life in recurrent cyclical and interrelated patterns, does not encourage the development of the Western-style unilinear plot; second, the preferred plot structure in Chinese fiction is borrowed from drama, in which the climax or pivotal point in a work occurs not at the end but two-thirds or three-fourths of the way through the story. Whereas Western audiences may see the concluding, rather quiet, section of such a work as anticlimactic and therefore unsatisfying, Chinese appreciate in the final calming "afterglow" a sense of the completion of a cycle, the implicit assumption that "life goes on" and that the completion of one cycle is the prologue of another.[6] This insistence on seeing life as the ceaseless alternation and interplay of life and death, joy and sorrow, summer and winter, order and chaos, has been an awe-inspiring vision the Chinese have found deeply satisfying and meaningful. Such a worldview goes far to account for the relative absence of tragedy and nonlinear plots in Chinese fiction.

I have described some of the main characteristics of Chinese fiction and have compared in very broad terms the traditions of storytelling in China and the West. In the remainder of this chapter I focus on Chinese fiction itself. After touching very briefly on the major categories of fiction in China and noting the development of different types of short stories from the tenth century onward, I conclude with a discussion of the most famous traditional Chinese novels written from the fourteenth to the nineteenth centuries.

Patrick Hanan has identified three distinct literatures in the Chinese tradition corresponding to three general audiences. The bulk of the population, illiterate and relatively poor, enjoyed an oral tradition, consisting of stories told in vernacular Chinese at marketplaces and in urban entertainment districts. For the highly educated literati class, literature included the short tale in classical Chinese, the highly allusive written language of officialdom (little changed from the time of Confucius to the twentieth century) that required years of study to master. From at least the fourteenth century onward a written vernacular literature that drew on both oral and classical traditions also developed; it appealed especially to an urban "middle class" of semiliterate shopkeepers, merchants, artisans, clerks, bookkeepers, and low-level officials. Scholars once assumed that the written vernacular stories were composed primarily by urban storytellers themselves as promptbooks for their live performances. This may have happened in some cases, but we now know that many highly educated writers also borrowed the storytellers' conventions in writing these stories for a relatively well-educated reading public.

These three literatures, Hanan is quick to point out, have always existed in close proximity, and there is a good deal of overlapping and mutual influence among them.[7] The written vernacular, as a kind of middle-level literature, is no doubt the most eclectic of the three and by far the most fertile in the development of the Chinese novel. Both written traditions borrowed heavily from oral storytelling conventions as well as from music, drama, and poetry. The vernacular authors commonly interspersed their narratives with verses (in classical Chinese), popular songs, sayings, and ballads, occasionally in such profusion as to overshadow the prose narration itself.

In general Chinese storytellers, novelists, and compilers of stories have been voracious borrowers of plots, dialogue, poems, and sayings from any and all available sources. As a result, a common stock of plot lines has been cycled and recycled through all the main types of literature. Some stories exist in dozens of different versions, ranging from classical tales to poetic ballads (*chantefables*) to dramas to vernacular tales, and even novels that might string together a number of preexisting stories. This profusion of recycled stories makes the history of Chinese fiction especially complex for scholars tracing the entangled webs of borrowed sources. What mattered most to a traditional Chinese audience was not an author's originality but the cleverness with which he could weave borrowed material into a believable pattern with no seams showing.

As in the West, fiction in China evolved from shorter to longer forms. The earliest written fiction in China (popular by the fourth century A.D.) consisted of very short notes, tales, observations, and anecdotes called *biji*, or simply jottings, mostly a paragraph or two in length. In the Tang period (seventh to tenth centuries) a somewhat longer and more precisely defined type of story evolved called *chuanqi* (literally meaning "propagation of wonders"). Both *biji* and *chuanqi* authors delighted in the strange, the supernatural, and the bizarre, although the *chuanqi* stories dealt with a broader range of fictional topics, including love, knight-errantry, and a variety of historical themes. In the seventeenth century the *chuanqi* reached its greatest perfection in the work of Pu Songling, who wrote a marvelous collection titled *Strange Stories from Liaozhai* (Pu's studio). Pu's tales are an eerie blend of humor, satire, mild eroticism, reports of exotic or strange phenomena, and terrifyingly vivid descriptions of suffering and injustice.[8]

Two short story forms that particularly reflect the didactic emphasis of Chinese fiction are the *bianwen*, Buddhist-inspired tales of moral retribution in parallel prose or alternating verse and prose, and the *gong'an*, or detective story. Partly spoken and partly sung or canted, the *bianwen* apparently flourished in the ninth and tenth centuries, but they were rediscovered only in the twentieth century in the caves of Dunhuang, after lying unnoticed for nearly a thousand years. Their emphasis on moral retribution came to be a main feature of most later Chinese short stories. The detective story has probably enjoyed a longer run in China than in any civilization (roughly from the eleventh century to the twentieth). In the *gong'an* (literally, "court case"), a crime is committed, often in full view of the reader. A magistrate then proceeds to solve the crime, usually through elaborate and clever stratagems. The suspense is not in discovering the criminal but in following the magistrate's thought and action to see *how* justice will be served.

The most important short stories in the Chinese tradition are the vernacular tales, *huaben* (usually called "promptbooks"), which became increasingly popular from the eleventh century onward. Originally thought to have been nothing more than the notes of oral storytellers, *huaben* are now recognized as a fully developed written genre in vernacular Chinese that borrowed the conventions of the storyteller but were written for and sold to the literate reading public. These stories cover a broader range of subjects than the literary tales, and they reflect the growth of cities and the spread of printing and literacy in China from the Song period onward. They were especially popular in the late Ming period (sixteenth and seventeenth centuries) when they were first published by professional writers and compilers, who signed their works and defended fiction as a worthwhile and even noble endeavor.[9]

When we consider the traditional Chinese novel, an almost universal consensus affirms six works as truly great. These books were created from the sixteenth through the eighteenth centuries. Although many other novels were written during these years, these six almost alone have been widely known, read, and loved by educated Chinese from the time they were first published (usually some years after their author's death) to the present. These novels are comparable in scope, ambition, and narrative skill to the Western novel from the sixteenth through the nineteenth centuries.[10]

Given the strong influence of historical narrative on Chinese fiction, it is not surprising that the earliest great work of extended prose narrative is *Romance of the Three Kingdoms* (*Sanguozhi yenyi*), a historical narrative based on the dissolution of the Han Dynasty into three competing kingdoms after A.D. 220.[11] Although traditionally attributed to Luo Guanzhong (1330–1400), the earliest extant version of *Romance of the Three Kingdoms* dates only from the early sixteenth century. It was probably compiled by a number of anonymous authors and editors over several generations. All the characters are historical, the general plot outline is based on historical fact, and the mode of narration is little different from that of official histories. The purpose of the work is also (ostensibly at least) the same as the historian's: to give meaning to the past through the preservation and presentation of a moral order in history.

The main characters in *Three Kingdoms* are heroic in stature. Three men, Liu Bei, Guan Yu, and Zhang Fei swear an oath of brotherhood at the beginning of the story, and much of the rest of the tale follows as a consequence of this act. This brotherhood celebrates the Confucian virtue that personal loyalty in a good cause assumes and even surpasses the force of blood ties. Liu Bei is the rightful heir of the Han throne; his chief foe is Cao Cao, a high Han official with his own dynastic ambitions. Cao Cao, perhaps the most famous "villain" in popular Chinese historiography, is one of Luo Guanzhong's greatest triumphs in characterization. An ambitious man adept at manipulating Confucian symbols while violating Confucian virtue, Cao Cao is ruthless in his quest for fame and power. But he is also a sensitive poet and an impulsive man vulnerable to anxieties and violent swings of mood.

One of the chief virtues of Luo's *Three Kingdoms* is its level of complexity and irony in narrating the struggle for power in an era of dynastic collapse. With its vast canvas encompassing the length and breadth of China over a century of political and military turmoil, this novel shows the great generals and statesmen of that era as mortal men with very human passions (the chief ones being the desire for fame and power) and ultimately with little individual power to change the inexorable sweep of great historical events. The virtue of Liu Bei, in accord with orthodox Confucian theory, wins him loyal followers and retainers, but virtue alone is not enough to overcome bad decisions, bad strategy, and (perhaps) the workings of fate or Heaven.

Even more than in China's dynastic histories, *Three Kingdoms* reveals history to be a seamless web of closely interwoven factors. Morality and Heaven are important but no more so than courageous fighting, daring maneuvers, clever tactics, and sagacious strategies; and the ability of the evil general may even surpass that of the virtuous one in these areas. Blind luck and supernatural phenomena may occasionally intervene, but it is abundantly clear that treachery and deceit can at times pay handsome dividends. The only consolation seems to be that those short-term gains at the cost of virtue stand condemned forever in the cold and clear-eyed assessment of the chronicler.

Three Kingdoms approaches a tragic view of human life in its often pessimistic picture of dynastic collapse, but the view is ultimately too long-term and too morally confident to be defined as tragic. The assumption remains that human life goes on, and the narrator (and implicitly his audience) appreciates and affirms the good cause. The confident hope also remains, whatever the concrete evidence to the contrary, that the people will ultimately flock to support the virtuous ruler and allow him to reestablish a just order. It may take centuries, but China's experience is so long and the Chinese viewpoint so long-term that centuries of disorder, even a few in succession, are not enough to shake this confidence in the eventual return to virtue, peace, and harmony. In its complexity and irony, *Three Kingdoms* has given Chinese through the centuries a relatively sophisticated picture of politico-military history that is ultimately affirmative, even though focused on some of history's darker sides. The virtues and failings of its characters have also given the Chinese a rich shorthand vocabulary in the politics of intrigue, warfare, villainy, and statesmanship.

The next great novel in the Chinese tradition, *Water Margin* (*Shuihu zhuan*, also available in translations titled *All Men Are Brothers* and *Outlaws of the Marsh*)[12] also evolved over a long period and passed through the hands of numerous authors, editors, and compilers. *Water Margin* is the story of a band of outlaws, some of whom really existed, in the Northern Song dynasty (1101–1125). But compared with *Three Kingdoms* it is far less rooted in historical events and far more indebted to the vernacular short story tradition. Its origins in the vernacular short story can be seen in its language, which is far more colloquial than that of *Three Kingdoms*, and in its style, which is far less dependent on historical narratives and more indebted to the storyteller's conventions of stock phrases, poems, songs, and parallel prose interspersed throughout the narrative. In its theme *Water Margin* is also more potentially subversive than *Three Kingdoms* because its bandits are frequently the heroes of the story and government officials, right up to the emperor, are either ignored or portrayed as weak, misguided, venal, and corrupt.

In a sense *Water Margin* celebrates the virtues of righteousness, loyalty, and justice, which are quite respectable Confucian virtues. In Confucian terms the problem with the book is that these virtues seem to be the monopoly of outlaws, and they are often carried to such excess that they violate all sense of Confucian propriety and moderation. The impetuous righteousness of the heroes leads them to break the law and join the bandit brotherhood under the leadership of Song Jiang in his mountain lair of Liangshanbo (named for Mt. Liang and its marshy and conveniently inaccessible borders in Shandong province). Eventually, 108 of these heroes find their way to Liangshanbo in a rambling series of discrete episodes (taking up much of the novel's one hundred chapters) that culminate when all the heroes celebrate a banquet on the mountain. From this high point the excitement tapers off as the heroes gradually disperse, die out, or surrender to the government.

There is a good deal of blood and gore in this novel, albeit in the name of justice and righteous vengeance. Some Chinese editors have attempted to impart the story with socially redeeming value by having the rebels finally surrender to the throne and begin to work for the state by turning their wrath on other presumably less virtuous rebels. *Water Margin* has frequently been condemned by modern critics for its brutality (the righteous rebels sometimes eat their defeated rivals), its misogyny (promiscuous women are brutally slain by the self-righteous and sexually puritanical bandits), and its gang morality (outlaws who join the Liangshan group are often oppressed in turn by the strict but selective mores and social pressures of the outlaw band).

Andrew Plaks has argued that *Water Margin*, at least in one sixteenth-century version, is actually an ironic Neo-Confucian critique of its popular heroes; their brutality is exaggerated so as to undercut all the surface praise of their heroism.[13] Despite Plaks's ironic interpretation and despite the criticism of other nonironic interpreters of the novel, *Water Margins* has always been a favorite of young Chinese readers who appreciate it for its vivid characterizations of brave exciting heroes who are larger than life, fun-loving, hard-drinking, loyal companions to the death. As a tale of adventure, it has been appreciated for its drama and not for its morality; in the service of excitement its brutality has been accepted without many qualms. In a society where learning to read and write has been a tedious task inextricably bound up with submission to the authority of the past and to one's elders, *Water Margin* has afforded each new generation the vicarious thrill of rebellion and revenge.[14]

The next great Chinese novel, *Journey to the West* (*Xiyou ji*, known as *Monkey* in Arthur Waley's abridged translation),[15] was also inspired by an actual historical event: the pilgrimage of Xuanzang, a pious Buddhist monk, to India in the seventh century to bring important Buddhist scriptures back to China. Xuanzang's courageous seventeen-year journey inspired many tales of adventure and religious devotion, particularly useful to Buddhist proselytizers in search of an audience. In the sixteenth century many of these popular stories and legends were woven together, perhaps (although we cannot say with certainty) by Wu Cheng'en, a witty poet and minor official. In any case, *Journey to the West* was first published in 1592, a decade after Wu's death.

In its form *Journey to the West* marks a significant advance in the Chinese novel. Far more than embellished history or loosely connected short stories, *Journey* is a coherent work of fantasy; it incorporates a far wider range of sources than its predecessors, and it also shows a much higher degree of control by an individual author. It is as interlaced with poetry as *Water Margin*, but most of the poetry in *Journey* is original and inventive, whereas *Water Margin* tends to rely heavily on popular songs, stock phrases, and preexisting poems that are little better than doggerel. The plot of *Journey* is also more unified than those of its predecessors. The personalities of its heroes (although not explored in great depth) are more consistent and complex than the generals and bandits of the more historical novels. Particularly striking is the comic interplay between the novel's main characters.

In *Journey* the serious moral story of a pious monk becomes intertwined with countless supernatural figures and fables and is transformed into a sprawling comic allegory full of gentle and humane satire. The vast stretches of desert and mountains in China's "wild west" had inspired a rich Chinese lore of monsters and perils, a lore deeply tapped by Wu Cheng'en. Xuanzang is about the only "normal" human being in a world of gods, monsters, fallen angels, and wizards of all shapes and sizes; but unlike his historical model, the novelist's Xuanzang is hopelessly incompetent and dull. He despairs over the slightest obstacle in his path and is successful in the end almost in spite of himself. The real heroes of *Journey* are Xuanzang's assistants, protectors, and guides, Zhu Bajie and Sun Wukong, both "fallen angels" expelled from Heaven for misdeeds, and both trying (or at least willing to appear to try) to regain their heavenly status by assisting the poor lonely monk on his treacherous pilgrimage. Zhu Bajie is a pig (Pigsy in Arthur Waley's translation), embodying all the earthly appetites and inclinations associated with that animal. Sun Wukong (whose name, "Aware of Vacuity," ironically suggests enlightenment) is a magical monkey, as quick-witted, energetic, and anarchistic as Xuanzang is slow, dull, and orderly.

Much of the comic content of this novel rests on the interplay of the hedonistic Pigsy, the irrepressible Monkey, and their "master," the helpless plodding monk. In the world of this journey all the gods, goddesses, demons, and devils who threaten the pilgrims are utterly self-seeking, lustful, petty, and corrupt; they mirror every imaginable human weakness. Xuanzang finds his life or his purity constantly threatened; the female demons pose a particularly frightful threat for they believe having sexual intercourse with a human being will prolong their lives. The cumulative effect of the journey is to make of Xuanzang a nervous wreck lacking the courage and imagination even to face each new day. Pigsy, utterly practical and unconcerned about purity, constantly looks out for the short run, ever hopeful of finding a good hot meal, a warm lover, and a soft bed.

Xuanzang's timidity and Pigsy's laziness leave Monkey as the principal fighter and strategist against all comers. Fortunately, Monkey has innumerable powers of transformation, including the possession of a magical, toothpick-sized instrument that can be expanded into a great deadly cudgel when the need arises (giving Freudian interpreters much cause for fascination with "Monkey's rod"). Although Xuanzang depends entirely on Monkey's powers for his own safety, Monkey's impulsive audacity poses threats of its own, for the little ape is so quick, so energetic, and so uninhibited that he is constantly on the verge of forgetting the religious purpose of the journey and seeking adventure purely for its own sake. What ultimately keeps Monkey in line is his slim metal headband controlled by Xuanzang; the monk can tighten the band to produce such excruciating headaches that Monkey simply has to obey despite all his contrary instincts. The interplay of Xuanzang, Pigsy, and Monkey is reminiscent of the dialogue between that great duo of Western literature, Don Quixote and Sancho Panza. Monkey's imagination and energy propel him beyond the wildest thoughts of Xuanzang and Pigsy, yet their commonsense survival instincts are occasionally all that save Monkey from self-destruction.

Journey is a complex novel that can be read and enjoyed on many levels. Although technically a Buddhist novel on the quest for enlightenment, it pokes as much fun at Buddhism as at any other human institution. The entourage of the Buddha himself is as corrupt as any customs office in the underpaid Confucian bureaucracy. Yet for all its satiric barbs aimed at the Buddhists, the novel also lends itself to a Buddhist—or, more broadly, a Buddhist-Daoist-Confucian-allegorical interpretation. The journey of Xuanzang and his companions is a religious quest, and each of the quest's participants faces a different kind of temptation. If Pigsy needs to overcome animal appetites and lust, Xuanzang must try to conquer his own self-centered fears and anxieties, and Monkey has to learn the humility to accept limitations in his quest for power and knowledge. Through all the comedy and satire shine what we might call a Daoist amusement at human absurdities, a Buddhist critique of greed and materialism, and a Confucian appreciation for moderation in all things. In *Journey* Wu Cheng'en (and/or other anonymous authors) created a universal fable of human foibles in a unified work of inventive imagination, comic whimsy, and philosophical insight.

Another late-sixteenth-century work of a very different kind marks a similar advance in the art of the Chinese novel. *Jin Ping Mei* (which is also translated under the title of *The Golden Lotus* and *The Plum in the Golden Vase*)[16] is the first great Chinese novel of morals and manners, a meticulously detailed portrait of the daily lives of a Chinese merchant, Ximen Qing, and the many members of his household. Perhaps one should call *Jin Ping Mei* the great Chinese novel of the absence of morals and (good) manners because it has long been recognized as one of the least inhibited works of erotic and pornographic literature in the relatively rich Chinese tradition.

As I noted earlier, didacticism has been one trademark of Chinese literature, and certainly many Chinese moralists (not to mention parents) have condemned *Jin Ping Mei* for its most imaginative and unrelenting eroticism. However, the whole framework of the novel is a moral hedonism. What is more important in an artistic sense is the stark realism of the novel, which makes it a truly compelling multidimensional portrait of a rapidly changing, money- and status-crazed society.

Jin Ping Mei is far more firmly rooted in everyday life than any of the other works thus far discussed. As Patrick Hanan astutely observes: "If one defines the novel as in some way concerned with depicting social change or conflict by the careful documentation of the texture of society, then the *Chin P'ing Mei* is the first true Chinese novel."[17] Not surprisingly, this work appeared at the turn of the seventeenth century, a time of rapid economic expansion, the growth of cities, and the increased use of money. The seventeenth century was also a time of considerable philosophical ferment in China; the Confucian world was shaken by the growth of an iconoclastic, idealistic, and individualistic school of thought that attacked conservative orthodoxy; and the literary world witnessed similarly shocking changes as a movement sprang up to proclaim fiction as a valuable and worthwhile pursuit.

Such Western critics as Lionel Trilling and Ian Watt have noted the importance of economic growth, social mobility, and urbanization in the rise of the Western novel.[18] The anonymity of city life allows for the fascinating interaction of many different types of people; the decline of a stable rural society, together with the corresponding increase in social mobility (both upward and downward), provides authors with many new plot possibilities; the increasing pace of social and economic change gives authors and audiences alike a new and often intense fascination with questions of status, wealth, and power. Economic expansion and urbanization also stimulate the entertainment industry and the growth of publishing. In some ways these kinds of changes had already occurred in China in the Song period (from the tenth century onward), but the sixteenth and seventeenth centuries marked an acceleration of long-term trends in economic growth and urbanization. The changes that occurred in the last century of the Ming dynasty (roughly 1540–1640) were as dramatic in literature and philosophy as in the economy and society. Jin Ping Mei, with its unprecedented level of social realism, is in both form and content a vivid reminder of the rapid social and intellectual change that occurred in late Ming China.

The plot of Jin Ping Mei is more unified and focused than any of China's earlier novels, even though the anonymous author seems deliberately to quote popular songs and to make references to other stories, dramas, and novels at every conceivable opportunity. As a result of such borrowing, the novel is a kind of encyclopedia of literary and dramatic quotation, an unprecedented eclectic creation that weaves disparate materials into a coherent story. Jin Ping Mei is framed as a spin-off from the plot of the Water Margin: Wu Song, one of the toughest heroes of Song Jiang's band, avenges the murder of his brother by killing his brother's former wife and murderess, Pan Jinlian (the Golden Lotus). But the incident involving Wu Song is in fact only a tiny thread that appears at the beginning and the end of the Jin Ping Mei; in between is a vast tapestry totally different from Water Margin in almost every way.

In some respects Jin Ping Mei is a parody of Water Margin's heroes. Like Song Jiang, Ximen Qing is also surrounded by a group of "sworn brothers," but in contrast to the courage and derring-do of the Liangshan bandits, Ximen Qing's entourage is made up entirely of weak ciphers, social climbers, and hangers-on. There is nothing remotely heroic in this group. Ximen Qing is not a malicious person, but he has his weaknesses: chief among them is an insatiable lust. Almost a tragicomic figure, Ximen Qing is at the center of a whirlwind he cannot control. When he finally dies of sexual overexertion, his friends, who depended entirely on his largesse for their lives of ease and pleasure, are sorry chiefly for themselves. To express their deep respect, they jointly compose a eulogy for their benefactor that is notable primarily as hymn of praise that describes him in unmistakably phallic terms.

Perhaps the most striking innovation of Jin Ping Mei lies in its characterization of women. We might not think of an erotic and pornographic novel as the likeliest place to find psychological insights regarding women, but by focusing on domestic life in a well-to-do urban household the author of Jin Ping Mei took a much closer look at the psychology of women than any earlier Chinese novelist. Ximen Qing has six wives, all of them bound to serve him and, if possible, to produce strong, healthy male heirs. Their utter dependency on his favor produces a palpable air of lethal competition in the household, in large part because of the machinations of the fifth wife, Lotus (the same Golden Lotus Wu Song eventually kills). As a former slave who has suffered much abuse, Lotus is driven by insecurity and insatiable desires for power and sexual pleasure. Because Lotus is a stronger personality than Ximen Qing, he is unable to bring order to his household or to resist her manipulations even when his own interests are threatened. She finally drives him to sexual exhaustion and death in a chilling series of scenes where she keeps him sexually aroused with aphrodisiacs and ointments even after he falls in a coma.

Jin Ping Mei contains some of the most sexually gruesome scenes in Chinese literature, but it also exhibits a great deal of lighter satire and comedy (often involving sex) before turning dark and ugly near the end of the work. Despite the heavy erotic and comic emphasis, however, the novel remains a serious work of literature that integrates its moral message convincingly into the fabric of the story. Buddhist reincarnation and moral retribution are central to the novel; the main sinners all come to a bad end, and eventually Ximen Qing's son (who may or may not be his own reincarnated soul) becomes a monk in order to compensate for his father's misdeeds. The novel also lends itself to a Confucian interpretation: Ximen Qing fails to cultivate virtue in his own person; failing that, he also fails to order his own household; and as a prominent merchant with good political connections, Ximen in his failure symbolizes a larger social and political failure in Ming China. By the end of the novel the entire state is near collapse, and the cause is clearly a moral one that ascends from the individual to the family to the bureaucracy and finally to the court. The eclectic author of Jin Ping Mei assumes a compatibility between Buddhist and Confucian messages and an inseparable bond linking the individual, the society, and the state.[19]

In a tour de force of literary historical scholarship Andrew Plaks has analyzed the four novels discussed so far as serious works of Neo-Confucian commentary on sixteenth-century Chinese society. Drawing on all available critical scholarship in Chinese, Japanese, and Western languages, Plaks interprets these works with special attention to their sixteenth-century editors, authors, and commentators. He notes the many structural features the works have in common, including their paradigmatic length of one hundred chapters [with one exception], narrative rhythms based on division into ten-chapter units, further subdivision into building blocks of three- or four-chapter episodes, contrived symmetries between the first and second halves of the texts, special exploitation of opening and closing sections, as well as certain other schemes of spatial and temporal ordering, notably the plotting of events on seasonal or geographical grids.[20]

In contrast to the earlier emphasis in much scholarship on the origins of these novels in popular storytelling, Plaks demonstrates how the sophisticated and highly literate authors and compilers of these works manipulated the conventions of popular storytelling in a variety of subtle ways so as to assume an ironic stance toward the surface meaning of the texts. Thus, *Three Kingdoms* contrasts the ideal of dynastic order with the realities of dynastic collapse and disorder; *Water Margin* deflates the heroic myths and stereotypes of the popular tradition; *Journey to the West*, in more comic ways, undercuts the proclaimed high seriousness of the religious quest; and *Jin Ping Mei*, most clearly of all, satirizes the moral bankruptcy of society by juxtaposing pedestrian proclamations of conventional piety with the grossest immoral behavior.[21]

Plaks may not win universal assent on all points, but he has raised the level of criticism of the traditional Chinese novel to new heights of sophistication. His emphasis on the progressive development of irony is particularly useful and illuminating for my purposes in this discussion because irony reached its fullest development in the Chinese tradition in the two great works of the eighteenth century, *The Scholars* and *Dream of the Red Chamber*.[22]

The Scholars was written nearly two centuries after *Jin Ping Mei* and one full century after the tumultuous collapse of the Ming dynasty and the conquest of China by the Manchus.[23] A satirical novel above all else, *The Scholars* resembles *Jin Ping Mei* in its focus on ordinary people and everyday life, its didactic assumptions, and its obsession with questions of money and status, but it differs from that erotic novel in most other ways. The author of *The Scholars*, Wu Jingzi (1701–1754), focuses not on the bedroom but rather on the public aspects of urban life, particularly the life of the literati class. Wu Jingzi borrowed jokes, anecdotes, and subplots from a variety of sources, but his borrowing was far less extensive than that of any earlier Chinese novelist. Poems and stock storyteller phrases still appear at chapter breaks in *The Scholars*, but they no longer bear much burden in carrying the story along. Instead, a relatively objective narrator sets scenes in which the characters reveal themselves entirely through their own words and deeds. Wu Jingzi's vernacular prose description and his heavy incorporation of autobiographical experience into the fabric of his work were major developments in the Chinese narrative tradition.

The Chinese title of this work is *Rulin waishi* (An informal history of the literati). *Rulin*, literally, "forest of Confucian scholars," was a category of orthodox Confucian historiography. The *rulin* section of official histories (following the example of the great Han historian, Sima Qian) consisted of biographies of important scholars. *Waishi*, "outer history," denotes an informal history (often including gossip and hearsay) as opposed to the orthodox *zhengshi*, or official history. Whereas the orthodox Chinese historian emphasizes the major events, offices, honors, and accomplishments of the great and near-great (as well as the evil deeds of great villains), Wu Jingzi in his informal history concentrates on the daily lives, the petty cares and concerns, and the pretensions and posturings of the literate and semiliterate aspirants to elite status.

In Wu Jingzi's novel, status is the most important thing in existence; it is a tangible commodity avidly sought through success in the civil service examinations and readily bought, sold, traded, or stolen in many ways. The biographies in *The Scholars* amount to a veritable catalogue of status-seekers. Examination success is of course the first and most assured route to high status, but failing that, one can ingratiate oneself with those who have won examination degrees, marry one's children into prominent families, impersonate famous poets and scholars, or edit and publish selections of "successful" or "model" essays for the preparation of examination candidates. If one finds these strategies too demeaning, as Wu Jingzi himself clearly did, one could adopt the opposite position of the proud eccentric, hold in contempt all examination candidates and their feeble examination essays, sponsor poetry outings and drama contests with one's like-minded friends, lavish money on all "good causes" that come along, and generally thumb one's nose at the establishment. The middle part of *The Scholars* describes one such proud eccentric, Du Shaoqing (a self-portrait of Wu), who adopts this latter strategy so enthusiastically that he squanders his rather substantial family inheritance.

The satire of *The Scholars* is somewhat uneven and alternately mixed with slapstick comedy and heavy-handed invective. The plot is a loose and rambling affair that seems particularly unfocused in the last third of the story. Yet this work has long been cherished by Chinese readers for the purity of its vernacular prose, for its distinctive and self-assured authorial personality, and for its vivid gallery of unforgettable social types from the hurly-burly of an increasingly urban society "on the make" in eighteenth-century China. A civilization as old as China's invites, almost requires, a burdensome pedantry in its intellectuals, and Wu Jingzi provides a delightful pinprick in the balloon of intellectual pomposity. As China's first long work of sustained social satire, *The Scholars* has continued to inspire Chinese writers into the nineteenth and twentieth centuries.[24]

The greatest Chinese novel, all agree, is Cao Xueqin's *Dream of the Red Chamber* (*Honglou meng*), also known as *The Story of the Stone*.[25] First published in 1792, *Dream of the Red Chamber* is unparalleled by any other Chinese novel in its psychological depth, philosophical ambition, and multilayered complexity. Unfinished at the time of Cao Xueqin's death, *Dream of the Red Chamber* has provoked more textual and interpretive controversies than all other traditional Chinese novels combined. In the twentieth century research on this work has grown into a virtual industry called "Red Studies" (*hongxue*) in which hundreds of scholars and students have tried to resolve questions concerning its authorship, early commentators, different editions and manuscripts, and hidden meanings. The novel has been proclaimed, among other things, an autobiographical confession, a tragic triangular love story, an apolitical Buddhist allegory, an elaborate anti-Manchu tract in disguise, an encyclopedic summation of Chinese civilization, and a revolutionary attack on a decadent feudal culture.

The complexity of *Dream of the Red Chamber* begins with its language. The work is full of homonyms and homophones with double and triple meanings. The surname of the main family is Jia, a pun on "false"; there is also a Zhen (which sounds like the Chinese word for "real") family that mirrors the Jia family in all details. The novelist delights in foreshadowing events and dropping everywhere hints of predestination and reincarnation. There is a running dialogue through 120 chapters on the alternation and confusion between illusion and reality. The possibilities for allegorical readings are almost endless, and the messy textual history of the novel insures against any one interpretation ever becoming definitive.

On one level *Dream of the Red Chamber* is a Buddhist work on the theme of the illusory and transitory nature of the material world. A stone, literally a discarded piece of Heaven, is curious about the human world of the "red dust" (Buddhism's term for the illusory world of material things and human attachments and entanglements) and so is incarnated in the human form of Jia Baoyu, the young protagonist of the novel, whose name means Precious Jade to signify the magical piece of jade found in his mouth at birth. Baoyu is plunged into this world of human attachments to experience all its suffering so that he may eventually attain enlightenment and detachment from the material and psychological world of the "red dust." As the stone is disillusioned, the whole story of its astonishing experience is carved out on the very piece of jade originally found in Baoyu's mouth. The story of the stone is also the story on the stone.[26]

On another level *Dream of the Red Chamber* is an exciting human story of a large complex family on the decline. The Jia family is prominent: a daughter serves as an imperial concubine, and the father is a respected official. Yet the future of the family is in doubt because none of the young males is responsible or capable. Befitting its high status, the family must keep up appearances—weddings and funerals, for example, must be lavish—but ample funds for such elaborate displays have long ago disappeared. As the family slips into financial trouble, it also gradually loses favor at court. Eventually, the family's property is confiscated, its once-high position is destroyed, and the novel ends on a despairing note of disillusionment. Downward social mobility is a common theme in Chinese fiction, but nowhere else in the Chinese novel is its psychological pain spelled out in such vivid detail.

The main narrative of *Dream of the Red Chamber* focuses on the young people of the Jia family, particularly the youngest son, Jia Baoyu, his maids, and his female relatives (sisters, cousins, aunts, mother, and grandmother). Baoyu, patterned at least in part after Cao Xueqin himself, is a thoroughly irresponsible young man. He cares nothing for appearances (except in girls' faces and clothes), nor for success, fame, orthodoxy, respectability, or work. In these traits he is the exact opposite of his father, who cares precisely and exclusively for these things. Baoyu is usually protected from his father's wrath by his mother and especially his grandmother, a fun-loving and compassionate old lady who is unspoiled by the artificiality and pretensions of aristocratic and official life.

As a pampered young aristocrat, Jia Baoyu lives in a magnificent garden compound along with several female cousins and their many solicitous serving maids. In intimate daily contact they enjoy feasts of the richest food, dramatic performances, parties, wine, and poetry-writing games and contests. Baoyu is a sensitive friend of all the young women in the household. He prefers the company of girls over boys, but to the puzzlement (or disbelief) of his elders, he seems relatively indifferent to female sexual enticements. Except for a few elegant young men who excite him, all other males in his story appear to be vulgar bores to Baoyu. Most of Baoyu's male cousins seem obsessed with sex, an obsession he finds both strange and disgusting.

The novel's most popular subplot revolves around the important question of Baoyu's marriage. He loves his beautiful hypersensitive cousin Lin Daiyu above all others. Her name means Black Jade, after her own jade locket that matches Baoyu's jade piece. In addition to their common stones the two share artistic temperaments that love true beauty and detest shallow superficiality in all forms and guises. Unfortunately, Daiyu is too frail and neurotic to be judged an acceptable mate by the senior women in the Jia household. They conspire instead to arrange Baoyu's marriage to another beautiful cousin, Xue Baochai, who is much more conventional, sane, and healthy than the increasingly ill Daiyu. As the marriage takes place, Daiyu dies a pitiful death, feeling abandoned by Baoyu and everyone else.

One of the many titles this novel has been given in its various stages is *The Twelve Beauties of Jinling*, after twelve of the main young women in the Jia household (located in Jinling, or Nanjing). One by one these women come to a tragic end: maids and mistresses alike are forcibly married to undesirable mates; several take refuge in Buddhist nunneries; some are cruelly expelled from the idyllic life of the garden; others commit suicide in protest against unjust accusations of wrongdoing; and several die painful deaths as much from psychological as physical causes. For all his sympathy for these women, Baoyu is weak and incapable of doing anything to help them avoid their painful fates. The novel is especially revealing in its portrait of family dynamics and the psychological development of the Jia women. Details of dress, gestures, makeup, tone of voice, dreams, intimate conversations, and confessions are all used most effectively in creating vivid portraits of individual personalities. *Dream of the Red Chamber* is unique in the Chinese tradition in its apparent obsession with individual feelings and the smallest details of daily life.

By the end of the novel Baoyu, who earlier detested all thought of examination competition, relents, studies, and passes the all-important examination that will admit him to the elite status of officialdom. But instead of returning home to enjoy his moment of glory as the savior of the Jia family, he abandons his wife and infant son and disappears with the Buddhist priest and Daoist monk who have wandered in and out of the story from the beginning proclaiming the vanity of the world of the red dust and the virtue of detachment and withdrawal.

The intense contradiction at the heart of *Dream of the Red Chamber*, between human passion and Buddhist detachment, is thus ultimately resolved in favor of enlightenment and withdrawal. Or is it? Ironically, this novel, which proclaims the illusory nature of the world of the red dust, has recreated that world so lovingly and artfully that it gives that world the permanence in art that it lacked in the painful experience of Cao Xueqin and his family. For all its proclamations of Buddhist meanings, this work remains the sharpest example of social realism in the Chinese tradition. No other Chinese novel relates such an entire world so believably. The real allegiance of Cao in the final analysis would seem to be not to Confucian familial responsibility or Buddhist-Daoist detachment but to the truth of the novelist's art and to the magic of storytelling.[27]

The classic Chinese novel reached its apogee with *Dream of the Red Chamber* but did not end there. In the early nineteenth century two works in particular deserve mention: *Six Chapters of a Floating Life*, by Shen Fu, and *Flowers in the Mirror*, by Li Ruzhen.[28] *Six Chapters* (of which only four chapters survive) is more an autobiography than a novel, but its casual, simple, and straightforward style, its intensity of feeling, and its intimate description of married love make it a minor landmark in the Chinese narrative tradition. *Flowers in the Mirror* is a mixture of fantasy and satire that marks the culmination of the traditional scholarly Chinese novel. It is most famous in the modern West as a work sympathetic to women; a few of its chapters portray a Kingdom of Women where traditional Chinese gender roles are completely reversed, with predictable consequences for the male Chinese travelers who visit there hoping to make their fortune selling cosmetics. *Flowers in the Mirror* is a gentle satire of all kinds of human quirks and shortcomings and a clever vehicle for Li Ruzhen to show off his esoteric knowledge of everything from table games and poetry to phonetics and etymology. It combines the air of fantasy of *Journey to the West* and the social commentary of *The Scholars*.

Six Chapters of a Floating Life and *Flowers in the Mirror* are charming if minor works and they mark a logical conclusion to this survey of traditional Chinese fiction. The genre of the Chinese novel seems in its conclusion to imitate the internal architecture of the novel itself. *Dream of the Red Chamber* marks the climax of the tradition, and the two later works form a kind of after-glow, a quiet and final recycling of earlier themes in a less ambitious and slightly minor key. When more Chinese novels were written in the late nineteenth century, followed by still more in the twentieth, they had begun to absorb Western influences.

As I noted earlier, the development of the Chinese novel offers many illuminating contrasts and parallels with the Western novel. In China, as in the West, from the sixteenth century to the nineteenth century the novel came to be recognized by some as a serious intellectual endeavor capable of addressing and illuminating the most important social, political, and philosophical issues of an entire civilization. Drawing on the tradition of classical commentaries, Chinese fiction critics and editors wrote detailed chapter-by-chapter or even line-by-line commentaries on all the major novels. They analyzed these works from many different perspectives including narrative structure and composition, style and pacing, artistic and philosophical strengths and weaknesses, and the relationship of each work to the major intellectual traditions of Confucianism, Buddhism, and Daoism. Although these commentators remained something of a minority within the Chinese intellectual elite, they articulated a kind of poetics of the novel that can be extremely valuable to the modern student hoping to understand these works and their original authors on their own terms.[29] The traditional Chinese commentators remained less secure and more defensive than their Western contemporaries in proclaiming the legitimacy of fiction, but their efforts clearly parallel Western development in the growing intellectual respectability of prose fiction.

One of the most striking differences between the novel in China and the West lies in the absence in China of anything approaching the great explosion of works of genius in the nineteenth-century West. There were notable works written in nineteenth-century China, but nothing to compare with the amazing production of the Western greats: Austen, Thackeray, Dickens, the Brontes, Eliot, and Hardy in England; Stendhal, Balzac, Dumas, Hugo, Sand, Baudelaire, and Zola in France; Gogol, Turgenev, Dostoevsky, and Tolstoy in Russia; Hawthorne, Melville, Twain, and James in the United States. The list could be longer, but one has only to hear the Western novelists' names to realize the enormous contrast with nineteenth-century China.

Instead of the geometrical growth of great works as the novel matured, the Chinese tradition seemed to leapfrog along at a leisurely pace, producing several great novels every other century. Despite a far less spectacular flowering, however, in a rough way the changes in these two-century leaps parallel the Western experience: with increasing narrative sophistication came a deepening sense of irony toward society's mainstream values, a gradual decline in mythic and supernatural elements, and a corresponding increase in reliance on individual authorial experience and creativity.

What does not occur in China is an artistic declaration of independence or autonomy for literature. In one of the classics of Western literary criticism, *The Mirror and the Lamp*, M. H. Abrams sees in Western romanticism of the early nineteenth century a radical break with the previous two thousand years of Western critical thought. Whereas the Western poet had earlier been identified with the image of the mirror, passively reflecting external objects, the romantic movement identified the poet with the image of a lamp, an active illuminator that shines on reality and thus transforms it literally into something new. In the nineteenth century Western romantic view the individual author thus assumed a role of tremendous power and importance. Although dealing explicitly with poetry rather than fiction, Abrams draws attention to the kind of revolutionary changes that occurred in European literary traditions only as recently as the nineteenth century.[30]

In China, by contrast, the novelist remained as much a peripheral figure in the nineteenth century as in the sixteenth. Despite the minority movement extolling the importance of fiction in the sixteenth century, the Chinese novelist was not prominent, powerful, or influential until the twentieth century, and even then prominence more often brought persecution than power. Of the six major novels I discuss, only the last two—*The Scholars* and *Dream of the Red Chamber*—have clearly identifiable individual authors, and their identity was not known with certainty until the 1920s. In some ways Wu Jingzi and Cao Xueqin fit the stereotype of the modern Western alienated artist, but even in alienation the modern Western artist has had a powerful sense of importance, of widely shared artistic traditions and assumptions, and of artistic autonomy from political and economic forces. The traditional Chinese novelist did not enjoy such a sense of importance and autonomy. In the light of this difference the accomplishments of the Chinese novelists from the sixteenth to the nineteenth centuries are more striking than their shortcomings: their works are among the most accessible, enjoyable, illuminating, and inspiring documents from China's late imperial era.

NOTES

1. Although I have not always been able to implement their suggestions, I am very grateful to the following people for very helpful criticisms of earlier drafts of this chapter: Sunhee Kim Gertz, G. T. Hsia, David L. Rolston, Yaohua Shi, Virginia

Vaughan, and Judith Zeitlin. Four useful introductory works illustrating different approaches to the study of fiction are Rene Wellek and Austin Warren, *Theory of Literature*, 3rd ed. (New York: Harcourt, Brace and World, 1956); Wilbur Scott, ed., *Five Approaches of Literary Criticism* (New York: Collier-Macmillan, 1962); Elizabeth Burns and Tom Burns, eds., *Sociology of Literature and Drama* (Harmondsworth: Penguin, 1973); and Terry Eagleton, *Literary Theory: An Introduction* (Minneapolis: University of Minnesota Press, 1983).

2. An excellent discussion of the development of the novel in China and the West is by Andrew H. Plaks, "Full-length *Hsiao-shuo* and the Western Novel: A Generic Reappraisal," *New Asia Academic Bulletin 1* (1978): 163–76.

3. Michael Sullivan, "Chinese Art and Its Impact on the West," in Paul S. Ropp, ed., *Heritage of China: Contemporary Perspectives on Chinese Civilization* (Berkeley: University of California Press, 1990), 282.

4. The triumph of the entertainer over the moralist among the writers of erotic fiction that poses as "avoidance" literature may be seen from the titles of two representative works in English translation: Li Yu, *The Carnal Prayer Mat*, trans. by Patrick Hanan (New York: Ballantine Books, 1990), and John Scott, trans., *The Lecherous Academician and Other Tales by Master Ling Mengchu* (London: Rapp and Whiting, 1973). A detailed and insightful study of eighteenth-century Chinese erotic fiction is Keith McMahon, *Misers, Shrews, and Polygamists: Sexuality and Male-Female Relations in Eighteenth-Century Chinese Fiction* (Durham: Duke University Press, 1995).

5. David N. Keightley, "Early Civilization in China: Reflections on How It Became Chinese," in Ropp, *Heritage of China*, esp. 20–21, 32–35.

6. Andrew H. Plaks, "Towards a Critical Theory of Chinese Narrative," in *Chinese Narrative: Critical and Theoretical Essays*, ed. Andrew H. Plaks (Princeton: Princeton University Press, 1977), 334–39.

7. Patrick Hannan, "The Development of Fiction and Drama," in *The Legacy of China*, ed. Raymond Dawson (London: Oxford University Press, 1964), 115–43.

8. Two translations of selected stories from Pu's work are P'u Sung-ling, *Strange Stories from a Chinese Studio*, trans. Herbert Giles (reprint, New York: Dover, 1969), and Pu Songling, *Strange Tales from Make-Do Studio*, trans. Denis C. and Victor H. Mair (Beijing: Foreign Languages Press, 1989). An insightful study of Pu's art is Judith Zeitlin, *Historian of the Strange: Pu Songling and the Chinese Classical Tale* (Stanford: Stanford University Press, 1993). One can also gain a sense of Pu's narrative power from the elegant translations of his stories sprinkled throughout Jonathan Spence, *Death of Woman Wang* (New York: Knopf, 1978).

9. An excellent small collection of *huaben* stories is Cyril Birch, ed., *Stories from a Ming Collection* (New York: Grove Press, 1958). The most comprehensive sampling of all the major Chinese short story forms in English translation is Y. W. Ma and Joseph S. M. Lau, eds., *Traditional Chinese Stories: Themes and Variations* (New York: Columbia

University Press, 1978) a fine critical history of *huaben* stories is Patrick Hanan, *The Chinese Vernacular Story* (Cambridge: Harvard University Press, 1981).

10. For a far more detailed introduction to these major Chinese novels, including numerous critical comparisons between Chinese and Western literature, see C. T. Hsia, *The Classic Chinese Novel* (New York: Columbia University Press, 1968). As will be clear to Hsia's readers, my assessment of these novels is deeply indebted to his work. A superb study of the publishing and illustration of popular fiction in the late imperial period is Robert E. Hegel, *Reading Illustrated Fiction in Late Imperial China* (Stanford: Stanford University Press, 1998).

11. The best English translation of this novel is Luo Guanzhong, *Three Kingdoms: A Historical Novel* (Beijing: Foreign Languages Press, 1994, and Berkeley: University of California Press, 1991). See also the excellent one-volume abridgment by Moss Roberts, *Three Kingdoms: A Historical Novel*, abridged edition (Berkeley: University of California Press, 1999).

12. There are three complete English translations of this novel: J. H. Jackson, trans., *Water Margin*, 2 vols. (reprint, Boston: Cheng and Tsui, 1976); Pearl S. Buck, trans., *All Men Are Brothers*, 2 vols. (reprint, New York: Crowell, 1968); and Sidney Shapiro, trans., *Outlaws of the Marsh*, 2 vols. (Beijing and Bloomington: Foreign Languages Press and Indiana University Press, 1981; one-volume abridged reprint, Boston: Cheng and Tsui, 1991). The text of *Water Margin* has had a messy history; countless different versions have been compiled and published by many different (usually anonymous) editors. Different versions have ranged from seventy to one hundred and twenty chapters. The shorter versions, especially a seventy-one-chapter edition published in the seventeenth century, have generally been more popular and critically praised than the longer versions. The Jackson and Buck translations are based on the popular seventy-one-chapter edition; the recent Shapiro translation is taken from an earlier one-hundred-chapter edition.

13. Andrew H. Plaks, *The Four Masterworks of the Ming Novel* (Princeton: Princeton University Press, 1987), chap. 4.

14. An excellent study of a seventeenth-century sequel to *Water Margin, Shuihu houzhuan*, written to express the author's Ming loyalist opposition to the Manchu conquest of China, is Ellen Widmer, *The Margins of Utopia: Shui-hu hou-chuan and the Literature of Ming Loyalism* (Cambridge: Harvard University Press, 1987).

15. Arthur Waley, trans., *Monkey* (New York: Grove Press, 1958), includes less than one-fourth of the entire novel, but it is remarkably true to the original spirit of the work. A masterful complete translation is Anthony C. Yu, trans., *Journey to the West*, 4 vols. (Chicago: University of Chicago Press, 1977–1984).

16. The best translation of this novel is currently in progress, with the following two volumes now available: David Tod Roy, trans., *The Plum in the Golden Vase, or Chin P'ing Mei*, vols. 1 and 2 (Princeton: Princeton University Press, 1993 and 2001).

There also exists in a one-volume abridgment, [Bernard Miall, trans.], *Chin P'ing* Mei, [translated from a German version by Franz Kuhn] (Toms River, N.J.: Capricorn, 1960), and a more complete but still abridged scholarly translation, Clement Egerton, trans., *The Golden Lotus*, 4 vols. (reprint, London: Routledge and Kegan Paul, 1972).

17. Hanan, "The Development of Fiction and Drama," 134. Hanan elaborates further on this theme in another essay, "A Landmark of the Chinese Novel." *University of Toronto Quarterly* 30, no. 3 (April 1961): 325–35.

18. See, for example, Lionel Trilling, "Manners, Morals, and the Novel," in *The Liberal Imaginations*, by Lionel Trilling (New York: Viking Press, 1951), and Ian Watt, *The Rise of the Novel* (Berkeley: University of California Press, 1972).

19. An illuminating study of *Jin Ping Mei* that highlights the Confucian interpretation of the novel is Katherine Carlitz, *The Rhetoric of "Chin P'ing Mei"* (Bloomington: Indiana University Press, 1986). A recent study of the sexual politics of the novel is Ding Naifei, *Obscene Things: Sexual Politics in "Jin Ping Mei"* (Durham: Duke University Press, 2002). A new study of androgyny in late Ming and early Qing literature that begins with an insightful discussion of *Jin Ping Mei* is Zhou Zuyan, *Androgyny in Late Ming and Early Qing Literature* (Honolulu: University of Hawaii Press, 2003).

20. Plaks, *Four Masterworks of the Ming Novel*, 497–98.

21. Plaks summarizes his closely reasoned book-length argument in *Four Masterworks of the Ming Novel*, chap. 6.

22. Although I do not have the space to discuss them here, a variety of interesting novels were written in the seventeenth century. They are expertly analyzed in Robert E. Hegel, *The Novel in Seventeenth Century China* (New York: Columbia University Press, 1981).

23. The only English translation of the novel is Wu Ching-tzu, *The Scholars*, trans. Hsien-yi Yang and Gladys Yang (Peking: Foreign Languages Press, 1957).

24. For a useful study of Wu Ching-tzu's satirical art, see Timothy C. Wong, *Wu Ching-tzu* (Boston: Twayne, 1978). Illuminating works on this novel in relation to several others include Martin W. Huang, *Literati and Self Re/Presentation: Autobiographical Sensibility in the Eighteenth-Century Novel* (Stanford: Stanford University Press, 1995) and Stephen J. Roddy, *Literati Identity and Its Fictional Representations in Late Imperial China* (Stanford: Stanford University Press, 1998). Social criticism in *The Scholars* is the subject of Paul S. Ropp, *Dissent in Early Modern China: "Ju-lin wai-shih" and Ch'ing Social Criticism* (Ann Arbor: University of Michigan Press, 1981).

25. The most elegant translation of Cao Xueqin's novel is David Hawkes and John Minford, trans., *The Story of the Stone*, 5 vols. (Harmondsworth: Penguin, 1973–1986). Another complete translation is Hsien-yi Yang and Gladys Yang, trans., *A Dream of Red Mansions*, 3 vols. (Peking: Foreign Languages Press, 1978–1980). This translation has been abridged in a one-volume edition and published by Cheng and

Tsui of Boston in 1996. Other one-volume abridgements include: Florence McHugh and Isabel McHugh, trans., *Dream of the Red Chamber* (reprint, Westport, Conn.: Greenwood Press, 1975), and Chi-chen Wang, trans., *Dream of the Red Chamber* (New York: Anchor, 1958).

26. An inventive study of the stone imagery in this novel as well as *Water Margin* and *Journey to the West* is Jing Wang, *The Story of Stone: Intertextuality, Ancient Chinese Stone Lore, and the Stone Symbolism of "Dream of the Red Chamber," "Water Margin," and "The Journey to the West"* (Durham: Duke University Press, 1992).

27. Fine literary studies of *Dream of the Red Chamber* include Lucien Miller, *Masks of Fiction in "Dream of the Red Chamber": Myth, Mimesis, and Persona* (Tucson: University of Arizona Press, 1975); Andrew H. Plaks, *Archetype and Allegory in "Dream of the Red Chamber"* (Princeton: Princeton University Press, 1976); Louise Edwards, *Men and Women in Qing China: Gender in "The Red Chamber Dream"* (Leiden: E. J. Brill, 1994); Anthony C. Yu, *Rereading the Stone: Desire and the Making of Fiction in "Dream of the Red Chamber"* (Princeton: Princeton University Press, 1997); Dore J. Levy, *Ideal and Actual in "The Story of the Stone"* (New York: Columbia University Press, 1999); and Xiao Chi, *The Chinese Garden as Lyric Enclave: A Generic Study of "The Story of the Stone"* (Ann Arbor: University of Michigan Center for Chinese Studies, 2001). In addition, the following important studies deal with issues of gender, sexuality, and desire in *Dream of the Red Chamber* and several other novels from late imperial China: Li Wai-yee, *Enchantment and Disenchantment: Love and Illusion in Chinese Literature* (Princeton: Princeton University Press, 1993); Maram Epstein, *Competing Discourses: Orthodoxy, Authenticity, and Engendered Meanings in Late Imperial Chinese Fiction* (Cambridge: Harvard University Asia Center, 2001); Martin W. Huang, *Desire and Fictional Narrative in Late Imperial China* (Cambridge: Harvard University Asia Center, 2001); and Zhou Zuyan, *Androgyny in Late Ming and Early Qing Literature*.

28. The most recent and accurate translation of Shen Fu's work is Leonard Pratt, trans., *Six Chapters of a Floating Life* (Harmondsworth: Penguin, 1983). An effective abridged translation of *Flowers in the Mirror* is by Dai-yi Lin (Berkeley: University of California Press, 1965).

29. For an introduction to these traditional Chinese commentators, with full translations of important commentaries on the six "classic novels," see David L. Rolston, ed., *How to Read the Chinese Novel* (Princeton: Princeton University Press, 1989).

30. M. H. Abrams, *The Mirror and the Lamp: Romantic Theory and the Critical Tradition* (Oxford: Oxford University Press, 1953).

chapter eight

BEIJING OPERA PLAYS AND PERFORMANCE

Elizabeth Wichmann-Walczak

Editor's note: Wichmann-Walczak introduces the aesthetic aims and elements of traditional Beijing Opera, addressing all the performance aspects of this popular theater genre—"story, music, voice, movement, makeup, costume, and stage properties." The aesthetic aim of Beijing Opera is to convey essence—a beautiful evocation rather than a realistic representation. The beautiful is the reigning value behind the three aesthetic principles of synthesis ("integration for one effect"), stylization (the elevation of the ordinary though "roundness"), and conventions (setting, gesture, music, and character type).

THE AURAL DIMENSION of Beijing Opera is so fundamentally important to the identity of this theatrical form that attending a Beijing opera performance is traditionally referred to as "listening to theatre" (*tingxi*), and acting in a play is termed "singing theatre" (*changxi*). But when Beijing opera singers apply stylized makeup, dress in elaborate costumes, and go onstage to "sing theatre," they actually do much more than sing and speak. Beijing opera singers are in fact consummate performers who act, sing, speak, dance, and often perform acrobatics as well. A general understanding of the aesthetics that apply to the total performance of Beijing opera, and of the plays that provide the characters, plots, and overall performance structure, is therefore a prerequisite to the discussion of aural performance.

THE TOTAL PERFORMANCE OF BEIJING OPERA

The total performance of Beijing opera presents a kaleidoscopic array of theatrical elements—story, music, voice, movement, makeup, costume, and stage properties. The presence of these numerous elements justifies calling Beijing opera "total theatre," according to E. T. Kirby's general definition of the term: "Theatre as the place of intersection of all the arts is . . . the meaning of 'total theatre.' We most often find this totality indicated by a list of components such as music, movement, voice, scenery, lighting, etc." Kirby, however, goes on to establish a more specific criterion for "total theatre":

> More important . . . is the understanding that there must be an effective inter-
> play among the various elements, or a significant synthesis of them. Totality may,
> in this sense, be more or less extensive, including a greater or lesser number of
> aspects, but it must always be intensive, effecting an integration of the com-
> ponents. While totality as an ideal is extensive and all-inclusive, it is this rela-
> tionship between elements, rather than an accumulation of means, which actually
> distinguishes the form.[1]

By this more specific standard, Beijing opera not only qualifies as "total theatre" but in fact exemplifies the concept. Its performance elements are bound together—are almost organically related to one another—by the fundamental aesthetics of traditional Beijing opera performance: the aesthetic aim, the basic aesthetic principles, and the role types of its dramatic characters. Beijing opera performers refer to the importance of these fundamental aesthetics by saying that they make Beijing opera a complete, integrated art (*wanzheng yishu*), possessed of "a complete set of things" (*yitao dongxi*)—that is, a complete set of performance elements and techniques.

AESTHETIC AIM

In the performance of traditional Beijing opera, the stage is perceived as a platform upon which to display the performers' four skills (*gong*): song (*chang*); speech (*nian*); dance-acting (*zuo*), which includes pure dance, pantomime, and all the visible, physical results of "acting" in the Western sense; and combat (*da*), which encompasses not only actual fighting with fists, knives, swords, and spears, but also acrobatics as well. These skills are displayed within the context of a drama, in which each performer portrays a dramatic character.

The display of skills, however, is not an end in itself. Even the most virtuoso technique will be criticized as "empty" (*kong*) if in performance it does not contribute to the pursuit of a larger aesthetic aim. The fundamental aesthetic aim of traditional Chinese painting, to "write [i.e., draw/paint] the meaning" (*xieyi*) rather than to "write realistically" (*xieshi*), is frequently referred to by Beijing opera practitioners as being analogous to their own. Traditional painting is not realistic in the Western sense; for example, landscape paintings are rarely identifiable as portraying a precise portion of a specific place. Rather, a painting of a particular mountain will resemble that mountain in broad terms, and will convey the essence of that mountain and the spirit of the total concept "mountain." Beijing opera likewise aims first to strike the audience with a resemblance to life—and then to convey the very essence of life. It is through the display of skills, externalizing the thoughts

and feelings of major characters and elaborating upon their actions and interactions, that Beijing opera performance transcends a resemblance to life and
builds an overall effect that conveys its essence.

In the pursuit of this aesthetic aim, performers adhere strictly to a basic
aesthetic value: everything within the world of the play must above all be
beautiful (*mei*). In its simplest applications the demand for beauty requires,
for instance, that a beggar be dressed in a black silk robe covered with multicolored silk patches rather than in actually dirty or tattered clothes, which
would not be considered beautiful.

The demand for beauty also affects the portrayal of certain emotions; a
performer playing a young woman who has just received heart-breaking news
should never cry real tears, for the accompanying red eyes and runny nose are
considered anything but beautiful. Instead, the act of crying is suggested, both
vocally and physically; when done skillfully, the resulting portrayal is very
moving as well as almost painfully beautiful.

The demand for beauty actually affects the display of every performance
skill. Song, speech, dance-acting, and combat should at all times appear effort-
less (*bu shi li*) in order to be beautiful. Any hint of strain at hitting a high
note, performing a complex series of somersaults and flips, or speaking an
extended declamatory passage is perceived as indicating that the performer's
command of technique is insufficient. When skills are not displayed
adequately—when strain or effort is noticeable—the build to an overall effect
capable of conveying the essence of life rather than its mere resemblance is
destroyed by the evident, un-beautiful actuality of a struggling performer.

In training schools and rehearsal halls, the criticism heard with much the
greatest frequency, directed at song, speech, dance-acting, and combat alike,
is that the particular sound or action being performed is incorrect because it
is not beautiful. And the highest praise that can be given a performance is to
say that it is beautiful. Ultimately, beauty as an aesthetic value connotes con-
formance to the aesthetic aim and principles of Beijing opera—anything that
is not within the aesthetic parameters of Beijing opera is not beautiful within
that world.

AESTHETIC PRINCIPLES

Every aspect of traditional Beijing opera performance is governed by three
aesthetic principles: synthesis, stylization, and convention. Together, these
principles provide the basic fabric of Beijing opera performance—the overall
patterns (*guilü*) that characterize each aspect of Beijing opera performance, as
well as the relationships among them.

Synthesis.   Story, music, song, speech, and dance-acting are present in almost
every Beijing opera performance; many include stage combat and acrobatics

as well. These elements are not simply presented in sequence, however. It is their synthesis (*zonghexing*) that is characteristic of Beijing opera performances.

Song and speech in performance occur simultaneously with the dance-like movement of the performer; dance-acting and combat are interwoven on the stage with melodic and/or percussive accompaniment. The primary skill displayed in some passages is an aural one—song or speech. In others it is visual—dance-acting or combat. However, if the focus at a given moment is aural, as when a singer relates a sad separation from a loved one, that song is performed within the complementary visual fabric presented by the unceasing gentle synchronized movements of eyes, hands, torso, feet, and often the body through space. And if the focus is visual, as upon a brave warrior ascending a steep mountain, that pantomime is enacted within a texture of percussive sound provided by the orchestra. Percussive sound also provides aural punctuation to speech, which is performed within a visual fabric of movement punctuation as well. Extended speech and song without dance-like movement and accompanying melodic or percussive sound rarely occur in traditional Beijing opera, nor does dance-acting or combat without melodic or percussive accompaniment. Both the eyes and the ears of the audience are engaged at all times.

Stylization.   Stylization refers to the divergence between the behaviors of daily life and their presentation on the stage—that is, the representation of those behaviors in performance, within a particular style. In Beijing opera, stylization is considered to be the act of raising and refining (*tilian*) the behaviors of daily life, with the aim of making them beautiful—making them a part of the world of Beijing opera performance.

The most basic physical, visually perceived characteristic of stylization in the performance of Beijing opera is roundness (*yuanxing*). Roundness applies to posture and movement, both of various parts of the body in isolation and of the entire body in or through space. Straight lines and angles are to be avoided; positive aesthetic value is perceived in the presentation of a three-dimensional network of circles, arcs, and curved lines.

In stasis, this means, for instance, that an outstretched arm will be held in an extended curve unbroken at either the shoulder or elbow by angles. In movement, this aesthetic applies to action as small as the gaze of an eye, and as large as the blocking of major characters. For many types of characters, the performer's eyes are used to focus the attention of the audience; to lead it with the movement of a gaze. In such an instance, if the performer intends to indicate an object on the ground, the gaze of his or her eyes will begin away from the object with a sweep up, and then curve down to rest on the object. Conversely, if the gaze is to end in an indication of something above eye level, it will travel down as it moves toward that object and then sweep up to light upon it. This same use of the arc is made in pointing gestures, which first curve away from the direction in which the hand will ultimately point; to point directly in front of his or her body, a performer will begin by sweeping the pointing hand in towards the body before sending it out to point. To point to the left, the performer will begin with a sweep of the pointing hand to the right, and vice versa.

In movement through space, the performer similarly avoids straight lines and angles. For instance, a move from facing downstage at downstage center to facing downstage in front of a chair at upstage center is begun by circling to either the left or the right while gradually turning the entire body to face upstage. The performer then crosses upstage on a slight diagonal to the side of the chair and circles again in the opposite direction to face downstage once more, this time directly in front of the chair. The resulting S-shaped curve has been compared to the movement of a marionette puppet, necessary to keep the puppet's strings from entangling, and hypotheses have been drawn on this basis concerning the origins of traditional theatre movement in puppet theatre.[2] Whatever the origin, the ceaseless pattern of curved lines, arcs, and circles running throughout all Beijing opera performances helps to create a characteristic visual world for Beijing opera.

The foundation for Beijing opera's aurally perceived stylization is its musical system (shengqiang xitong); the elements of the musical system as presented orchestrally and vocally in the performance of Beijing opera plays serve to create a characteristic aural world for Beijing opera. This aural dimension, like the visual one, is perceived by the practitioners and connoisseurs of Beijing opera as being characterized by roundness. But while roundness in visual stylization is fairly direct and therefore readily appreciated by Western audiences, roundness in aural stylization is a more complex concept. Its appreciation requires that the auditor be cognizant of the aesthetics, elements, and techniques of the musical system, and of composition and performance within that system.

Conventions. In the broadest sense, conventions (chengshi) are an aspect of stylization; conventions are also departures from daily reality. But conventions are more specialized: they include specific practices to which fairly precise meanings have been ascribed by tradition. The use of a particular conventional sign serves to signal its ascribed meaning to the audience. A great many such conventions are utilized in Beijing opera performance; the meanings of some are immediately recognizable to an uninitiated audience member while others require preknowledge for comprehension.

Dance-acting conventions most frequently fall in the former category, especially pantomimic actions such as opening and closing doors and windows, mounting and descending stairs, tending fowl, sewing, and movement over rough terrain and in conditions of darkness, heat, cold, rain, and wind—these actions are directly communicative and require no informed expertise of the spectator. Other dance-acting conventions are more formal, such as the act of walking in a large circle, which connotes traveling a considerable distance, and the straightening of costume and headdress parts upon entrance to signal the presence of an important character who is about to speak; these conventions do require familiarity from audience members, as do the visual conventions associated with the staging of Beijing opera.

The traditional Beijing opera stage is bare, with a decorative rather than realistic backdrop, and a carpet covering the floor for the protection of acrobatic performers. The only scenery used is one or more tables and one or more chairs. Although recent years have seen the advent of more elaborate scenery and certain technological innovations—including lighting and sound effects—in the performance of some plays, the staging of Beijing opera remains fundamentally quite simple.

This simple staging achieves a high degree of plasticity through the use of conventions. The table(s) and chair(s), through their placement and use, conventionally serve as a city wall, a mountain, a bed, a throne, or simply as a table and one or two chairs. Conventional use of stage properties frequently signals the presence and use of large objects not visually present on the stage; a whip signals the presence of a horse, an oar that of a boat, and large blue banners swung in wide arcs close to the stage floor that of rushing water.

Aural conventions require that audience members learn beforehand their ascribed meanings—very few aural conventions are immediately understandable without preknowledge of their significance. The most important aural conventions are individual elements of the musical system, which through their appropriate combination conventionally express specific emotions.

Role Types

The four principal role types in Beijing opera are *sheng* (standard male characters), *dan* (female characters), *jing* (painted-face male characters), and *chou* (lit. "ugly" characters, who are usually male). During Beijing opera's early development and nineteenth-century maturation, all were played by men. Although the majority of performers in contemporary China play role types of their own gender, most major subcategories in most role types do have both male and female performers. Each of the role types, and even more specifically each of their major subcategories, is itself indicative of a particular age, gender, and level of dignity; makeup, headdress, and costume conventions indicate visually the role type and subcategory of every character in each play.

Most Beijing opera performers specialize in the performance of only one role type—for instance, the term *sheng* refers both to *sheng* characters and to performers who play *sheng* characters—and most perform only one particular subcategory. This does not imply that actors perform stereotypes, however;

the characters included in each of the several role types and subcategories may be good or bad, strong or weak, intelligent or stupid. Role-type special-ization produces patterns (*guilü*) of performance technique rather than dramatic characters with stereotyped personalities. Performers of each role type specialize in the display of certain selected performance skills. And the performance of each role type is characterized by certain physical and vocal conventions and patterns of stylization specific to it. Although some of the major physical conventions and patterns of stylization are touched upon in the following descriptions of each role type, the fundamental role-specific vocal characteristics are not discussed here.

Sheng. *Sheng* characters are intrinsically dignified male characters. Generally, they are of high social status or deserving of such. There are three major subcategories of *sheng* roles: older *sheng* (*laosheng*), martial *sheng* (*wusheng*), and young *sheng* (*xiaosheng*).

Older *sheng* roles are those of scholars, statesmen, and faithful retainers; although the vagaries of fortune as dictated by the plot may place them in positions of low social status, the intrinsic dignity of older *sheng* implies that they are deserving of respect. Their makeup is fairly simple, consisting of black-rimmed eyes and sharply rising black eyebrows on a flesh-colored face tinged slightly peach around the eyes and in the center of the forehead. All older *sheng* wear beards (*rankou*), which are usually waist-length and may be black, gray, or white depending upon the age of the specific character being portrayed. Every beard is divided into three separate parts—two sideburns and a central chin portion. Black cloth boots with thick white wooden soles (*guan xue*, also called *houdi xue*, lit. "thick bottom boots") enhance the dignity of the older *sheng*'s gait, lending weight and solidity to each step. Costumes for older *sheng* frequently include water sleeves (*shuixiu*); these are extensions of the sleeves proper, made of white silk from twelve to eighteen inches long. They may be held folded at the wrist, or dropped and moved by the arm in a variety of gestural patterns. Older *sheng* roles feature primarily song, speech, and dance-acting skills. There is an important further subdivision of the role, martial older *sheng* (*wulao-sheng*), in which combat skills are featured as well. These characters wear stage armor (*kao*), which may include four flags attached to the back at the shoulders.

Martial *sheng* roles are those of warriors and bandits. Their makeup is identical with that of older *sheng*, but they usually do not wear beards. In some cases, however, martial *sheng* characters who are over thirty years old and/or married are bearded.

There are two major subcategories of martial *sheng*: *changkao* (lit. "long armor") and *duanda* (lit. "short combat"). The former are high-ranking war-riors and are dressed in stage armor, like the martial older *sheng*. *Duanda* martial *sheng* are lower-ranking warriors, bandits, criminals, or supernatural characters. They wear close-fitting costumes that facilitate movement, flat soft-soled boots (*bodi xue*, lit. "thin bottom boots"), and rarely use water sleeves. The major skills of all martial *sheng* are combat and dance-acting, though some song and speech are used, most extensively by the *changkao* martial *sheng*, who tend to be more dignified.

Young *sheng* characters are under thirty and/or unmarried. Their make-up follows the overall design of the older *sheng*'s; however, the basic color is much paler, and the tinge around the eyes pinker. Young *sheng* are always unbearded but usually wear the thick-soled boots. Their major skills are song, speech, and dance-acting. Lovers and young scholars are played by civil young *sheng* (*wenxiaosheng*) actors; they frequently use water sleeves and folding fans. Princes and young warriors are played by martial young *sheng* (*wuxiaosheng*) actors; they often wear two long pheasant feathers (*zhiwei*, also called *lingzi*) attached to their headdresses that figure prominently in their gestures, and utilize combat skills as well.

Dan.   The second principle role type in Beijing opera is *dan*, female characters. There are four major subdivisions: older *dan* (*laodan*), "blue cloth" *dan* (*qingyi*), "flower" *dan* (*huadan*), and martial *dan* (*wudan*).

Older *dan* are almost always dignified characters, respected because of their great age. They wear essentially no makeup and have unadorned hair in a simple bun on the top of the head. Older *dan* usually walk with a long staff (*guaizhang*) in a quite realistic portrayal of extreme old age, with a bent back and a slow and painful gait. Most older *dan* roles use costumes with water sleeves. Their major skills are song and speech, supported by dance-acting.

The remaining subcategories of *dan* are all young women. Although hair styles and headdresses differ among the subcategories and for specific roles within them, the makeup is the same throughout. It is similar to that of the young *sheng*, but the tinge around the eyes and on the cheeks is a deep rose that does not appear on the center of the forehead, and the mouth is red or deep rose and quite small.

Blue cloth *dan* are demure young and middle-aged women, usually of high social status and/or high intrinsic dignity. The name for the role type may come from the fact that a blue cloth is used to wrap the head of blue cloth *dan* who are poverty-stricken or traveling.[3] Blue cloth *dan* usually wear costumes with long skirts and water sleeves. Their main skill is song, supported by speech and dance-acting. Very young blue cloth *dan* are sometimes called "boudoir" *dan* (*guimendan*). They are usually of high social status, but have a somewhat livelier movement style than other blue cloth *dan* because of their extreme youth.

Flower *dan* are vivacious young women, usually of fairly low social status. They may be dressed in either long skirts or trousers but rarely use water sleeves since the role type features much hand gesture. Whereas the eyes of blue cloth *dan* are usually downcast, those of flower *dan* are used extensively and flirtatiously. And while blue cloth *dan* roles are usually serious, flower *dan* roles generally are quite humorous. The main skill of flower *dan* performers is dance-acting, supported by speech and sometimes song.

Martial *dan* characters may be of high or low social status; they are generally more dignified than flower *dan* but less so than blue cloth *dan*. They may be dressed in the female version of stage armor, often with pheasant feathers in their headdresses, or in a feminine version of the close-fitting garments of the *duanda* martial *sheng*; the latter are sometimes called "sword and horse" *dan* (*daomadan*). The main skill of martial *dan* is combat, supported by dance-acting, speech, and in some instances song.

A fifth major subcategory of *dan*, the "flower shirt" (*huashan*), was developed by *dan* performers of the first half of the twentieth century, including Mei Lanfang (1894–1961), one of the foremost Beijing opera actors of all time. The flower shirt role is a combination of the three young *dan* role types. Such characters may or may not use water sleeves, depending upon the particular play being performed. Flower shirt roles combine the natures and skills of martial, blue cloth, and flower *dan*, allowing the performer to display all four skills: song, speech, dance-acting, and combat.

Jing.   The third principal role type in Beijing opera, *jing*, is also known as "painted face" (*hualian*, lit. "flower face"). Painted-face characters are men of great strength—men with suprahuman physical or mental powers, or supernatural beings. One of the most striking features of the role type is its makeup. The entire face is completely painted in bright colors and striking designs from high on the forehead, which is shaved, to the jawline. The designs of painted-face makeups (*lianpu*) range from faces that are a single, solid, brilliant primary color, broken only by white eye areas between black eyebrows and black-rimmed eyes, to complex, multicolored abstract designs and carefully rendered, realistic paintings of real and mythical animals that are totally unrelated to the natural features of the face. The colors and designs used have specific connotations, telegraphing every character's nature to the audience and identifying many characters specifically. Most painted-face characters wear beards that are as long as or longer than those of *sheng* characters and are broad and solid rather than in three separate parts. All painted-face characters wear padded shoulder jackets under their costumes and very high thick-soled boots to increase their physical size.

There are three main categories of painted-face roles: great-painted-face (*dahualian*), supporting *jing* (*fujing*), and martial *jing* (*wujing*). Great-painted-face roles, also called "great face" (*damian*), "black head" (*heitou*), and "copper hammer" (*tongchui*), are usually major roles, and feature singing skill. Supporting *jing* roles, also called "posture-painted-face" (*jiazi hualian*) and "second-painted-face" (*erhualian*), are usually secondary roles, and feature speech and dance-acting skill. Characters in both of these civil role categories frequently use water sleeves. Martial *jing* roles feature dance-acting and combat skills, and in some cases acrobatics; such characters often wear stage armor (*kao*).

Chou.   The fourth principal role type in Beijing opera, *chou*, is often referred to in English translation as "clown" or "jester." Although they frequently portray humorous characters, the actors of this role type may also play villains, young lovers, and other characters who are not necessarily humorous. The major distinguishing features of the role are that actors in performance may improvise, ad lib, and talk directly to the audience as actors, activities in which performers of other role types generally do not engage. *Chou* characters therefore serve as a direct link to the audience, clarifying and commenting upon the actions of other characters. Perhaps for this reason, *chou* characters are rarely leading characters but are important supporting characters.

There are three major subcategories of *chou*: civil *chou* (*wenchou*), marital *chou* (*wuchou*), and *choudan*. Civil and martial chou are male characters of less intrinsic dignity than *sheng*, though they may be of any social status, high or low. They are often called "small-painted-face" (*xiaohualian*) because of their makeup—a patch of white in the center of the face, enclosing their eyes and nose. Black eyebrows, soft red blush on the cheeks, and black-outlined reddish-brown mouths are frequently featured in their makeup as well. *Chou* may wear beards when appropriate for the age of the character being portrayed—most *chou* beards, however, are short and patchy in comparison with those of *sheng* and *jing*. Civil *chou* often use water sleeves and feature speech and dance-acting skills in their performance. Martial *chou* dress in the manner of *duanda* martial *sheng* and feature combat skills supported by dance-acting and speech.

Choudan (also called *chou* "old ladies," *choupozi*) are usually somewhat older, ugly female characters—matchmakers, nagging wives, and other older women who usually have certain undesirable qualities and are of rather low social status. Though younger *choudan* characters (sometimes called "colored" *dan, caidan*) were once the province of *dan* performers, all *choudan* characters are now usually considered to be *chou* roles.[4] The makeup, hair, and costume for *choudan* are designed for each specific character, often in parody of the young *dan* aesthetics—tiny eyes, large red mouths and red circles on the cheeks, faint downward curving eyebrows, and large black moles are common makeup features, accompanied by skirts that are too long or too short, water sleeves that are too narrow or improperly manipulated, or other comically reinterpreted young *dan* costume features. *Choudan* roles, like civil *chou* roles, feature speech and dance-acting skills in performance.

Every Beijing opera troupe aims for a playable balance of role types. This balance is often described through analogy to a table whose top is supported by four beams that in turn are supported by four legs. The top represents the full repertoire of Beijing opera plays; to perform them, four "beams," i.e., four principal performers, are required to portray leading roles. These principal performers are an older *sheng*, a martial *sheng*, a young *dan*, and either a young *sheng* or a *jing*. These four "beams" are then supported by four "legs," the absolutely essential performers of supporting roles: a secondary older *sheng*, an older *dan*, a *chou*, and a young *sheng* or *jing* (whichever has not already been employed as a "beam").[5] Every troupe also requires a number of tertiary performers to serve as additional supporting characters, foot soldiers, attendants, and servants of both sexes.

THE PLAYS

Most Beijing opera plays are anonymous, having been devised by actors as vehicles through which to display their own performance skills. Many have never been published and exist only as part of the oral acting tradition or in handwritten copies in the possession of individual actors. Many of those that have been published contain no stage directions or descriptions of action; they include only the language that is spoken and sung in performance. In addition to this important component of aural performance, however, Beijing opera plays provide the plots and thereby the characters in whose portrayal performers display their skills, as well as the overall structure of each performance.

PLOT

The plots of most Beijing opera plays are well-known stories concerning familiar characters. Most early plays were adaptations of the *chuanqi* plays of *kunqu*, the predominant national theatre form before the ascent of Beijing opera, or of the plays of *kunqu*'s major predecessors, *nanxi* and *zaju*. At least half of the 272 Beijing opera plays listed in 1824 had the same titles as plays performed in those earlier theatre forms.[6] The most comprehensive listing of Beijing opera plays to date, Tao Junqi's *Jingju jumu chu tan* (An initial exploration of the Beijing opera repertoire), first published in 1957 and updated in 1964 and 1980, includes 1,389 play synopses. According to the scholar Hwang Mei-shu, the plots of more than one-third of these plays can be found in just thirteen novels. Most of the remaining plays in the Beijing opera repertoire are based upon "history, true stories, sketches, notebooks, legends, [other] novels, and earlier plays."[7]

The "earlier plays" to which Hwang refers include not only *kunqu*'s *chuanqi* plays, *nanxi* plays, and *zaju* plays, but also plays from other regional forms of *xiqu*, forms that developed earlier than or concurrently with Beijing opera. Many of these plays are also based upon the sources listed by Hwang. In quite a few cases, a single plot has been dramatized in a number of regional forms, and several of these versions have been separately adopted by Beijing opera. Often, these different versions of what is essentially the same play have different titles as well. For instance, *The Fisherman's Revenge* (*Dayu sha jia*), *The Lucky Pearl* (*Qing ding zhu*), and *Demanding Fish Tax* (*Tao yu shui*) share the same plot and characters; the story of *The Butterfly Dream* (*Hudie meng*) also occurs as *Zhuangzi Fanning the Grave* (*Zhuangzi shan fen*) and *Breaking Open the Coffin* (*Da pi guan*).[8]

Because they are based upon well-known stories, the plots of Beijing opera plays may "unfold in a leisurely and natural way, without the tension and violence that characterize Western plays. . . ."[9] Dramatic interest does not arise from the plot, for there is very little question as to eventual outcome. As Sophia Delza points out, "This theatre is not one of suspense, as is our Western theatre."[10] Dramatic interest instead arises from the interpretations given these familiar characters, and especially from the expression of their reactions to the circumstances in which they find themselves. In the expression of those feelings and emotions, performers make the greatest, most concentrated display of their performance skills.

Not surprisingly, this large body of plays with overlapping plots and characters has been classified according to a number of systems during the course of its development.[11] In contemporary China, Beijing opera plays are classified according to three main systems. Although each system is concerned primarily with plot and subject matter, all are related to performance as well. In the first classification system, inaugurated after Liberation in 1949, plays are each placed in one of three categories according to thematic content. This system is based upon the various historical periods during which Beijing opera plays were developed and reflects certain basic, overall performance considerations. The second two systems are traditional and can be represented as continuums along which each given play is placed. The characterizing extremes of the continuum in the first system are civil (*wen*) and martial (*wu*), and those in the second system are serious (*daxi*, lit. "great play") and light or comic (*xiaoxi*, lit. "small play"). These two classification systems reflect the different purposes served by each of the four performance skills—song, speech, dance-acting, and combat—and the relationship of these skills to one another in performance.

Thematic Content.   Since the establishment of the Drama Reform Committee in July of 1950, less than a year after Liberation, all Beijing opera plays have been divided into three categories that are based upon the thematic content of the plays and the historical period in which they were created.[12] The first category, that of traditional plays (*chuantongju/chuantongxi*), includes all plays that were in performance before 1949 and were devised or written without the intention of conveying post-Liberation values and concerns. Some of them have been altered somewhat to remove or replace objectionable attitudes and situations, particularly those with overt erotic content. But the aesthetic prin-ciples and performance techniques of all aspects of traditional Beijing opera performance are exemplified in the performance of these plays.

The second category is most often referred to as newly written historical plays (*xinbian de lishiju/lishixi*), though it is sometimes given broader names, such as newly written ancient plays (*xinbian de guzhuangju/guzhuangxi*). When the term "historical" is used, it is used loosely—although some of these plays do concern historical figures, many have well-known mythological heroes such as the Monkey King Sun Wukong and the legendary Judge Bao. Whether strictly historical or not, these plays have newly created plots, many of which are constructed to consciously embody contemporary values and concerns and all of which are set in the past. Although no newly written historical plays were produced from 1966 to 1976, from the beginning of the Cultural Revolution until the overthrow of the Gang of Four, they are currently a major focus for many Beijing opera playwrights. Because newly written historical plays are set in the past—usually the traditional Chinese past—the entire body of traditional performance techniques may be utilized in their perfor-mance. Except for their thematic content, such plays are therefore often quite similar to traditional plays in both script and performance.

The final category of plays is termed contemporary plays (*xiandaiju/ xiandaixi*). Like many newly written historical plays, contemporary plays con-sciously embody contemporary values and concerns. However, their plots and characters are all of the twentieth century. The aesthetic principles and per-formance techniques of traditional Beijing opera, developed for the presen-tation of plays concerning familiar characters in traditional Chinese society, are not necessarily directly applicable to the performance of contemporary plays. Contemporary plays in performance are experimental theatre pieces. Though they share the basic aesthetic aim of all Beijing opera plays, con-temporary plays require the creative adaptation of aesthetic principles and the development of new performance techniques.

Civil and Martial.   The civil and martial classification system is the oldest and most generally used. In this system, civil plays (*wenxi*) have plots involv-ing personal, social, domestic, and romantic situations; the plots of martial plays (*wuxi*) center upon wars, military encounters, the activities of bandits, and other such situations that feature heroic, martial activity.

The performance skills of Beijing opera serve different purposes, purposes that are related to these two types of plots. Civil plays are concerned with the relationships between characters, and especially with those characters' feelings and emotions. In the performance of civil plays, the expression of feelings and emotions is achieved primarily through the display of song skill. Although martial plays also include sometimes highly emotional character portrayal, they are generally more concerned with situation and action—with the representation of martial activity, portrayed through the display of combat skill. Dance-acting occurs in both types of plays. It is always performed in syn-thesis with song, combat, and/or speech, its display supporting the display of those skills. Dance-acting may also be featured as a major display of skill; in such cases, it usually serves to establish environment and in some instances to advance the plot. The display of speech skill occurs in all civil plays, and in most martial plays as well, serving in both types of plays primarily as the means of interaction—i.e., communication between characters, and therefore as a major means of furthering the plot. The content of dialogue in Beijing opera (though not necessarily the style) is quite accurate in its reflection of conversation in daily life. In traditional Chinese society, the direct expression of emotion, both physically and vocally, is strongly discouraged. In the civil plays of Beijing opera, where the expression of emotion is a major aim, emo-tions are most often expressed through the stylized display of song skill—a departure from the standard modes of social interaction.

In keeping with this distribution of performance skills, civil and martial plays feature those role types whose performers specialize in the appropriate skills. The leading performers in martial plays are martial *sheng*, martial young *sheng*, martial *dan*, and martial *jing* actors, supported by martial *chou* actors. Civil plays feature performers of the older *sheng*, civil young *sheng*, older *dan*, blue cloth *dan*, flower *dan*, and civil *jing* role types, supported by actors of civil *chou* and *choudan* roles.

Very few full-length plays, however, are limited entirely to either civil or martial elements. Most predominantly civil plays feature some martial ele-ments, usually performed by supporting martial-role characters. Sometimes, however, combat skills are displayed by the leading characters as well. The play *The White Snake* (*Bai she zhuan*) provides a good example. In this pri-marily civil play, a white and a blue snake spirit descend to earth in human form—that of a blue cloth *dan* and a flower *dan*, respectively. The love affair between the White Snake and a young man (a young *sheng*), their marriage, and their domestic life together are portrayed through song, speech, and dance-acting skills. However, after the young man is turned against his wife by a powerful Buddhist monk and locked away from her in that monk's impregnable temple, the two snakes lead an army of water spirits in an attack upon the temple—and the two leading performers playing the snakes are called upon to display combat skills themselves during the battle. In such cases, performers such as flower shirt *dan* actors, capable of displaying all four skills—song, speech, dance-acting, and combat—are required if the major characters are to be played by the same performers throughout. The majority of predominantly martial plays likewise include some civil elements. However, the song and speech skills in martial plays are almost always displayed by the performers playing the leading roles.

Whatever the balance of martial and civil elements in a given play, the inclusion of both is in keeping with the basic aesthetic principle of synthesis. It also requires that performers of all role types be trained in the aural performance skills—song and speech—because at least one of those skills is displayed in the vast majority of plays. Even in those few strictly martial plays, such as *Yandang Mountain* (*Yandang shan*), in which no song or speech is performed, there remains a strong aural dimension to performance, for the percussive orchestra accompanies and punctuates all displays of combat and dance-acting skill.

Serious and Light.   Every Beijing opera play is also classified as being a predominantly serious play (*daxi*, lit. "great play") or a primarily light or comic play (*xiaoxi*, lit. "small play"). The play *Silang Visits His Mother* (*Silang tan mu*) is one of the most serious. It concerns divided national and familial loyalties and a conflict between the considerations due past and future generations in terms of filial piety. Among the lightest are plays involving the Monkey King Sun Wukong and plays of lighthearted romance, such as *Picking Up the Jade Bracelet* (*Shi yu zhuo*), in which the only real hindrance to the joining of two lovers is their own shyness.

The performance skills of Beijing opera serve different purposes in relation to serious and light plays, purposes that parallel their functions as represented by the civil and martial classification system. In civil plays, the display of song skill is the primary means whereby the feelings and emotions of major characters are expressed to the audience; it is therefore the major source of serious elements. In martial plays, combat skill is used to portray the serious, martial activity with which these plays are concerned. Light elements in both civil and martial plays are presented primarily through the display of speech and dance-acting skills.

This does not imply that speech and dance-acting skills are always a source of humor. In both civil and martial plays, as discussed above, they are important means of advancing the plot and establishing environment as well. And dance-acting may even serve as the primary, serious dramatic focus, as in the danced portrayal of tragic suicide in *Investigating the Jade Bracelets* (*Kan yu chuan*), and of the death of a fallen horse and his heroic rider in *Overturning the War Machine* (*Tiao huache*). However, in the vast majority of serious civil plays, serious emotions are expressed through song. "The more complicated the internal feelings and emotions of the major characters, the more song is needed." And in martial plays, "the more immediate the martial situation [i.e., the more serious], the more combat is needed."[13] The aural performance of serious civil plays features the display of both song and speech skill, as well as the music of the orchestra. The aural performance of light civil plays features primarily speech skill and orchestral music. In the performance of martial plays, whether serious or light, speech is often the major aural performance skill, and the percussive accompaniment of the orchestra is an important component of the aural performance.

Even the most serious plays are by no means required to end tragically. The vast majority of traditional Beijing opera plays, no matter how serious, are given *tuanyuan* endings. *Tuanyuan*, which literally means "round round" and in common usage connotes "reunion," is perhaps best defined theatrically as a "modified happy" ending. Even if the major positive character(s) dies as a result of the machinations of negative characters or the general pressures of an unjust society, he or she will be vindicated in the end, his or her name cleared or revered, and his or her descendants rewarded for the virtue of their ancestor. And much more often than not, the still-living major positive character(s) is cleared and rewarded for his or her virtue by the end of the play.

Furthermore, even the most serious plays include some light elements, provided in the aural dimension of performance through the display of speech skills. The serious, primarily civil *Silang Visits His Mother* provides a good example.

While the barbarian Princess is trying to come to terms with the fact that for fifteen years she has not known the true identity of her husband, and Silang is tearfully mustering the courage to tell her his real name, their baby son, Ah Ge, cries, and she holds him off to the side so that he can urinate through the slit in his trousers. Silang says, "Ah, Princess, I am talking to you. Why are you disturbing Ah Ge in this way?" And the Princess replies, "Say what you have to say but don't prevent my son from making water."[14] Performers usually must pause after this exchange to allow the audience's laughter to die down before proceeding to the more serious matter of Silang's real identity. Because the Princess is a flower shirt *dan* role, which includes the skills of flower *dan*, and comedy is primarily the province of flower *dan* and *chou* roles, it is not surprising that humorous elements are to be found in scenes involving this character.

The basic aesthetic principle of synthesis supports the practice of mixing serious and light elements, as well as civil and martial elements, in one play. Humor as conveyed through speech also increases the variety of skill displayed in the performance of speech, thereby enriching the aural dimension of performance.

STRUCTURE

In Beijing opera, play structure is generated by the demands of performance. The structure of every play is designed to display the skills of major performers through the portrayal of the feelings and reactions of major characters arising from the dramatic situation provided by the plot. Generally the focus is on one skill at any given time, with a second and often a third skill simultaneously displayed in support of the first. As discussed above, when song or speech is the featured skill, dance-acting supports it; when combat is the featured skill, it is also supported by dance-acting, and occasionally by brief displays of speech or song skill as well.

Many Beijing opera performances in pre-Liberation China consisted of *zhezixi*, short plays or selected scenes from longer plays; several *zhezixi* were performed together as a single bill.[15] Although such performances are no longer as common as they once were, they do still occur; this performance practice is directly related to the structure of Beijing opera plays. The short plays have simple plots featuring one basic situation. In civil plays, the major character expresses his or her emotional reaction to the situation; in martial plays, he or she carries out a plan of action arising from the situation. The performer portrays these emotions or actions through several virtuoso displays of skill. The longer plays may have much more complex plots but are also structured to feature one basic situation and a concentrated display of skill in each major scene; these scenes, when excerpted, can stand alone as complete performance pieces. Generally, a bill of *zhezixi* is composed to feature as wide a range of the four performance skills as possible.

A short play usually consists of one act. In Chinese such a play is termed a *xiaoxi* (lit. "small play"), the same designation used for a light, or comic, play. A longer play, which may consist of from six to fifteen or more scenes, is called a *daxi* (lit. "great play"), the same designation used for a serious play. Since the introduction of Western drama into China in the late nineteenth and early twentieth centuries, a short Beijing opera play may also be referred to as a one-act play (*dumuxi*, lit. "single curtain play"), and a long play is often referred to as a full-length play (*quanbenxi*) or multi-scene play (*duochangxi*). For purposes of clarity, they will be referred to in this study as one-act plays and multi-scene plays, respectively.

All plays—light and serious, civil and martial—may be composed in either one-act or multi-scene structure. In the following description of play structure, the examples cited are from serious civil plays because these plays feature the aural performance skills—song and speech—most predominantly. In light civil plays, the same types of structure are used to feature dance-acting, speech, and sometimes song; in martial plays, to feature combat and dance-acting, and in many instances speech and song as well.

The primary structural features that will be discussed are the use of emotional-progression structure (*cengcixing buju*, lit. "progressional composition") and the conceptions of time (*shijian de gainian*). These features are fundamental to the structure of both one-act and multi-scene plays.[16]

Emotional-Progression Structure.   The structure of most one-act plays and of most major scenes in multi-scene plays consists of a series of emotional states, each the reaction of the major character(s) to developments in the basic situation. After presenting as little expositional material as possible through speech and dance-acting, the major part of each one-act play and major scene is devoted to the concentrated display of performance skill in the presentation of these successive emotional states. When song is the featured skill, the successive emotional states of the major character(s) being portrayed are the foundation of musical composition.

In the one-act play *The Favorite Concubine Becomes Intoxicated* (*Guifei zui jiu*, sometimes translated as *The Drunken Beauty*), the first emotional state is the proud joy the Favorite Concubine feels in strolling through the moonlit gardens to an appointed rendezvous with the Emperor. This is expressed through song, speech, and dance-acting skills. She is then informed by her attendants that the Emperor has gone to visit another concubine instead, and enters a second emotional state. Her anger and jealousy are controlled by her desire to appear undisturbed before her attendants; after an initial outburst in a short monologue conventionally not overheard by the other characters onstage (*beigong*), she proceeds to drink the wines of the feast alone in an attempt to demonstrate the desired lack of concern. The performer conveys this emotional conflict through dance-acting skills. The character enters the third emotional state through increasing intoxication. Playfulness alternates with progressively more obvious displays of anger and jealousy, conveyed by song and dance-acting skills. In the fourth, very brief emotional state she accepts defeat and the uncertainties of her fate; sadness and loneliness are expressed through song, speech, and dance-acting skills as the character submits to the urging of her attendants and departs for her chambers without seeing the Emperor.

Not all scenes in multi-scene plays are composed in emotional-progression structure. The simplest multi-scene plays use an overall structure pattern termed focal-scene structure (*zhongdian tuchuxing buju*, lit. "highlighting the focus composition"). Such plays feature only one or two major focal scene(s). The major focal scene(s) is preceded by several shorter, expositional scenes and often followed by one or more concluding scenes as well. Only the major focal scene(s) is composed in emotional-progression structure, and may be excerpted for performance as *zhezixi*.

More complex multi-scene plays are composed in contrast structure (*duibixing buju*, lit. "contrast nature composition") and feature several major scenes, most of which are composed in emotional-progression structure and may be performed as *zhezixi*. Contrast in such plays is achieved by alternating between scenes concerned with positive characters (*zhengmian renwu*) and scenes concerned with negative characters (*fanmian renwu*), between civil (*wen*) and martial (*wu*) scenes, or between scenes set in two different "worlds" (*shijie*).

In the first two instances, one type of scene usually features the major character(s), and the other, the supporting characters; the scenes featuring the major character(s) are of course the major scenes. For instance, in the six-scene play *The Fisherman's Revenge* (*Dayu sha jia*), the scenes alternate between those concerned with the fisherman and his daughter, the positive characters, and those concerned with the negative characters and their attempts to tax and drive out the fisherman and his daughter. However, the scenes that feature the older *sheng* actor playing the fisherman and the young *dan* performer playing his daughter include more extensive, concentrated displays of song, speech, and dance-acting skills than those featuring the negative characters; generally, only the former are excerpted for performance as *zhexi*.

Plays concerning the exploits of the legendary Judge Bao perhaps best exemplify the contrast between "worlds." They often alternate between scenes involving officials and aristocrats, and those concerned with peasants and outcast members of society. The Judge himself then moves between these two "worlds" of society in the course of making his investigation, and arrives at a true and just solution. In most such plays, there are several major scenes in which the great-painted-face actor playing Judge Bao has ample opportunity to display song, speech, and dance-acting skills. These major scenes are usually composed in emotional-progression structure and can be excerpted for performance as *zhexi*.

The most complex multi-scene plays are said to follow emotional-progression structure throughout. In such plays the majority of scenes are composed in emotional-progression structure, with each scene beginning its emotional build at the point where the preceding scene concluded. The performance of these plays requires enormous stamina of their leading performer(s), who must almost constantly perform concentrated displays of skill. The thirteen-scene play *Silang Visits His Mother* (*Silang tan mu*), a virtuoso performance piece for the older *sheng* actor in the title role, provides a good example.

Within the overall emotional-progression structure of this complex play, contrast structure is also utilized. There are seven major scenes: the first two are set in the "barbarian world" of which Silang has become a member through marriage, as is the final scene in the play. Scenes seven through ten occur in the "Chinese world" where Silang's Chinese family is encamped. Scenes three through six, eleven, and twelve are short and transitional. All major "Chinese world" and "barbarian world" scenes are civil, with martial scenes performed "on horseback" occurring in the transitions from one world to the other.

In the first two scenes, Silang reveals his true identity and persuades his barbarian wife to help him in his effort to visit his Chinese family, and she tricks her mother the Empress into giving her a pass, good until dawn, with which Silang may cross the border. During the first transition, the first transitional scene is set in the "barbarian world" (scene three) and is civil; the last is set in "Chinese world" (scene six) and is martial. The two intervening scenes occur on the border rather than in either world and are both martial. This progression takes Silang from the peaceful life he has known for fifteen years and thrusts him into the tense, unsettled milieu of the deposed Chinese ruling class in exile.

In the four major scenes set in the "Chinese world," Silang is briefly joined with his Chinese family in tearful reunion. Then, despite their protests, he painfully tears himself away and returns to the "barbarian world" to prevent his barbarian wife and son from suffering for their part in his unlawful visit to enemy territory. Upon his return, he once again passes through the martial border transition (scenes eleven and twelve), and once again suffers for having done so; he is imprisoned and sentenced to death. However, in the final scene of the play, the barbarian Princess pleads with her mother and succeeds in saving her husband's life. This tight structure of multiple contrasts—Chinese and barbarian worlds and the transitions between, and civil and martial activities—creates a total theatrical piece of strong cohesion. None of the major "world" scenes is of less importance than any other, and each features major displays of song and speech skills. Furthermore, all thirteen scenes are integral, successively building parts of the full play.

Nonetheless, four separate zhexixi, each an integral theatrical piece in itself, can be excerpted from the play. The first, second, and final scenes, each of the major scenes of the "barbarian world," are composed in emotional-progression structure. Each may be performed alone as a complete theatrical piece. The major "Chinese world" scenes are usually not separated from one another because together they constitute a single, unbroken emotional progression for the major character, Silang. However, as a set they are frequently performed as a single, complete, and quite complex zhexixi.

Multi-scene plays composed in focal-scene structure with only one focal scene are rarely performed in their entirety. Such plays simply do not present enough concentrated display of skill. This concentration is best created by zhexixi, each of which is a focal scene or one-act play composed in emotional-progression structure, or by a multi-scene play composed in contrast structure or in emotional-progression structure throughout, in the manner of Silang Visits His Mother.

The Conception of Time.   Time on the Beijing opera stage is conceptualized in three separate ways: as stage time (*wutai shijian*), also referred to as the span of time covered by the action of the play (*juqing shijian de kuandu*, lit. "breadth of dramatic plot time"); as performance time (*yanchu shijian*); and as script length (*juben changdu*).[17]

In terms of stage time, a number of Beijing opera plays cover very short periods of time; the action of *Silang Visits His Mother* occurs within a twenty-four-hour period, from early morning of one day, when the barbarian Princess learns of Silang's plight and helps him to visit his Chinese family, to early morning of the next day, when he returns from that visit and the Princess must plead for his life. However, many plays may be considered "epic" in the sense that the action of the play may span years or even decades; *The White Snake*, with its final scene in which the Blue Snake returns to free her friend and mistress from imprisonment, spans more than thirty years.

In the exposition of plot, stage and performance time in a Beijing opera play are often compressed. For instance, a journey or several hours' or months' duration may be portrayed by a few lines of speech and several circles of the stage. The passage of many years may not even be enacted at all, with a character simply stating at the beginning of a scene that a certain number of years have passed since the last action portrayed.

In the expression of emotional states, however, the opposite phenomenon often occurs; stage and performance time are expanded, with, for instance, several minutes of song or speech occurring in the several "seconds" it takes a watchman to strike the hour. Reactions to surprising events are often extended in this manner, so that every step and realization of the reaction may be fully portrayed through song, speech, and/or dance-acting. This manipulation of time serves an important purpose: it allows a greater proportion of performance time to be devoted to the display of skill.

One-act plays usually have a performance time of approximately one hour, and multi-scene plays generally take from two to three hours to perform. Because most post-Liberation performances are approximately three hours in length, one or two complete traditional plays may be performed on one bill. A single bill may therefore consist of a single, long multi-scene play, or of a one-act play and a short multi-scene play. In either case, the multi-scene play selected for this type of performance generally utilizes contrast structure or emotional-progression structure throughout, rather than focal-scene structure, in order to provide the concentrated display of skill necessary to create a build of effect; this is especially true when only one long multi-scene play is performed. And, as previously noted, a single performance may also consist of *zhezixi*; a combination of from three to five one-act plays or excerpted scenes may be performed on one bill, the number depending upon the exact performance time of each piece.

Performance time is not necessarily reflected in script length, however. Because many published scripts contain no stage directions or descriptions of action, dance-acting and combat skills do not appear; but the display of these skills may occupy a considerable portion of actual performance time. Scripts for predominantly civil plays are therefore in most cases considerably longer than those for predominantly martial plays, because civil plays contain more song and speech. Even with civil plays, however, the scripts for two plays with the same performance time vary markedly in length if one features more song than speech; the performance time required to sing a given number of written-characters (zi) is often much longer than that needed to speak the same number.

When compared with the scripts of plays for Western-style Chinese theatre (*huaju*, lit. "spoken drama") and translated realistic Western plays of the same performance time, even the scripts for predominantly civil Beijing opera plays are quite short. The Western and Western-style plays average ten thousand written-characters each, while the longest multi-scene civil plays of Beijing opera contain approximately five thousand written-characters, and most multi-scene Beijing opera plays average only two thousand five hundred written-characters.[18] This difference in script length of course reflects the importance of dance-acting and combat skills. However, it is also due in large measure to the display of aural performance skills in Beijing opera; whereas speech in Western and Western-style realistic theatre is delivered rather naturalistically, and therefore fairly rapidly, a large portion of the performance time of civil Beijing opera plays is occupied by the music to which song lyrics are sung, and by the stylization of the spoken passages. The unique language of Beijing opera facilitates this prolonged delivery.

NOTES

1. E. T. Kirby, "Introduction," in *Total Theatre: A Critical Anthology*, ed. E. T. Kirby (New York: E. P. Dutton, 1969), xiii.

2. See Sun Kaidi, *Kuilei xi kao yuan* (An examination of origins in puppet theatre) (Shanghai: Shangza Chubanshe, 1953) for a well-supported thesis aiming to prove that puppetry was the origin of theatre in China, and that theatre therefore imitates the techniques of puppetry. See Sun Rongbai, *Jingju changshi jianghua* (A guide to general knowledge of Beijing opera) (Beijing: Zhongguo Xiju Chubanshe, 1959), 7, for a description of S-shaped movement patterns in Beijing opera.

3. The origin of the name for this role type, *qingyi*, is somewhat obscure. *Qing* may mean blue, green, or black. *Yi* means clothing, clothes, or garment. Poverty-stricken blue cloth *dan* in fact wear black robes, trimmed in turquoise-blue piping; when they are traveling, their heads are wrapped in a cloth of the same blue color. Because the majority of blue cloth *dan* performers with whom I worked equated the name to the blue head covering, I have followed that interpretation in my translation of the name.

4. See A. C. Scott, *The Classical Theatre of China* (London: Allen and Unwin, 1957), 74.

5. Gui Weizhen and Wang Qinsheng of the Jianjsu Province Beijing Opera Company.

6. Zhou Yibai, *Zhongguo xiju shi* (History of Chinese theatre), 3 vols (Shanghai: Zhonghua Shuju, 1953), 682. See William Dolby, *A History of Chinese Drama* (New York: Barnes and Noble, 1976) and Colin Mackerras, ed., *Chinese Theatre: From Its Origins to the Present Day* (Honolulu: University of Hawaii Press, 1983) for descriptions of these three important predecessors of Beijing opera.

7. Hwang Mei-shu, "Peking Opera: A Study of the Art of Translating the Scripts with Special Reference to Structure and Conventions" (Ph.D. diss., Florida State University, 1976), 29–31.

8. Ibid., 34–35. In Toa's listing, all plays with essentially the same plot are listed only once, with alternate titles following each play synopsis.

9. Liu Wu-ch'i, *An Introduction to Chinese Literature* (Bloomington: Indiana University Press, 1966), 174.

10. Sophia Delza, "The Classical Theatre of China," in *Total Theatre: A Critical Anthology*, ed. E. T. Kirby (New York: E. P. Dutton, 1969), 228.

11. See Dolby, *History of Chinese Drama*, and Lo Chin-t'ang, *Zhongguo xiqu zongmu huibian*, (A comprehensive bibliography of China's *xiqu*) (Hong Kong: Wanyou Tushu Gongsi, 1966) for descriptions, analyses, and applications of these earlier systems; Lo's work includes synthesis of antecedent classification systems as well.

12. The policy of "simultaneously develop the three" (*san zhe bing ju*), prevalent throughout the late 1970s and early 1980s, is associated with Zhou Enlai's policies of the 1950s and early 1960s regarding theatrical development. For a fairly comprehensive history of theatre in China from the perspective of cultural officials in the late 1970s, see "Zai Zhongguo Xijujia Xiehui disanci huiyuan daibiao dahui shang, Zhao Xun tongxhi zuo Ju Xie gongzuo baogao" (At the third general meeting of member delegates of the Association of Chinese Theatre Artists, comrade Zhao Xun reports on the work of the Association), *Renmin xiju* (People's theatre), no. 12 (1979): 8–16.

13. Wu Junda of the Jiangsu Province School of Xiqu; translations of quotations from personal interviews and conversations here and throughout are by the author.

14. Translation by A. C. Scott, *Traditional Chinese Plays*, vols. 1 and 3 (Madison: University of Wisconsin Press, 1967 and 1975), 1: 45.

15. Technically speaking, only short scenes from longer plays were traditionally considered *zhezixi*, although both complete short plays and selected scenes from longer plays were performed together on the same program. Perhaps because of this performance practice, both short plays and selected scenes have come to be referred to individually as *zhezixi*; a program of such pieces is also referred to as *zhezixi*.

16. The discussions of emotional-progression structure and the conceptions of time are based primarily on information provided by Wu Junda and Liu Jingjie of the Jiangsu Province School of Xiqu and Huang Yuqi of the Jiangsu Province Beijing Opera Company, and on analysis of live and recorded performances and available play scripts.

17. Although contemporary practitioners and connoisseurs frequently refer to these conceptualizations, they are not in fact traditional. As articulated concepts, they are products of the introduction of Western dramatic theory into China in the twentieth century. See Zhang Geng, *Xiqu yishu lun* (On *xiqu* art) (Beijing: Zhongguo Xiju Chubanshe, 1980).

18. Wu Junda.

chapter nine

REFLECTIONS ON CHANGE AND
CONTINUITY IN MODERN
CHINESE FICTION

Leo Ou-fan Lee

Editor's note: Leo Ou-fan Lee examines the impact of social revolution on the aesthetics of modern Chinese fiction. Since the May
Fourth Revolution, writers have called for realism, vernacular language, and a popular audience. This politicized realism has served
as self-expression and also as an expression of ideology. Lee considers the fiction of the Cultural Revolution (1966–1976) to be a
return to the comic-satiric mode of traditional literature. He
describes the post-Mao literature of the 1980s as self-emancipated
search for roots and reinventions of the past using experimental
forms.

IN HIS CLASSIC ESSAY "Change and Continuity in
Chinese Fiction," Cyril Birch raises a most intriguing issue concerning the
place of May Fourth fiction in the historical schema of Chinese literature. He
places what he aptly characterizes as the tragic-ironic mode of May Fourth
fiction between the comic-satiric tradition of late Qing writings and the
highly didactic political allegory of Hao Ran's novels produced at the height
of the Cultural Revolution. Thus sandwiched between two native traditions,
the May Fourth phase of realism seems like a brief aberration—a small, though
revolutionary, change within mainstream continuity. This is what Birch predicted in 1974, when his essay was written (for the Dedham Conference on
Modern Chinese Literature), two years before anyone could predict the
Cultural Revolution would soon be over:

> These new writers of the People's Republic are engaged in a kind of Great Return.
> Whatever comparative judgments we may wish to make, we are bound to find
> the new mainland fiction "more Chinese," and it is demonstrably more popular.
> In all of Chinese narrative and dramatic literature, there is a strong urge toward
> the exemplary. We must be prepared to see this urge expressed again and again
> in writings of the future. There is, after all, no reason why the realist phase, which
> so dominated the literature of nineteenth-century Europe, should occupy China

153

for any more than the space this paper has indicated, the brief decades subsequent to May 4, 1919.[1]

If we look back over the past fifteen years since Birch's essay was written, it would seem that his prediction about the May Fourth legacy was too pessimistic: not only did the urge toward the exemplary dissipate itself, but shortly after the end of the Cultural Revolution, the May Fourth legacy of realism was restored as a corrective to the Maoist excesses of revolutionary romanticism. Post-Mao literature does not effect a "great return" to native forms of collectivity and populism. Rather, it is the theme of self and its emancipation—surely a May Fourth tenet—that has been celebrated. At the same time, Birch was not entirely wrong about the persistence of the communal impulse and the limited phase of realism; what he did not envision was the far more radical prospect that, a decade after 1974, a younger generation of writers on the mainland would become dissatisfied with both legacies and wish to cast their creative writing in new directions that go beyond the native and realist realms.

Before we explore this new phenomenon, it may be useful at this critical juncture in time to reflect once again on the May Fourth legacy in modern Chinese literature and to reconsider Birch's realist paradigm.

That the concept of realism was invested from the very beginning with a high seriousness is common knowledge. It may be recalled that in Chen Duxiu's famous 1917 article proclaiming the Literary Revolution, realism was one of the three central principles on the banner of "revolutionary army."[2] In Chen's original formulation, the word was placed in a semantic context in which a "fresh and sincere literature of realism" was opposed to "the stereotyped, ornamental literature of classicism" in the same way that the other two tenets—a "simple, expressive literature of the people" and a "plain-speaking and popular literature of society"—were made to oppose and replace the pedantic, obscure, and ornamental literature of the traditional elite. In other words, realism was regarded as a mode of direct, untrammeled expression of popular society. Insofar as this injunction was followed in the fictional works of early May Fourth writers, the practice of realism nevertheless presented a number of problems, both normative and technical. How do we define such terms as "fresh and sincere," "simple and expressive," and "plain-speaking and popular"? It seems that some of the subsequent literary debates—on the use of dialects, on popularization and proletarianization, on the "Europeanization" of the May Fourth vernacular—harked back to these unclear initial tenets. At the same time, however, the literary controversies in the early 1930s became dominated by an increasingly doctrinaire view of language that in its excessive emphasis on the need of the mass audience left out certain crucial epistemological and technical questions: What constitutes reality from the May Fourth perspective? How can the Real be represented in a literary—particularly fictional—text? How is it possible to make the literary text "speak" the voices of popular society?

In a recent book, Marston Anderson subjects these complex questions to a nuanced and masterful analysis by drawing upon the fictional works of half a dozen May Fourth writers.[3] Basing his analysis on matters of fictional form, Anderson sees May Fourth realism as derived from an essentially Western epistemology. Western realism, which is part of a mimetic tradition, rests on the assumption that a fundamental schism exists between the word and reality, and "the exploration of this divide is realism's hidden agenda."[4] In the case of May Fourth fiction, the task of bridging this paradoxical gap—as "realist works are at once distinct from and dependent on the world they describe"[5]— became all but impossible. The realization of its limitations—its formal incapacity to either "mirror" or "frame" the totality of the Real—coupled with an increasingly heightened sense of social activism finally led to the decline of the May Fourth brand of realism:

> By the 1930s most saw that critical realism was not the simple tool for social regeneration its advocates had once believed it to be. In working with the mode, Chinese writers and critics had come increasingly to understand that realism did not naturally lend itself to the activism and populism that Chinese radicals felt the times demanded.[6]

Thus increasingly, this awareness of the "social impediments" paved the way for the eruption and triumph of the "crowd," the massification of literature into communal forms of socialist realism in which the "distinction between 'I' and 'they'—between self and society—that had been an indispensable basis for the practice of critical realism" is subsumed in a "collective we."[7] Thus after much brilliant analysis, Anderson joins Birch in concluding that the journey beyond realism signaled a "great return" to the "communal."

The issues raised by Anderson deserve careful scrutiny. His emphasis on the technical aspect of realism is valid when we recall that the Chinese phrase for "realism" used in the early May Fourth period was indeed *xieshi zhuyi*, which seems to give as much weight to "writing about" reality as to reality itself. In other words, technique becomes an essential component of realism. By the 1930s, however, the phrase had changed to *xianshi zhuyi*, or literally the doctrine of contemporary reality, for which Reality assumes almost an ontological status and the technique of writing is deemphasized. At the same time, we must also remember that from the very beginning the early May Fourth practice of realism involved both a formal/technical dimension and a moral intention of the author. Anderson has in fact cited Ye Shaojun to the effect that "true literature originates in the author's deep feelings" and that "the truth of a literary work is dependent on the sincerity of the emotions expressed in it."[8] That is to say, what Lionel Trilling calls the virtue of "sincerity"—or "to thine own self be true"—has much to do with writing about reality. Although Ye's views may have been indebted to the neo-Confucian notion of self-cultivation, it is equally important to note that, as Trilling has reminded us, the virtue of sincerity was also linked historically to the rise of the concept of the individual with a new awareness of his or her "internal space."[9] In the May Fourth context, this means essentially that realism may in fact have been part of a manifestation of individualism—that the technique of realistic observation and description carries with it a perspectivism anchored in the sense of truthfulness to both external reality and the author's internal self. Simply put, it means that the sincerity of the author must be a precondition of the technique of realism.

This is indeed the argument of a brilliant new book by Rey Chow, who, citing the seminal work of Prusek, sees a close connection between what Prusek calls "subjectivism and individualism"—the lyrical impulse expressed in autobiographical writings and confessional narratives—and the program of nation building and social reform.[10] Prusek saw May Fourth writers as inheritors of two tendencies from traditional literature—what he called the "lyrical" and the "epic." If May Fourth fiction is affiliated with the "epic" narrative tradition, which in turn provides the formal ground for the social ethos of nationalism and reform or revolution, this does not mean that the lyrical tendency was entirely taken over: in fact "the emphasis on individual emancipation . . . gives to the prominence of lyricism a *revolutionary* significance."[11] Thus both epic and lyrical forms can be made to cohere with the demands of "reality." From Prusek's insight, Chow also sees in the May Fourth preoccupation with "reality" an inheritance from classical Chinese notions of "truthfulness" (*zhen*) and "fullness" (*shi*), according to which "'good' literature is by necessity morally sound writing, which is considered 'truthful' because 'full,' whereas 'fictional' works, which often foreground the vicissitudes of language, are idiomatically associated with 'emptiness' and 'falsehood.'"[12] As Chow aptly puts it, this is indeed the dilemma of realism in the May Fourth period— a "recurrent obsession with 'reality' which sees itself as revolutionary and defines 'truth' as personal and historical *at once*."[13] In my view, this morally tinged conjunction of individualism and collectivism, reality and fiction, cannot be fully understood, its underlying tensions and contradictions resolved, purely in linguistic or formal terms. If one should dare to reverse the current poststructuralist injunction and resurrect the status of the author as both a textual and an external agent, it would seem that sincerity in the self-perception of the May Fourth author enters directly into the production of the literary text as a crucial factor governing its formal operation.

To put the argument in the form of a generic question: How do we explain the fact that the primary genre for the operation of the early May Fourth realistic mode was the short story and *not* the long novel? How then do we account for the obvious rise of the novel form after 1930? (Not to mention the equally obvious issue that the long novel never attained the kind of literary privilege and prevalence once accorded the *sida qishu*, or the four great "novel" books, of the late Ming or the "four great novels" of the late Qing?) Following Birch, are we ready to assign a more prominent place to the long novel—instead of the May Fourth short story—as the exemplary communal form in Chinese fiction, past and present? Insofar as these generic distinctions make both formal and "moral" sense, I would like to argue, somewhat contrary to Anderson's position, that instead of its formal "limitations," it was precisely the opposite traits of the short story form—freedom, brevity, and a lack of constraints—that appealed to the romantic temper of most early May Fourth writers. In fact, it has been noted that the short story can be considered the "romantic prose form" in the West: "Whereas the conventional nineteenth-century novel normally accommodates the processes of a dense, ordered society, the short story had been by its very nature remote from the community—romantic, individualistic, and intransigent," for "in its normally limited scope and subjective orientation it corresponds to the lyric poem, as the novel does to the epic."[14] Accordingly, the modern vernacular (*baihua*) short story, one could argue, was the appropriate vehicle—a free form that registers the spontaneous ebb and flow of personal emotions (hence a more subjective form than the traditional novel) or presents a slice of life vividly from a subjective angle or an individual focal consciousness—especially when that consciousness springs from a newly discovered "gendered self" of the woman writer. One need only mention Ding Ling's famous story "Diary of Miss Sophie" as a pioneering example, in which the protagonist seeks to construct her own "subjectivity" by rewriting herself into a different text—a diary in which she is in the process of becoming an autonomous subject.[15]

It was only when the technique of realism as an individualistic mode (*xieshi*, an extension of *xieyi*) was replaced by the more embracing and imposing demand of Reality (*xianshi*) that the problematic of the "great divide" between word and reality was set in motion and given an enormous ideological burden by its pointed reference to the ills of contemporary Chinese society. Again, if we consider the possible role of the (real) author in textual production, not only does Anderson's formal thesis make eminent sense, but what C. T. Hsia calls the "obsession with China" takes on a dimension of ontological meaning. That is to say, the external social reality becomes the only Reality that exists for the writer and that also brings about artistically the "achieved reality" of the fictional universe. Here the issues are likewise more complicated than what can be seen from a purely formal analysis.

With a few exceptions the realistic novel of the 1930s was rural in the sense that its main "chronotope" was the Chinese village or small town. Even in such seemingly urban works as Lao She's *Luotuo Xiangzi* (Rickshaw), the evocation of old Peking has a predominantly rural character. One can almost make the generalization that the evolution of modern Chinese fiction is a narrative of urban-rural transition—from the urban-based subjective short story to the more objective rural novels of the 1930s. This is in sharp contrast to the development of English literature, which Raymond Williams has traced as a shift from the pastoral, "knowable communities" of the countryside to the "cities of darkness and light."[16] How might we account for this contrary development? In my view, extraliterary factors—the historical situation in the first half of the twentieth century—did indeed intrude upon both the collective consciousness of writers and their fictional worlds—so much so that the real and the fictional became closely intertwined.

It was at this juncture that the Soviet Marxist notion of "reflectionism" began to exert a powerful impact by its injunction that literature must reflect the reality of social life. In its Chinese formulation introduced by leftist theoreticians such as Zhou Yang, reflectionism assumed both a passive and a positive role: the fictional text was seen as a reflecting mirror at the same time as the act of writing was assigned the function of active critique of societal evils. In other words, the problem of realism took on an ideological dimension in which the fictional form—particularly the novel—was made not only to reproduce a broad mosaic of life but also to articulate a wide range of societal discontent. As evidenced in the polemical essays by Qu Qiubai and a host of leftists, popularity of language became increasingly a populist matter in which the issue of the mass audience was considered more vital that the creative intention of the author.

This more ideological mode of realism demands a more "committed" interpretive strategy than is given in Anderson's rather formal and negative appraisal. If we take an author-oriented approach, it would seem that in their eagerness to have their fictional canvas encompass a totality of social life, the socially committed writers of the 1930s were caught in the very chaos and disarray of reality itself—to the extent that just as real life itself continued to unfold and baffle the author, its fictional representation likewise led to no neat closure. Some of the long novels written in the 1930s and 1940s are sprawling narratives, forming (sometimes incomplete) trilogies or tetralogies, such as Ba Jin's trilogy *Jiliu* (Torrent) or Lao She's *Sishi tongtang* (Four generations under one roof). It seems as if these fictional narratives strove to approximate the process of modern Chinese history by highlighting some of its important moments in the spatial frames of a village or a family. In fact, this narrative "imitation" of history became a significant creative ethos. Even Lin Yutang, an otherwise apolitical author, wrote his only novel "of contemporary Chinese life," *Moment in Peking*[17] (rendered in Chinese as *Jinghua Yanyun*), as a narrative of family history.

Thus Chinese literary practice in the 1930s tended to make a dual demand upon author and text—for both sincerity and authenticity—in order to realize the cathartic effect of an imagined sharing of experience between author and reader(s). In this context of sharing, the literary text becomes ill-defined: its language tends to refer as much to what lies outside—that is, the real external world—as to the literary elements within it. In sum, literary or formalistic consciousness is cut through by reality and emotion in the raw. It is this "hybrid" quality that has served for Chinese readers and critics as the general yardstick by which to judge the artistic quality of modern Chinese fiction. We may consider this stance as the "realism of conscience": it "confesses that it owes a duty, some kind of reparation, to the real world—a real world to which it submits itself unquestionably."[18] It compels the reader to become involved emotionally in the fictional world to the point of total identification with its authentic reality because it is thought to stem from "authentic reality." The sheer length of the novel, therefore, becomes an advantage as it serves to build up an accumulated impact, and in its sprawling "structure" some segments can be more gripping than others. This is what Lao She rather humorously calls "stealing a hand" (*toushou*) to allow a degree of flexibility and freedom in the long novel that is more difficult to achieve in the short story.[19] To this extent, we may push Lao She's argument a step further by stating that the modern Chinese realistic novel does not seem to fulfill what one Western scholar calls "the coherence theory of realism," in which the effect of realism is achieved "not by imitation, but by creation; a creation which, working with the materials of life, absolves these by the intercession of the imagination from mere factuality and translates them into a higher order."[20]

There is no need, of course, to draw a clear line between these two superficial stances—realism of conscience and realism of coherence—and categorize modern Chinese fiction accordingly as belonging predominantly to the former. What complicates the matter further is the obvious issue of intention versus realization. For all its manifested sincerity of intention, a literary text of social conscience depends nevertheless on its formal properties in order to realize its didactic content or its external "ambition." What needs to be (re)emphasized is that what Anderson regards as the "eruption of the crowd" represents both a reconfiguration of voices in the text (in which the hitherto silenced collective takes on a commanding presence) and a conscious authorial reorientation concerning the social purpose of fiction. If this reorientation from self to society can no longer be contained (as Anderson would argue) by the realist form of the May Fourth story, it does not follow that it would lead inevitably to the demise of the realist form itself. In other words, as it often happens when we read the novels of the 1930s, different texts of realism, even if animated by similar social impulses, are enriched in different ways by the uses of language. Here we are not merely talking about regional dialects or the other populist concerns raised by leftist critics. Indeed we must be concerned with the literary uses of narrative language (in such matters as plot, character, tone, voice, etc.). In a work like Xia Hong's "short" novel *Shengsi chang* (Field of life and death), for example, we can argue that a sincere impulse of social conscience is translated into an authentic art of evocation in which the materials of her familiar life are absolved by the intercession of the author's unique imagination and language. Another of her novels, *Hulanhe zhuan* (Tales of Hulan River), does not even read like an average novel, in the opinion of Mao Dun: "It is a narrative poem, a colorful genre painting, a haunting song."[21] One should also add that in this work of "disconnected fragments" the most conscience-ridden moment—the episode about the child-bride—is also structurally and symbolically the most significant, as it brings a purposely intrusive feminist perspective to bear on a narrative of remembrance of her "native soil" (*xiangtu*).

In fact, those works of realist fiction that have endured are precisely those that combine conscience with imagination, social content with formal consciousness. Recent mainland Chinese scholars are beginning to differentiate several varieties of realism in the regional fiction of the 1930s. More specifically, they have seen fit to recover a more "cultured" variety of fiction known as the "Beijing School," consisting of such writers as Fei Ming, Shen Congwen, Ling Shuhua, Xiao Qian, and Wang Zengqi.[22] Among them, the name of Shen Congwen enjoys an exalted position as a writer whose visions of rural reality do not fall into the same revolutionary mode. Interestingly, it is also Shen's more lyrical type of regional fiction that proved to be particularly inspiring to the young generation of writers associated with the "search for roots" (*xungen*) movement in the mid-1980s than the more politically conscientious realism of Wu Zuxiang, Zhang Tianyi, Sha Ting, and Ai Wu.

What distinguishes the "homeland" fiction of Shen Congwen from the usual mode of critical realism is its treatment of the rural locality not merely as critical leverage for dramatizing a social message. According to David Wang's analysis, West Hunan, Shen's homeland, is both a barbarous country and a landscape rich with literary allusions, in particular to the two great masterpieces of classical Chinese literature: Qu Yuan's *Chuci* (Songs of the south) and Tao Qian's "Taohua yuan ji" (Peach blossom spring). Shen is fully aware that he is writing within this illustrious tradition. Thus his native soil fiction comprises both a biographical attachment and an imaginative tie to the literary place. But Shen also knows only too well that the present reality of his native land is anything but idyllic. The inevitable tension generated by the "dialogic" relationship between past and present becomes the source of a unique vision of reality. Unlike other writers concerned only with contemporary social injustice and suffering, Shen projects a pastoral world that is based on what Wang calls the "poetics of imaginary nostalgia," a paradox of authentic loss and imagined retrieval that characterizes this specific "tragic-ironic" mode of writing rooted in the conscience of homeland or native soil.

Native soil literature is literally and rhetorically a "rootless" literature, a kind of literature whose meaning hinges on the simultaneous (re)discovery and erasure of the treasured image of the homeland. Native soil writers come forth to write out what they fail to experience in reality. Their imagination plays just as important a role as their lived experience, and their "gesture" of remembering is no less important than the things remembered. Insofar as the lost past can only be regained through the act of writing, the "form" of remembrance may become itself the content of what is remembered. . . . Insofar as the "real" native soil and homeland can only be recapitulated in the form of continuous regression, native soil literature always appears as a "belated" form of writing, nurtured ironically on the "imagination" of loss that calls itself nostalgia.[23]

This paradigm of "nostalgia" not only provides an apt characterization of the work of Shen Congwen and Xiao Hong; it has also had an unintended bearing on the *xungen* fiction of the 1980s. For unlike the fiction of critical realism that emphasizes the immediate linkage between the reality depicted within the text and the Reality without, Shen's evocative powers rise beyond the demands of narrow reflectionism—so much so that his homeland becomes both realistic and allegorical: it refers to both the actual place of his birth and "a textual locus where his discourse 'about' the homeland has germinated, and through which he transports his social/political ideas. In its textual transcription, West Hunan is as much a 'homeland' for Shen Congwen as it is for his readers, wherever their actual homelands are."[24] In this regard, we can also redefine Shen's imaginary nostalgia as a discourse on the paradox of modernity, as he himself made explicit in *Xiangxing sanji* (Random sketches of a trip to Hunan), or even something of a national allegory viewed from a schizophrenic perspective. That is to say, Shen's "homeland" represents a displaced "communal" world alienated and uprooted, ironically, by the rootless native soil writer's impulse to construct a coherent narrative about it—an "external" impulse derived from a belief in a new Chinese nationhood as a product of modernity. Whether or not we have stretched his "imaginary" boundaries too far afield, there can be no doubt that Shen Congwen's fiction has enriched the artistic resources and expanded the cultural horizons of modern Chinese realism.

When we think about the post-Mao literature of the 1980s, the immediate background against which we should measure its achievements must be the literature produced during the Cultural Revolution—not Shen Congwen, but Hao Ran and the "mass style" of revolutionary romanticism: what Birch extolled as the great return of the "communal" in the mode of heroic hagiography. In this regard, Birch's many insights are still valid: the renewed sense of social order, the return of didacticism, the formula writing, the popular desire to entertain, and the appearance of the positive hero as either peasant or cadre. Above all, Birch argues that with this great return to the comic-satiric mode, realism of the May Fourth variety becomes all but impossible:

The post-1942 work of fiction can be assigned to the realist mode only if we accept the arrival of the millennium on the mainland. We would have to believe that human nature itself has been fundamentally changed there before we could find realism in fiction where all behavior patterns are dictated by class origin, where the motivation of positive types can be paralleled only by the lives of epic heroes or saints in other literatures, and where the happy ending is mandatory, a formal requirement. What Hao Ran offers us is allegory.[25]

Birch's ironic doubt is apposite because, as he remarks, with the changed definition of human nature there is no room in the fictional text for "the implied author as an individual taking an independent stand."[26] However, the ethos of "taking an individual stand" was not entirely dead: from Ding Ling, Wang Shiwei, and Xiao Jun in the 1940s to Hu Feng, Qian Gurong, Feng Xuefeng, Qin Zhaoyang, Wang Meng, and Liu Binyan in the 1950s and early 1960s, the history of political campaigns has been "littered" with "fallen" heroes who in different ways continued to demand an individual voice without challenging entirely the Party's collective goals. It is not surprising, therefore, that we have witnessed, after Mao's death, "another return"—on the part of these dedicated Party or non-Party "individualists" who were castigated as "rightists." Their mental journey is vividly portrayed in Wang Meng's story "Buli" (Bolshevik salute).[27] And as the story's title clearly reveals, the intellectual outlook of this entire generation born after May Fourth had been shaped most significantly by Soviet revolutionary literature and thought.

This is not the place to enter into a lengthy discussion of the tradition of Soviet socialist realism. Suffice it to say that it by no means can be reduced to a fictional mode of hagiography about Stakhanovite heroes. To be sure, Chinese writers, like Ai Wu and Xiao Jun, had consciously imitated the Soviet model—with disastrous political consequences: in particular, Xiao Jun's novel, *Wuyue de kuangshan* (Coal mines in May) received severe criticism for its "unrealistic" portrait of superheroes. But the central Soviet legacy bequeathed to a generation of Party intellectuals and writers in China, especially from the early 1950s to the early 1960s, was a cluster of literary works translated into Chinese and published primarily in *Yiwen*, the translation journal that was instrumental in introducing not only the new crop of Soviet literature after Stalin's death but also a mental attitude and a way of personal behavior that served as model for the intellectuals who blossomed during the Hundred Flowers movement and soon faded into the countryside as "rightists."[28] To put it simplistically, this mental outlook is grounded in a romantic *ressentiment* centering on the conflict between revolutionary commitment to collective goals on the one hand and personal yearning for romantic love and fulfillment on the other. Compared with the Chinese model—the "combination of revolutionary realism and revolutionary romanticism" first proclaimed during the Great Leap Forward campaign in 1958—the Soviet model still retains a "bourgeois" edge in its insistence on the sincerity of individual feeling and perception. In the case of Hao Ran's *Jinguang dadao* (The Golden Great Way), however, the heroism of Gao Daquan contains no residual individualism but the personification of purely ideological traits: a heroic figure, so to speak, in a new collective allegorical tale.

It is intriguing to note that in the first crop of works published after Mao's death, known as *shanghen wenxue* (literature of the wounded), a striking feature is the portrait of a committed Party cadre who has suffered unjustly as a victim of the wrongdoing of the Gang of Four. Whereas the ideological gloss comes clearly from the Party's new policy, both in characterization and in "sentiment" they are reminiscent of the Soviet model. In a work such as Zhang Jie's "Love Must Not Be Forgotten," blatant intertextual references to Soviet and Russian literature become the central clue to understanding the past of the heroine's mother, whose romance with another cadre is the focal point of the plot. The real "didactic" agenda of the story is to restore the sacredness of this "Bolshevik" revolutionary sentiment. And to the extent that the reha-bilitated writers of the 1950s—Liu Binyan, Wang Meng, Qin Zhaoyang, Liu Shaotang, among others—once again found themselves in a dominant posi-tion, we can chart a different course of return, a return both to a Soviet style of revolutionary romanticism that privileges the individualism of the wronged Party cadre and to a mode of critical realism focusing once again on the ills of socialist society. The reportage of Liu Binyan exemplifies this trend.

It would be an easy task to follow the trend and seek out its obvious affini-ties with the critical realism of the 1930s—a further "return" that would provide an alternative line of "change and continuity" to Birch's thesis. With the demise of Hao Ran's communal utopia, post-Cultural Revolution litera-ture seems to bring us back not to a "more Chinese" and popular route of exemplary didacticism (as Birch prophesied) but directly to the May Fourth tradition of critical realism. In some ways, this is precisely the argument of a large number of Chinese scholars and Western observers, essentially with regard to the renewed emphasis on individualism and its attendant stance on literature as a form of subjective critique of society. But I would like to differ from this assessment and agree with Birch's and Anderson's position (though for different reasons) that for all its past literary glory, realism as a technical mode and as a May Fourth legacy is found indeed to be deficient—this time by another, and much younger, generation of writers who emerged after the Cultural Revolution.

During the mid-1980s, two creative and controversial trends on the lit-erary scene captured considerable attention: the movement known as "search for roots" and the related phenomenon of "modernistic" experimentalism. I have written elsewhere in general terms about both.[29] In this essay I will merely single out a few issues in order to look at Birch's thesis in a new light.

The impetus for a modernist mode of writing certainly grows out of a sense of deep-seated frustration of the self in its dealing with the external world, a world so enveloped by the Party's frequent shifts of ideological policy that socialist Reality as defined by the Party ceases to command any belief. The reaction of the younger generation, therefore, is not only to recover a sense of selfhood in writing but to "deconstruct" the Party's vision by renouncing its very ideological "master-narrative" through which reality is constituted. Thus the need to experiment with a new fictional language and vision becomes the new "revolutionary" credo. As the critic Li Tuo has argued, the initial step had been taken in the late 1970s by the young poets associated with the unofficial literary journal *Jintian* (Today), and what followed from its example of "obscure poetry" was a mode of writing that ran counter to the "mainstream" of post-Mao realism—from the "literature of the wounded" and "reform literature" (such as Jiang Zilong's "Manager Qiao assumes office" and Ke Yunlu's "New Star") and critical reportage.[30] Interestingly, Li Tuo includes both the *xungen* and experimental fiction (*shiyan xiaoshuo*) in the counterrealist trend and traces their origins to the initial position of *Today* magazine— a stance that defines literature as a purely aesthetic endeavor to be separated from politics. Since realism in the socialist mode has been so heavily politicized, the writers of this countermovement have also embarked upon another task—a purposeful deconstruction of the Chinese realist paradigm by stripping away its most sacred tenets: its reflectionism, its linear narrative and "present" time frame, its lifelike or positive characters, and above all its close and critical linkage with external social reality. Their primary "tool" is an invented "poetic" language that owes an intellectual debt to such diverse sources as Baudelaire, Kafka, García Márquez, and Shen Congwen.

That the fiction of Shen Congwen should have attained such an exalted status in their minds is not hard to explain. He was discovered for a practical purpose by the writers from Hunan—Gu Hua, He Liwie, and Han Shaogong—who consciously imitated his lyrical style (He Liwei) or turned his imaginary landscape into a land of political turmoil (Gu Hua's *Fuyong zhen*, or *A town called Hibiscus*) or mythic chaos (Han Shaogong's "Ba Ba Ba"). But more important, Shen Congwen's fiction as analyzed above opens up new possibilities for reinventing reality. If for Shen (as David Wang argues) writing fiction about the "native soil" is an act of nostalgic retrieval and artistic representation, the young writers of the 1980s have replaced Shen's "poetics of imaginary nostalgia" with a poetics of cultural reinvention. In Han Shaogong's story "Gui qulai" (The homecoming), for instance, the plot is clearly embedded in the "Peach Blossom Spring" tale, thus harking back to a regional literary heritage, but the time frame is the "present" of the Cultural Revolution. The juxtaposition of past and present creates a different kind of tension from that found in Shen's stories: instead of overcoming the power of time by the imaginary reconstruction of memory, the "present" reality of the Cultural Revolution is ruptured by the foregrounded "presence" of a mythic past that claims belief. In a way, this mythic voice of the Other reality, reinvented from cultural memory, becomes in Han's other fictional stories even more significant.

For, as Han and the other *xungen* writers would argue, the present reality as defined by the Party culture is but a dead "crust" overlaid on the seedbed of a vibrant mixture of several ancient and unorthodox cultures.

And this is precisely the gist of the *xungen* writers' argument: that they have been cut off from the deepest layers, the dormant "lava," of Chinese culture. Their search for "roots" cannot be a nostalgic act but an active effort of imaginary reinvention, so as to revitalize these long absent cultural resources as a way to reconstruct a more meaningful reality (in terms of art) and as a countermyth to the Party's master allegory of revolutionary history. Here I see their project—still ongoing—to be twofold, having to do with their own creative resources of language and their mythic uses of reality and history.

When we examine the works of *xungen* fiction in geographical terms, it would seem that they betray both a regional association and a "marginal" position. Like Shen Congwen, most writers purposefully paint a "border town" landscape by situating their fictional setting in the peripheral regions: the Xing'an mountains in Heilongjiang (Zheng Wanglong), the southwest province of Yunnan (Ah Cheng), northern Shanxi and Shenxi (Shi Tiesheng), and Tibet (Zhaxi Dawa). There is an evident fascination with the minority ethnic cultures of these remote regions that provide an exotic contrast to the dominant Han culture. But if we bear in mind the somewhat ironic fact that most *xungen* writers reside in the urban centers, it is not surprising that they, too, are strangers to these peripheral regions that they wish to uncover as authentic "centers" of Chinese civilization. Herein lies their paradox (somewhat reminiscent of Shen Congwen once again): like exiles returning home after a long absence, they have found the "homeland" of their own culture foreign, and the journey to their "roots" becomes one of increasing "defamiliarization." However, what matters is precisely their attempt to set up by various narrative devices an imaginary boundary between the familiar real world, which continues to be dominated by ideologies of the Party center, and the unfamiliar "other" world they imagine to have existed. To this extent, their imagined roots pose a direct cultural challenge—from the real or imagined margins—to the political center.

At the same time, after separating their "marginal" world from the central sphere of the Party, some writers have become more "localized," using fiction to construct a genealogy of their own region as a more authentic form of history that threatens to substitute for the Party's own hegemonic, but false, History. Jia Pingwa, a writer from Shanxi, wrote a series of fictional sketches of his hometown, Shangzhou, in a reinvented traditional *biji* style. Mo Yan, a writer from Shandong (a region geographically rather close to the Party center in Beijing), produced his most celebrated novel, *Hong gaoliang* (Red sorghum), as a familial and "tribal" record (*zupu*) in which the implied author takes painstaking steps to "reconstruct" the heroic feats of his grandparents' generation during the Sino-Japanese war. The novel becomes a double narrative framed by seemingly meticulous research: the more the implied author throws in fragments of documents from the local gazetteers and other historical sources (a clever meta-fictional device), the more the story gains authenticity and plausibility, and the more the reader is made aware of the distance that separates that past world from present reality. Certainly for Mo Yan, familial and local history is the only history that counts.

It can be argued that this desire to (re)construct a family or regional history is itself the result of an obsession with history, which is certainly a dominant Chinese cultural trait. In modern Chinese literature, that obsession is expressed by fictional narratives in which history presents itself not only as the background of reality but as a governing structural principle. Thus it is common to construct fictional trilogies or tetralogies about several generations in one family as something of a microcosm of the historical process. Some works by Ba Jin and Lao She, mentioned earlier, are famous examples. It was only when modern Chinese history was appropriated by the Chinese Communist Party and turned into revolutionary canon and sanctified as the only History that recent fiction departed from its ideological grip and sought to attain a "history" of its own. One finds such a new historical move in Mo Yan's novel—a family chronicle that ironically replicates the same historical moments as in the Party's History. The Party's glorious revolutionary past in guerilla warfare during the Sino-Japanese War has been a recurrent *topos* for a large number of revolutionary novels and operas produced before and during the Cultural Revolution. In Mo Yan's *Red Sorghum*, the war becomes a family saga in which the "real" heroes and heroines are family ancestors and their bandit friends, thus edging out the Party's commanding role. At the same time, the novel does not merely offer a new version of history; more significantly it lays bare a realm of desire and violence that has never existed in the Party's canonical literature—as if releasing from long repression certain primordial libidinous forces that clamor for narrative recognition. Lurking in the family saga is a subtext of the "collective unconscious" of Chinese life, a record of totems and taboos. This has become increasingly the new "obsession" of a number of writers: Liu Heng's "Fuxi Fuxi," a story of a sexual obsession between aunt and nephew, ends with a blatant reference to the size of the dead nephew's sexual organ. Male sexual prowess thus becomes a new "totemic" force governing the regional universe of peasant life—a far cry from Hao Ran's world of the "golden way" in which the physical power of the tall, big, and perfect hero (Gao Daquan) reveals no trace of sexual energy, only abundant ideological fervor.[31]

It seems that in searching for the "roots" of Chinese culture, *xungen* fiction has unveiled several "realities"—mythic, historical, sexual—that combine to form a new "regional" universe encased in a radically different narrative structure in which the old revolutionary formula no longer holds. Reading such texts as Han Shaogong's "Ba Ba Ba," Mo Yan's *Hong Gaoliang*,

Liu Heng's "Fuxi Fuxi," and Ge Fei's "Danian," not to mention the works of Can Xue and Yu Hua, I am reminded, ironically, of what Cyril Birch said about the tragic-ironic mode of May Fourth fiction: "The old feeling of order disrupted and restored is gone; order itself is gone, the world is in chaos, any kind of happy ending unthinkable."[32] And instead of the formulaic closure in pointing to the shining vista of the "correct" way toward communism, the plot of the *xungen* works seems only to lead to a clash of some primordial and irrational forces out of human control and beyond the realm of any bright reality. Tragedy and the "supernatural" (in terms of the ironic workings of nature and fate) wait in the wings—wait for liberation via fiction. It is fair to say that, whatever its intentions, Chinese "roots" fiction has not only pushed old realism to new frontiers; it has gone beyond realism.

The key issue for this transformation of realism is language—and a new consciousness of the function of language in fiction. As Li Tuo has remarked, the theory of realism had attained great popularity in China because it "recognizes the transparency of language; it recognizes that language is indeed capable of reaching the reality it depicts." But the writers of "obscure poetry" began to emphasize just the opposite—"the subjectivity of poetry": "They focus on the self—completeness of language itself and the feasibility of treating the literary text as a system of signs. It does not need to have any corresponding relation with the real world."[33] This new conception of literary language becomes the starting point of experimental fiction. According to Li Tuo, this experimental trend began with Ma Yuan, who constantly seeks to subvert and deconstruct the narrative process itself—hence meta-fiction—and Can Xue, who expands the visual and imagistic properties of the Chinese language so as to render "narration into an endless accumulative process"[34]—piling up rows of distorted images to create a nightmarish landscape of decay and death. It reaches a height in the recent works of Yu Hua, whose experiments take on another macabre dimension by subverting the conventional reading habits of Chinese readers. Aside from these three, a host of younger experimentalists crowded the literary scene in 1987 and 1988—Ye Zhaoyan, Ge Fei, Su Tong, Sun Ganlu, among others—so much so that Li Tuo (in his preface to a collection of Yu Hua's stories) ceremoniously announces the end of the Party's "worker-peasant-soldier" literature.[35]

It may be too early to assess the implications of this new "linguistic turn" for creative writing. If we place it side by side with *xungen* fiction and treat it as two complementary aspects of the same phenomenon (in another, more unilinear division, the *xungen* trend is said to have ended around 1987 to be "followed" by experimental fiction), it would seem that the writers associated with these trends are terribly ambitious: they would like to go back to the "roots" of the *baihua* language itself, together with its repository of dialects, in order to recover its potential "allure," thereby fashioning a prose unsullied by the present ideological language of the "Mao discourse" (*Mao wenti*, in Li

Tuo's phraseology). A few of the practitioners have presumably returned to the "purity" of the personal prose tradition of the Ming dynasty (Wang Zengqi) or scaled down modern prose's vocabulary to its bare essentials in order to sharpen its oral quality (as in Ah Cheng's most recent "*biji* stories," for which the reading process should be both intellectual and verbal, as if reading aloud in one's mind). Most writer's, however, experiment by reinventing their own language and fictional form.

Interestingly, the generic form found most useful is neither the short story nor the long novel, but the in-between form of "medium-length" novella (*zhongpian xiaoshuo*, consisting of anywhere between fifty thousand and eighty thousand Chinese characters). No critic seems to have studied the origins and evolution of the form or accounted for its privileged position in the writings of "roots" and experimental fiction. To recall a quote about Western realistic genres used earlier in this essay: "Whereas the conventional nineteenth-century novel normally accommodates the processes of a dense, ordered society, the short story has been by its very nature remote from the community—romantic, individualistic, and intransigent." If this statement still holds any relevance, it would seem that at one level the new writers are still negotiating uneasily within the formal constraints of the fictional narrative—undecided, as it were, between conformity and intransigence. On the other hand, the brevity of the short story form obviously cannot accommodate the process of constructing an alternative history or myth. The novella becomes, therefore, the fitting form that offers sufficient freedom for exploration without imposing an overall structure or "order." The technical problem becomes, therefore, not so much whether the fictional form is adequate to frame a full range of social reality as whether it can give some shape to the unformed workings of a fertile imagination. To some extent, as Han Shaogong's novella "Ba Ba Ba" has shown, the thematic material is too copious to be contained in a short story; at the same time, however, the conceptual structure of the story has the pretension of being a long novel, for which Han's narrative language cannot fully sustain itself. In other words, there remains a gap—not necessarily between word and reality, but between intention and realization. In some cases, the scope of a vision is undercut by the limitations of the language; in others, the inventive flourishes of language all but saturate the text and submerge the vision.

The case of Yu Hua's fiction again offers a revealing example. Several kinds of language experiment are undertaken—a violent parody of a Ming *sanyan* story ("Gudian aiqing," or "Classical Romance") written in imitation classical vernacular; a melodrama about fratricide ("Xianshi yizhong," or "A Kind of Reality") with an ornate "overworked" naturalistic language that depicts torture and killing in minute detail as if to test the reader's endurance of cruelty; a "semiotic" story ("Shishi ruyan," or "A world of affairs like smoke") in which human characters become nameless numbers and the fragmented plot brings no cohesion or sequence of time. It is certainly true, as Li Tuo argues, that Yu Hua's language constantly subverts the typical reading expectations of the Chinese readership who wishes to be either entertained or instructed.[36] Instead, Yu Hua's narrative proceeds coldly and cruelly, using the visual capacities of the language to give the most frightening spectacles of violence and death. In so doing, the narrative challenges the reader either to give up reading altogether or to change old reading habits in order to accommodate to the text. Despite its brilliant surfaces, which make the first reading an equally violent experience of shock and dismay, the effect of the challenge gradually wears off. And one finds that the fictional text resembles rather a chessboard on which showy linguistic moves are made to win a language game. (One would not be surprised to detect traces of Alain Robbe-Grillet.) In this sense, Yu Hua's experimental fiction is a bold exercise, but not in my view a mature work of art.

These avant-garde ventures in language do not necessarily entail a journey into High Modernism. One is yet to find any experiment in the vein of Joyce's *Ulysses* or *Finnegan's Wake*, where fictional language becomes a labyrinthean unfolding of a highly subjective "focal consciousness" from an individual character. (In this connection, the modernist writer from Taiwan, Wang Wen-hsing, is much closer to Joyce than is any mainland writer.) On the contrary, what Birch might call the "communal" impulses—from the more traditional attitude of norm sharing and communal celebration that is clearly evident in communist fiction, to the 1930s mode of rural fiction that seeks to represent the whole world of a village or town—are not entirely dead in current mainland Chinese writing. (In the case of Taiwanese fiction one might add, this communal impulse is expressed by the native soil writers in their strong reaction against the excesses of urban individualism and alienation.) Even in Yu Hua's linguistic universe, one nevertheless detects a vaguely "communal" space that is shared by all the "characters." One wonders if the Chinese attraction to García Márquez's *One Hundred Years of Solitude* may not have something to do with his "magic" evocation of a mythic/historical village, Macondo, which represents his homeland—or even with Faulkner's Yoknapatawpha. Perhaps there has always been in contemporary Chinese writing, hidden behind all the avant-gardist displays of language and distortions of reality, an "imaginary nostalgia" about China after all.

NOTES

1. Cyril Birch, "Change and Continuity in Chinese Fiction," in *Modern Chinese Literature in the May Fourth Era*, ed. Merle Goldman (Cambridge: Harvard University Press, 1977), 404.

2. Chow Tse-tsung, *The May Fourth Movement* (Cambridge: Harvard University Press, 1960), 276.

3. Marston Anderson, *The Limits of Realism: Chinese Fiction in the Revolutionary Period* (Berkeley: University of California Press, 1990), esp. chap. 1 and 2.

4. Ibid., 200.

5. Ibid., 200–01.

6. Ibid., 200.

7. Ibid., 202.

8. Ibid., 40–41.

9. Lionel Trilling, *Sincerity and Authenticity* (Cambridge: Harvard University Press, 1972), 24.

10. Rey Chow, *Women and Chinese Modernity: The Politics of Reading between West and East* (Minneapolis: University of Minnesota Press, 1991), 92–95. See also Jaroslav Prusek, *The Lyrical and the Epic: Studies of Modern Chinese Literature*, ed. Leo Ou-fan Lee (Bloomington: Indiana University Pres, 1980).

11. Chow, 93.

12. Ibid., 94.

13. Ibid., 95.

14. Ian Reid, *The Short Story* (London: Methuen, 1977), 27–28.

15. See Lydia H. Lieu, "Invention and Intervention: The Making of a Female Tradition in Modern Chinese Literature," in *From May Fourth to June Fourth: Fiction and Film in Twentieth-Century China*, eds. Ellen Widmer and David Der-wei Wang (Cambridge: Harvard University Press, 1993), 194–220.

16. Raymond Williams, *The Country and the City* (New York: Oxford University Press, 1973), chap. 14.

17. Lin Yutang, *Moment in Peking: A Novel of Contemporary Life* (New York: John Day, 1939).

18. Damian Grant, *Realism* (London: Methuen, 1970; reprinted 1981), 14.

19. Lao She, "Wo zenyang xie duanpian xiaoshuo" (How I wrote short stories), Laoniu poche (Old ox and broken car; Hong Kong, reprint, 1961), 53.

20. Grant, 15.

21. Hsiao Hung, *The Field of Life and Death and Tales of Hulan River*, trans. Howard Goldblatt (Bloomington: Indiana University Press, 1979), appendix, 288–89.

22. Yan Jiayan, *Zhongguo xiandai xiaoshuo liupai shi* (History of schools in modern Chinese fiction) (Beijing: Renmin wenxue chubanshe, 1989), chap. 6.

23. David Der-wie Wang, *Mao Dun, Lao, She, Shen Congwen: Chinese Fiction in the Twentieth Century* (New York: Columbia University Press, 1992), chap. 7, 8, 13; quoted with the author's permission.

24. Ibid., 11.

25. Birch, 403–04.

26. Ibid., 403.

27. Yi-tsi Mei Feuerwerker, "Text, Intertext, and the Representation of the Writing Self in Lu Xun, Yu Dafu, and Wang Meng," in *From May Fourth to June Fourth: Fiction and Film in Twentieth-Century China*, eds. Ellen Widmer and David Der-wei Wang (Cambridge: Harvard University Press, 1993), 167–93.

28. See Rudolph Wagner's paper for the Harvard conference, "Life as a Quote from a Foreign Book: Love, Paul and Rita," esp. 10–12.

29. See also Leo Ou-fan Lee, "Beyond Realism: Thoughts on Modernist Experiments in Contemporary Chinese Writing," in *Worlds Apart: Recent Chinese Writing and Its Audiences*, ed. Howard Goldblatt (Armonk: M. E. Sharpe, 1990), 64–77. For a brief introduction to *Xungen* fiction, see my introduction to Jeanne Tai, ed., *Spring Bamboo: A Collection of Contemporary Chinese Short Stories* (New York: Random House, 1989).

30. Li Tuo, Talks at the Symposium of Overseas Chinese Writers (Oslo), *Jintian* (Today) 2: 94 (1990).

31. By contrast, when sexuality is depicted by Wang Anyi, a female writer, repression and desire spring from a more human-life world, in which consuming of obsessive love replaces the flaunting of male physical prowess. A good example is her novella "Xiaocheng zhilian" (Love in a small town). The issue of male narcissism—certainly a prevalent hallmark of works by a number of male authors, particularly Zhang Xianliang—awaits more critical study. Rey Chow finds such a symptom even in the works of film director Chen Kaige (see Rey Chow, "Male Narcissism and National Culture: Subjectivity in Chen Kaige's *King of the Children*," in *From May Fourth to June Fourth: Fiction and Film in Twentieth-Century China*, eds. Ellen Widmer and David Der-wei Wang (Cambridge: Harvard University Press, 1993), 327–60.

32. Birch, 391.

33. Li Tuo, 97.

34. Ibid., 98.

35. I am obviously indebted to Li Tuo for having introduced me to the works of these new writers and for sharing with me his insights and papers such as his introduction to Yu Hua's fiction.

36. Li Tuo, 98.

chapter ten

THEATER AND SOCIETY: AN INTRODUCTION TO CONTEMPORARY CHINESE DRAMA

Yan Haiping

Editor's note: Yan Haiping discusses five contemporary texts—from regional musical drama, spoken drama, and film—demonstrating how they register China's social, economic, political, and cultural transformations since 1979. Originally written as the introduction to her anthology, Yan's essay charts the initial reactions against the persecutions of the Cultural Revolution, the early hope for socialist reforms, and the current struggle with the increasingly market-driven economy. Contemporary Chinese dramatists reevaluate China's past, sometimes juxtaposing dynastic turmoil with Maoist socialism. They critique Western modernism as well as they evaluate and define post-Maoist China.

THE FIVE TEXTS discussed here are selected from the hundreds of plays and film scripts written and produced each year in China since 1979. Registering the nation's social, economic, political, and cultural transformations, these works have been published in leading journals and staged in major theaters, provoked powerful responses from Chinese audiences, and caused heated discussions, controversies, and confrontations on a national scale. Representing the most important achievements of contemporary Chinese theater, they also cover its two leading genres, namely traditional regional music drama and modern spoken drama.[1] The one film script included here, *Old Well*, is nationally and internationally acclaimed. These texts offer both vital information about what has come to be called "the dramatic renaissance of the new period" and significant insights into a society that has been undergoing complex structural changes.

"Drama of the new period," like other forms of art and literature of the era, began as a critical response to the Cultural Revolution (1966–1976). Upon emerging from these ten years of civil strife and political fragmentation, many people were frustrated, angry, and deeply shaken. The shared need to express long-stifled emotions found one effective medium in drama, especially modern spoken drama. The first wave of this theatrical movement lasted approximately two years. From 1976 to 1978, two major kinds of plays were produced on stage nationwide. The first comprised new productions of some of the best-known plays created before 1966, such as *Nihongdeng xiade shaobing* (Sentries under the neon light) and *Jiang jie* (Elder sister Jiang). The former is about a group of young soldiers of the People's Liberation Army who come from rural backgrounds but have learned to deal successfully with their new and challenging experiences in Shanghai, the largest and most westernized city in China; the latter is based on the life of a woman revolutionary who maintained her integrity while being imprisoned, tortured, and finally executed by the Guomindang government in the 1940s.[2]

As dramatizations embodying the social, cultural, and political values of a "socialist new China," these plays were extremely popular when staged in the 1950s and the early 1960s. During the Cultural Revolution, along with most other literary and artistic works produced since 1949, they were denounced as "poisonous weeds" and consequently banned.[3] The creators of those works were accused of various political crimes and many of them died of persecution.[4] While violent social forces were released in the course of the Cultural Revolution to attack "traditional culture," eight "model plays" in the forms of the Beijing Opera and sinicized Western ballet monopolized the stage of Chinese performing art. Professional theater in general was suppressed; many theater companies were disbanded; modern spoken drama in particular was proclaimed "dead" by Jiang Qing and her followers.[5] The restaging at the national level in the late 1970s of the dramas popular before 1966, therefore, indicated the ending of an era in the nation's cultural and political life and the beginning of what has been called "a dramatic renaissance."

Condemnation of the massive political persecution enforced during the Cultural Revolution was more directly expressed in the second group of plays staged in the late 1970s—plays newly written by both professional and nonprofessional playwrights, including Zong Fuxian's *Yu wusheng chu* (From the depth of silence), Sha Yexin's *Chenyi shizhang* (Mayor Chenyi), Cui Dezhi's *Baochun hua* (Spring flowers), Xing Yixun's *Quan yu fa* (Power versus law), and Su Shuyang's *Danxin pu* (Noble hearts).[6] These plays were constructed with two prominent features: a bitter condemnation of the Gang of Four and an ardent affirmation of senior revolutionary figures who were persecuted during the Cultural Revolution.[7] A nostalgia for the early years of the People's Republic of China (PRC) lent these plays an unspoken sense of tragedy. The tears in the eyes of theatergoers when these dramas premiered marked one of the most intense moments in the nation's contemporary emotional and cultural life.

This nationally shared moment, characterized by its emotional reaction to the repression of the Cultural Revolution and nostalgia for the hopeful and more open early years of the People's Republic, was soon replaced by another wave of more complex theatrical representations. Rather than evoking memories of the past, beginning in the spring of 1979 an increasing number of plays generated debates over the present and its relation to the past and the future. *You zheyang yige xiaoyuan* (There is such a small compound) in Beijing, *Paobing siling de er'zi* (The artillery commander's son) in Shanghai, *Yige wuangu de shengchan duizhang* (A stubborn production team leader) in Anhui, and *Kaolü kaolü* (We shall consider) in Hubei, to name a few, explored sensitive issues such as social inequality and government bureaucracy, touching off debates where they were staged.[8] Finally, a national controversy quickly developed over the one-act play *Jiaru woshi zhende* (If I were real) by Sha Yexin, produced in Shanghai, based on the true story of a young man who manipulated various government officials and gained privileges by impersonating the son of a high-ranking official before being exposed and sentenced to jail.[9] These plays were short and many were crudely crafted, but their appearance indicated that a substantial reexamination of the nation's past, present, and future was under way. After having been forced like most literary and theater journals to cease publication during the Cultural Revolution, the monthly *Jüben* (Drama)—the authoritative forum of the theater world since 1952—resumed its publication and its leadership role in 1979. In the following years the theater world was full of significant controversies. Leading dramatists, critics, theoreticians, and cultural administrators, once allied in their bitter rejection of the repressive policies of the Cultural Revolution, quickly split into different, shifting, and opposing camps over these controversies and the emergence in the early 1980s of a group of assertive playwrights who called their work "the school of critical realism."

One of the most representative controversies generated by these "critical realists" centered on *Xiaojing hutong* (Small Well alley), a five-act drama published in 1981.[10] Its author, Li Longyun, an "educated youth" from Beijing who had worked for many years on an army land reclamation farm, depicted a group of urban residents living in a courtyard named "Small Well" from 1949 to the early 1980s. After surviving various hardships under the Guomindang regime, these hardworking common folk embrace the 1949 revolution with great enthusiasm. Experiencing the remarkable first decade of the People's Republic, they develop a strong sense of national identity and shared social purpose, as well as unconditional belief in the new government and its policies. They throw themselves into the Great Leap Forward of 1958, sacrificing all they have for an imagined national paradise, only to suffer irretrievable individual and collective losses.[11] During the Cultural Revolution, they are in turn confused, frightened, split against one another, and devastated, but they finally reunite in resistance to the political opportunists who seek power while destroying many people's lives in the name of leftist radicalism. The Gang of Four is shown to be sustained by such powerseekers operating at every level of the society including that of the residential neighborhood committee, and their downfall means for the common folk of Small Well a "second liberation." Unlike after their first liberation of 1949, however, in 1979 these common folk take initiatives in asserting their rights to elect their neighborhood committee and democratically organize their community and its leadership. With a cast of nearly thirty characters of different social and individual constitutions and identities, the play presents a nuanced portrayal of the lives of urban working people in Beijing over four decades with a profound sense of history and emotional poignancy.

The Beijing People's Art Theater Company produced the play in 1983. Certain leading figures in dramatic circles and cultural administration in Beijing, however, questioned the decision to bring the play before the public. Although the first act shows that the people of Small Well welcomed the 1949 liberation, they argued, the following acts show only how things went from bad to worse, focusing only on people's "suffering": "It seems as if the Great Leap Forward and the Cultural Revolution were the only two things that we [the Communist Party] have done since liberation—such a representation of PRC history appears rather lopsided."[12] Contending that he was a dramatist, not a historian, the playwright and his supporters argued that a play was not a historical textbook and should not be judged as such. But the play was permitted to run for just three performances with invited guests only. The subsequent bitter controversy involved playwrights, novelists, journalists, critics, theoreticians, and members of the cultural administration at the national level.

The question at the core of the controversy was how to reevaluate and represent some of the most critical and complex experiences of the nation since 1949. Through its portrayal of several moments of socioeconomic and political crisis in the People's Republic, the play captures and explores the problems of the historically conditioned and changing relationship between the socialist state and its citizens, the national body of policymakers and ordinary members of the society. It is imperative, the Small Well story argues, for the Chinese leaders and all citizens to recognize the vital importance of socialist democracy and to develop effective forms of such democracy through which the common folk can employ critical thinking and genuinely participate in the decision-making process of the nation. It was due to unconditional belief in the policies made by the ever narrowing circles of the central leadership and the lack of a community-based participatory socialist democracy that China had suffered such economic fiascoes as the Great Leap Forward and such political disasters as the Cultural Revolution. Underlying such an argument is a conviction that the well-being of the common folk is the ultimate standard for evaluating success and failure in Chinese history. Such a conviction is based upon the author's understanding of his role as a playwright whose vocation is to "speak for the ordinary citizens."

This conviction underlying Li Longyun's emotionally charged play shapes one of the primary principles and organizing features of the school of critical realism. Playwrights such as Zong Fuxian (Shanghai), Zhong Jieying (Beijing), Yao Yuan (Jiangsu Province), and Li Jie (Jilin Province) who loosely gathered under the banners of this school, despite their many differences, shared the basic view that working people's daily experiences and ethical sentiments were the sources of their creative activity, and that enacting social and cultural critiques in dramatically effective ways was the essential function of theater. Their pointed critiques of contemporary Chinese society were therefore woven together with their pronounced emotional attachment to the well-being of the ordinary majority, a commitment that had been one of the essential components in the legitimacy of the PRC government and its proclaimed programs. Li Longyun once summarized his thoughts on playwriting in the following lines.

> I grew up in the southern part of the old city of Beijing, the little alley where we lived had a rather civilized name, "the small well." The small well alley looked old and tumbledown, but in my heart and in my memories it is lively and filled with tenderness. Like a gracious mother, it offered me a gentle breast to rest upon, provided me a space to begin my toddling. I believe that every writer has a piece of land that his heart calls home, and every homeland has its own smell, color, ethos, and culture. It is upon this homeland a writer's life is dependent and by which a writer's death is defined. My homeland has formed the most essential feelings in the depth of my heart, it has shaped a particular sense of self-respect in me, it tells me about kindness and beauty, about integrity and firmness, and what is the dignity of common folk living at the bottom of a society.[13]

The sentiments expressed by Li Longyun in these lines were shared by many playwrights of critical realism active in the first half of the 1980s. It is the working people's lives and their profound sense of human dignity and equality that render *Small Well Alley* and its likes critical of aspects of the PRC's history and affirmative of the values of a socialist morality deeply resonating with Chinese folk egalitarian ethics.

Responding to these ethical sentiments from another angle but sharing similar views on socialist democracy and socially engaged theater, another group of playwrights in the early 1980s sought to employ premodern historical materials to create dramas that were allegorically relevant to the contemporary social situation. They employed the form of modern historical drama that was invented by Guo Moruo in the 1920s and has been developed by spoken dramatists ever since, and they drew upon Chinese history for dramatic motives. Among the modern historical plays produced in the early 1980s, *Li Shimin, Prince of Qin* was one of the most influential.[14] Written by Yan Haiping (the author of this essay), then a student at Fudan University in Shanghai, *Li Shimin, Prince of Qin* dramatizes the early years in the political life of Li Shimin, later the grand emperor of the Tang dynasty—a dynasty that represents the pinnacle of China's imperial history (A.D. 627–650). Exploring the turbulent events that led to the founding of the Tang dynasty, the play's thematic vision is based on the classical concept of *minben* (民本), a prominent concept in Chinese political philosophy and history which asserts that the foundation of any dynasty lies in the common people and their minds and hearts, reminding its audience that "the commoners are the currents of the river, and the kings and the nobles are the boats riding it; the river carries the boats but also buries the boats."[15] With its epic-style dramatization of the conflict between Li Shimin, who was pressured to recognize the demands of the peasants and their essentiality to the lasting stability of the Tang dynasty, and his father, Li Yuan, and elder brother, Li Jiancheng, who adhered to the desires of the nobility and the supremacy of imperial authority, the play reenacts a historical story with critical significations relevant to post-Cultural Revolution society.

The production of the play by the Shanghai Youth Theater Company in 1981 created a stir nationwide. While the enthusiastic audience crowded in for ninety performances in the heat of Shanghai's summer and some critics embraced it with even greater enthusiasm, other critics, newspaper editors, and cultural administrators denounced it for deviating from Marxist historical materialism. Li Shimin and his father, Li Yuan, and brother, Li Jiancheng, they argued, were all members of the imperial ruling class; their conflict was a pure power struggle among the members of the ruling elite and did not concern any significant policy difference. That the author chose an emperor as her protagonist showed how far she had wandered from Marxist class theory and how "dangerously she had gone astray."[16] The author responded that the core of Marxism was its historical dialectic, and that vulgar materialism would only lead to nihilistic attitudes toward the nation's rich and complex history.[17] Focusing on the tensions between the commoners' needs and the ways in which the members of the governing body come to terms with such needs, the author summarized her reading of Li Shimin's story:

> Witnessing how the peasants rebelled against the Sui dynasty, Li Shimin was awestruck; searching into the rise and the fall of past dynasties, Li Shimin further recognized the formidable forces of the commoners and their importance to the long-term stability and prosperity of his dynasty. "The Son of Heaven," he wrote, "if he follows *Dao* [Heaven], people will support him, and if he violates *Dao*, people will discard him," because "*Dao* sees as the people see, *Dao* hears as the people hear." This is the lesson that Li Shimin learned from his experiences as one of the founding generals of the Tang dynasty as well as from his understanding of history, this is the core of his thoughts on policymaking and governing. Those who respond to the needs of the people will govern, and those who ignore the needs of the people will perish. In the past, in the present, as in the future, even the greatest leaders of our nation have to be tested and judged by this basic law of historical process.[18]

Such a rereading of history has an interesting doubleness. Clearly criticizing the PRC leadership—especially Mao Zedong—for the destructive consequences of such social turmoils as the Cultural Revolution, it at the same time registers deep influences of Mao's teaching on human history and the relationship between "the commoners" and "the kings and the ministers." By remembering the past in such a way, it reevaluates the present and leaves no room for any leaderships—past or present—to be exempt from the "historical judgment" of the commoners. Although a symposium on the play organized by the Shanghai branch of the Association of Chinese Dramatists was riven with high political tension and deep divisions among participants of considerable sociocultural status and influence, subsequent discussions became increasingly enthusiastic, involving all the major theater journals and critics in the country.[19] The play was soon made into a television series shown nationwide and was adapted into regional music forms and performed in small cities and towns.[20] While other modern historical plays of the same period have different thematic concentrations and theatrical effects, their dramatic constitutions are woven with similar convictions of the historical inescapability and ethical legitimation of the judgment on any governing body from "the commoners." Chen Baichen's *Dafengge* (Song of the wind), Lu Jianzhi and Fang Jiaji's *kunqü*-style *Tangtaizong* (The Grand emperor of Tang), and Zhen Huaixi's *puxian*-style music drama *Xintinglei* (Tears shed at the Xin Pavilion) are among the most significant examples.[21]

Rereading the nation's past on the one hand and examining the current conditions of working people and their needs on the other, many of the critical realists of the early 1980s sought to rediscover history and to confront the severe problems and crises in Chinese society in order to revitalize what they saw as the spirit of socialist modernization. Such efforts were questioned by other dramatic activities with more individualist impulses. There emerged another group of playwrights who attempted to break away from what they saw as the alienating, antiartistic, and ultimately illusory role of social and moral leadership with which Chinese intellectuals—including the critical realists—seemed obsessed. Looking to the West for inspiration, these playwrights discovered Western modernism in their eager, albeit tentative, pursuit of "the modern."[22] As early as 1980, some influence of the theater of the absurd appeared in works by such playwrights as Jia Hongyuan and Ma Zhongjun in Shanghai, and very quickly such influences appeared with more thematic substance in theater circles in Beijing.[23] A formally experimental play titled *Absolute Signals*, by Gao Xingjian, a scholar in modern French literature, was produced in 1982 in Beijing; its dramatization of the sensitive social issues of youth unemployment and juvenile delinquency attracted positive responses, though its highly innovative visual image of socially detached individuals went largely uncommented.[24] The following year, *Bus Stop*, by the same author, was staged by the People's Art Theater Company, and with it

Western-style experimental modernism came of age in China. Still interacting with the social concerns of realist playwrights, the play shows certain structural and ideological departures—much more significantly than most works of critical realism at the time—from traditions of the theater in particular and Chinese culture in general since the 1950s.

A seemingly Beckettian play, *Bus Stop* dramatizes a group of people who have been waiting for ten years at a bus station somewhere between country and city for a bus that is to take them to the city. One bus after another passes but none stops at their station. While waiting and agonizing over their individual dreams and desires, they hardly notice that one silent, middle-aged man leaves the bus station after several buses have passed: "He strides away without turning his head even once. Music rises, the melody evoking a painful and persistent search."[25] By the end of the play, people begin to realize that perhaps this bus stop has been suspended and the bus route changed; they finally decide to stop waiting and get ready to walk on their own feet to the city. Realistic in characterization and symbolistic in overall structure, the play provoked immediate controversy in Beijing cultural circles, followed by heated discussion in major cultural centers throughout the nation. Some critics stressed the play's creativity and hailed its message that people should actively take charge of their lives rather than waste their lives in passive waiting. Other critics contended that the play contained a basic questioning if not a fundamental negation of the organization of contemporary Chinese society, a condescending attitude toward the deluded "pitiable multitude," and an elitist and individualistic impulse embodied in the "silent man" walking alone to the city.[26] The controversy occurred in 1983, a time when a serious debate at the highest levels of the state and cultural spheres was intensifying, and a socioideological metamorphosis in the world of literature and art was quickly unfolding. At the center of the debate were efforts to read the economic and political disasters and implied theoretical problematics of PRC history as symptoms of a systematic "alienation" inherent in socialist theory and practice. Led by senior theorists such as Wang Ruoshui, then the deputy editor of *People's Daily*, and supported by such figures as Zhou Yang, then the minister of culture, the theory of "socialist alienation" was proposed while a rediscovery of humanist discourse in the early writings of Karl Marx was conducted.[27] Wang, Zhou, and their supporters were arguing that the Chinese socialist project had over the decades turned into the opposite of the ideal of socialism—had become alienated from itself—and that the Marxist theory of class struggle in the hands of the "ultraleftists" had been used to fabricate class struggles in a socialist society; such fabrications served not only to legitimize their violation of many people's personal freedom and their denial of the human dignity of the citizens but to "justify sheer cruelty in their pursuit of power."[28]

Responding to this theory of socialist alienation and the proposed humanistic remedy, former Politburo member Hu Qiaomu and other theorists insisted upon two major points. First, the problems that occurred in Chinese socialist practice could be rectified while the socialist system as a whole still had its great vitality and could further mature. That such disasters as the Great Leap Forward and the Cultural Revolution were stopped, criticized, and indeed denounced provided the evidence that the socialist system had in itself an effective rectifying mechanism. The problems that Wang, Zhou, and their supporters pointed to, therefore, could not be defined as predetermined results of the systematic alienation of socialism itself, and to define them as such could lead to the dangerous conclusion that socialism was intrinsically alienating if not fundamentally flawed. Second, humanism and its variants, including the version in the young Marx, was historically inseparable from and in fact a vital part of the ideology of the bourgeoisie. This was why Marx himself in his mature writings turned away from this creed and developed his dialectic and historical materialism. Adopting this Western and bourgeois ideology to solve the problems in Chinese socialist practice was therefore historically utopian and theoretically misleading.[29] The appearance of *Bus Stop* added to this debate a particular dimension by providing Hu Qiaomu and his supporters, including He Jingzhi and Feng Mu, a dramatic illustration of bourgeois humanist individualism with an overall negation of the socialist practice and history of contemporary China.

The significant critical attention the play received can be seen in the discussion organized by the editorial committee of *Xijübao* (On theater), the equivalent of *People's Daily* in the theater world, and participated in by Tang Yin, Du Gao, and Zhen Bonong, three important cultural critics. In their response to the play, these critics also articulated their views on the forces operative in the formation of the school of "Western modernism," on the debate about socialist alienation theory and humanism, and on the general climate in the cultural world at the time. They saw in all these "theories of socialist alienation" and "schools of Western modernism" a fundamental rejection of socialism and Marxism and, by implication, a crisis of the socialist consciousness that could undermine the "foundation of our country":

Some of our theorists tend to view and judge our historical experiences of socialist practice and its problems with pessimism and formulate the misleading theory claiming that the socialist system constantly generates its own "alienation." . . . This theory can easily be accepted by some of our young writers who have become fundamentally doubtful about socialism. When we are criticizing ultraleftism and its effects on art and literature, creative experiments in the theater are the refreshing fruits with which we have every reason to be pleased. Yet our critiques of ultraleftism seem to have caused serious confusion in the minds of some young

authors as well. They take the critique of ultraleftism as a fundamental aban-
donment of Marxist views on art and culture and total denunciation of the
achievements of socialist literature and art and its revolutionary tradition. And
their "innovations" turn out to be mere echoes of Western modernists. Taking
the capitalist art of the West as the ultimate "world art" and canceling the fundamental distinctions between socialist art and capitalist art, their dramatic
"innovations," as a result, become imitations of "the theater of the absurd," products of the declining Western culture.[30]

The response from these critics was consequential. *Bus Stop* was stopped after
ten performances in July 1983, and the play was judged "seriously flawed." At
about the same time, the debates on "alienation theory" and "the young
Marx's humanism" *vs* "the old Marx's class struggle" concluded with Zhou
Yang's self-criticism for having misunderstood Marx and Wang Ruoshui's
removal from office. Such administrative conclusions, however, did not
resolve the complex questions raised in these debates and certainly did not
prevent enthusiasm for Western culture and ideology from further growing in
the Chinese cultural world.

More books on Western modernist theater were quickly and often inad-
equately translated into Chinese and disseminated in literary, dramatic, and
theoretical circles. Plays by emerging Chinese playwrights of various schools
ranging from "absurdism" to "surrealism" continued to be staged in rapidly
increasing quantity from 1983, and the first peak of experimental modernism
was reached in the mid-1980s. *Jieshang liuxing hongqunzi* (Red skirts are the
fashion) by Jia Hongyuan and Ma Zhongjun and *Yige shengzhe dui sizhe de
fangwen* (A visit from a dead man) by Liu Shugang were among the most
acclaimed and controversial plays.[31] In *Red Skirts*, a "model socialist worker"
alienates her coworkers because of her ideological pretension—however reluctant—of being a virtuous role model and her socially induced dishonesty. In
A Visit, a fashion designer fights the "social prejudices" against private own-
ership and courageously sets up and runs her own business, while her lover,
who is marginalized by his temporary working status in a state-run theater
company, emerges as the true moral hero by saving a passenger assaulted by
a murderous criminal on a public bus at the expense of his own life. Despite
the measures taken by some cultural administrators to criticize or ban some
of those plays, their rising popularity testified that theater circles in particular and the cultural world in general were living in a profoundly different
climate—one in which not only Marxist notions of class and class struggle
were questioned in their relation to Chinese society but a whole range of
social ethics and moral values established since 1949 were, implicitly or
explicitly, deconstructed as forms of "hypocrisy of ultraleftism." As an "era of
pluralism" in the cultural arena was heralded by some quickly rising new
writers,[32] it appeared clear that the value system of humanistic individualism

was reshaping the orientation and organizing features of Chinese art and literature. It was represented in literary, artistic, critical, and theoretical works in rapidly increasing quantity, although such individualism was harshly and constantly criticized and indeed denounced from on high.

The quest for "modern subjectivity," proclaimed by leading modernists and indicated by the bulk of modernist plays produced since the mid-1980s, is at the heart of Western-inspired and Western-oriented experimental modernism. Among the features of "modern subjectivity," the claim of individuality and individual creativity is most prominent. The theory of "socialist and revolutionary realism," which stressed the sociopolitical nature and function of art and literature and had been the dominant theory in China since the 1950s, was rejected by the modernists, who asserted that such theory over the decades had become a political cliché that had frozen the natural blossoming of modern Chinese culture. To liberate Chinese literature and art from stifling orthodoxy, many experimental modernists declared that art in its essence was independent of politics, not representing any socioeconomic group or class. Rather, artistic works were expressions of individual creativity and universal humanity. In searching for such expressions of transcendental individual-universal humanity, they embraced and absorbed Western modernism with great enthusiasm while undergoing a process of multilayered psychocultural transference.

The thematic motives of modernism, such as epistemological uncertainty, existential agony and despair, and ontological nothingness, articulated in the West by the post-World War II generation, in short, were captured, appropriated, transplanted, and reproduced in a radically different sociohistorical context, namely, post-Mao China. Such a practice was of course not, as modernists themselves claimed, apolitical or cleansed of sociopolitical implications. They were both socially and politically charged expressions rooted in the desire to break away from particular sociopolitical constraints. But contrary to the assertions of Du Gao and others, they were not mere imitations of European modernist theater either. The historically specific dynamics in this complex process of discovery, appropriation, and reproduction can be seen in all the works of experimental modernism mentioned above and others. In his essay on modernism and contemporary Chinese literature, written in 1987, Gao Xingjian articulates the features of such Chinese modernist organizing principles quite clearly:

> The movement of contemporary Chinese literature toward modernity shares some features with Western modernism, but it cannot possibly repeat the process of development of modern Western literature. The school of modernism that has emerged in China, in general terms, is rather different from that of Western modernism . . . . Unlike Western modernism, which is underlined by a negation of the self, Chinese modernism is founded on an affirmation of the self; it exposes the

absurdities in the realities of Chinese society but does not—as Western modernism does—take absurdity as constitutive of the existential conditions of
humanity. . . . A critical skepticism about the old humanism is the point of departure for Western modernism; but for Chinese modernists, the rediscovery of
humanism that was lost under the social conditions of modern and contemporary Chinese society is their core. Such rediscovered humanism is imbued, in
effect, with the spirit of romanticism.[33]

Such a "rediscovered humanism" filled with the spirit of "romanticism,"
while not overtly rejecting collectivism, focuses on the individuality of the
citizens that had been radically deemphasized if not erased in contemporary
Chinese public discourses. Gao's Bus Stop, the earliest modernist play, is certainly one of the representative works of this dramatic school. Samuel
Beckett's Waiting for Godot provided a situational structure and dramatic
impulse for Gao's play, but Bus Stop has an unmistakably Chinese quality in
its individual characterizations and structural implications, which are both
underlined by the social and historical conditions of Chinese society in the
post-Mao era. Beckett's play, more specifically, explores the loss of the
meaning of humanity in the postwar West, and Gao's play centers on what
he sees as the blindness of the multitude who have been trapped by illusory
group-bound conventions and promises throughout their lives. As an embodiment of epistemological negation of Western modernity, Godot offers
nothing, indeed cancels almost any possibility, for change. As an embodiment
of disillusionment about Chinese socialist practices, Bus Stop offers the "silent
man," who is clearly a trope for humanistic enlightenment and an individual
search for direction in a moment of social transformation and political
uncertainty.

Situated in and responding to this moment of transformation and uncertainty, dramatists writing in the vein of critical realism and experimental modernism in the first half of the 1980s adopted distinctively different organizing
principles in their playwriting and theatrical production. Their differences,
however, were largely submerged by their shared support of Wang Ruoshui
and Zhou Yang, first for their advocacy of "humanism in early Marx," and
later through a variety of confrontations with what both called "ultraleftism,"
namely, the complex and by no means homogeneous cultural and political
forces persisting in the society that were critical of their dramatic and theatrical practices. The battle waged over the banning of the play WM (We) in
1985 shows how the major members of both schools functioned as allies in a
national controversy. The play WM is hence chosen as the second text in this
discussion.

Written by Wang Peigong and produced by the Theater Troupe of the
Air Force in Beijing, WM offers a tender and nearly melancholic portrayal of
"educated youth" in their struggle to cope with their drastically changing

living conditions and to find meaning in their lives. The play begins with a scene of a "collective household" in the countryside during the Cultural Revolution and ends with a reunion at a fancy city restaurant in the mid-1980s. The seven characters in the play are from different social and family backgrounds: the status and identities of their parents range from those of a senior army officer, a cadre who gained power during the Cultural Revolution, and a hardworking industrial worker to those of intellectuals, a "rightist," and a "capitalist roader."[34] Their lives, registering important aspects of Chinese society over a decade and capturing significant historical moments of these years, are characterized by emotional ruptures and political disillusionments. Despite all they have suffered, however, they remain deeply bound by their shared youth spent in the "collective" and their memories of a sunny childhood in the 1950s, crystallized in the team song of the "Young Socialist Pioneers." The play ends with them humming the melody of the song and poignantly echoing—with explicit mockery and implicit nostalgia—a group of children, another generation of Young Pioneers, singing in the distance.

Structurally, the play is divided into four parts, with a series of intertwined individual stories using two drummers to set the rhythm of the unfolding events and accentuate each character's often unspoken feelings or subconscious. Drawing on such modernist elements as stream of consciousness in the forms of overlapping or parallel monologues, WM is substantiated by a realistic characterization. The significance of such structural innovation certainly goes beyond the realm of pure theatrical techniques. Registering such sentiments of experimental modernism as an ever-growing sense of alienation among once genuinely connected characters, the play is at the same time suffused with a longing for social justice, equality, and the ideals that informed most plays of critical realism in the early 1980s. The reform era in WM is no longer an imagined future invested with hope for socialist democracy (as in Small Well), belief in the "laws of history" in accordance with which the will of the commoners prevails (as in Li Shimin), or desires of romantic individualism (as in Bus Stop). The reform era in the play has turned into a trying reality in which some old problems persist and new problems emerge while drastic social changes dislocate everyone and redefine everything. Compared with the three texts discussed above, WM offers a much more fluid narrative that aims to capture these complex social conditions and the individuals who feel caught in them without any conclusive evaluations. As the author said in an interview, "We don't want to define those characters in ready-made categories of good or bad, . . . we just want to accurately represent their experiences, their emotional crises, to show the barely discernible changes in human relations under changing social realities."[35] In fact, WM is one of the few plays of the mid-1980s that touches upon the subtle disintegration of the moral fabric of human relations under the gradually developing commodification of society.

Some leading members of the Air Force Cultural Bureau were displeased with the play. The young people, they argued, all appeared self-serving and petty; they lacked a belief in socialism and a sense of purpose for their lives. The only person among the seven characters who had kept his ideals and integrity appeared most abstract, and he was literally losing his eyesight. One sees in the play how these young people had lost their socialist dreams but no indication of how they could regain their ideals. The production, judged too "gloomy, low-spirited, and decadent," was permitted two dress rehearsals with a small group of invited guests to solicit comments and suggestions for its revision.[36] Wang Gui, the director of WM and also the head of the troupe, rejected these criticisms as ultraleft orthodoxy. Arguing that the play realistically reflected the life experiences of the generation of "educated youth," he refused to make any revisions and turned the first "dress rehearsal with invited guests only" into a full-fledged evening performance witnessed by a large group of critics, reporters, writers, and theorists. Although praise quickly appeared in major newspapers and journals, the Air Force Cultural Bureau canceled all rehearsals and further possibilities for public performance.

The controversy immediately reached the national level, and the decision to ban the play provoked anger and protest. Numerous dramatists from the schools of critical realism and experimental modernism protested the decision, calling it "brutal and confused administrative interference."[37] The Society of Dramatic Literature, a newly established subgroup of the Association of Chinese Dramatists, soon decided to sponsor a production of the play by collecting donations from such sympathetic groups as the Chinese Society of the Disabled, led by Deng Xiaoping's elder son, Deng Pufang.[38] They then invited artists from different theater companies to perform it. The Shanghai People's Theater Company, meanwhile, also decided to stage the play. While the rehearsals were proceeding in both cities, numerous newspapers and journals reported on the play and its surrounding controversy, and when the two productions were brought to the public in October, the reviews were full of unanimous praise.

The overwhelming praise for WM, like the resolute ban it provoked, indicate as much about the complexity of the moment in which it appeared as about the meaning of the production itself. With the decollectivization being enforced in the rural areas, by 1985 the urban economy had entered preliminary stages of denationalization. The cultural climate, the most sensitive barometer of Chinese socioeconomic and political life, was likewise transforming. In late 1984 the Fourth Congress of Literature took place in Beijing, and Hu Qili, then a standing member of the Politburo, gave a keynote speech promoting efforts to create "a vast sky of artistic freedom" and denouncing "inappropriate administrative interference" in literature and art.[39] In the early spring of 1985, the Fourth Congress of Theater also took place in Beijing, at which Xi Zhongxun, then secretary of the Central Disciplinary Committee of the Communist Party, made a speech similarly denouncing "ultraleft inter-ference." The institutional implications of these speeches were demonstrated in the striking reconfigurations of the standing committees of the Writers Association and the Dramatists Association that were accomplished at both congresses: a significant number of those who had supported the controver-sial "new works of the new period" since the early 1980s were elected to replace some of the increasingly unpopular previous members of both com-mittees;[40] and the once controversial writer Wang Meng was soon to assume the office of Minister of Culture. The production of *WM* was hailed as "a new chapter of modern Chinese spoken drama," and *Small Well Alley* was finally restaged for the public in the spring of 1985 after its five painful years of being kept at bay.[41]

The *WM* production, therefore, occurred at a significant transitional moment in the world of art and literature. The transition, however, was far more complex than what the performance of the play and its emotionally charged controversy had contained. The appearance of *Small Well Alley* looked tragically belated on the changing Chinese sociocultural scene. "Chinese reform" as a synonym for "Chinese modernization" was by now iden-tified not only with the decollectivization of the rural economy but with the partial denationalization, commodification, and internationalization of the urban economy, and voices echoing such socialist ethics as the collective well-being of the working people were likely to be judged old, outdated, and some-what "ultraleft." Welcomed by its Beijing audience, *Small Well* was received as a gesture about a dispute in the past rather than as an artistic work augur-ing the future, and the moral values of the honest, hardworking common folk with their preference for the collective well-being affirmed in the play appeared out of step with the culture of the day. That none of the plays Li Longyun wrote after *Small Well* was nearly as influential indicates the changed sociopolitical conditions following in the wake of the reform process. Leading critical realists, after their hard-won battles over the "ultraleftists" who often attempted to ban their works in the first half of the 1980s, were confronted with growing new problems after the mid-1980s.

The cultural world of these years embraced Western-style modernism that was accompanied by escalating importation of European and American cul-tural products; books on Western literature, philosophy, political science, art, and theories were hastily translated and published. The theater world from 1985 onward was increasingly dominated by "modernist" dramas. These dramas, like some of the earlier modernist experiments, absorbed certain Western modernist sentiments on alienation from the state and a rebellious spirit toward sociocultural orthodoxy. More important, and unlike some of the earlier modernist dramas, they further inherited great amounts of sociocul-tural nihilism built within the organizing principles of Western modernist theater, in the light of which the ideology of Marxist socialism and its moral traditions were rejected. The spirit of individual rebellion against society embodied in Western modernism was transplanted into the Chinese context to deconstruct established cultural and moral systems, even as the conventional values of Western modernity were penetrating China to fill the ideological void created by such modernist deconstruction and the furthering of economic denationalization and internationalization. As such literary terms as "absurdism," "surrealism," "expressionism," or simply "modernism" were dancing through theater or literary journals and cultural circles, waves of Western consumer goods were sweeping across Chinese society. There appeared in cultural circles an equation of the modern West with the modern world, modernization with Westernization, and Western-style modernity with universal humanity. While this Western-oriented modernism was reaching its second apex in the latter half of the 1980s, "the West is best" sentiments began to dominate the theater world as well as the society at large.[42]

Responding to the challenges that modernist theater with a nihilistic turn posed, but insisting on the "Chineseness" of their theatrical practices, some of the critical realists consciously appropriated the modernist techniques. Among the innovations in playwriting evident since the mid-1980s were structural changes: well-made plots often gave way to series of episodes; the orderly unfolding of stories began to split into multiple lines of development in which time and space or past and present were manipulated with greater flexibility; complex, ambiguous, and at times allegorical images increasingly replaced well-defined and linearly developed characters. When realists employed these putatively Western modernist techniques, they began to appear more familiar to Chinese eyes and even turned out to be something very close to many aesthetic formulations of Chinese traditional music drama. The rich trove of traditional music drama then was emphatically rediscovered by critical realists. Such features of Western modernist theater as the fluidity of time and space, symbolism of imagery, and performative theatricality, some critical realists asserted, were in fact originally borrowed by Western dramatists from dramatic cultures of the East. Bertolt Brecht's interest in Beijing Opera, which inspired him to crystallize his theories of alienation effect and the epic theater, was the most cited and discussed example. Creative combinations of European modernist semiotics and the aesthetic codes of traditional Chinese drama, some of the leading dramatists of critical realism argued, marked the most promising direction for modern Chinese theater. The effort to carry out such combinations resulted in one of the most influential and provocative dramas of the 1980s: the *chuanjü*-style play *Pan Jinlian: The History of a Fallen Woman* of 1986, a realist redramatization of an ancient Chinese story in the form of regional music drama that rather consciously and effectively incorporated Western modernist elements.[43]

Written by well-known playwright Wei Minglun in the form of traditional *chuanjü* with one prelude and four parts, *Pan Jinlian* reappropriates the traditional story of "lascivious" Pan Jinlian by recontextualizing her life in juxtaposition with various fictional and historical characters from different times and places. Jia Baoyü, the hero of the Qing-period novel *The Dream of the Red Chamber*, Wu Zetian, the female emperor of the Tang dynasty, Anna Karenina, the heroine of Leo Tolstoy's classic novel, *Feifei*, a divorcée of modern China, and her friend, a contemporary woman judge, are but a few of those presented in this representation of Pan Jinlian's tragic story. The play, the author announced, is a protest against the "oppression of the female gender" rooted in Chinese traditional culture and persisting in different forms in modern Chinese society.[44] Moreover, the place where the story takes place is "across countries and continents, unconstrained by specific locations," implying that this protest is relevant to cultures and societies everywhere.[45] The "fallen" woman, Pan Jinlian, viewed as one among all the women in the world who have suffered male oppression, is reevaluated from cross-national, transhistorical, and multicultural perspectives as the victim of patriarchal power structures. Compared with such plays as *WM* that also incorporate traditional Chinese and Western modernist techniques, *Pan Jinlian*, with a regional music form and folk-style language familiar to Chinese audiences in both urban and rural areas, appears more coherent and complete in its aesthetic stylization and more dynamic and effective in its dramatization. The play creates virtually an entirely new form of Chinese regional music drama that cannot be fully defined by reference to categories of realism or modernism, traditional or modern. The author himself styled it "*chuanjü of the absurd.*"

Stimulating many theatergoers of both traditional music drama and modern spoken drama with its refreshing thematic treatment and formal innovations, and disturbing some others with its radically different reinterpretation of the traditional story, *Pan Jinlian* touched off another heated nationwide debate. Some acclaimed the play as a milestone in contemporary cultural history and a powerful protest against Chinese "feudal morality" and its contemporary variation, "ultraleft orthodox morality," which imposed feudalistic restrictions on relations between male and female citizens. Wei Minglun's redramatization of *Pan Jinlian*, they argued, revealed the necessity of "sexual liberation" not only for Chinese women but for the nation's search for sociocultural modernity.[46] The concept of "sexual liberation," directly translated from English, was thus formally introduced and quickly disseminated in contemporary Chinese literary criticism. Others, however, denounced the play as a grave sociocultural misrepresentation in which a hedonistic, self-indulgent, and thoroughly traditional woman is glorified as an icon for women's liberation. "This play is written and produced with explicit pragmatic social purpose," a senior critic wrote; "it is certainly not just about a traditional story and a woman who was victimized by China's feudal tradition. The play's immediate implications for Chinese society in the 1980s are more than visible, as the author himself also declared. In our society today, while rapidly increasing numbers of middle-aged and younger men are carrying on extra-marital and premarital affairs, and the percentage of teenagers' love affairs has also been quickly rising, Wei's Pan Jinlian, who is driven by her impulsive individual sexual desires to 'justifiably' murder her husband, can indeed help those men to achieve and justify their 'sexual liberation.' The sex is liberated, but this has nothing to do with women's liberation."[47] As in some of the previous controversies, the oppositions had little interest in the complexity of the play as a many-layered artistic work and less patience to explore the issues broached by it: problems of gender in the gender-blind discourse of state socialism, the issue of sex in a society in which only four decades earlier Confucian patriarchy was still the official ideology and concubinage was legal, and the changing configurations of gender, sex, and class in a women-friendly and at the same time paternalistic state that is presently dismantling some of its established social mechanisms while generating a market economy, with all its usual women-hostile consequences, such as the return of the oldest form of sexual exploitation—prostitution. All these issues and more that are contained in this play and its receptions, unfortunately, have not been explicated in this debate.

Unlike the debates over Small Well or WM, however, the controversy about Pan Jinlian was quickly concluded with a general affirmation of the play as a great artistic work offering a powerful critique of both "feudalist moral codes" and "ultraleft orthodoxy" about human sexuality. It is significant that although leading cultural luminaries of the reform era such as Wang Meng and Liu Zaifu celebrated the flourishing of an "era of cultural pluralism,[48] in the theater world Pan Jinlian hardly engendered genuine critical exchanges and substantial controversy at all. Instead, Chinese dramas written and produced in the late 1980s were regularly acclaimed by critics as protests against "feudal ultraleftism" or as arguments for "reform and open-door policy," "modernity," and "individuality." Until, that is, the social and political explosion of 1989 and the imposed silence that followed June 4. The national success of Pan Jinlian, and the brief but highly visible controversy it aroused, temporarily masked the disturbing fact that from the mid-1980s the theater world as a whole was drastically declining. Film, television, and various popular entertainments flourishing in urban areas since the mid-1980s surpassed theater as the medium attracting national attention. As early as 1983, more than one hundred new films were released annually, and 87 percent of the households in Beijing and Shanghai already had television sets.[49] "Every evening," a noted dramatist wrote in 1983, "several TV channels offer interesting programs, more than ten cinemas show various Chinese and foreign films, each theater stages musical dramas, dancing dramas, and other popular performances—people now have many choices for a leisured evening. If we want to attract the audience to come and see our spoken dramas, we have to offer something special."[50] Theater, in short, had been increasingly challenged by the rapidly changing social conditions and larger patterns of the nation's cultural life.

Emblematic of those changes, the Chinese film and television industries had been visibly rising since the mid-1980s. As the percentage of urban households that had television sets increased with unprecedented speed and programs and channels with commercial advertisements multiplied, so did the time that people spent in front of the television. Although the sociocultural impact of the television industry on the general public was increasing in the mid-1980s, the film industry, which reached its most productive period in its quantity and technical quality, captured most of the public attention.[51] The rise of the once humble Xian Film Studio best exemplified such changes. Led by Wu Tianming, appointed manager of Xian Film in 1983, the studio produced a series of national hits and, in 1985, sold more copies of its films than any other studio in the country. In 1987, its films won seven of the eleven national Golden Rooster Awards and several prestigious international prizes.[52] Provoking strong responses at a variety of international film festivals while stirring excitement and controversy within China, these films registered the dynamics of modern Chinese history as much as the changes in the history of Chinese film.

Wu Tianming was recognized as one of the most forceful figures in film by the mid-1980s and an outstanding director in national and international film circles. Among eleven awards he received as a film director, five were international; among the five films he had directed, Old Well, released in 1986, was awarded two national and three international prizes.[53] With a narrative style strikingly distinguished from those of realist films made by such leading senior directors as Xie Jin and Wu Yigong, Old Well fascinated audiences with its innovative use of heavy color and strong light, creative appropriation of folk and rural imageries, highly assertive and theatrical cinematic representation, and enormous emotional energy. The film focuses on villagers who live and labor under the harshest physical conditions. Generation after generation of these villagers searched for water, the most precious source of life and hope, in a severely barren mountainous area. Their heroic-tragic persistence and the allegorical significance of their struggles are powerfully revealed through the cinematic narration, which is at once brutally realistic and intensely symbolic. Rewriting the realist tradition of Chinese film with its allegorical narrativity, Old Well paved the way for and heralded most creative features of the "fifth generation" of Chinese film directors. Embraced by Chinese viewers and acclaimed by Western critics, it significantly altered the landscape of Chinese cinematic culture.

The national and international recognition of Wu Tianming's Old Well caused complex but positive reactions as well as nationwide controversy in China. Some cultural critics and administrators asserted that the film gained attention in the West by representing Chinese society and people's lives in a most degrading way, exaggerating and even fabricating China's dehumanizing rural poverty and backwardness to please Western critics and audiences who held culturally and racially prejudiced stereotypes about the inferior "yellow race." Others contended that the film embodied the most precious spirit of the Chinese people and its culture, namely, the indomitable tenacity and determination to live and to develop under the most severe natural and social conditions. The international recognition the film won, they further argued, should be celebrated as a victory of Chinese culture asserting itself in the world and not taken as negative evidence against the film itself. As the Chinese economy, according to the general orientation set up by the reform policies of the nation, must find ways to enter the international economy, Chinese cultural production must make every effort to enter the global cultural market. *Old Well* was exemplary in taking the lead in "going into the world."[54]

The debate over *Old Well* concluded with unequivocal praise of the work by most members of the Chinese cultural world, but the complex questions regarding export-oriented cultural products in the international economic and cultural market were far from being resolved. Although 1985 to 1987 became known as the "golden years of Chinese film" for the unprecedented influence that film exerted throughout the nation compared with other performing arts, particularly spoken drama, financial support from the government for the film industry soon declined. This reduction of government financial support generated an urgent need for alternative resources. From 1987 onward, driven by the need to find more adequate financial support, attracted by the glamour and wealth that international recognition implied, and further pushed by the policies designed by the Chinese reform leadership to promote production for export, the Chinese film industry resorted to foreign investment and to making films for international markets. Competition for overseas financing among film directors intensified, and some turned completely to the Western film market starting in the late 1980s. Zhang Yimou's *Raise the Red Lantern* (1991) and *Shanghai Triad* (1995) and Chen Kaige's *Farewell My Concubine* (1993) and *Temptress Moon* (1997) were among the latest sensations so created. That the majority of the Chinese audience showed less and less interest in these films, even deeply disliking Zhang's *Red Lantern* in particular, contrasted sharply with the nationwide enthusiasm that Wu Tianming's *Old Well* once evoked.[55]

The problematic implications of the increasing fame of certain Chinese films since the late 1980s in the world film market can be partly seen in the marketing and distribution of Zhang Yimou's *Red Lantern*. Financed from Hong Kong and Japan and catering to the Eurocentric mindset that has dominated the international cultural market in general and film market in particular, *Red Lantern* offered a brilliant cinematic fabrication and a conscious exoticization of the Chinese concubine system in the 1920s and its erotic politics. The high-profile coverage and sensational praise the film received in the Western media contrasted with the ambiguous comments in Chinese newspapers, revealing an emerging process of "orientalizing" Chinese culture and people, a process consciously joined by some Chinese artists who won international fame bestowed by Western patronage with monetary rewards.[56] This process has begun to induce serious critical examinations.

Meanwhile, the television industry had been undergoing intensifying commercialization since the late 1980s. Media products from Hong Kong, Taiwan, Japan, and the West were imported in increasing quantities, and by 1988 nearly 60 percent of television programs in Shanghai and Beijing were imported from the West or Japan or patterned after Hong Kong and Taiwan commercial styles.[57] As many Western scholars of contemporary China have emphasized, the rise of the television industry in the 1980s was one of the most significant developments in modern Chinese cultural history. Unlike its counterpart in the West, however, its rapid development since the mid-1980s was generated not only by the growing forces of the domestic economy and technology but also by the aggressive expansion of Western consumer culture and its variations in the "Kong/Tai" (Hong Kong and Taiwan) style into China.[58]

These changes in film production and the rise of the television industry, emblematic of the formation of a performing arts market in China and the changes in the nation's cultural life, were inseparable from, and to a certain degree illustrative of, an overall economic and social transformation. The increasing commodification of society and the further opening of the nation to Western multinational capital and ideology, particularly since the late 1980s, have been structurally redefining the modes of production and the fundamental ways of life of the Chinese. When pursuit of material wealth began to dominate society's imagination and dictate the lives of individual citizens, cultural activity that was not yet commercialized appeared increasingly superfluous and anachronistic. While the government was cutting funds on one hand and the declining audience was cutting the box office on the other, the theater world as a whole was rapidly sinking into total crisis. By 1988, in the words of Yin Ruocheng, then vice minister of culture, "a large percentage of spoken drama companies nationwide are nearly dead." His solution: "We must disband more theater companies at all levels, adopt a contract system, and promote tourist performances."[59]

Confronted with this crisis, dramatists of critical realist and experimental modernist persuasions responded in very different ways. Many of the realists were disturbed by commercialization and what they called "Hongkongization" and "Taiwanization" of Chinese culture. As early as 1985, after Hu Qili's speech on artistic freedom, leading dramatists of critical realism gathered in Beijing to discuss "freedom of artistic creation and artists' historical missions."

Wang Peigong, the author of *WM*, evoked the threat of cultural commodification to spoken drama in the following comments:

All the programs produced by the central television network for the Spring Festival this year, including that Hong Kong-style "New Year's Eve Show" and that traditional music drama preluded by a comic actor embracing a big shoe-shaped piece of gold, were utterly disappointing to the mass audience. "So this is called 'freedom of art?!'" many asked. Some answered: "Why make such a fuss? This is merely the beginning!" If such a "beginning" continues, more of the audience will be driven out of theater and cinema. How then can we talk about literary and artistic prosperity? Such a "beginning," I don't need to repeat, will make some men of letters "freely" run into fatal pitfalls![60]

Echoing Wang's comments, Zhong Jieying, another noted playwright of the Beijing People's Art Theater Company, warned: "Please cherish what we have finally won, namely, the right to write what we truly feel and think about our lives. If we let our art be dominated by those fashionable performances that imitate Hong Kong and Taiwan tastes and let money-dictated publications including pornography dominate our society, freedom will lose its true value and become just another form of falsehood."[61] Most dramatists of the critical realism school shared these views, as many essays printed in journals and speeches made at meetings indicate; yet how to further understand or deal with those "pitfalls" and "falsehoods," few of them seemed to know.

Similarly uncertain about the fate of modern Chinese drama, and indeed the future direction of the country as a whole, dramatists of experimental modernism responded to the changing situation with diverse views. Some followed the impulses offered by European modernist "negative theology" and went further and further into an isolated agony and despair over the "ultimate meaninglessness of being"; others turned into unconditional admirers and proponents of Western modernity and its ideology, identifying the idealized images created by eighteenth-century European rhetoric of "liberty," "equality," and "fraternity" with historical realities. They shared, however, the rhetorical assertion that the socially engaged and committed tradition of modern and contemporary Chinese literature and art was the culprit responsible for the multiple crises of Chinese culture in general and Chinese drama in particular.[62] Literature and art, some of them insisted, were expressions of individual subjectivity endowed with universal humanity, and anything that involved social issues was doomed as pseudoart repugnant to "our modern audience." Such pseudo art and literature, it was further argued, were deeply rooted in the tradition of classical Chinese aesthetics, which emphasized the social and ethical function of literary activity and was simply a feudal legacy that should be eradicated from "modern" ways of artistic thinking.[63] Critical realism, with its announced engagement with the social, political, cultural, and emotional conditions of the nation, was thereby viewed as another variant of "ideological orthodoxy," a descendant of "feudalism" and its modern reincarnation, "ultraleftism," outdated, petrified, and bound to be discarded by "new waves of world history."[64] Increasing numbers of playwrights of critical realism, including Zong Fuxian, Xin Yixun, Li Jie, and Li Longyun were implicitly criticized and at times explicitly ridiculed.[65]

It is here that the problematic tensions between the school of critical realism and that of experimental modernism became explicit. As early as 1985, in an interview with an American journalist, Li Longyun made the following comments:

> What's most attractive about a writer is his or her own character, and what is most appealing about a nation is its own cultural spirit and form of living . . . . A play is significant internationally if it is characterized by its own unique artistic style and resonates with its own profound cultural traditions. I believe that our productions of plays like Rhinoceros and Bald Soprano cannot surpass the productions by Western theater companies, but I dare say that there is no theater in the entire world that can produce a better production of Teahouse than the Beijing's People's Art Theater Company.[66]

More polemical phrases like "superficial imitators," "self-styled westernizers," and "trick players and claptrappers" were coined by some critics to characterize some of the modernists, indicating the degree to which this conflict was emotionalized.[67] While modernist plays staged in cities like Shanghai accounted 74 percent of all the productions mounted in the years from 1985 to 1989, a large proportion of these dramas, with intentionally obscure language and westernized images, were less and less appealing to the general public.[68] Despite the effusive praise they received from some theater critics, the theater of experimental modernism in the late 1980s was losing the genuine cultural energies and critical thrusts operating in the pioneering modernist works of the earlier years and, more important, was losing the remaining part of the general audience for spoken drama.

The deep tension between the two drama schools voiced by some critics and dramatists, such as Wang Peigong and Li Longyun, interestingly enough, has never been adequately explored in the theater world. As China's structural economic changes encouraged further commodification of society and were closing the social spaces once occupied by such noncommercial forms of culture as spoken drama, a sizable proportion of the nation's leading playwrights and drama theoreticians either remained silent on topics of urgent social relevance or stretched themselves to comply with whatever currents that were carrying the day. Those who insisted upon the organizing principles of socially engaged critical realism and "Chinese cultural styles" in their literary practice and theories often appeared defensive and reactive rather than creative or initiative; Zong Fuxian and Xi Yixun, among others, managed to criticize their own playwriting with explicit anxiety and hidden ambivalence.[69] While further socioeconomic changes forced even the most ontolog-ical or transcendental modernists to confront the empty theater houses in the late 1980s, most of them seemed desperately frustrated and deeply lost rather than capable of asserting alternatives as they once appeared so confident in doing. The ambivalent responses of some—and the significantly absent responses of others—to the crises of Chinese spoken drama since the mid-1980s indicate the historical profundity and complexity of the crisis in rela-tion to a changing society.

As the decade of the 1980s was ending, financial support for theater from the government was further reduced to subsistence or a lower than subsistence level. The Ministry of Culture in 1987–1988 began to enforce an "employee contract system" in theater companies for their new hiring, and such basic principles as job security, free medical care, and other benefits were done away with. For those dramatists who joined the companies before this contract system was enforced and hence still retained some benefits, particularly free medical care, the State Council adopted a new policy that "strongly encour-aged" them to stop being dependent on the company for their income and to take the initiative to organize individual performances to make a living for themselves. Meanwhile, more theater companies were disbanded. In 1987 alone, for instance, five spoken drama troupes in Liaoning Province were closed.[70] The degree of change in government policy in the late 1980s was demonstrated emphatically when *Jüben* (Drama), the national drama journal that was founded in 1952 and contained essentially the entire history of con-temporary Chinese drama ever since—except during the Cultural Revolution years—lost its annual funding from the cultural administration in 1988.[71] The editors and staff members of the journal refused to let it be closed. They made a historically unprecedented and emotionally charged national appeal for donations, and managed to continue its publication. The national theater journal *Xijübao* (On theater), on the other hand, did not lose its funding entirely. But with its funding drastically reduced it was compelled to change its title to *Zhongguo xiju* (Chinese theater), and it started issuing "popular edi-tions" containing photos of sexualized women and violent, sensational stories to increase revenues.[72] Moneymaking had become the real priority for theater companies and drama publishing houses at all levels, and more theater com-panies were turned into nightclubs.[73] A large number of playwrights gave up playwriting and started working for the television industry or joined other lucrative commercial activities; a larger number of actors left the stage of spoken drama and contracted for various commercial performances to make a living; driven by the profit-making pressures at home and lured by the spells of Hollywood films and American-style mass culture industries abroad, many artists left the country altogether and joined the largest "brain drain" from China in the twentieth century.[74]

Still, some of the finest playwrights, directors, and dramatic artists of the nation remained with their chosen vocation and continued their creative efforts. The dramatic works of fine artistic quality written and produced in the last two years of the 1980s, therefore, cannot be fully appreciated without understanding the turbulent social, economic, and cultural situation in which Chinese dramatists struggled. Faced with a wide array of night entertainment, neon-light advertisements for Western consumer goods such as MTV, legal or illegal imported videotapes, magazines, and pornography, Hong Kong, Taiwan, and American television programs and Rambo films, discos and Japanese-style karaoke singing, theater productions appearing in the last years of the 1980s were not only outstanding artistic works but heroic triumphs for the much undermined, confused, and distressed world of Chinese spoken drama. *Sangshuping jishi* (Sangshuping chronicles) was such a play, and it is therefore chosen as the last dramatic text in this discussion.[75]

Staged by the Central Drama Academy in Beijing in 1988, *Sangshuping* is set in a northern Chinese village during the late years of the Cultural Revolution. It dramatizes how the "high rhetoric" of militant radicalism during the Cultural Revolution had no real connection at all with the villagers' lives and was used only by traditional patriarchal forces in the socioeconomically backward countryside. The patriarchal tradition perpetuated by rural poverty and the victimization of women by such cultural traditions and economic conditions are both emphatically dramatized. The love stories of the young and their tragic endings are movingly represented. As a condemnation of the die-hard patriarchal and traditional forces operating through "ultraleftism" during the Cultural Revolution, the play did not go beyond the accomplishment of plays of critical realism like *Small Well Alley*. The crucial difference between the plays produced in previous years and *Sangshuping Chronicles*, however, lies in the fact that the former's critiques of social, political, and cultural illnesses were intertwined with their authors' call for a genuine practice of socialist ethics and democracy in accordance with the common folk's needs and desires, while the latter holds the patriarchal mentality of "the common folk" in rural China perpetuated by their extreme economic poverty as one more major source of the social illnesses persisting in society. The causes of the tragedies of Sangshuping, the play suggests, are not only the abuse of power by officials and their institutional mechanisms, but the extreme rural poverty and the cruel ignorance of the peasantry rooted in their poverty and associated traditional values.

Such a difference is particularly striking when one compares this play with the film *Old Well*, which deals with a similar type of rural lives. While *Old Well's* villagers share many of Sangshuping's problems, their human spirit to not only persist but struggle to change their lives is recognized and represented with intimate understanding and deep emotional resonance. In Sangshuping, no such spirit survives. Whereas the two leading women characters in *Old Well* assert their strong individualities and their ability to define their own forms and values of living, in *Sangshuping* the two leading women characters become simply victims—one goes insane and the other commits suicide. *Old Well* unfolds with the life of Wangquan, a young man with a modern education who returns to his home village to live, suffer, work, and fight; *Sangshuping* is seen through the observant eye of Zhu Xiaoping, in whom the authorial voice speaks. Unlike Wangquan, Zhu is the only character in the play who is not from the village but from another world—China's large urban centers. Although his sociopolitically privileged family background is presented with critical reflection in the play when Zhu is shown using it to help the villagers, his constant gaze is clearly enacted as a perspective of "the modern" that organizes this dramatic narrative of "the traditional." Indeed, one may well argue that *Old Well* is a story told as the villagers live through it, while the *Sangshuping* story is told as a self-conscious modernist sees it. Many of the critical insights into the Chinese peasantry in the play are certainly invaluable in heightening the sense of urgency to "enforce fundamental social reform" and "eliminate feudalistic ignorance," as the director of the play puts it.[76] But the structuring of the play is also underlined by a narrative distance that allows a fair amount of objectification of the villagers. By turning them into carriers and victims of "feudalistic" ignorance and cruelty without any intrinsic resources for effective change, the play implies a prescription for saving the Chinese peasantry from itself—a "modernization" that seems a negation of the "backward lives" of the Sangshuping village rather than a consolidation of the desires and strengths for change coming from its inhabitants.

The much emphasized focus of the production is on aesthetic experimentation. Incorporating elements of traditional Chinese music drama and techniques of Western modernist theater in an innovative, unique, and coherent performing style, the play is full of images of poetic richness and allegorical suggestiveness, fluid spatial constructions and temporal transmutations, and expressive representations of individual characters' feelings and their shared living situation. As the performance was going on in the Academy's little theater, all noted theater critics and cultural administrators in Beijing, including Yin Ruocheng, then the minister of culture, hailed it as "the crystallization of the finest achievements of contemporary Chinese dramatic art."[77] While such celebration is grounded in the remarkable aesthetic experimentation of this production, it cannot substitute for substantial explication of the complex signification of the play and its prescriptive "call for fundamental social reform." As if being somewhat displaced by the promotion of its aesthetic innovation in itself, discussions of any substance about the play—its form in relation to its content, for instance—were visibly absent in the entire celebration of this "theatrical triumph." The show "closed after fewer than twenty performances at the Academy's little theater."[78]

Such triumphs on stage, moreover, were fewer and fewer, as the prescriptions for the nation's modernization with a "global vision" were intensifying in the public discourse, indicating the degree to which tensions between the public program for "national progress" and the lives of China's ordinary citizens were growing. After the tragic events of 1989, no one can say that the theater world remained unchanged, but the essential tensions and crises discussed above persisted and developed. While market-led reform was in temporary retrenchment from late 1989 to late 1991, there appeared a momentary resurgence of spoken dramas reasserting "socialist spirit and morality."[79] After Deng Xiaoping's trip to southern China in the spring of 1992 and the Fourteenth Party Congress in the fall calling for speeding up the implementation of reform policies gearing the society toward a "socialist market economy," however, this momentary resurgence was eclipsed and commodification further dictated sociocultural trends.[80] Although a "middleclass theater" was advocated by some critics and dramatists in the late 1980s and then again in the early 1990s, most Chinese artists who remained in their profession seemed to have realized that they were living in a painful period during which the most they could do might be to keep their dramatic activity alive on a small scale and continue to prepare for a resurgence in the future—whatever that might be.[81] In his essay "Our Hope for Spoken Drama Lies in the New Century," Zhao Yaoming, a noted playwright in Nanjing, predicted that it would take thirty or so years for China to succeed with its market reforms and to turn itself into "a prosperous, democratic, socially integrated, and culturally developed country" with a fully established middle class. Until then, it seemed to Zhao, modern spoken drama, conditioned by the necessities of Chinese social history, had no alternative but to continue its struggle to survive in its diminished and diminishing social spaces.[82]

While hope for the revitalization of modern Chinese drama seemed to be placed by some critics and dramatists in the twenty-first century, with an ideal audience of an imagined Chinese middle class, some American- and Western-run commercial theaters began to gain social and institutional ground in cities like Shanghai.[83] Meanwhile, the last group of playwrights and dramatists were leaving the realm of spoken drama; 95 percent of the students in the 1992 class at the Shanghai Drama Academy chose to write television scripts to fulfill the requirements for their degrees.[84] A news item in South Evenings on July 21, 1993, reported that playwrights in Beijing had all stopped writing plays; some retired, some started working for commercial television, and some "jumped into" the "sea of business." The situation in such provincial centers of spoken drama as Hubei and Liaoning was even worse than in Beijing. In the south, Shanghai, Nanjing, and Guangzhou are faring slightly better; there have been occasional productions of spoken dramas, but they are by and large not well attended.[85] Among the few plays to win some national media coverage in the beginning of the 1990s, one was an adaptation of

Harold Pinter's *The Lover* in Shanghai in August 1992, containing a love-making scene; another was a new play called *Taiyang wan* (Harbor of the sun) by Chu Yue in Beijing in May 1993, which had a female nude scene.[86] While female nudity was certainly not the sole attraction of these two plays, they did not seem to offer much for sustained artistic or social discussion. As a Chinese scholar noted in 1994: "Since a certain kind of capitalism is developing in China now, theater companies can no longer operate as they have since the inception of the People's Republic in 1949."[87]

Modern Chinese drama continues to exist, however, no matter how small its scale of production and how limited its social influence may be for the moment. Contemporary dramatists are still searching for ways to keep their art alive, no matter how much they have to turn to commercial activities for their living.[88] In the early 1990s in Nanjing a series of innovative performances in small and at times temporary theaters were produced by artists who put their limited individual financial resources together, and "the Nanjing little theater movement" became nationally known.[89] In Beijing, there also appeared various sponsoring programs, and all the shows produced in the 1990s have had substantial public or private donations. *Niao ren* (Bird men), a three-act spoken drama, was mounted by the People's Art Theater in April–May 1993 with such subsidies and was extremely well received by the audience.[90] In Shanghai, artists organized stage readings of noncommercial scripts, and some of them led to formal and successful public productions. *Loushang de marjin* (The karaoke upstairs), staged by the Shanghai People's Theater in June 1994, was one such success. In all these productions supported by various financial sources, the organizing principles of experimental modernism developed since the early 1980s clearly leave their marks on dramatic texts and performances, particularly in their structural constitutions and technical effects; but a return of critical realism in their dramatic narratives is also undeniable and potent.

The return of critical realism in the first half of the 1990s is in fact beginning to show increasing prominence in the struggling theater world. *The Karaoke Upstairs* is a case in point. Written by Zhang Xian, formerly a student of Shanghai Drama Academy and currently the most active playwright in Shanghai, the play dramatizes the life of a young female receptionist at a luxury hotel who prostitutes her body to help her struggling working-class family, and the life of a female stockbroker who has done away with any family ties while devoting her body and soul to the speculations at the newly opened and fluid "futures market." The former has an elder brother whose salary as a factory worker cannot keep the family going but who condemns his once "sweetest baby sister" for being "brazenly immoral," and the latter has a temporary lover from Taiwan who seems to be plunged into a desperate search for "human feelings" in Shanghai by his transnational property and wealth. As the brother is reduced to seeking help from his sister after he admits that he actually wants "the immoral money," the love-hungry man from Taiwan sinks into a hysterical rant on the inhumanity of the world after he realizes that his longing for "feelings" is returned with the financial calculation of his Shanghai female partner for "blue chips." The play ends with the stockbroker sitting at the window of her hotel room gazing into the silent starry sky of a busy Shanghai night, as the "sweetest baby sister"-turned-prostitute at the hotel reception desk hums the "Team Song of the Young Pioneers" that every Chinese child since 1949 knows by heart, remembering her elementary-school days when she was the youngest and most beloved of her class: "Father," she says with a choking voice, "I have received an A again for my Chinese literature test." The production had five evening performances, and each had a full house in attendance.[91]

Sharing the dramatic dynamics of critical realism but with more allegorical significance, *Bird Men* is also among the noteworthy plays of the 1990s. Centering on a group of Beijing residents who love Beijing Opera and the traditional culture of bird breeding, the play dramatizes how their encounters with Westerners and overseas Chinese generate tensions. As the story unfolds, a sociocultural gathering place for those who breed their birds and practice the art of Beijing Opera is one day taken over by an overseas Chinese and turned into a psychoanalysis clinic, holding all those bird breeders and Opera lovers as patients. The place is visited by a representative of an international organization for bird protection; through an English translator, this representative accuses the bird breeders of various cruelties against birds, including violating bird rights by putting them into beautiful cages. Meanwhile, he awards a medal to a Chinese Dr. Chen, who specializes in "birdcology" and makes vivid specimens out of living rare birds, asserting that "specimen making of rarity is a great contribution to preserving and collecting rare birds and animals of the world."[92] As the overseas Chinese uses Freud to analyze the "Chinese neuroses" and the Western representative actively forces "international regulations" into the culture of Chinese bird breeding, the leading character of the play—a longtime Beijing Opera performer—turns both of them into objects of investigation. By showing how the overseas Chinese knows precious little about China and Freud and is fundamentally incoherent, he unmasks this expert on "Chinese neuroses" as a cultural charlatan. By showing how Dr. Chen is a bird killer with obsessive compulsions for sinister acquisition, he tells the representative of "bird protectors international" to never again "come and issue these sorts of medals!" When the representative protests his right to come and issue medals since "now we live in a single globalized world," the Beijing Opera performer replies: "You are protected by the consular jurisdiction; otherwise you need to worry about your doggy-life! Now guys, get him out!"[93] Although the play never spares the Beijing Opera master his sense of profound crisis, it offers an allegorical story that clearly registers not only a probing self-reflection but a certain nationalist impulse that is critical of both the Chinese Dr. Chen and the Western representatives. With its mixture of Chinese and Western humor, modern and traditional as well as official and colloquial language styles, the play seized the imagination of the audience in Beijing and topped the list of most popular shows in 1994.

Despite the often overwhelming difficulties in mounting them on the public stage, the return of critical realist dramas with an allegorical turn persists. Such a return can also be seen in the continuing efforts to stage modern historical dramas of realist-allegorical significance in the mid-1990s. *Xinhai chao* (The tidal currents in the year Xinhai), a powerful dramatization of the mass movement in Sichuan Province in 1911 to protect the Chinese railway construction against the encroachment of Western imperialist forces with which the Manchu court was collaborating, was produced in 1991. *Shangyang*, a play about a famous minister in the Warring States (17–11 B.C.) who resolutely sought to reform the court, promote economic growth, and consolidate the state by establishing the legal system and carrying out its enforcement, was staged in 1996. Shangyang was put to death by the nobility after the old emperor died, but the systems and mechanisms established by his reform remained as the core of the great success of the state of Qin.[94] The implications of both plays for the continuing Chinese reform and its shifting, contested, and contradictory orientations in the late twentieth century are striking and certainly complex. Dramatists of the 1990s return to history and the lives of ordinary citizens for their artistic inspiration under extremely difficult conditions and with enormous tenacity. The scope of their activity and the influence of their works is nowhere near those of the critical realists in the early 1980s, certainly. The spirit with which they probe the problems and crises in a structurally changed and changing China through dramatic creations, however, will register as a unique chapter with yet-to-be-recognized significance in the history of modern Chinese drama.

The future of modern Chinese drama and dramatists, as a leading scholar of Chinese theater in the modern West once remarked, depends on the future of China's modernization and its repositioning in a "global village" that seems increasingly dominated by multinational and transnational capital.[95] Caught in the historical confluence that has transformed a reform that inspired hopes for socialist democracy into a reform led by the market economy, the playwrights who emerged in the early 1980s and their younger colleagues have to structurally reconstitute themselves and their art while keeping their creative spirit and social commitment alive, confronting the drastically altered conditions of their lives and their country in ever more complex relations to the world at large. A rethinking of their professional mission and a redefinition of their identities are essential to the survival of modern Chinese dramatists and the development of Chinese dramatic culture. It is indeed time to anthologize contemporary Chinese drama, including film scripts, that have been produced since the beginning of the reform era. [These texts offer] those who

love Chinese theater and Chinese culture in particular, and love human creativity and human creations in general, an opportunity to reflect upon what
has happened in the turbulent past two decades and to ponder what might be
created in the future—in China as in the world.

NOTES

1. There is another category of Chinese dramatic literature, namely, "modern historical drama." Regional music drama (which has had a long history beginning in the
twelfth century) and modern spoken drama (which made its appearance in 1907 and
has been developing since) are often viewed as the two major genres of modern
Chinese theater. Modern historical drama, created by Guo Moruo in 1923 and practiced by many distinguished Chinese dramatists ever since, may well be ranked as
another major genre in modern Chinese theater. For more information on the aesthetic features and significance of this genre, see Yan Haiping, "Modern Chinese
Drama and Its Western Models: A Critical Reconstruction of Chinese Subjectivity,"
Modern Drama, March 1992, 54–64; Yan Haiping, "Male Ideology and Female Identity: Images of Women in Four Modern Chinese Historical Plays," *Journal of Dramatic
Theory and Criticism*, fall 1993, 61–81.

2. The government under the Nationalist Party (Guomindang), headed by
Chiang Kai-shek, ruled China from 1928 to 1949 before the Chinese Communist
Party, led by Mao Zedong, came to power and founded the People's Republic of China.

3. Colin Mackerras, *Chinese Drama: A Historical Survey* (Beijing: New World Press
1990), 167.

4. Lao She and Tian Han were among the most prominent spoken dramatists who
died during the Cultural Revolution. Between the years 1966 and 1976, the member-
ship of the Writers Association dropped from 1,059 to 865. Most of the decrease was
due to deaths, and most of these deaths occurred between 1966 and 1969, the height
of the Cultural Revolution. See Bonnie S. McDougall, "Writers and Performers, Their
Works, and Their Audiences in the First Three Decades," in *Popular Chinese Literature and Performing Arts in the People's Republic of China, 1949–1979*, ed. Bonnie S.
McDougall (Berkeley and Los Angeles: University of California Press, 1984), 304 n.
69.

5. See "Xinchangzheng yü xinshiming: fukan zhi duzhe" (New long march and
new mission: to the readers on the day when *Drama* resumes its publication), *Jüben*
(Drama), January 1979, 2. Mao Zedong's wife, Jiang Qing, was one of the members of
the Cultural Revolution Committee in 1966 and leader of its radical "Gang of Four."
The very few spoken dramas that were allowed to be staged professionally during the
decade, carrying political messages promoted by the Gang of Four, indicated the
minimal possibility of survival for spoken drama on the professional stage as a whole.
It should be noted, however, that amateur performances of dramatic stories created by

amateur writers in factories, schools, and other working units in urban areas were widespread. Those performers also brought their shows to rural areas. In the rural areas where the land was fertile and farming was comparatively advanced, many production teams used their resources to organize young people to create their own amateur performances as well.

6. Zong Fuxian, *Yü wusheng chu* (From the depth of silence), *Renmin xijü* (People's theater), December 1978, 49–76; Sha Yexin, *Chenyi shizhang* (Mayor Chenyi), *Jüben* (Drama), May 1997, 2–40; Cui Dezhi, *Baochun hua* (Spring flower), *Jüben* (Drama), April 1979, 2–47; Xing Yixun, *Quan yü fa* (Power versus law), *Jüben* (Drama), October 1979, 2–34; Su Shuyang, *Danxin pu* (Noble hearts), *Renmin xijü* (People's theatre), May 1978, 16–80.

7. Zhang Chunqiao, Yao Wenyuan, Jiang Qing, and Wang Hongwen represented the radical forces during the Cultural Revolution. The term "the Gang of Four" was used by Mao Zedong in referring to them critically at a Politburo meeting in the late 1960s and has been used extensively since 1979, when the four were arrested by Ye Jianying, one of the ten marshals of China, with the support of the army and Hua Guofeng, then the first vice chairman of the Chinese Communist Party and the prime minister of the PRC. Many of those plays are fictional, of course, but some were dramatizations of the lives of senior revolutionaries. For example, *Shuguang* (Dawn), by Zhao Huan (1977), is about the life of He Long; *Chen Yi chushan* (Chen Yi coming out of the mountains), by Ding Yishan (1979), is about the life of Chen Yi. Both He and Chen were among the ten marshals of the PRC.

8. Li Longyun, *You zheyang yige xiaoyuan* (There is such a small compound), staged by the Children's Repertoires Theater of China in Beijing, April 1979; Zhou Weipo et al., *Paobing siling de er'zi* (The artillery commander's son), *Wenhui bao* (Wenhui daily), Shanghai, June 10, 1979; Li Min, *Yige wuangu de shengchan duizhang* (The stubborn production team leader), *Anhui xiju* (Anhui drama), March 1979; Xue Zheng, *Kaolü kaolü* (We shall consider), *Jüben* (Drama), August 1979.

9. Sha Yexin, *Jiaru woshi zhende* (If I were real), *Qishi niandai* (The seventies), Hong Kong, January 1980.

10. Li Longyun, *Xiaojing hutong* (Small Well alley), *Jüben*, May 1981, 3676. A complete English translation of the play by Jiang Hong and Timothy Cheek of Colorado College is available upon request.

11. The Great Leap Forward was launched by Mao Zedong and the PRC leadership in 1958 to speed up growth of the national economy. The movement failed, resulting in a widespread famine from 1959 to 1963. See Maurice Meisner, *Mao's China and After* (New York: Free Press, 1986), 204–51.

12. Archivists of *Jüben*, "Guanyü jige huaju de zhengyi" (Regarding the debates on several spoken dramas), *Jüben* (Drama), February 1985, 94.

13. Li Longyun, "Yü meiguo jizhe de tanhua" (A conversation with an American journalist), *Yingju yuekan* (Film and drama monthly), July 1985, 7.

14. Yan Haiping, *Qinwang Li Shimin* (Li Shimin, prince of Qin), *Jüben* (Drama), October 1981, 10–47.

15. See Yan Haiping, "Xizuo *Qinwang Lishimin* de yixie xiangfa" (Reflections on writing *Li Shimin, prince of Qin*), *Jüben* (Drama), September 1982, 87–90.

16. Wang Guorong, "Ping *Qinwang Lishimin*" (On *Li Shimin, prince of Qin*), *Jiefang ribao* (Liberation daily), July 1, 1982.

17. Yan Haiping, *Qinwang Li Shimin: jüben yü pinglun* (Li Shimin, prince of Qin: Text and Criticism) (Beijing: Chinese Drama Publishing House, 1985), 144–68.

18. Yan Haiping, "Jinjin shi kaishi: Woxie *Qinwang Li Shimin* ("This is just the beginning: I write *Li Shimin, Prince of Qin*") in *Li Shimin, Prince of Qin: Text and Criticism*, 150.

19. Li Zehou's review of the play is one of the fine examples. See *Li Zehou shinianji: 1979–1989* (Collections of Li Zehou's writings from 1979–1989) (Anhui: Anhui's Publishing House for Art and Literature, 1994), 49–51.

20. The television series, *Qinwang Li Shimin* (Li Shimin, prince of Qin), was written by Yan Haiping, directed by Zhang Ge, and produced by Shanghai Television Station, December 1982. In 1982, the play was awarded the national prize for excellence in drama by the Association of Chinese Dramatists and the Chinese Ministry of Culture.

21. Chen Baichen, *Dafengge* (Song of the wind), *Jüben* (Drama), January 1979; Lu Jianzhi and Fang Jiaji, *Tangtaizong* (Grand emperor of Tang), *Jüben* (Drama), April 1982; Zhen Huaixi, *Xintinglei* (Tears shed at the Xin Pavilion), *Jüben* (Drama), August 1982.

22. See "Daoyan de hua" (Words from the director), in the program for the production of Samuel Beckett's *Waiting for Godot* by the Shanghai Drama Academy, 1987.

23. Ma Zhongjun, Jia Hongyuan, and Jü Xinhua, *Wuwai you reliu* (There are warm currents outside of this house), *Jüben* (Drama), June 1980, 55–65.

24. Gao Xingjian and Liu Huiyuan, *Juedui xinghao* (Absolute signals), *Shiyue* (October), a literary quarterly, no. 5, 1982.

25. Gao Xingjian, *Chezhan* (Bus stop), *Shiyue* (October), no. 3, 1983, 119–38.

26. See "Bianzhe an" (Notes from the editor) to "*Chezhan* sanren tan" (A dialogue among three critics on *Bus Stop*), *Xijübao* (On theater), March 1984, 3–7.

27. Wang Ruoshui, "Wei rendaozhuyi bianhu" (An apology for humanism), *Wenhui bao* (Wenhui daily), Shanghai, January 17, 1983.

28. Wang Ruoshui, "Lun yihua" (On alienation), *Xinwen jie* (News front), no. 2, 1980; Zhou Yang, "Makesizhuyi de jige wenti" (On several theoretical issues in Marxism), *Renmin ribao* (People's daily), March 9, 1983.

29. Hu Qiaomu, "Guanyu rendaozhuyi he yihua wenti" (On humanism and the question of alienation), *Xinhua wenzhai* (New China digest), March 1998, 1–17.

30. "Chezhan sanren tan" (A dialogue among three critics on *Bus Stop*) *Xijübao* (On theater), March 1984, 3–7.

31. Jia Hongyuan and Ma Zhongjun, *Jieshang liuxing hongqunzi* (Red skirts are the fashion), staged by the Youth Theater Company of China, June 1984; Liu Shugang, *Yige shengzhe dui sizhe de fangwen* (A visit from a dead man), *Jüben* (Drama), May 1985.

32. See Liu Xinwu and Li Li, "Liu Xinwu tan xingshiqi de bianhua" (Liu Xinwu on the literary changes in the new era), *Wenhui yuekan* (Wenhui monthly) no. 5, 1988.

33. Gao Xingjian, "*Chidao de xiandaizhuyi yü dangjin zhongguo wenxue*" (The slow arrival of modernism and contemporary Chinese literature), a speech at the Conference on Contemporary Chinese Literature and Modernism held in Hong Kong, October 11, 1987, in Gao Xingjian, *Meiyou zhuyi* (No-isms) (Hong Kong: Tiandi Publishing House, 1996), 102.

34. Wang Peigong and Wang Gui, "*WM*" (We), *Jüben* (Drama), September 1985, 6–23. "Rightist" is a political category formally coined and used in the political campaign of 1957 in which half a million people (most of them intellectuals) were labeled as "antisocialist rightists" and punished accordingly. The category continued to exist in Chinese political life until the end of the Cultural Revolution. "Capitalist roader" was a political label coined and used during the Cultural Revolution (1966–1976), referring to those political leaders who allegedly wanted "to restore capitalism in China instead of developing socialism." See Meisner, *Mao's China and After*, 167–397.

35. Staff reporter of *Jüben*, "Fang Women de zuozhe" (An interview with the author of *WM*), *Jüben* (Drama), August 1985, 51.

36. See Yi Min, "*Women fengbo de shizhong*" (The beginning and the end of the controversy on *WM*), *Jüben* (Drama), November 1990, 18–26.

37. Ibid., 18–26.

38. The Society of Dramatic Literature was established in 1985, included many active playwrights of the Dramatists Association, and was chaired by Wang Zhen, the former director of the Chinese Drama Publishing House. See *Jüben* (Drama), November 1985, 91.

39. "Xuexi Hu Qili tongzhi zai zhongguo zuojia di sici daibiao dahui shang de zhuci" (Discussions on Hu Qili's speech at the Fourth Chinese Writers' Congress), *Jüben* (Drama), March 1985, 27–30.

40. "Cong minzhu dao tuanjie de dahui" (A democratic and unifying conference on the Fourth Congress of Theater), *Yingjü yuekan* (Film and drama monthly), June 1985, 3–5. For the names of the members in the newly elected secretariat of the Association of Chinese Dramatists, see *Xijübao* (On theater), June 1985, 3.

41. Wang Buping, "Huajü yishu de xinpianzhang" (A new chapter of modern Chinese spoken drama), *Jüben* (Drama), September 1985, 25–27; Wang Yüsheng,

"Wei xiaojing hutong gongyan erzuo" (For the eventual public production of *Small Well Alley*), *Xijübao* (On theater), March 1985, 12–13.

42. Wan Shuyuan, "Xijü chongbai yü guannian cuojue" (On the phenomenon of worshiping Western theater and its implied conceptual illusions), *Yingjü yuekan* (Film and drama monthly), July 1987, 17–19; Bai Ren, "Waiguo ren shuo . . ." (The foreigners say . . .), *Xijübao* (On theater), July 1986, 50; Ye Tingfang, "Women de shenmei yishi yao jinru xiandai lingyü" (Our aesthetic consciousness should be modernized), *Xijübao* (On theater), October 1985, 18–21.

43. Wei Minglun, *Pan Jinlian: yige nüren de chenlunshi* (Pan Jinlian: The history of a fallen woman), *Xinhua wenzhai* (New China digest), February 1986, 87–99. *Chuanjü* is one of the major Chinese regional music theater forms, originated in Sichuan province; "chuan" means Sichuan, and "jü" means drama.

44. Wei Minglun, "Wo zuozhe feichang huandan de men—Pan Jinlian xiaxiang" (I am having a very absurd dream—some fanciful thoughts on Pan Jinlian), *Xinhua wenzhai* (New China digest), February 1986, 101.

45. Wei Minglun, *Pan Jinlian*, *Xinhua wenzhai* (New China digest), February 1986, 87.

46. Liu Binyan, "Cixiang fengjian youling de lijian-ping chuanjü *Pan Jinlian*" (A sharp sword against feudalism—on *Pan Jinlian*), *Xinhua wenzhai*, (New China digest), September 1986, 102–04.

47. Zhang Yihe, "Chuanjü *Pan Jinlian* de wenti yü qüshi" (The pitfalls and trendy impulses in chuanjü *Pan Jinlian*), *Xijübao* (On theater), October 1986, 40–45.

48. See *Renmin wenxue* (People's literature), January–February 1987. Gao Xingjian, *Meiyou zhuyi* (No-isms), 105.

49. Huang Weijun, "Wodui huajü qiantu zhi duanxiang" (My thoughts on spoken drama's future), *Xijübao*, July 1983, 34.

50. Wang Zhen, "Huajü de miren, caiyou huajümi" (Spoken drama has to be fascinating to have its fans), *Xijübao* (On theater), May 1983, 14.

51. *Zhong guo wenhua nianjian* (Yearbook of Chinese culture) (Beijing: People's Publishing House, 1986–1987).

52. Lan Mu, "Wu Tianming yü xiying de qiji" (Wu Tianming and the miracle of Xian Film Studio), in *Laojing: zhongguo mingzuoxuan-dianying* (*Old Well*: Chinese masterpieces—film), vol. 1, ed. Jiao Xiongping (Taipei: Wanxiang Publishing, 1990), 127.

53. Ibid.

54. Chen Kun, "Yangwang Chang'an—zheli you ge Wu Tianming" (Look up toward Chang'an—there is a Wu Tianming), *Dazhong dianying* (Popular films), September 1987.

55. See, for instance, Dang Yang, *Haiwai feihong* (Letters from overseas) (Beijing: Chinese Federation of Arts and Literature Publishing House, 1996), 93–103; Zhu Ling, "A Brave New World? On the Construction of 'Masculinity' and 'Femininity' in *The Red Sorghum Family*," in *Gender and Sexuality in Twentieth-Century Chinese Literature and Society*, ed. Lu Tonglin (Albany: State University of New York Press, 1993).

56. I use the concept of "orientalizing" in the way that Edward Said articulates it in his *Orientalism* (New York: Vintage Books, 1978). Orientalism, simply put, is a way of defining, creating, controlling, manipulating, and maintaining the cognitive dichotomy between the Western Self and its Other—the Orient and the Oriental—with the former occupying certain "positional superiority" to the latter politically, intellectually, culturally, and morally.

57. This percentage is based on unpublished letters from television producers and critics in both cities from 1987 to 1988.

58. Herbert I. Schiller's essay, "Transnational Media: Creating Consumers World-wide," *Journal of International Affairs* 47 (summer 1993), contains important information regarding this aspect of Chinese media.

59. Ling Sheng, "Huaju jiang zouchudigu: ji Yin Ruocheng buzhang yü xijüjie renshi de tanhua" (Spoken drama will overcome its crisis: the conversations between Minister Yin Ruocheng and representatives of the theater circles from northeastern provinces), *Xijübao* (On theater), January 1988, 4–8.

60. "Chuangzuo ziyou yü lishi shiming" (Artistic freedom and historical mission—a group discussion), *Jüben* (Drama), April 1985, 33.

61. Ibid., 34.

62. Xia Yan, "Guanyü wenxue yü yishu" (On literature and the arts), an interview with Xia Yan by Li Ziyun, *Renmin wenxue* (People's literature), May 1988.

63. Ibid.

64. Deng Hindun, "Zhongguo xiandai xijü meixue yantao de lishi huigu" (Historical reflections on the studies of modern Chinese dramatic aesthetics), *Shanghai xijü* (Shanghai theater), April 1987, 8; Qian Jianping, "Huaju wutai de zaodong—jianlun yizhong xijü pinge" (The restless forces in spoken drama—considerations on a new dramatic style), *Shanghai xijü* (Shanghai theater), February 1988, 33–34.

65. See, for instance, Yü Jun, "Xiandai yishi yü xijü fazhan" (Modern consciousness and the development of drama), *Jüben* (Drama), June 1988, 77; many articles of a similar kind can be found in Shanghai's *Shanghai xijü*, 1986–1989; Beijing's *Xijübao*, 1986–1989; and Nanjing's *Yingjü yuekan*, 1986–1989.

66. Li Longyun, "Yü meiguo jizhe de tanhua" (A conversation with an American journalist), *Yingjü yuekan* (Film and drama monthly), July 1985, 8.

67. Dong Jian, "Lishi de zhuanzhe yü huajü de mingyun" (The transformation of history and the fate of drama), in *Wenxue yü lishi* (Literature and history) (Nanjing: Jiangsu People's Publishing House, 1992).

68. Yü Shuqing, "Xianshi, youzai zhaohuan xianshi zhuyi—jian tan xinshiqi Shanghai de huajü wutai" (Reality is again calling for realism—spoken drama in Shanghai during the reform era), *Shanghai xijü* (Shanghai theater), February 1990, 7.

69. Zong Fuxian, "Wode kunhuo yü zhuiqiu" (My confusions and my searches), *Jüben* (Drama), August 1988.

70. From the archives of the Liaoning Province Branch of the Association of Chinese Dramatists.

71. The editors, "Zhi duzhe" (To the readers), *Jüben* (Drama), December 1988, 27.

72. See *Zhongguo xijü* (Chinese theater), January–March 1989.

73. Feng Zi, "Jüzuojia de shiming" (Playwrights' vocation), *Jüben* (Drama), July 1988, 27.

74. The real number of artists who left China in and since the early 1980s is not adequately documented, although it is well known that the losses of artistic talent across the nation are considerable. The Shanghai Philharmonic Orchestra, for instance, had lost one-third of its musicians by 1986 to Western Europe, the United States, and Canada, among others. After losing 111 members over the past two decades, it currently has 155 musicians and staff members, among whom twenty or so hold passports and reportedly wish to go abroad, according to the orchestra's personnel archives for 1986–1990.

75. Chen Zidu, Yang Jian, and Zhu Xianping, "*Sangshuping jishi*" (Sangshuping chronicles), *Jüben* (Drama), April 1988, 4–28.

76. Xu Xiaozhong, "Sangshuping jishi shiyan baogao" (A report on the stories of Mulberry village experiment), trans. Faye C. Fei, *TDR*, summer 1994, 106–09.

77. Ibid.; also *Xijübao* (On theater), June–August, 1988.

78. Faye C. Fei and William H. Sun, "Stories of Mulberry Village and the End of Modern Chinese Theatre," *TDR*, summer 1994, 132.

79. See *Jüben* (Drama), 1990–1992. *Rishi* (Eclipse, 1990), by Tong Dinmiao, Fang Zi, and Gu Tiangao (from Beijing), *Tianbian you yizu shenghuo* (Sacred fires burning on the horizon, 1990), by Zhen Zhenghuan (from Shandong), *Qingjie* (The complex, 1991), by Xü Yan (from Guangzhou), *Fuqin de chezhan* (Father's station, 1991), by Su Lei (from Beijing), and *Daqiao* (The grand bridge, 1991), by He Guofu (from Shanghai), were among the most notable.

80. In 1992, Deng Xiaoping visited the special economic zones in the coastal areas of southern China. The speeches he made during the visit virtually ended the debates on "the nature of the Chinese reform" that had been escalating after the tragedy of June 4, 1989, centering on the differences between socialist reform and cap-

italist reform. The core of his speech was as follows: "Socialism's real nature is to liberate the productive forces, and the ultimate goal of socialism is to achieve common prosperity." See Maurice Meisner, *The Deng Xiaoping Era* (New York: Hill and Wang, 1996), 516. Deng's proposals for achieving a more rapid pace of development through the adoption of capitalist methods were canonized at the Fourteenth Congress of the Communist Party of China, which met in Beijing from October 12 to October 18, 1992. See Meisner, *Deng Xiaoping Era*, 480.

81. See, for instance, Shao Hongda, "Guanyü huajü fazhan de da shihua" (Some honest remarks on the development of spoken drama), *Jüben* (Drama), February 1988, 58.

82. Zhao Yaoming, "Women ji xiwang yü xinshiji de huajü" (Our hope lies in spoken drama of the new century), *Yingjü yuekan* (Film and drama monthly), February 1992.

83. The theater built in the American International Center-Shanghai Center located on the Nanjing Road is a prominent example.

84. *Shanghai xijü* (Shanghai theater), September 1992.

85. "Jüzuojia zai zuoshenme?" (What have the playwrights been doing lately?), *Nanfang wanbao* (South evening news), July 21, 1993.

86. See *Qiaobao* (The China press), August 31, 1992; *Zhongguo ribao* (China daily), May 2, 1993.

87. David Jiang, "Shanghai Revisited," *TDR*, summer 1994, 79.

88. Ibid., 75–80.

89. The "little theater movement" was described in a letter by Dong Jian, the leading theater scholar and critic in Nanjing, dated June 5, 1994.

90. Gou Shixing, *Niao ren* (Bird men), *Xin jüben* (New drama), March 1993, 3–21.

91. The play has not been published yet. For a brief report on the production, see the Shanghai *Xinmin wanbao* (Xinmin evening news), June 16, 1994, when it was staged in June 1994 in the small theater of the Shanghai People's Theater. The audience, a mixture of university students and urban residents, was very responsive to the emotional turbulence enacted among the four characters in the play.

92. Guo Shixing, *Niao ren* (Bird men), *Xin jüben* (New drama), March 1993, 17.

93. Ibid., 21.

94. He Feng, *Xinhai chao* (The tidal currents in the year Xinhai), *Jüben* (Drama), May 1991, 23–46; Yao Yuan, *Shangyang* (Shangyang), see Li Rong's report, "Lishijü nenfou zaidu huihuang?" (Can modern historical dramas regain their glory?), *Jiefang ribao* (Liberation daily), September 12, 1996.

95. Mackerras, *Chinese Drama*, 223.

chapter eleven

BORDER CROSSINGS:
CHINESE WRITING, IN THEIR
WORLD AND OURS

Howard Goldblatt

Editor's note: Howard Goldblatt reminds the reader of the fundamental role of the translator as "cultural mediator" or "gate-
keeper," who chooses which texts will enter the English-reading
world. Admitting that personal preference influences his own
choice of Chinese texts to translate, Goldblatt argues that increasingly since the 1980s, he has been impressed by Chinese writers
who have abandoned socialist realism and ideology and developed
experimental forms and personal—often alienated and violent—
visions.

*Novelists are totally unethical beings: when the truth of fact and the needs
of fiction conflict, the novelist will always favour the latter.*
—David Lodge, *The Practice of Writing*

NOVELS AND POEMS. Why do we read them? How do we
read them? A puzzling question, perhaps, but the range of answers can be
instructive when dealing with the literary output of China and with its reception in the West. Historically, that is, throughout the twentieth century, the
socio-political intentions and applications of Chinese literature have frequently overshadowed the belletristic for a "foreign" audience; read more as a
window onto contemporary events and society than for its aesthetic or entertainment values, modern and contemporary fiction and verse have tended to
follow, and sometimes subvert, the political and ideological twists and turns
of the nation. Whether because of the nature of the writing or because China,
like so many countries, appears so culturally remote to Western readers, those
few novels, stories, and poems that migrate beyond China's geographical and
linguistic borders attract an audience made up primarily of those who wish to
"learn about China" in a more reader-friendly format than a textbook. Take,
for instance, the following comments from a *New York Times* review of Mo
Yan's "breakthrough" novel, *Red Sorghum*, "In 'Red Sorghum,' Mo Yan intro-

duces Western readers to the unfamiliar culture of provincial China through dozens of vivid characters. By the end, they and Mo Yan have put Northeast Gaomi Township securely on the map of world literature,"[1] or on Jia Pingwa's *Turbulence*, "The Chinese countryside, home to nearly a billion peasants, is described in ways that are both instructive and moving."

That "instructive" precedes "moving" is in itself instructive, for that implies a predetermined, and probably nonliterary, motivation for coming to the Chinese novel in the first place. Novels as textbooks, fiction as sociology, facts over imagination. That, in spite of the verity that "literature is not the best way to learn about other lands and cultures, especially when the literature appears in our own culture's forms, that is, when the literature is familiar in form . . . bent on telling a story in a way we like our stories told."[2] At the risk of seeming overly idealistic, it seems to me that writing from another culture, at its best, tells us not so much about that particular culture as it does about the similarities and dissimilarities of individuals who are nurtured in that culture with those from other societies; a fine point, perhaps, but significant, in that human truths tend not, I believe, to be restricted by spatial or temporal borders, while the various ways to those truths and how they are articulated and experienced give them greater universal meaning.

Sometimes, of course, the works of Chinese authors are praised for their artistic achievements, if not always on their own terms, as illustrated in *Kirkus Reviews*:

> Balzac and Zola would have recognized a kindred spirit in our author, whose extraordinary pictures of the extremes to which human beings drive one another and themselves seem scarcely inferior to their own;

or, as the novelist Amy Tan states on the cover of *Red Sorghum*:

> Having read *Red Sorghum*, I believe Mo Yan deserves a place in world literature. His imagery is astounding, sensual and visceral. His story is electrifying and epic. I am convinced that this book will successfully leap over the international boundaries that many translated works face . . . and that his voice will find its way into the heart of the American reader, just as Kundera and García Márquez have.

This essay has been undertaken in part to supply a "non-Other" context, however superficial or preliminary, to contemporary writing from China, and in part as an introduction for readers who come to that writing in translation, for whatever reason. As a translator first and a critic second, my personal biases will become transparently obvious. That I tend to deal with works and authors I have translated is not as self-serving as it may seem; in a field of endeavor that has attracted few practitioners, I am fortunate to have been free to select and work on much of the best and most appealing fiction written in Chinese, and I cite it here for the reasons that drew me to it, not for the results of the translation. In the role of cultural mediator, for that is what a literary translator becomes, the responsibilities toward authors, texts, and readers are themselves mediated by the pleasures obtained from wrestling with words, concepts, and images from one culture and clothing them in new garb for another.

FROM THERE . . .

Much has changed in Chinese literature since the days of political and ideological extremism ended in the mid 1970s. Writers, who had been hobbled by Maoist demands for socialist-realist literary production for nearly three decades, began to enjoy a bit more freedom in the choice of subject matter and modes of writing, a phenomenon that has continued to the present, with a brief but tragic interruption in June 1989. Poets and novelists, in line with Dengist liberalization/reform policies and a bit of double-edged neglect during the economic boom, have continually pushed the envelope, taking on increasingly controversial topics and experimenting with a variety of writing styles.[3]

While cognizant of the risk of essentialism when characterizing the corpus of writing that has emerged from China over the past decade, I think it is constructive to identify some of its most prominent features, especially in regard to fiction, which is still the most commercially popular, the most engaging, and perhaps the liveliest genre. Foremost among these features is a move away from mimetic realism, that which strives to imitate the real world, toward new forms of expression. The critic David Wang agrees:

> The best contemporary Chinese fiction cannot be classified as realistic in a traditional sense. For those used to seeing modern Chinese fiction as a supplement to social history or as a predictable Jamesonian "national allegory" of sociopolitics, the fiction produced since the late eighties may tell a different story. It shows that literature in the post-Tian'anmen period has not harked back to the old formulas of reflectionism. Precisely because of their refusal either to remain silent or to cry out in an acceptably "realist" way, the new writers see life as an ongoing process, a conglomeration of possibilities and impossibilities. Precisely because of their inability to believe in the one true path through realism to modernism and then postmodernism, or in any melodramatically predictable path through history, contemporary Chinese writers promise new and lively beginnings for the end-of-the-century Chinese imagination.[4]

These "lively beginnings" are most notably anchored in China's past. In encountering novels and stories from fin-de-siècle China, one is struck by an obsession with history and with memory, individual and collective. That is so, I think, for a variety of reasons: First, successful and widely read contemporary writers, most of them in their thirties and forties, are fascinated by China's past, having lost so much of their recent history through the political process. Second, as the cultural critic Rey Chow has stated, "The weight of history bears upon the writing of 'fiction' in such a way as to force one to reflect critically on the space in which the Chinese intellectual has had to live. This is a space without fresh air."[5] Recapturing that past and subjecting it to renewed scrutiny is at the core of some of the most successful fiction in the post-Mao era.

Prominent among this group of writers is Mo Yan, whose re-creations of early twentieth-century Chinese history, especially the war years, in such powerful and panoramic novels as *Red Sorghum* evoke a sense of futility and loss. By merging myth and reality, biographical and historical incidents, heroic and mundane activities, Mo Yan makes a case for cultural degeneration while drawing attention to the way the past is reconstructed, a narrative process that has been characterized as "one that oscillates and mediates between remembered history and imaginative reconstruction." Referring to his hometown and, perhaps, by extension, all of China, as "the most beautiful and most repulsive, most unusual and most common, most sacred and most corrupt, most heroic and most bastardly, hardest-drinking and hardest-loving place in the world," he cries out against China's blind rush to modernity, the human cost of which appears to be civility and morality: "Now I stood before Second Grandma's grave, affecting the hypocritical display of affection I had learned from high society, with a body immersed so long in the filth of urban life that a foul stench oozed from my pores."[6] Modernity as a national icon takes a substantial drubbing from this "peasant writer," while historiography, and perhaps history itself, is problematized, to the horror of the literary establishment and the government it represents.

For writers like Mo Yan, and so many of his contemporaries, history is neither circular nor linear but random and shifting, until the boundaries between past and present blur into obscurity. By denying history its traditional authority, they raise fundamental questions about contemporary life, politics, and values. Historical fiction, once a refuge for writers intent on buttressing or criticizing specific politics or ideologies, has become a showcase of human nature, frequently at its most despicable. The past is now open to a plethora of interpretations by China's writers, who refuse to accept official versions and, in the most extreme cases, do not admit the "possibility" of knowing history at all. The sanctity of history, we learn from these Chinese authors, exists in its mystery and in its possibilities, not in either its glorification or manipulation by ideologues.

Often characterized as members of a lost generation, writers such as these, whose childhood and teen years were spent "making (or, for the youngest, playing at) revolution" in the service of Mao, only to be abandoned by him and left to contemplate their enormous losses in education, family cohesion, and the little pleasures of life, turned naturally to the theme of alienation, especially in the wake of the Tian'anmen Massacre of 1989. Coupled with the heady delights of commercialization, this trend has produced a coterie of novelists and poets whose work reveals a place where surface stability uneasily masks a society in turmoil and whose cynicism has alarmed the official literary community while capturing a considerable readership of like-minded urbanites.

Themes (contents), of course, do not tell all the story. As China stumbles along toward modernity and international respect, its writers have become more experimental, more daring, more self-consciously iconoclastic than ever before. Topics and a host of hybrid narrative strategies once considered taboo now inform the works of many of the writers of fin-de-siècle China. Opaque language, self-reflective and disjointed narratives have, along with unthinkable acts and ideas—from cannibalism to perverted sex—become trademarks of the most conspicuous among them. While they are sometimes accused of pandering to Western tastes, either by filling their work with sensationalist descriptions or dissident views, or by consciously striving for writing with a high degree of "translatability,"[7] these writers are nevertheless becoming more defiant and much more self-assured.

It may seem bewildering that they are published at all, given the seemingly subversive nature of much of their writing; indeed, some of their work does disappear from bookstores under withering attacks by conservative critics. Yet so long as they do not openly attack the Party and leadership or call for a new system of government, the limitations of book distribution, contrasted, say, with movies, and, one hopes, the unrelenting pressure of freedom-to-write advocates and the attention of readers around the world conspire to keep iconoclasm alive and visible. While some of these writers must sometimes publish their work first in Taiwan or, less often, in foreign translation, none with whom I am familiar has yet wound up in jail for a novel, a story, or a poem.

The issue of Western influence, not just on the exploration of nontraditional, even corrupting, topics, but on styles of writing as well, has been widely, and emotionally, debated. Few will deny the influence of the magic-realists of Latin America or the more self-conscious collagistic writings of the Czech novelist Milan Kundera and the like on aspiring writers in the wake of the Cultural Revolution, yet those influences have led to transformations more readily suited to the linguistic, semantic, and cultural realities of China. The highly allusive, myth-laden, and enigmatic stories of a clutch of avant-gardists have plumbed the descriptive powers of the Chinese language as authors have set out to shock and alienate a readership more comfortable with a "reality-anchored" style of writing, whether it is "hard-core" realism or grotesque exposé. In speaking of the avant-garde school, the critic Jing Wang has written:

> [I]ts irreverent attitude toward history and culture is decipherable only when seen
> against the historical context from which it emerged [the economic boom of the

late 1980s]. The young heretics' fabrication of a rootless subject, devoid of memory, was not a mindless pursuit. The making of a subject without a core who narrates without a purpose was a highly subversive act. What the avant-gardists sneered at was the sublime subject construed for a decade by humanist writers and intellectuals. Theirs was a socio-politically centered and culturally invested subject invigorated with a teleological and utopian vision toward life . . . . Posing as seditious elements in the post-Mao era, the avant-gardists adopted an impious attitude toward history. Those who look in their stories for trenchant critiques of the Cultural Revolution will be disappointed. What they display, instead, is a voracious appetite for the clinical depiction of unmotivated violence, which represents a metonymy, rather than just a metaphor, of the historical cataclysm of the Cultural Revolution.[8]

In the sweep of Chinese literary history of this century, this constitutes an unprecedented change in attitude. In characterizing the goals of writers from the pre-communist period, the critic C. T. Hsia has observed that "what distinguishes this 'modern' phase of Chinese literature alike from the traditional and Communist phases is rather its burden of moral contemplation: its obsessive concern with China as a nation afflicted with a spiritual disease and therefore unable to strengthen itself or change its set ways of inhumanity."[9] As the twenty-first century begins, that no longer holds true, at least not for members of the post-Cultural Revolution generation. One defiantly individualistic novelist, for instance, has claimed tersely: "I can't stand people with a sense of mission."[10] Concurrent with recent changes in the way novelists are writing these days are changes in the way they view their role as artists. No longer interested in placing their pens in the service of society, which seems to be unraveling in the midst of economic reforms intended to fulfill the national dream of becoming rich and powerful, they view the xenophobic zeal of their parents' generation with skepticism at best, contempt at worst. They see themselves as independent artists whose works can, and should, appeal to readers and viewers all over the world.[11] In their truth-telling about contemporary and historical China, they present a picture of a nation that is turning away from its past and demanding new paths to an urbanized, entrepreneurial, less static future; it may turn out that in the long run they are appreciated less in their own country than elsewhere.

In fact, in this era of increasing globalization and information overload, these young writers speak to the rest of the world precisely because they no longer care to speak *for* China. The common thread of misanthropy running through much of their work and the emphasis on skewed, anti-Confucian family relations, including incest, rape, murder, voyeurism, and more, underscore a belief that they are no more responsible for social instability in their country than are entrepreneurs who want only to get rich, students who want only to leave, or petty bureaucrats who want only to enlarge themselves at public expense. Whether their pessimistic views of China turn out to be prophetic, mimetic, or even wrong, it is now as hard to make arguments for a benign Chinese exoticism as it was to evoke visions of a genteel, kimono-clad Japan in the wake of novels by "postmodernists" Murakami Haruki and Murakami Ryu, and even the trendy Banana Yoshimoto, who speaks to the fantasies and perplexities of her thirty-something generation.

In the urban centers of China, where images have eroded the power of ideas and where the pace and nature of MTV, rock concerts, and soap operas dominate culture, darkly cinematic writings are winning over a materialistic and cynical readership that is caught up in a rush to embrace capitalist consumerism and experience as much decadence as they can squeeze into their young lives.

The reader will note that up to this point I have focused on fiction, both because its narrative possibilities, its spatial and temporal sweep, more neatly accommodate the demands of national modernity and more closely capture (or subvert) the *zeitgeist* of the age, and, of course, because a lot more people read novels and stories—and watch the movies that are adapted from them—than go to the theater or curl up with a book of verse. With the exception of small coteries of intellectuals and esthetes who write, read, and view performances of contemporary Chinese plays—many of which are performed only outside the country—drama has fallen on hard times in the People's Republic and, for that matter, other Chinese communities. If the term *avant-garde* has a home, it is not in the Chinese novel or short story, but on the stages and in the chapbooks that struggle to retain a dwindling audience/readership. Gao Xingjian, now a full-fledged expatriate in Paris, is both the best known and the most prolific dramatist working in Chinese today; his recent plays, extremely opaque and accessible only to the most dedicated viewers and critics, are performed in Europe and America to small but enthusiastic audiences. Several Taiwanese and Hong Kong dramatists, plus a few on the mainland, keep the experiment going, and while their work is occasionally translated into Western languages, it does not travel well.[12]

Poets, on the other hand, do attract readers in the original and in translation. Language, of course, is the supreme barrier, for the highly allusive, concise nature of Chinese is a constant frustration to translators, whose creative talents are strained to the limit. Much in the mold of Western poets such as John Ashbery, whose quest to tease the most out of poetic language has taken him into "slippery syntax, elusive personae, narrative uncertainty, the blending of incongruous dictions,"[13] today's poets from the Cultural Revolution generation are turning more inward, more subjective, and more elusive in their writing. What was once characterized as "misty poetry" has, for many at least, become a dense fog through which beauty pokes here and there without ever forming a recognizable whole.

Only one poet, Bei Dao, has had his work published in the West to any significant degree. And he, like a disproportionate number of poets from the People's Republic, has lived in the West in exile since the bloodshed in Beijing a decade ago.[14] It is, in fact, the plight of the displaced artist that most compellingly informs, and internationalizes, contemporary Chinese poetry, at least that which is published in Western languages. Some poets have begun writing in English; most, however, have continued to write in Chinese while living abroad, becoming more nostalgic and more cynical as their exile deepens.[15]

. . . TO HERE

Writing in the *New York Times* (June 18, 1998), Martin Arnold states that "the sale of foreign translations in the United States is generally like a nearly empty can of shaving cream: a little air and a few bubbles." As recently as 1990, the percentages of all translated titles were nearly 10 percent for France, over 25 percent for Italy, and under 3 percent for the United States; no figures are available for China, although the number is surely quite high. While this points to the growing influence of English-language production throughout the world, it also leads one to speculate that cultural xenophobia is alive and well in the United States.

The implications are clear: The selection criteria—who to introduce, what to translate, and when to do so—are critical, if Chinese writers are to receive even a fraction of the attention they deserve. And it is virtually impossible for contemporary Chinese writing to enter the Western literary mainstream, as have, for instance, the novels of Gabriel García Márquez, Mario Vargas Llosa, Milan Kundera, and others. As Rey Chow points out:

> While the "world" significance of modern Chinese literature derives from its status as minority discourse, it is precisely this minority status that makes it so difficult for modern Chinese literature to be legitimized as "world" literature, while other *national* literatures, notably English, French, and Russian, have had much wider claims to an international modernity in spite of their historical and geographical specificity.[16]

Without a broad and representative corpus of fiction and verse available in translation, Chinese books cannot exert much artistic influence on Western writers. Which takes us back to the prior issue of selection, the one area in which translators can make a difference. But before examining the particulars of what gets translated, and why, it is worth our time to look at some underlying concerns about literary translation in general.

In an essay devoted to an exploration of the latest crop of English-language translations of Chinese fiction, the critic Kam Louie quotes Liu Sola, a well-known (and reasonably well-translated) Chinese novelist who has asserted "the popular proposition that only Chinese can fully appreciate Chinese literature—no matter how skilled the translator, foreigners can never fully understand Chinese writing since they have not experienced the Cultural Revolution, the anti-Japanese War, or the recent reform policies." Complaining, perhaps in contradictory fashion, that "the world has been Westernized to a degree where everything is judged from the perspective of Europe/America," Liu expresses "the frustrations felt by some Chinese writers at the tardy and often reluctant recognition of their works on the international literary scene."[17] While sympathizing with the author's frustrations—who wouldn't?—both Louie and I take strong exception to the claim that cultural interchange is an impossibility, even between China and the West. Beyond Liu's apparent negation of the power of the imagination, what lies at the heart of this debate is the dialectic between national/indigenous peculiarities and universal issues of humanity. Although the concept of a "world literature" may be too laden with economic, even imperialist and hegemonic baggage, too insular a view of cultural boundaries smacks of cultural relativism, wherein the experiences of one community cannot be understood, appreciated, or shared by another.[18] Furthermore, Liu's argument leads too easily, and quite uncomfortably, to similar restrictions on age, gender, class, and more. It is not somewhere we want to go if literature is to remain a viable form of "interchange."

To be sure, the nature and quality of the translated "product" play an important role in the possibility of translinguistic/transcultural exchange. Quality, easily recognized in only the very best and the very worst translations, is too reliant upon subjective criteria for us to consider here. Needless to say, such concerns as fidelity (getting it "right"), understandability, and literariness determine how well a text is rendered from one language into another. On the other hand, the goals and approaches of a translator can be readily determined. Some observers and practitioners of translation insist that a translator is obligated to bring the reader toward the author and not the other way around. To them, a "foreignized text" (a literal translation, for lack of a better word) has become an ideological necessity, a work that happily disrupts cultural codes in the target language, unlike a domesticated (or literary) translation, which is an appropriation of a foreign culture that denies the opportunity of revealing stylistic possibilities in one's own language that are different from the original.

The "literary" school, exemplified by works that read as if they were actually written in the target language, appears to be winning the publishing lottery, because those are the translations that emerge from the editorial offices of commercial and university presses; whether one celebrates that trend or laments it, the fact remains that "readable" translations of "translatable" books are the ones that get published.

So what does the English-language reader of contemporary Chinese writing have to look forward to? I shall end this essay with some answers to that question, based upon my personal experience as a translator. To that end, I shall focus my examination on three recent, and quite disparate, novels on which I have worked.

Over the past two decades, I have been involved in the production of two dozen or more translations of modern and contemporary Chinese fiction, and while the results of those endeavors can in no way reflect all the literary twists and turns in post-Mao China, they fairly represent my own tastes in literature, some of the strictures within which I work, and, most important, the essence of Chinese novels and short stories to which English-language readers have been exposed.[19]

Contemporary writing dates from the early 1980s. The earliest creations of the post-Cultural Revolution period, while dealing with issues of reform in the Dengist era, were not all that different from the socialist-realist writing that had monopolized the first three decades of the People's Republic. Oh, we Western readers were pleased to see that the ideologues were no longer in the spotlight, that reformers were beginning to get their way, and that just plain folk could finally fall in love with something other than a tractor. But the themes and the writing style—hard-core, representational realism—continued to reflect Party and governmental policy; in other words, these novels and many more like them from the early to mid-1980s fulfilled the role of state-sponsored art (if this sounds harsh, it must be remembered that virtually all professional writers at this time were, in fact, on the national payroll and were well paid for their efforts).[20] No breakthrough yet, although more liberal views of sexuality, the autonomy of the individual, and unflattering descriptions of the behavior of Party and government representatives were beginning to appear, however tentatively.

Not until the arrival of members of the generation who were children or teenagers during the Cultural Revolution and who were just beginning their writing careers when the Tian'anmen Massacre of June 4, 1989, occurred did a remarkable change in the very nature of writing take place. Holding themselves blameless for the horrific excesses of the Maoist era and finding great intellectual and creative stimulation from the nascent internationalist climate in (the cities of) China, they began producing works that excited domestic readers as well as those of us who, in order to practice our craft, had been seeing ourselves as unwitting supporters of "socialist art," that is, "portrayals of the social state and social space that corresponds to reality and to the possibilities hidden in reality."[21]

It is now possible to choose works to translate based primarily on aesthetic or other literary criteria, although political and market considerations continue to play a role. While it may be true that more critical or darker works are chosen over works that paint a rosier picture of historical or contemporary Chinese society, it is also highly likely that those works are more artistically and intellectually satisfying. I do not think that literature is well served if the translator's choices are ideologically motivated.

As post-Deng turned into postmodern, the very ethos of literary writing, at least among a talented coterie of experimental and often self-indulgent young men and women, changed dramatically. As I implied earlier, personal vision supplanted national policy in their fiction, poetry, and plays, and the tendency was toward an increasingly solipsistic form of writing, that which refers only to itself (sometimes referred to as "art for art's sake"). Not surprisingly, that vision is dark, often nihilistic, even, at times, perverse. And it has struck a resonant chord with readers outside China. The reasons for this are complex but include, I think, a diminution of the long-held dreamily exotic view of China in the West (with a concomitant lessening of tolerance toward the positivistic brand of writing with which we have become familiar), a global fin-de-siècle anxiety (which informs the sexual and social behavior of characters in recent writing from China), and a fear that the world has become apocalyptically violent. With images of June 4, 1989, still fresh in the public consciousness, in recent literature from China, selected and mediated by translators, we see more currents of commonality than ever before.

The most disturbing Chinese writing to appear in English is laden with graphic depictions of horrific violence, often in elegiacal proportions. One critic's comment on the novelist Yu Hua could easily be applied to many young Chinese writers: "To journey through his fictional universe is to subject oneself to a harrowing series of depictions of death, dismembered bodies, and acts of extreme and seemingly gratuitous cruelty."[22] Disorienting stories of grotesque brutality, layered with symbolism and often lacking the traditional markers—time, place, names—that is, stories incorporating a sense of universality, bestow upon the numbing violence in them a true metonymic quality. Savage, homicidal fictions, while seemingly "ready-made for appropriation into the critique of the antihumanistic ravage of the Cultural Revolution," nonetheless have become "a heresy to the older generation of writers and critics for whom violence [is] a political act and a symptom, albeit an irrational one, of history. The pure consumption of violence as an aesthetic form [is] inconceivable, and not surprisingly, utterly sacrilegious, to survivors of turbulent historical trauma."[23] But these claustrophobic worlds of depravity and bestiality (not unlike that of the Polish writer Bruno Schulz, a Jew who was killed in the Holocaust) epitomizes what David Wang has called a "familiarization of the uncanny. [B]y turning the world into a realm of fantastic and uncanny elements or by identifying normalcy with the grotesque and insane, writers awaken their readers from aesthetic and ideological inertia, initiating them into a new kind of reality."[24]

Violence and evil, with all their metonymic possibilities, are nowhere more powerfully evoked than in Su Tong's catalogue of horrors with the

innocuous title of *Rice*. The tale of a thoroughly malign individual who cor-
rupts (or kills) every person with whom he comes into contact during the
course of his self-consuming life, the novel portrays a society (pre-war China)
bent on self-destruction and, in the view of many critics, the pervasive dehumanizing climate of contemporary society. *Rice* is a grim, numbing, disturbing, even profane work that, with all its exaggerated grotesqueries, is all too
believable. One reviewer, having posed the question "Why would anyone read
this book in the first place?" supplies her own thoughtful answer: "Because Su
Tong renders these people so vividly that they possess, for us, the individuality that they deny one another. Even their rampant misogyny . . . tells us how
willfully alone each is, how frightened and defensive. And because when we
read about bad things happening to bad people, we feel bad—and that's good.
That's what makes us human."[25] Su Tong's novel, and many of his stories,
paint China's recent history—and by allusive implication, its present—in
unrelieved darkness. Fiction with a historical setting, particularly during the
Republican era, that is, the first half of the twentieth century, presents an
opportunity to deal obliquely with contemporary events with a measure of
safety; one can, however disingenuously, point to the damning visions in one's
writing and imply that the setting, now past, would be impossible in the socialist context, and that is precisely how many of them refute the accusations of
conservative critics that their work is somehow "unhealthy."

No one has been accused of writing "unhealthy" fiction more than Mo
Yan, until recently a member of the Cultural Section of the People's Liberation Army. With *Red Sorghum* he created sympathetic heroes out of bandits,
adulterers, murderers, and anti-Party activists. With his second novel, *The
Garlic Ballads*, he went further, examining the precarious, even antagonistic,
relationship between the Chinese peasantry and the Communist government
in his most transparently ideological novel. In *Large Breasts and Full Hips*, the
focus is on sex, politics, and, echoing *Red Sorghum*, China's frightful modern
history. None of these works, each unique in its own right, prepared the reader
for what, in my opinion, may be the most astonishing novel to appear from
China in this century, *Republic of Wine*.

Hailed by one critic as a "twentieth-century fin-de-siècle masterpiece,"
this experiment in narrative technique is a multi-layered work of fiction that
confronts the Chinese trait of gluttony, a national discomfort with the issue
of sex, and a host of human relationships, many of them quite bizarre. Reminiscent of, if not exactly parallel to, Swift's "A Modest Proposal," the novel
explodes the myths of a benevolent government ruling over a civilized nation;
while it is but the latest in a long tradition of literature dealing with cannibalism in China, the novel views the aberrant behavior as an extreme example
of China's vaunted gourmandism in the context of a racy parade of sexual
misconduct and ultimately constitutes an attack by Mo Yan on some of

China's cultural sacred cows, as well as a reaction by him to the horrors of June 4th at Tian'anmen Square.

Beyond that, *Republic of Wine* is concerned not only with issues of culture and humanity, but with the process of writing as well, a self-conscious "retrospective" of the author's oeuvre. The text includes a series of fictional correspondences between an amateur writer who lives in Republic of Wine and engages "Mo Yan" in discussions of fiction, of the novel in which he appears, and of food, liquor, and sex. The dialogue between the two characters is further enhanced by the inclusion of stories by the amateur, stories that get increasingly bizarre and intriguing as the novel progresses. Finally, it is a novel about liquor, whose paradoxical social functions—an elevation of the spirit as well as the epitome of excess[26]—undergird the structure of the novel as a whole. If I were to be asked the same question the reviewer asked in regard to Su Tong's *Rice*—Why would anyone read this book in the first place?—the answer would have to include the sheer joy of his Rabelaisian humor and gusto, the structural artistry, and the satirical barbs, much, but not all, of which is apparent even in translation.

Su Tong and Mo Yan, pretty heavy stuff. But what about the young novelist who "can't stand people with a sense of mission"? He reigned as China's most popular writer for much of this decade, and the powers that be dislike him as much as the reading public, particularly the young, adores him. Wang Shuo, in whose novels self-indulgence, hedonism, and the pride of sociopathy mock both the establishment and the vaunted reforms of the Dengist era, has been called Beijing's "bad boy" and worse (or better, depending upon your point of view). The characters of his short novel *The Operators*, for instance, are unprincipled young men who sell their services as proxies—for lovers, people in trouble, henpecked husbands—thus thumbing their nose at social norms: anything for a buck. In *Please Don't Consider Me Human*, a satirical farce that mocks the campaign to recoup feelings of national pride in the wake of the loss of the bid to host the 2000 Olympics, a pedicab driver is chosen by a group of Beijing punks to defend the nation's honor by getting castrated in order to participate in an international sporting event as a woman. Wang Shuo, it has been pointed out in the *New York Times*, "romanticizes young alienated rebels in much the same way that Jack Kerouac did. He explores the paradoxes and absurdities of society, as Joseph Heller and Kurt Vonnegut do."[27]

Instead of criticizing the Communists for being autocratic, Wang Shuo does what is far more devastating: he mocks them for being uncool. In *Playing for Thrills*, Wang Shuo plays with the mystery genre by building a story about a murder that might have occurred and the young hedonist who might have committed it. The "thrill" for Wang Shuo is in describing the Beijing "lower depths" and weaving a tale that mystifies as it delights, sending the reader off with at least as many questions as answers. For some, like mystery mogul Stephen King, who provided a cover blurb for the novel, Wang has written a book for everyone:

> Playing for Thrills is perhaps the most brilliantly entertaining "hardboiled" novel of the 90s . . . and maybe of the 80s, as well. It constitutes a genre by itself, call it China noir, and offers guilty pleasures beyond any most readers will encounter in a bound set of Kinsey Milhones or Lucan Davenports. What the hell is this anyway? Jack Kerouac unbound? I don't think so . . . you have to experience this in order to really get it. Most ultimately cool.[28]

. . . AND BEYOND . . .

More translations of contemporary Chinese literature are appearing these days than ever before; whether this means that the readership base is expanding at the same time, that more people from different walks of life are switching to fuller "cans of shaving cream," is impossible to determine. There is, of course, the fluctuation principle to consider, that literary works from China gain popularity every time China is in the news and disappear from bookstore shelves during more quiescent periods; also at play is the coattail effect, in that as the number of people who travel to China to work or visit increases, so, too, do the quantity and diversity of reading material, including literature.

Another encouraging factor is the trend among U.S. trade publishers toward enriching their lists by adding Chinese authors—not just individual books—and promoting them with at least modest enthusiasm. Unhappily, however, as the burgeoning market economy in China holds out the promise for the more enterprising among its population to enjoy unprecedented material comforts, many writers find it increasingly less rewarding to employ their talents in an endeavor that is not well appreciated in a consumer-capitalist climate. Jianying Zha is correct when she writes:

> Every Chinese intellectual is waking up to one common fact: no longer is the government the only thing they must deal with. Now they must reckon with forces of commercialism. They can't kid themselves anymore: the days of huge readerships are gone, along with the feeling that a writer is the beloved and needed spokesman of the people and the conscience of society.[29]

Many promising young novelists appear to have abandoned their quest for artistic perfection for the more lucrative fields of commerce, TV script-writing, and the like. In my view, this could actually work to the advantage of belles lettres in and from the People's Republic, in effect a winnowing process that will leave only the most dedicated and talented writers on the scene and will motivate them to further polish their craft in the face of a smaller though more demanding readership, both in China and abroad. At present, no more than a dozen novelists, most in their middle years, are regularly published in the West; they are becoming identifiable on an international basis and are being read as much for their literary talents as for the windows onto contemporary Chinese society they inevitably provide.

It is, of course, an uphill struggle. Yet even with all the perils inherent in the translation process, and the "Third-World" status of literature from China, contemporary literary works, however mediated, can be uniquely satisfying for, and revealing to, readers beyond China's borders; there is no reason why the words of one critic cannot apply to Chinese literary works rendered into foreign languages: "A translation gives us access to the literature of the world. It allows us to enter the minds of people from other times and places. It is a celebration of otherness, a truly multicultural event without all the balloons and noisemakers. And it enriches not only our personal knowledge and artistic sense, but also our culture's literature, language, and thought."[30] And if it is true that "translating authors from other cultures can prevent a literature from becoming too nationalistic or too provincial,"[31] then the literary borders between China and the rest of the world must, and will, remain open for free movement in both directions.

NOTES

1. Wilborn Hampton, "Anarchy and Plain Bad Luck," *New York Times Book Review*, April 18, 1993. Edward Hower is more concise: "*Red Sorghum* is a book that anyone interested in China will have to read" (*New York Newsday*, May 2, 1993). Andrew F. Jones has dealt in detail with the marketing of Chinese literature abroad in his essay "Chinese Literature in the 'World' Literary Economy," *Modern Chinese Literature*, vol. 8 (1994), 171–90. In this essay I have not considered the literature from Taiwan, Hong Kong, or any of the other places where fiction, drama, and prose are written in Chinese. The interested reader may consult *The Columbia Anthology of Modern Chinese Literature*, ed. Joseph S. M. Lau and Howard Goldblatt (New York: Columbia University Press, 1995). More can be found in the Columbia University Press series "Modern Literature from Taiwan" and the Hong Kong translation journal *Renditions*, which also publishes books.

2. Robert Wechsler, *Performing Without a Stage: The Art of Literary Translation* (North Haven, Conn.: Catbird Press, 1998), 246.

3. Needless to say, a substantial amount of writing that hews more closely to Party ideals continues to be published in China; it, too, has a loyal readership, as do all the popular genres—detective fiction, science fiction, romance, even pornography—and bad writing generally. Little of it gains serious attention within China and hardly any gets translated.

4. David Der-wei Wang, "Chinese Fiction for the Nineties," in *Running Wild: New Chinese Writers*, ed. David Der-wei Wang and Jeanne Tai (New York: Columbia University Press, 1994), 242.

5. *Writing Diaspora: Tactic of Intervention in Contemporary Cultural Studies* (Bloomington: Indiana University Press, 1993), 74.

6. Mo Yan, *Red Sorghum*, trans. Howard Goldblatt (New York: Penguin Books, 1994), 4, 356. See, too, his second novel, *The Garlic Ballads* (1996).

7. This is the charge leveled against the poetry of Bei Dao (and, by extension, most modern Chinese poets) by the classical Chinese literature specialist Stephen Owen, in "What Is World Poetry? The Anxiety of Global Influence," in *The New Republic* (November 19, 1990): 28–32. Domestic critics, too, have stated their concern over a tendency by writers and moviemakers to cater to Western tastes. The journalist Dai Qing has written of Zhang Yimou's film adaptation of Su Tong's *Raise the Red Lantern*, "this kind of film is really shot for the casual pleasures of foreigners." Quoted in Jianying Zha, *China Pop: How Soap Operas, Tabloids, and Bestsellers Are Transforming a Culture* (New York: The New Press, 1995), 94.

8. Jing Wang, ed. *China's Avant-Garde Fiction* (Durham: Duke University Press, 1998), 4.

9. "Obsession with China: "The Moral Burden of Modern Chinese Literature," in *A History of Modern Chinese Fiction*, 2nd ed. (New Haven: Yale University Press, 1971), 533–34.

10. Contemporary fiction writer, Wang Shuo, as quoted in Jianying Zha, *China Pop*, 110.

11. While these writers have taken heart in the rather amazing reception of Chinese films around the world (do, in fact, participate in the scriptwriting), they are puzzled that their books do not generate the same enthusiasm.

12. For a sampling of contemporary drama, the reader may consult *An Oxford Anthology of Contemporary Chinese Drama*, ed. Martha P. Y. Cheung and Janet C. C. Lai (Hong Kong: Oxford University Press, 1997); and *Theater and Society: An Anthology of Contemporary Chinese Drama*, ed. Haiping Yan (Armonk, N.Y.: M. E. Sharpe, 1998). Both anthologies provide illuminating introductions.

13. Mark Ford, *Times Literary Supplement*, in review of John Ashbery's *Can You Hear, Bird* (1995).

14. Several anthologies of Bei Dao's poems have been translated into English, including *The August Sleepwalker*, trans. Bonnie S. McDougall (1990), and *Landscape over Zero*, trans. David Hinton (1995), both from New Directions. Bei Dao continues to edit the literary quarterly *Jintian* (*Today*), begun during the heady "Democracy Wall" movement in 1979, which includes fiction, poetry, criticism, and a feature entitled "Rewriting Literary History." The most comprehensive view of contemporary Chinese

poetry is provided in Bonnie S. McDougall and Kam Louie, *The Literature of China in the Twentieth Century* (New York: Columbia University Press, 1997).

15. It is not surprising, given the marginalization of Asia generally and China specifically in Western literary studies, that only two contemporary writers from Asia, the Japanese novelist Yasunari Kawabata and the Chinese short-story writer A-cheng, appear in two recent books on exile: *Exile and the Writer*, Bettina L. Knapp (University Park: Pennsylvania State University Press, 1991) and *Altogether Elsewhere: Writers on Exile*, ed. Marc Robinson (Boston and London: Faber and Faber, 1994), both in the former.

16. Chow, *Writing Diaspora*, 101.

17. Kam Louie, "The Translatability of Chinese Culture in Contemporary Chinese Fiction," in *Modern Chinese Literature* (1994): 216.

18. The ideal of a world literature (*weltliteratur*) originated with Goethe, who wrote that "there can be no question of the nations thinking alike, the aim is simply that they shall grow aware of one another, understand each other, and even where they may not be able to love, may at least tolerate one another." This statement has been adopted as a motto of sorts by the literary quarterly *World Literature Today*.

19. In recent years, about a half dozen anthologies of contemporary Chinese literature in English translation have been published in the West; added to that are a couple of dozen novels or single-author story collections and a few books of poetry. Not a large figure, by any stretch of the imagination, but a broad enough cross-section of offerings in Chinese to give English-language readers an idea of the quality and type of available writing and a wide-ranging glimpse of the society that has spawned it. Most have been published by commercial presses, but university presses have added to the number. Worthy of note is the "Fiction from Modern China" series from the University of Hawaii Press. Foreign Languages Press in Beijing also publishes work by contemporary writers.

20. The Hungarian poet Miklós Haraszti writes: "Before socialism, the function of art had been simply to preserve its own autonomy, or, in a wider sense, to preserve the possibility of autonomy within society at large. In the culture of social commitment it has a new function: to enlarge, direct, and give cohesion to an organized public, the nucleus of the future society." This socialist art, he continues, "neither hates nor worships 'reality'; it merely denies reality the chance to be mysterious." *The Velvet Prison: Artists under State Socialism* (New York: Basic Books, 1987), 37, 38.

21. Ibid., 129.

22. Andrew Jones, "Translator's Postscript," Yu Hua, *The Past and the Punishments* (Honolulu: University of Hawaii Press, 1996), 270.

23. Jing Wang, *China's Avant-Garde Fiction*, 4.

24. Wang, "Chinese Fiction for the Nineties," 243.

25. Kelly Cherry, "The Symbol of Plenty and Nothing," *Los Angeles Times*, January 28, 1996.

26. The multiple roles of alcohol, in the novel and in society in general, are treated in great detail in Xiaobin Yang, "The Republic of Wine: An Extravaganza of Decline," *positions: east asia cultures critique*, vol. 6, no. 1 (Summer 1998): 16.

27. Sheryl WuDunn, "The Word from China's Kerouac: The Communists Are Uncool," *New York Times Book Review*, January 10, 1993: 3.

28. Available in paperback in my translation from Penguin Books (1998).

29. Zha, *China Pop*, 46. According to Zha, the joke around Beijing a few short years ago was "there are more people writing novels than reading novels" (135).

30. Wechsler, *Performing without a Stage*, 11.

31. "Introduction," *Theories of Translation: An Anthology of Essays from Dryden to Derrida*, Rainer Schulte and John Biguenet, eds. (Chicago: University of Chicago Press, 1992), 8.

ANNOTATED BIBLIOGRAPHY

This selected bibliography lists general studies on Chinese aesthetics, literature, and culture by prominent scholars. These texts are accessible at most academic libraries. The primary texts themselves often offer excellent introductions and other materials also. Not included here are the many critical works that are more specifically focused on individual writers, texts, themes, and forms. The bibliographies noted below as well as the bibliographies found in many of the texts listed will help the reader locate more specialized studies. Audiovisual materials, including Chinese films, widely available on videotape, provide essential visual and auditory experiences and should be included in general humanities courses that deal with Chinese culture.

BIBLIOGRAPHIES AND REFERENCE BOOKS

Association for Asian Studies. *Bibliography of Asian Studies*. Ann Arbor, Michigan. The annual index for *Journal of Asian Studies*, covering journals, monographs, and book reviews, arranged by area and topic.

Brandon, James R., ed. *The Cambridge Guide to Asian Theatre*. Cambridge: Cambridge University Press, 1993. An authoritative and detailed guide to all aspects of Chinese drama and theatre, including an historical account of its development and regional forms.

Brandon, James R., with Elizabeth Wichmann, eds. *Asian Theatre: A Study Guide and Annotated Bibliography*. Washington: American Theatre Assoc., 1980. Extensive list of studies on Asian drama, both theatre and plays, divided by country and covering the history, theory, and practice of Asian theatre.

DeBary, William Theodore, and Irene Bloom, eds. *Sources of Chinese Tradition*. 2 vols. New York: Columbia University Press, 1999. Translations of key texts in classical Chinese philosophy, history, and religion.

Idema, Wilt, and Lloyd Haft. *A Guide to Chinese Literature*. Ann Arbor: Center for Chinese Studies, University of Michigan, 1997. A detailed history of Chinese writing, organized according to developments in writing technology, with a fifty-page introduction to traditional Chinese culture (excerpted here) and an extensive annotated bibliography.

Liu, James J. Y. *Essentials of Chinese Literary Art*. North Scituate, Mass.: Duxbury Press, 1979. Outline of general characteristics of Chinese poetry and drama, arranged chronologically.

Lynn, Richard John, ed. *Guide to Chinese Poetry and Drama*. 2nd ed. Original edition by Roger B. Bailey. *The Asian Literature Bibliography Series*. Boston: G. K. Hall, 1984. Annotated bibliography of these two genres, organized by historical periods, with introductions for each genre.

Nienhauser, William H., Jr., ed. *The Indiana Companion to Traditional Chinese Literature*. 2 vols. Bloomington: Indiana University Press, 1998. Bibliographical essays on classical Chinese writers.

Wu-chi Liu. *An Introduction to Chinese Literature*. Bloomington: Indiana University Press, 1966. Short essays for the general reader arranged chronologically by period and genre.

ANTHOLOGIES

Birch, Cyril, ed. *Anthology of Chinese Literature. From Earliest Times to the Fourteenth Century*, vol.1. New York: Grove Press, 1965. *From the Fourteenth Century to the Present Day*, vol.2. New York: Grove Press, 1972. An extensive collection of translated poetry, grouped by historical periods, with introductory essays to each volume and sectional notes that outline the historical contexts.

Chang, Kang-i Sun, and Haun Saussy, eds. *Women Writers of Traditional China: An Anthology of Poetry and Criticism*. Stanford: Stanford University Press, 1999. A collection representing the neglected female tradition in Chinese literature.

Cheung, Martha P. Y., and Jane C. C. Lai, eds. *An Oxford Anthology of Contemporary Chinese Drama*. Hong Kong: Oxford University Press, 1997. A collection of spoken drama from China, Taiwan, and Hong Kong.

Dooling, Amy D., and Kristina M. Torgeson, eds., *Writing Women in Modern China: An Anthology of Women's Literature from the Early Twentieth Century*. New York: Columbia University Press, 1998. A collection of writings by literary women who expressed their own experiences of gender at a time when the construction of gender in China was being revised.

Frankel, Hans H. *The Flowering Plum and the Palace Lady: Interpretations of Chinese Poetry*. New Haven: Yale University Press, 1976. Translations of 106 Chinese poems from tenth century B.C.E. to fourteenth century C.E., organized under thematic and stylistic headings, with analyses of traditional Chinese poetic structures.

Gunn, Edward M., ed. *Twentieth-Century Chinese Drama: An Anthology*. Bloomington: Indiana University Press, 1983. Includes historical introductions on social and political contexts.

Lau, Joseph S. M., and Howard Goldblatt, eds. *Columbia Anthology of Modern Chinese Literature*. New York: Columbia University Press, 1995. Modern writings of major genres from PRC, Taiwan, and Hong Kong.

Levy, Andre, ed. *Chinese Literature: Ancient and Classical*. Trans. William H. Nienhauser, Jr. Bloomington: Indiana University Press, 2000. Canonical texts arranged in four chapters: "Antiquity," "Prose," "Poetry," and "Literature of Entertainment: The Novel and Theatre."

Mair, Victor, ed. *The Columbia Book of Traditional Chinese Literature*. New York: Columbia University Press, 1994. Texts chosen to represent the full range of genres.

McDougall, Bonnie S., and Kam Louis, eds. *The Literature of China in the Twentieth Century*. New York: Columbia University Press, 1997. Separate essays on fiction, drama, and poetry in each of three modern periods: 1900–1937, 1938–1965, 1966–1989.

Minford, John, and Joseph S. M. Lau, eds. *Classical Chinese Literature: An Anthology of Translations*. New York: Columbia University Press, 2000. The three-thousand-year literary tradition as presented by Western translators of the past three hundred years.

Owen, Stephen, ed. and trans. *An Anthology of Chinese Literature: Beginnings to 1911*. New York: Norton, 1996. With period introductions on the technology and uses of writing.

Wang, David Der-wei, with Jeanne Tai, eds. *Running Wild: New Chinese Writers*. New York: Columbia University Press, 1994. With an afterward on contemporary Chinese fiction.

Watson, Burton, ed. and trans. *The Columbia Book of Chinese Poetry: From Early Times to the Thirteenth Century*. New York: Columbia University Press, 1984. An extensive collection, with a useful general introduction.

Wu-chi Liu and Irving Y. C. Lo, eds. *Sunflower Splendor: Three Thousand Years of Chinese Poetry*. Bloomington: Indiana University Press, 1975. Translations of an extensive collection of poetry, from earliest to contemporary times. Lo's introduction describes the development of Chinese poetry, featuring traditional forms, themes, and social functions.

Yan Haiping, ed. *Theater and Society: An Anthology of Contemporary Chinese Drama*. Armonk, N.Y.: M. E. Sharpe, 1998. Besides the introduction reprinted here, Yan Haiping includes translations of *Bus Stop* (1983), *WM* (1985), *Pan Jinlian: The History of a Fallen Woman* (1986), *Sangshuping Chronicles* (1988), and *Old Well* (1986).

Yip, Wai-lim, ed. and trans. Calligraphy by Kuo-hsiung Chen. *Chinese Poetry: Major Modes and Genres*. Berkeley: University of California Press, 1976. Translations of poetry, mostly from the Tang Dynasty, intended to redress translations that eclipse the grammatical and syntactical freedom of the originals.

Yu, Shiao-Ling S., ed. and trans. *Chinese Drama After the Cultural Revolution, 1979–1989: An Anthology*. *Chinese Studies*, vol. 3. Lewiston: Edwin Mellen Press,

1996. Includes an historical essay that focuses on Peking drama, Sichuan opera, and spoken drama.

GENERAL STUDIES

Ames, Roger T., Chan Sin-wai, and Mau-sang Ng, eds. *Interpreting Culture Through Translation: A Festschrift for D. C. Lau.* Ed. Hong Kong: The Chinese University Press, 1991. A collection of essays by translators on the interpretive art of translation. Ames' introduction is revised and included here as "Language and Interpretive Contexts."

Ames, Roger T., and Henry Rosemont, Jr., trans. *The Analects: A Philosophical Translation.* Albany: State University of New York Press, 1998. A translation that seeks to avoid reading Western metaphysics into Confucian concepts. Includes a thorough introduction to Confucius' life and thought and to the later interpretations and uses of Confucius' teachings.

Ban Wang. *In the Sublime Figure of History: Aesthetics and Politics in Twentieth-Century China.* Stanford: Stanford University Press, 1997. Discusses modern aesthetics, such as the development of the heroic individual, that emerged in China at the turn of the twentieth century as a self-conscious and defensive tactic by writers and intellectuals in response to China's demoralizing encounters with Western powers.

Callicott, J. Baird, and Roger T. Ames, eds. *Nature in Asian Traditions of Thought: Essays in Environmental Philosophy.* Albany: State University of New York Press, 1989. Essays on the ecological worldviews and traditions of China, Japan, and India, including "The Continuity of Being" by Tu Wei-ming reprinted here.

Chenyang Li, ed. *The Sage and the Second Sex: Confucianism, Ethics, and Gender.* Chicago: Open Court, 2000. Essays on the development of the female gender in Confucian thought.

Hall, David L., and Roger T. Ames. *Anticipating China: Thinking Through the Narratives of Chinese and Western Culture.* Albany: State University of New York Press, 1995. Thorough investigation of the different philosophical bases of oppositional cultures.

Li Zehou, Gong Lizeng, trans. *The Path of Beauty: A Study of Chinese Aesthetics.* Hong Kong: Oxford University Press, 1994. Essays on classical Chinese art and literature by Chinese scholars, who together represent the main aesthetic schools in contemporary China.

Ropp, Paul S., ed. *The Heritage of China: Contemporary Perspectives on Chinese Civilization.* Berkeley: University of California Press, 1990. Essays on the history of Chinese cultural traditions, including government, philosophy, science, economics, society, and the arts. Ropp's essay "The Distinctive Art of Chinese Fiction" is included here.

Spence, Jonathan. *The Chan's Great Continent: China in Western Minds*. Documents the history of the West's relationship with China as revealed in politics, literature, religion, and society.

Weston, Timothy B., and Lionel M. Jensen, eds. *China Behind the Headlines*. Lanham, Md.: Rowman and Littlefield, 2000. Essays that dispel false impressions of contemporary China fostered by the Western press. Includes "Border Crossings" by Howard Goldblatt, reprinted here.

Zhu Liyuan and Gene Blocker, eds. *Asian Thought and Culture: Contemporary Chinese Aesthetics*, vol. 17. New York: Peter Lang, 1995. Essays by contemporary Chinese scholars, reflecting modern Marxist thought, on Chinese aesthetics compared to Western traditions. Includes introductory essay by Blocker.

GENERAL LITERATURE STUDIES

Barlow, Tani, ed. *Gender Politics in Modern China: Writing and Feminism*. Durham: Duke University Press, 1993. Essays investigating the concepts of woman and man as new gender constructions developed since the mid-nineteenth century, contrasting with Western views of gender, and differentiating among treatments by individual Chinese writers.

Birch, Cyril, ed. *Studies in Chinese Literary Genres*. Berkeley: University of California Press, 1974. Collection of essays by eminent scholars arranged chronologically by genre.

Denton, Kirk A., ed. *Modern Chinese Literary Thought: Writings on Literature, 1893–1945*. Stanford: Stanford University Press, 1996. Essays by Chinese writers present Chinese literary modernism as a break with tradition and an appropriation of Western values.

Duke, Michael S., ed. *Modern Chinese Women Writers: Critical Appraisals*. Armonk, N.Y.: M. E. Sharpe, 1989. Series of essays focused on individual modern texts.

Eoyang, Eugene, and Lin Yao-fu, eds. *Translating Chinese Literature*. Bloomington: Indiana University Press, 1995. Translators, anthologists, and critics discuss the challenges of translating Chinese texts into English.

Goldblatt, Howard, ed. *Worlds Apart: Recent Chinese Writing and its Audiences*. Armonk, N.Y.: M. E. Sharpe, 1990. Studies of literature from the PRC and Taiwan.

Hegel, Robert E., and Richard C. Hessney, eds. *Expressions of Self in Chinese Literature*. New York: Columbia University Press, 1985. Essays on literary representations of the Chinese "self"—as opposed to the Western concept of self as independent individual.

Larson, Wendy. *Woman and Writing in Modern China*. Stanford: Stanford University Press, 1998. Considers two modern concepts, "new woman" and "new writing" developed as two theories of modernization: "women's liberation" and "autonomous aesthetic." Excerpts from the chapter "Woman, Moral Virtue, and Literary Text" are reprinted here.

Liu, James J. Y. *Language—Paradox—Poetics: A Chinese Perspective.* Princeton: Princeton University Press, 1988. Traditional Chinese poetics are juxtaposed with Western poetics, on the premise that language is inherently insufficient as a communicator of experience.

Lu, Tonglin, ed. *Gender and Sexuality in Twentieth-Century Chinese Literature and Society.* Albany: State University of N.Y. Press, 1993. Investigates the modern construction and uses of gender.

Miller, Barbara Stoler, ed. *Masterworks of Asian Literature in Comparative Perspective: A Guide for Teaching.* Armonk, N.Y.: M. E. Sharpe, 1994. Valuable guide for world literature and introductory literature courses, including an introduction to Chinese literature by Yu and Huters reprinted here.

Owen, Stephen, ed. *Readings in Chinese Literary Thought.* Cambridge: Harvard University Press, 1992. Discussions of key classic texts of Chinese literary theory.

Rickett, Adele Austin, ed., *Chinese Approaches to Literature from Confucius to Liang Chi'i-ch'ao.* Princeton: Princeton University Press, 1978. Essays on Chinese literary criticism.

Saussy, Haun. *The Problem of a Chinese Aesthetic.* Stanford: Stanford University Press, 1997. Discusses the question of allegorical, metaphorical and literal thinking in Chinese literature, as differentiated from the Western tradition of mimesis.

Watson, Burton. *Early Chinese Literature.* New York: Columbia University Press, 1962. Contains an essay on history, philosophy, and poetry from the earliest texts to 100 A.D.

Yu, Pauline, Peter Bol, Stephen Owen, and Willard Peterson, eds. *Ways with Words: Writing about Reading Texts from Early China.* Berkeley: University of California Press, 2000. Casebook on seven key texts, which includes for each a translation, several interpretations by scholars of different disciplines, and a "Perspective on Reading."

POETRY

Cooper, Arthur, ed. *Li Po and Tu Fu: Poems Selected and Translated with an Introduction and Notes.* London: Penguin Books, 1973. Introduction compares the two major poets as complementary contemporaries who exemplify Daoist and Confucian philosophies.

Hightower, James R., and Florence Chia-Ying Yeh. *Studies in Chinese Poetry.* Cambridge: Harvard University Asian Center, Harvard University Press, 1998.

A collection of critical essays by the two authors on specific Chinese poetry and Chinese poets.

Lin, Julia C. *Modern Chinese Poetry: An Introduction.* Seattle: University of Washington Press, 1972. Considers the untraditional poetic styles, themes, forms, and critical evaluations of twentieth-century poets, whose poetry is therefore more accessible to Westerners.

Liu, James J. Y. *The Art of Chinese Poetry.* Chicago: University of Chicago Press, 1974. A general introduction to Chinese poetry, including 1) "The Chinese Language as a Medium of Poetic Expression," 2) "Some Traditional Chinese Views of Poetry," and 3) "Poetry as Exploration of Worlds and of Language."

——. *The Interlingual Critic: Interpreting Chinese Poetry.* Bloomington: Indiana University Press, 1982. Explores the issue of the critic's identity and critical assumptions.

Owen, Stephen. *The End of the Chinese "Middle Ages": Essays in Mid-Tang Literary Culture.* Stanford: Stanford University Press, 1996. Historical essays by Owen on the diverse poetry practices of the period of 791–825 C.E.

——. *The Great Age of Chinese Poetry: The High Tang.* New Haven: Yale University Press, 1982. A literary history of the great age of classical poetry.

——. *Traditional Chinese Poetry and Poetics: Omen of the World.* Madison: University of Wisconsin Press, 1985. Discusses the art of lyric poetry and its social role, using texts from the fourth through the twelfth centuries. Includes the chapter printed here as "Omen of the World."

Shuen-fu Lin, and Stephen Owen, eds. *The Vitality of the Lyric Voice: Shih Poetry from the Late Han to the Tang.* Princeton: Princeton University Press, 1986. Essays from scholars, representing different nations and methodologies, on lyric poetry, its evolution from folk lyrics, its tradition, language, Eastern and Chinese critical concepts, nature, and form.

Watson, Burton. *Chinese Lyricism: Shih Poetry From the Second to the Twelfth Century.* New York: Columbia University Press, 1971. A critical and historical study of the thousand-year development of the central lyrical form in Chinese poetry.

Yu, Pauline. *The Reading of Imagery in the Chinese Poetic Tradition.* Princeton: Princeton University Press, 1987. Study of the concreteness and correlative meanings of poetic imagery, by focusing chronologically on key texts.

NARRATIVE

Elvin, Mark. *Changing Stories in the Chinese World.* Stanford: Stanford University Press, 1997. Discusses the celebration of Confucian civilization as the "drama of world history of humanity unfolding uniquely in China," and the criticism of this culture in satire and also in the Daoist vision of earthly life as a delusion.

Hanan, Patrick. *The Chinese Vernacular Story.* Cambridge: Harvard University Press, 1981. Traces the development of vernacular writing in novel, story, drama, and song as an alternative form to classical Chinese language and style.

Hegel, Robert E. *The Novel in Seventeenth-Century China.* New York: Columbia University Press, 1981. Discusses the cultural and literary contexts and the concept of the self during the great age of vernacular fiction.

Hsia, C. T. *A History of Modern Chinese Fiction.* Bloomington: Indiana University Press, 3rd ed., 1999. Hsia considers the Modern to be realistic and a rejection of Chinese culture rather than just a criticism of specific practices that are seen as aberrations of Chinese civilization.

——. *The Classic Chinese Novel.* New York: Columbia University Press, 1968. Introduction to the six greatest Chinese novels in comparison to Western fiction.

Huang, Martin W. *Literati and Self-Representation: Autobiographical Sensibility in the Eighteenth-Century Chinese Novel.* Stanford: Stanford University Press, 1995. Examines *The Scholars, Dream of the Red Chamber,* and *The Humble Words of an Old Rustic* to consider the autobiographical sensibilities that inform such eighteenth-century novels of the literati, who mask their concerns about the decline in their personal fortunes.

Jing Wang. *The Story of Stone: Intertextuality, Ancient Chinese Stone Myths, and the Stone Symbolism of* Dream of the Red Chamber, Water Margin, *and* Journey to the West. Durham: Duke University Press, 1992. 1–33. Demonstrates intertextuality as a critical approach that is congenial to Chinese studies, and investigates the stone image which begins and sustains the narratives of *Water Margin, Journey to the West,* and *Dream of the Red Chamber.*

Liu Ching-chih, ed. *The Question of Reception: Martial Arts Fiction in English Translation.* Monograph Series No. 1. Lingnon College: Centre for Literature and Translation, 1997. A collection of essays that examine culture from the perspective of this particular genre.

McMahon, Keith. *Misers, Shrews, and Polygamists: Sexuality and Male-Female Relations in Eighteenth-Century Chinese Fiction.* Durham: Duke University Press, 1995. In the context of polygamy in the Ming and Qing dynasties, McMahon examines the representations of sexuality and gender in the figures of the miser and the shrew.

Plaks, Andrew H., ed. *Chinese Narrative: Critical and Theoretical Essays.* Princeton: Princeton University Press, 1977. Essays on the narrative tradition to the early nineteenth century.

——. *Four Masterworks of the Ming Novel.* Princeton: Princeton University Press, 1987. Analysis of *Three Kingdoms, Water Margin, Journey to the West,* and *The Golden Lotus* as serious works of new-Confucian social criticism of sixteenth-century Chinese society.

Rolston, David L., ed. *How to Read a Chinese Novel: Traditional Chinese Fiction and Fiction Commentary.* Princeton: Princeton University Press, 1990. Chinese critical commentaries on the six greatest traditional Chinese novels, with annotations for the modern reader.

Widmer, Ellen, and David Der-wei Wang, eds. *From May Fourth to June Fourth: Fiction and Film in Twentieth-Century China.* Cambridge: Harvard University Press, 1993. Essays on May Fourth literature and the literature after the Cultural Revolution. Lee's "Reflections on Change and Continuity in Modern Chinese Fiction" is reprinted here.

DRAMA AND THEATRE

Dolby, William. *A History of Chinese Drama.* London: Paul Elek, 1976. Surveys the historical development of Chinese drama from its origins to the dramas of the People's Republic.

Fei, Faye Chunfan, ed. and trans. *Chinese Theories of Theater and Performance from Confucius to the Present.* Ann Arbor: University of Michigan Press, 1999. Chinese philosophers, scholars, artists, and critics discuss the origins, aesthetics, and functions of theater.

Mackerras, Colin. *Chinese Theater: From Its Origins to the Present Day.* Honolulu: University of Hawaii Press, 1983. Analysis of aesthetics in social and political contexts as well as the performance and training practices of Beijing Opera.

———. *The Performing Arts in Contemporary China.* London: Routledge and Kegan Paul, 1981. Discusses theater, film, and music after the fall of the Gang of Four in October 1976.

McDougall, Bonnie S. *Popular Chinese Literature and Performing Arts in the People's Republic of China, 1949–1979.* Berkeley: University of California Press, 1984. Essays on the aesthetic analyses of the oral and performing arts, poetry, fiction, and modern drama.

Wichmann, Elizabeth. *Listening to Theatre: The Aural Dimension of Beijing Opera.* Honolulu: University of Hawaii Press, 1991. Discusses the techniques and aesthetics of traditional Beijing Opera theatre, including "Beijing Opera Plays and Performance," reprinted here.

CINEMATOGRAPHY

Berry, Chris, ed. *Perspectives on Chinese Cinema.* Princeton: Princeton University Press, 2nd ed., 1991. Essays on the Fifth Generation filmmakers and the films that brought Chinese cinema to the international film scene and Chinese film studies to academia.

Browne, Nick, Paul G. Pickowicz, Vivian Sobchack, Ester Yau, eds. *New Chinese Cinemas: Forms, Identities, Politics*. New York: Cambridge University Press, 1994. Essays that analyze contemporary Chinese films as reflections of social changes in the 1980s.

Clark, Paul. *Chinese Cinema: Culture and Politics since 1949*. Cambridge: Cambridge University Press, 1987. Overview of film since 1949 in the context of mass national culture and Party demands on artists and audiences.

Ehrlich, Linda C., and David Desser, eds. *Cinematic Landscapes: Observations on the Visual Arts and Cinema of China and Japan*. Austin: University of Texas Press, 1994. Essays on Chinese painting and cinema.

Rayns, Tony. *King of the Children: Chen Kaige and Wan Zhi and the New Chinese Cinema*. London: Faber and Faber, 1989. Introduction describes film development in China since Mao's death in 1976 and the beginning of the New Wave in 1984 with *Yellow Earth*.

Semsel, George, ed. *Chinese Film: The State of the Art in the People's Republic*. New York: Praeger, 1987. Documents the views of leading Chinese film workers and experts in Chinese cinematography on such matters as the relationship of film to theatre, film as literature, and film as an independent art.

———. Xia Hong, and Hou Jianping, eds. Hou Jianping, Li Xiaohong, and Fan Yuan, trans. *Chinese Film Theory: A Guide to the New Era*. New York: Praeger, 1990. Film texts, interpretations, and theoretical essays by Chinese critics on contemporary film theory.

Semsel, George S., Chen Xihe, and Xia Hong, eds. *Film in Contemporary China: Critical Debates, 1979–1989*. Westport, Conn.: Praeger, 1993. A continuation of *Chinese Film Theory* cited above.

Silbergeld, Jerome. *China Into Film: Frames of Reference in Contemporary Chinese Cinema*. London: Reaktion Books, 1999. On traditionalism, nationality, allegory, gender, melodrama, No-drama, Pseudo-drama, Melodramatic Masquerade, and Deconstruction Drama.

Zhang, Xudong. *Chinese Modernism in the Era of Reforms: Cultural Fever, Avant-Garde Fiction, and the New Chinese Cinema*. Durham: Duke University Press, 1997. Critiques the "new waves" in Chinese literature, film, and other intellectual discourses.

CONTRIBUTORS

ROGER T. AMES is Professor of Philosophy at the University of Hawaii at Manoa and editor of *Philosophy East and West*. His recent translations of Chinese classics include *Sun-tzu: The Art of Warfare; Sun Pin: The Art of Warfare*; and *Tracing Dao to its Source* (all with D. C. Lau); *The Confucian Analects* (with H. Rosemont); *Focusing the Familiar: A Translation and Philosophical Interpretation of the Zhongyong*; and *A Philosophical Translation of the Daodejing: Making This Life Significant* (with D. L. Hall). He has authored *Thinking Through Confucius; Anticipating China: Thinking Through the Narratives of Chinese and Western Culture; Thinking From the Han: Self, Truth, and Transcendence in Chinese and Western Culture*; and *Democracy of the Dead: Dewey, Confucius, and the Hope for Democracy in China* (all with D. L. Hall).

HOWARD GOLDBLATT is Research Professor at the University of Notre Dame. Founding Editor of *Modern Chinese Literature* (now *Modern Chinese Literature and Culture*), he is the author or editor of studies of modern Chinese literature and culture. He has also translated many early twentieth-century novelists and the major figures of the post-Mao era, including *Notes of a Desolate Man* (with Sylvia Li-chun Lin) by Chu T'ien-wen (selected as 1999 Translation of the Year by the American Literary Translators Association).

LLOYD HAFT is Associate Professor of Chinese Literature at Leiden University, where he teaches modern and classical Chinese poetry. His special interests are in the interface of form and meaning and in the problems of translating poetry. His publications include his own poetry (nine volumes in English and Dutch) as well as *Pien Chih-lin: A Study in Modern Chinese Poetry; The Chinese Sonnet: Meanings of a Form*, and *A Guide to Chinese Literature*.

THEODORE HUTERS is Professor of East Asian Languages and Cultures at UCLA. His publications on modern Chinese literature and intellectual literary history include *Revolutionary Literature in China: An Anthology* (co-editor and co-contributor with John Berninghausen); *Qian Zhongshu, Twayne World Authors Series; Kaiming zhongji Hanyu* (Kaiming Intermediate Chinese) (co-editor with Sun Hui); *Reading the Modern Chinese Short Story* (editor and contributor); *Culture and State in Chinese History*; and *Bringing the World Home: Appropriating the West in Late Qing and Early Republican China*.

WILT L. IDEMA is Professor of Chinese Literature at Harvard University. His publications include *Chinese Vernacular Fiction: The Formative Period; Chinese Theater 1100–1450: A Source Book* (with Stephen H. West); *The Dramatic Oeuvre of Chu Yu-tan 1379–1439; Wang Shifu, The Mood and the Zither, The Story of the Western Wing* (with Stephen H. West). His publications in the Dutch language also include translations and an anthology.

WENDY LARSON is Professor of Modern Chinese Language, Literature, and Film at the University of Oregon. She is the author of *Woman and Writing in Modern China* and many articles on modern Chinese culture. Presently she is working on a study of the Cultural Revolution and sexuality in the works of post-Mao writers and filmmakers.

LEO OU-FAN LEE is Professor of Chinese Literature at Harvard. His publications on modern Chinese literature include *The Romantic Generation of Modern Chinese Writers; Voices from the Iron House: A Study of Lu Xun;* and *Shanghai Modern.*

STEPHEN OWEN is James Bryant Conant University Professor at Harvard University. His publications on Chinese poetry include *The Great Age of Chinese Poetry: The High T'ang; Traditional Chinese Poetry and Poetics: An Omen of the World; Remembrances: The Experience of the Past in Classical Chinese Literature; Readings in Chinese Literary Thought; An Anthology of Chinese Literature: Earliest Times to 1991* (American Literary Translators Association outstanding translation of 1997); *The End of the Chinese Middle Ages: Essays In Mid-Tang Literary Culture;* and *Borrowed Stone: Selected Essays of Stephen Owen.*

PAUL S. ROPP is Professor of History and Director of Asian Studies at Clark University in Worcester, Massachusetts. A specialist in late imperial China, he is the author of *Dissent in Early Modern China: "Ju-lin wai-shih" and Ch'ing Social Criticism* and *Banished Immortal: Searching for Shuangqing, China's Peasant Woman Poet.* He is also the editor of *Heritage of China: Contemporary Perspectives on Chinese Civilization* and co-editor, with Harriet Zurndorfer and Paola Zamperini, of *Passionate Women: Female Suicide in Late Imperial China.* He is a member of the National Committee on U.S.-China Relations and serves on the editorial board of the journal *Nannü: Men, Women, and Gender in Early and Imperial China,* published in Leiden.

TU WEI-MING is Harvard-Yenching Professor of Chinese History and Philosophy and of Confucian Studies, and serves as the Director of the Harvard-Yenching Institute. He received an honorary doctorate from Lehigh University in 2000 and that same year received the Thomas Berry Award. In

2001 he received the Ninth International T'oegye Studies Award. Among his numerous publications are *Humanity and Self-Cultivation: Essays in Confucian Thought; Confucian Thought: Selfhood as Creative Transformation; and The Way Learning, and Politics: Essays on the Confucian Intellectual.*

ELIZABETH WICHMANN-WALCZAK is Professor of Theatre and Director of the Asian Theatre Program at the University of Hawaii. Besides her critical studies and translations of Chinese theater, she has directed Jingju plays at the University of Hawaii and on tour in mainland China. The first non-Chinese to perform Beijing opera in the People's Republic of China, she is the first honorary (and first non-Chinese) member of the National Xiqu ("Chinese opera") Institute and of the Chinese Theatre Artists Associations of Shanghai and of Jiangsu Province and has received the National Xiqu Music Association's Kong Sanchuan award as well as the Second National Festival of Jingju Golden Chrysanthemum Award.

YAN HAIPING is Professor of Drama and Performance Studies at the University of Colorado, and Zijiang Chair Professor of Humanities at East China Normal University in Shanghai. Her publications include *Chinese Women Writers and the Feminist Imagination, 1905–1945; Theatre and Society: An Anthology of Contemporary Chinese Drama,* ed. and intro.; *The Journey of Homecoming: A Collection of Essays on Gender, Culture, and Global Politics; Li Shi-min, Prince of Qin,* a ten-act historical drama, and numerous scholarly essays. Recognized by CNN in 1999 as one of "six most influential Chinese cultural figures," she also was awarded China's 1980–1981 First Prize for Excellence in Drama.

PAULINE YU is Professor of East Asian Languages and Cultures and Dean of Humanities in the College of Letters and Science at UCLA. She has written numerous articles on classical Chinese poetry, literary theory, and comparative poetics as well as *The Poetry of Wang Wei: New Translations and Commentary* and *The Reading of Imagery in the Chinese Poetic Tradition.* She is the editor of *Voices of the Song Lyric in China,* and coeditor of *Culture and State in Chinese History* and *Ways with Words: Writing about Reading Texts from Early China.*

INDEX

Absolute Signals (Gao Xingjian), 179
Ah Cheng, 165, 168
Ai Wu, 160, 162
All Men Are Brothers. See *Outlaws of the Marsh*
ancestor worship, 45, 65
Anglo-Saxon, 19–25. See also Western philosophy
Apology for Poetry (Sir Philip Sydney), 2–3, 73. See also Western literature
Archimedes, 17. See also Western philosophy
Aristotle 17; Aristotelian, 6, 20. See also Western philosophy
"At Ch'ung-jang House, in the First Month of the Year" (Li Shang-yin), 85, 96, 100
Augustine, 21. See also Western philosophy
autobiography, 105, 118, 122, 156

Ba Ba Ba (Han Shaogong), 164–168
Ba Jin, *Torrent*, 158, 166
Beckett, Samuel, *Waiting for Godot*, 180–184. See also Western literature
Bei Dao, 218, 226n 7, n 14
biography, 3, 8, 61
Bird Men (Guo Shixing), 200–201
Bolshevik. See Marxism
"Bolshevik Salute" (Wang Meng), 27
Book of Changes, 36, 77, 94–96
Book of Songs, 4
Brecht, Bertolt, 188. See also Western literature
Buddhism, 6–7, 34, 46, 106, 109, 123; and *Journey to the West*, 10, 113–115; and *The Golden Lotus*, 117; and

Dream of the Red Chamber, 120–122; and *The White Snake*, 142
Bus Stop (Gao Xingjian), 179–185

Cao Xuequin, *Dream of the Red Chamber*, 9–11, 34, 118–124, 189
ch'i, 24, 28–38. See also Daoism
Chang Tsai, "Correcting Youthful Ignorance," 29–34; "Western Inscription," 33–34
Chen Kaige, *Farewell My Concubine*, *Temptress Moon*, 192
Christianity. See Western philosophy
civil examinations, 5, 50–53, 82–83. See also literati
Classics, The, 49
"Classical Romance" (Yu Hua), 168
Communism. See Marxism
Communist Party, 176, 187, 199, 203n 2, 204n 7, 215 and literature, 12, 121, 166, 162–166, 169. See also Marxism
Confucian thought, 5–10; and Daoism, 34, 42–44, 190; and disciples, 29; and fiction, 105–107, 111–119, 122–123; and neo-Confucian, 36, 156; and poetry, 83–84; and women, 59, 64
"Correcting Youthful Ignorance" (Chang Tsai), 29–34
critical realism, 155, 160–166, 177, 180, 184–188, 193–195, 197, 200–201. See also Marxism
critical reportage. See critical realism
Cultural Revolution, 12, 19, 66–76, 141, 153–154, 160–166, 173–188, 196–197, 203n 5, 204n 7, 215–222. See also Marxism